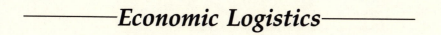

Economic Logistics

ECONOMIC
LOGISTICS

*The Optimization of Spatial
and Sectoral Resource, Production,
and Distribution Systems*

STEN THORE

The IC² Management and Management Science Series, Number 3
W. Cooper and George Kozmetsky, Series Editors

QUORUM BOOKS
New York • Westport, Connecticut • London

Library of Congress Cataloging-in-Publication Data

Thore, Sten A. O.
  Economic logistics : the optimization of spatial and sectoral
resource, production, and distribution systems / Sten Thore.
      p.   cm.—(The IC² management and management science series,
ISSN 1058-5036 ; no. 3)
  Includes bibliographical references and index.
  ISBN 0-89930-593-8 (alk. paper)
  1. Business logistics. 2. System theory. 3. Operations research.
I. Title. II. Series.
  HD38.5.T57   1991
  658.5—dc20   90-42970

British Library Cataloguing in Publication Data is available.

Library of Congress Catalog Card Number: 90-42970
ISBN: 0-89930-593-8
ISSN: 1058-5036

First published in 1991

Quorum Books, One Madison Avenue, New York, NY 10010
An imprint of Greenwood Publishing Group, Inc.

Printed in the United States of America

The paper used in this book complies with the
Permanent Paper Standard issued by the National
Information Standards Organization (Z39.48-1984).

10 9 8 7 6 5 4 3 2 1

Contents

Tables and Figures

TABLES

FIGURES

Acknowledgments

I have had the good fortune of having Dr. W.W. Cooper as my editor. I would like to convey my appreciation to him for his detailed and constructive criticism of this book, and for his continuing personal support. Chapter 2 ("Some Elements of Saddle-Point Theory") is a result of our close collaboration. It is authored jointly with W. W. Cooper.

I express my gratitude to Dr. G. Kozmetsky and my colleagues at the IC^2 Institute.

The leading idea of this book is to represent a spatial or sectoral economy as the optimal solution to some saddlepoint problem—as a saddle point. In the late 1970s I had the privilege of discussing these mathematical issues at length with A. Charnes. At that time, the seeds of this work were put in the ground.

Early versions of portions of this book were read by W. Barnett, L. Lasdon, and G. Thompson. D. Kendrick was helpful in providing an opportunity for me to teach a graduate course in the department of economics at the University of Texas–Austin, using my manuscript as a text. Over the years, M. Burtis, S. Isser, and T. Song have served as my research assistants. All computer runs for the numerical exercises were carried out by T. Song. The manuscript was typed by B. Jessee and R. Orendain. The in-house copyediting was done by L. Teague; she also drew the diagrams.

1

Introduction:
The Task Ahead

The Greek word *logistikos* simply means "calculatory," "rational." To the Romans, however, the main needs for calculation and computation arose within military science. And so, to them, the word came to mean the procurement, distribution, maintenance, and replacement of military materiel and personnel. This is the meaning that the term "military logistics" has today.

Within the field of operations research, it has long been recognized that the methods of military logistics transcend the applications to the military and can be applied to the production and distribution of civilian goods and services as well. The Institute of Management Sciences (TIMS) College on Logistics regularly sponsors research on multiechelon inventory systems, hierarchical production and distribution networks, and the optimal location of plants, inventories, and retail outlets.

The term "economic logistics" is used in this book to denote a field of economics: the analysis of resource, production, inventory, and distribution systems. The economist takes a somewhat broader view of these matters than the operations research specialist. The economist is concerned not only with the physical flow of goods along the production chain that extends from the initial employment of primary goods and services (such as labor and natural resources) to a finished consumer good bought in the supermarket, but also with the formation of markets and prices along this chain.

For example, consider the case of production, marketing, and distribution of vegetables in the State of Texas. Primary resources which are required include farmland of various categories, fertilizers, irrigation facilities, agricultural machinery, processing plants, manpower, and so on. The supply system can be viewed as a logistics system, converting resources into produce and distributing it to wholesalers and retailers in the various regions of the state. The economic problem is to determine the use of resources, the pricing of those resources, the flow of vegetables from the producer to the consumer, and the pricing of vegetables in different regions of the state.

For another example, consider the production and distribution of electric energy in the southwestern United States. Primary resources here are coal, hydroelectric installations, nuclear fuel, oil, and natural gas. There are alternative and parallel technologies of converting such resources into electric energy. In other words, the logistics system consists of many parallel paths all ending up in the same product: electric energy available for distribution in different locations in the Southwest. The economic problem is to determine the use of resources, the operation of alternative technologies in different regions, the need for manpower of different categories, the pricing of resources and manpower, the production and distribution of electric energy, and the demand and pricing of electric energy in different regions.

The characteristics of such a supply system may be specified in varying degrees of detail. Raw materials and capital goods used at any stage of production may be broken up into the underlying production processes of these goods themselves. The functioning of a logistics system will be specified using partial economic theory, keeping all variables outside the scope of the current investigation given and constant (the assumption of ceteris paribus). The partial theoretical construct may involve just a few variables at the end of the delivery system as endogenous variables (like relating the quantity supplied to prices—the so-called supply function) or the analyst may prefer to specify the details of the entire underlying logistics system of resource supply, production, and distribution. The form of theory should at all times be dictated by the actual problem at hand. Sometimes, it may even be preferred to direct the model toward some portion of the production chain, as in a study of the supply of steel or of fertilizers. (A supply analysis of steel would involve the production chain up to the point of making steel; the demand for steel would be taken as given and known.)

As now defined, the analysis of economic logistics systems would cover a major portion of the economic discipline. It includes resources, production, capital, inventories, distribution, marketing, and prices. The present book is concerned with exploring new structures in this large field, with developing new formats of analysis that can be used to investigate the joint determination of quantities and prices along the entire chain.

The conventional format for studying spatial distribution systems is the transportation problem, as encountered in operations research. The conventional format of analysis of production chains is activity analysis. Remarkably, the name of Tjalling Koopmans is associated with the development of both.[1] The transportation problem provides a format for the determination of the optimal shipping of a commodity through a transportation network with given origins and destinations. Activity analysis provides a framework of analysis of the conversion of primary inputs (like labor and minerals) into intermediate goods and final consumer goods.

The analysis of inventories to be developed in the present volume expands on the classic "warehouse problem," originally studied by A. S. Cahn in 1948. The solution provides an optimal time path of inventory, given the time path of the price of the commodity to be stored.

The transportation problem, activity analysis, and the warehouse problem all belong to the first round of pioneering work in linear programming carried out in the late 1940s and early 1950s. These three familiar model types are the three leitmotifs that will appear throughout this book. The transportation problem represents the *spatial* dimension of the logistics process—the movement of goods and services from the original locations where natural resources are being tapped to the retail outlets where the finished goods can be bought by consumers. Activity analysis represents the *vertical* dimension of the logistics process—the flow of commodities from one stage of production to the next. The warehouse problem provides the *time* dimension—the intertemporal problem of smoothing the time paths of inputs and outputs through the keeping of inventories.

Combining the transportation problem and activity analysis, we shall be able to investigate spatial networks of flows of goods throughout a production chain. Combining the transportation problem and the warehouse problem we find a tool for the analysis of regional warehouse systems. Combining activity analysis and the warehouse problem, we shall be able to understand multistage warehouse systems of intermediate goods cascading into the production and distribution of final consumer goods.

The full orchestration of these individual motifs, sometimes borrowing elements from one problem and transposing them onto another, modulating and intertwining them, will involve the use of nonlinear programming, goal programming, chance-constrained programming, and infinite games.

This book is a graduate textbook, intended for use in a master or Ph.D. program in economics. It is self-contained; all economic concepts and techniques of mathematical programming are explained, and the text is illustrated by many numerical examples.

1.1. ECONOMIC LOGISTICS: THE SPATIAL DIMENSION

It is rather curious that the spatial dimension is virtually absent from standard economic theory. Economic relationships are conventionally formulated with no reference to the geographical location of the participating economic subjects. (The obvious exception is the theory of international trade.)

And yet how can one understand the spectacular development of the modern economy without pointing at the development of new markets and the search for raw materials and energy sources? As transportation and distribution costs come down, the logistics networks that connect resources with final consumer demand become ever longer and more complex.

The key instrument of analysis of the routing of commodities from supply points to demand points is the transportation problem. It is usually not even mentioned in standard economic textbooks. Instead, it is taught in courses in production management and operations research. The problem is to determine the optimal routing of shipments of a commodity from a number of supply points (origins) to a number of demand points (destinations). The solution involves the minimization of total transportation costs subject to the condition that the demand at all destinations be covered.

This analysis is actually only part of what is required in order to understand the workings of an entire supply system. It focuses only on the transportation itself, and regards both supplies and demands as given and known. In energy economics, for instance, there obviously is the problem of determining the optimal routing of crude oil from the various oil fields in the world to consumer areas. But the larger problem is to determine the drilling of new wells and the quantity of oil pumped from each field in the face of the existing transportation capabilities and the size of current demand. What is needed is a system of micromodels that includes at the very least both some specification of the supply forthcoming at the various origins and the responsiveness of these supplies to price, and the transportation problem of shipping these supplies to the given destinations.

In a generalized transportation problem, there is a given supply function for the commodity in question at each origin and a given demand function at each destination. The task is to determine the optimal shipments along all routes and the equilibrium market prices at all origins and destinations.

Such problems of spatial equilibrium were originally treated by Paul Samuelson.[2] The literature flowing from his seminal work will be surveyed in chapter 3. Unfortunately, this body of analysis has not received the recognition that it deserves. It is well known in agricultural and regional economics but is not appreciated by economists at large. One of the aims of the presentation to follow is to show how Samuelson's analysis of spatial equilibrium can be woven together with elements of activity analysis and the warehouse problem to form a coherent body of analysis of the entire logistics process.

1.2. ECONOMIC LOGISTICS: THE VERTICAL DIMENSION

To the economists of the Austrian school, like Menger, Böhm-Bawerk, and Wicksell, the vertical dimension—or, as they put it, the "depth" dimension—of capital and production was of paramount importance. Essentially, they saw the Industrial Revolution which was gathering momentum in the Western world during the second half of the nineteenth century as an ever-continuing lengthening of the production chain and a "deepening" of capital. This theoretical heritage reached one of its high points in Wicksell's demonstration of how the optimal depth of capital is determined by the rate of interest.

A modern format of representation of the production chain is provided by activity analysis. Each elementary process of production is called an "activity"; operating any one single activity yields constant returns to scale. The quantities of inputs required per unit level of operation (the input coefficients) and the quantities of outputs obtained per unit level of operation (the output coefficients) are assumed to be fixed and known. A production chain may then be defined as a series of concatenated activities, where one or several outputs of any one activity along the chain are used as inputs for other activities at later stages. In other words, the activities are chained together as an activity network. An intermediate good is a good that is neither a primary resource nor a final demand; it is produced and used up along the path that leads from primary resources to final demand. The particular configuration of the activity network is defined by the coefficient matrices (the input coefficients and the output coefficients). In slightly different terms, the coefficient structure determines the morphology of the production chain.

Economists usually think of activity analysis as a model of the entire independent economy. Given a vector of endowments of nature, like natural resources and labor, the purpose of the model is to chart the optimal way of engaging various production activities in order to be able to satisfy final consumer demand. Our point of view is different. We shall present activity analysis as a tool of partial modeling, for the representation of an industry or a sector of the economy. In a study of the health care delivery system, for instance, activity analysis may be called on to establish how the possibilities for delivering health services at hospitals and clinics are related to the availability of doctors, nurses, and other trained medical personnel, and to the existing supply of hospital beds, diagnostic equipment, medical laboratories, and so on. An array of support functions are required even for such a routine task as the taking and running of a blood test. (The economic services now mentioned are an example of an intermediate good or service—the blood test is both an "output" and an "input" used by doctors for the purpose of diagnosis.) Activity analysis will deliver information about the menu of alternative health services that a given availability of scarce resources will permit, and the implied prices of these scarce resources. The network of activities ties the supplies of various resources together with the vector of final demand that those supplies can sustain.

1.3.   ECONOMIC LOGISTICS: THE TIME DIMENSION

Several authors writing in the late 1950s seized on Cahn's warehouse model, expanding it in different directions. Charnes and Cooper represented the intertemporal problem of finding an optimal path of purchases, inventory keeping and sales as a network problem over time.[3]

In the real world, warehousing problems commonly occur in conjunction with problems of production and distribution. A single firm holds inventories of raw materials, semifinished goods, and finished products. In an industry, there are inventories of raw materials and products along the entire production and distribution chain. If this chain is represented as a spatial and vertical network (see above), with each production, transportation, or distribution activity as a separate link, inventories may be held at every single node of the network.

In a transportation problem, there may be inventory at each origin (wholesale inventories) and inventory at each destination (retail inventories). The path from origins to delivery points may contain series of inventories, parallel alternate inventories, or even spatial hierarchies of inventories (spatial multiechelon inventory systems) through which goods have to pass before they reach the consumer.

In activity analysis, there may be inventories of primary goods, intermediate goods, or final goods. In activity networks, the network representation may be employed for both the successive concatenation of production activities and storage activities. Products may pass through simple vertically successive links of activities, alternate links, or even vertical hierarchies of inventories (vertical multiechelon inventory systems) before they reach the consumer.

This process may sound rather intimidating, but is actually only a matter of taking the time and the effort to spell out the details of the logistics system under consideration, joining together in the appropriate fashion the transportation problem, activity analysis, and the warehouse problem, and imbedding the entire model construct in a setting with given and known supply functions of all resources and labor, and given and known demand functions for all final goods.

But there is more to the time dimension: investment and capital. As it happens, the warehouse problem can be used as a point of entry into these subject matters as well. Consider a single warehouse with a given maximal storage capacity, and imagine the investment problem of building additional facilities so that the storage capacity increases. The simple investment problem now mentioned is quite instructive. For one thing, the returns on investment are not given and known, but depend upon the optimal operation of the investor (in this case the operator of the warehouse). For another, the cost of investment may be spread out over time, as a time path of costs.

Economists tend to look upon investment in terms slightly different from those used in finance and the analysis of investment of the firm. To the economist, investment is typically a matter of choosing from a menu of various interdependent projects. Investment in the publishing industry, for instance, is a question of—given the network of various spatial and vertical activities in that industry—purchasing offset presses, computer equipment, satellite channels, office space, and the like so that the total revenue obtained from operating this network optimally, calculated net of capital charges, becomes maximal.

Investment expands capacity limits—transportation capacities, production capacities, storage capacities. In order to determine optimal investment, it is necessary to logically inspect all conceivable such expansions along the spatial and vertical networks, to compare the resulting boost of revenue with the attendant time path of costs, and to select the time pattern that maximizes revenue net of cost charges.

1.4. ECONOMIC LOGISTICS AND OPERATIONS RESEARCH

The methods of operations research (OR) and management science were originally developed to analyze problems of production scheduling and sequencing of industrial operations, inventory control, and distribution—all of which are different aspects of the logistics process. The mathematical techniques that evolved in response to these and similar problems involve the optimization of large systems. They are usually referred to as mathematical programming.

A wide spectrum of OR models are available for the specification of the optimal behavior of firms, distributors, warehouses, and so on. Other formats have been developed to represent the interaction among several such units in the economic marketplace. The optimizing approach allows the model builder to provide quite detailed institutional specifications of the makeup of the various individual subjects and the economic environment in which they operate.

Economics needs the kind of operational significance that a sound use of OR methods can provide. There was a trend in economics to search for ever weaker assumptions and more general treatment (e.g., the search for "revealed preference" in an attempt to rid demand theory of all psychological underpinnings and instead rest it on an axiomatic framework). The problem with this outlook is that the weaker the assumptions, the weaker the conclusions. Today many economists would agree that the purpose of economic analysis is not to be as general as possible but rather to be as operational as possible. Analysis should be a useful instrument for transforming empirical observations of the real world into structures that can be used to answer relevant economic questions—often problems of economic policymaking.

Mathematical programming and game theory are prompting new and exciting departures in the discipline of economics at large. There is as of yet no accepted term for this kind of new economics. O. Morgenstern and G. L. Thompson have suggested the term "mathematical programming economics."[4]   Other possible terms include "extremal economics," "optimizing economics" or "operations research economics." It is the contention of the present author that during the last decades there have been developed a number of new mathematical tools in mathematical programming the full strength of which has yet to be tapped by economists. Several of these techniques (like goal programming and chance-constrained programming) were developed by the research team of A. Charnes, W. W. Cooper, and their numerous collaborators.[5]   As we shall see, these techniques are well suited to deal with the economics of logistics systems.

Since its inception, OR has delivered a series of new and powerful tools that have been adopted by economists and without which modern economics would not be what it is today. Activity analysis and game theory are just two examples of true innovations that originated in OR and subsequently were introduced into economics. This is not to say, of course, that any new OR model is destined for success as it is put into the hands of economists. But it is probably fair to say that economists would be well advised to keep an eye on what is going on in OR and, selectively, try to find out if there is anything new that fits what economics needs.

In the chapters that follow, we shall rummage about in the OR tool box and come up with some techniques that economists know well, and others that the reader may not be familiar with. Eclectically, we shall try to assemble and forge a series or model types which can be used to portray the economic behavior of an industry or a sector of the economy, and to solve for optimal decisions and market prices.

Perhaps the key word is "concatenation"—the joining together of a series of different OR micromodels to represent the economic behavior of a larger economic aggregate. Just as a cellulose molecule is constructed of thousands of individual atoms, arranged in mathematical combinations, we shall conceive of the economics of logistics systems as large concatenated aggregates of individual model types of individual producers, shippers, and warehouses. And, furthermore, it is suggested that the resulting theoretical structures and empirical model solutions is "economics," something that economists should care about.

1.5. THE NEOCLASSICAL SCHOOL, DISEQUILIBRIUM, AND ANTIEQUILIBRIUM

Economists are used to the idea of first developing suitable microtheory for individual participating market units, like firms and consumers, and then aggregating these units into larger systems (interdependent systems). These market units may be price takers, that is, taking all prices in the markets as fixed and known. Or, they may face, singly or collectively, given and known demand functions in markets where they sell, and given and known supply functions in markets where they act as purchasers.

The neoclassical school in economics further assumes that individual units are "rational," resting on behavior such as maximizing profits or utility, or minimizing costs.

Many of the models of economic logistics to be presented in this volume share these characteristics, and may thus be said to belong to the neoclassical tradition. A spatial system of operators of warehouses, for instance, purchasing a commodity in the marketplace (facing a given supply function at each location), storing it, distributing it, and selling it again in the markets (facing given and known demand functions at various locations), and looking for the maximal warehouse profit net of storage and transportation costs, certainly could properly be regarded as a specimen of a neoclassical model.

But other models cannot so easily be regarded as belonging to this category. The rationality of the decisionmaker(s) may be of a more complex nature in that there may be several objectives present at the same time, with some ranking of the priorities of these objectives. The programming format used to specify such a situation can be goal programming or goal focusing (see chap. 7).

In other models we shall rescind the assumption that markets clear, and allow for possible ex ante market gaps between demand and supply. Markets are then no longer in equilibrium but in disequilibrium (see chap. 8).

It is meaningless to pose the question whether the "real world" is in equilibrium or not. The sensible question is instead whether an equilibrium model or a disequilibrium model performs better in explaining empirical observations.

The disequilibrium approach to economics was developed by Swedish economists belonging to the so-called Stockholm school in the 1920s and 1930s. Elaborating on Wicksell's theory of the cumulative process, Lindahl, Myrdal, Ohlin, and others designed a framework for dynamic economic analysis, which the economic profession at large later came to associate with the terms "ex ante" and "ex post." In its later forms, in particular under the hands of Svennilson and Faxén, this dynamic theory evolved into highly formalized structures involving intertemporal planning under uncertainty and game theory.[6]

More recently, the French school led by Drèze, Malinvaud, Grandmont, and others has evolved a theory of interdependent systems with price rigidities. A key result in this field is the much-admired Drèze's theorem, which states that it is possible to replace any given economy subject to price rigidities (a disequilibrium economy) with an alternative equilibrium model featuring instead a system of properly designed quantity rations.[7]

The term "antiequilibrium" was coined by Kornai and used as the title for his monumental study. Thoroughly versed in the technicalities of the equilibrium school, he was still something of an outsider, with a background in mathematical programming. To him, the equilibrium school took too narrow an approach. The only signals transmitted through an equilibrium economy are prices. In Kornai's terms, the Walras system is "single-channel" and "single-level." He proposes alternative formats which are "multichannel" (transmitting information about prices and quantities) and "multilevel" (hierarchical systems).[8]

The issue of what kind of signals are transmitted throughout an economic system has to do with decentralization. How can an optimal plan for an entire logistics network, for the supply of resources, production, warehousing, and distribution be implemented in a market economy? If all markets are in equilibrium, decentralization can be achieved through price signals alone. In the language of mathematical programming, "decomposition" of the master program for the entire economy can be achieved through the delegation of prices to individual decisionmakers. But if markets do not clear, decomposition cannot be obtained through the delegation of prices alone.

1.6. THE ROLE OF THE ELECTRONIC COMPUTER

The electronic computer serves two functions in economics: as a medium for developing and storing economic theory, and as a means for numerical solution. In the chapters to follow, particular features of economic logistics will be discussed. Each one of these models is a complex system of theory. It is only by focusing on one aspect of the model-building task at a time that we shall be able to discuss these very large systems. Any attempt to adapt these constructs to an actual empirical situation will have to combine several features drawing upon various chapters. The resulting model of necessity becomes quite large, and it rapidly becomes difficult to keep track of the structure and the workings of the entire construct. Even in condensed mathematical notation, it may be difficult to get a comprehensive understanding of the model. And when it comes to the numerical details, it may rapidly become well-nigh impossible for the human brain to contemplate the joint workings of the entire theoretical assembly. Thus, we can use the computer as a device for recording, storing, inspecting, and manipulating the model. The striking thing about the computer is that it is a medium for both the specification of theory and the numerical solution of that theory. Theory and data are handled in one single medium as two different aspects of one and the same operation: mathematical programming.

A revolution is presently occurring in the numerical handling of mathematical programs. New software and hardware are coming on line, making nonlinear programming a routine operation that can be performed rapidly, at low cost, and with little prior knowledge of computer coding. The numerical exercises in this book were designated as required homework in a graduate class. Nonlinear programming as a practical tool has arrived in the classroom.

One gratifying consequence of these breakthroughs is that economists need no longer worry about algorithms. As we shall see, the earlier developments in the field of spatial equilibrium were hampered by a lack of efficient algorithms; this diverted the efforts of economists who had to spend time devising various methods of linear approximation. This period is now ended. Instead, there are "canned" nonlinear codes, and the economist need not even know how they were designed. It is enough to know how to use them.

The particular code used for the solution of the exercises in this book is GAMS, (General Algebraic Modeling System) developed by the World Bank. It features both a linear and a nonlinear option; a student can learn it in a few hours without any prior computer experience.[9]

1.7. LIMITATIONS

A key assumption in this volume is that the models of the economic logistics process are "integrable," that is, that the partial supply functions of various resources at each location and the partial demand functions of final consumer goods at each location can be integrated.

The detailed mathematical meaning of these expressions will be made clear as the text proceeds. The general idea, however, can be explained as follows. The mathematical programs to be formulated and solved throughout this book will involve the maximization or minimization, as the case may be, of some economic potential function, subject to constraints. Sometimes this economic potential function has an obvious and direct economic meaning, such as when one aims at minimizing total costs. In other cases, the potential has no immediately apparent economic meaning and is formed as a mathematical artifact for the purpose of generating the desired optimal solution. Whatever the case may be, however, it is necessary that the potential exists. The potential typically contains expressions involving integrated supply and demand functions. It is then necessary that these functions are indeed integrable so that the economic potential can be formed and so that the desired mathematical programming formulation can be arrived at. If the supply and demand functions are not integrable, the economic potential function does not exist and a programming formulation is not meaningful.

The integrability requirement should not be taken lightly. It imposes conditions on the mathematical form of the underlying utility functions which presumably would generate the supply and demand functions in the first place.[10]

What happens if the model is not integrable? In principle, nonintegrable models can be solved, but not by the techniques discussed in this book. Integrable and nonintegrable models are both specimens of so-called complementarity problems. They can be solved by complementarity methods. Recently, much progress has been made in constructing algorithms that can be used to solve nonlinear complementarity problems; in particular, reference may be made to the work of Mathiesen in solving such problems as a sequence of linear complementarity problems.[11] Also, several other numerical techniques are now becoming available to solve particular model types, such as nonintegrable models of spatial equilibrium networks (see chap. 3).

At this introductory stage, it is not easy to discuss technical concerns in a meaningful way. But perhaps the following comments are helpful. For any given nonlinear programming problem, one may write the so-called Kuhn–Tucker conditions characterizing a point of optimum solution. (Considerable effort will be spent in chap. 2 to explain the nature of these conditions.) Collectively, the Kuhn–Tucker conditions constitute a nonlinear complementarity problem. Solution of the given nonlinear programming problem and the Kuhn–Tucker conditions are then equivalent propositions. Now, if a model is not integrable, the nonlinear programming formulation does not exist. But the Kuhn–Tucker conditions may nevertheless exist in their own right, spelling out the desired economic characteristics of the optimal point that is sought. In order to determine such an optimum, methods of complementarity must then be invoked.

In the sense now indicated, the models in this book show the way for dealing with nonintegrable models as well. For every model treated, we shall carefully list all Kuhn–Tucker conditions and provide their economic interpretation. For a nonintegrable case, the reader will easily be able to list the corresponding set of conditions that an optimum should satisfy. This set of conditions will form a complementarity problem which can be solved by a suitable complementarity algorithm.

This volume deals only with ex ante analysis. Dynamic analysis is not covered. Economic analysis ex ante deals with plans and expectations. If the plans of the various participating economic subjects are compatible so that each subject can also carry out ("realize") these plans, ex ante will actually coincide with ex post and there is said to be equilibrium in the economy.[12] The ex ante economy then translates into a dynamic path of equilibrium. But if all economic subjects cannot realize their plans, some plans will have to give way (they have to be revised) and the ex ante economy does not by itself contain sufficient information to enable us to infer the subsequent dynamic evolution.

These limitations of the ex ante economy are serious. It means that we cannot cope with the rapid diffusion of scientific advances, extremely short technological lifecycles, comparatively brief generation times for new products, and the rapid appearance and disappearance of markets.[13] In sum, we are not well equipped to deal with change. This, of course, is unfortunate in a world where change is becoming crucial for the very survival of the modern firm in the marketplace.

Some tentative developments in the chapters to follow, however, point the way toward dynamics. In order to be able to deal with change realistically, we need to be able to deal with uncertainty. Uncertainty enters the models in two ways: technological uncertainty and price uncertainty. There is technological uncertainty when a producer applies new technology or develops new products which can be characterized by uncertain input requirements or uncertain outputs (or both). There is price uncertainty when the producer does not know in advance at which price his product is going to sell, or at which price he will be able to acquire the required inputs. If many producers face technological uncertainty, price uncertainty will arise in the marketplace. We shall attack these problems using methods of chance-constrained programming and game theory.

1.8. A GUIDE TO THE CHAPTERS

In order to make the book self-contained, chapter 2 (authored jointly by W. W. Cooper and Sten Thore) provides a review of some key results in mathematical programming and game theory that will be used in the subsequent chapters. The material is organized around the Kuhn–Tucker saddle-point theorem. From a pedagogical point of view, we believe that there is a new twist to the presentation in that the Kuhn–Tucker theorem for nonlinear programming, the dual theorem of linear programming, and the minimax theorem in the theory of games all flow from this saddle-point theorem.

The average reader should be able to leaf through this chapter fairly quickly, returning to it later as the need may arise. No attempt is made to provide complete proofs of all theoretical results; in several instances only the general nature of the proof is indicated. References to mathematical texts that provide complete treatment are given in the Bibliographic Notes.

The systematic treatment of economic logistics systems begins in chapter 3. After some introductory material the chapter turns to a presentation of Samuelson's model of spatial equilibrium. Next, the modern theory of equilibrium in spatial networks is covered. The chapter ends with the extension to several commodities and a discussion of the issue of integrability.

Chapter 4 deals with the vertical dimension—activity analysis, networks of intermediate goods, and the Takayama–Judge combination of spatial equilibrium and activity analysis. The intent of this chapter is not only to survey well-known theory but also to break some new ground in developing a combination of network theory and conventional activity analysis.

Chapter 5 presents the warehouse model, both independently and in a setting of spatial equilibrium. Next, there is an analysis of investment in storage capacity in a warehouse model. The resulting programming format is used as a stepping-stone to move on to models of investment in real capital quite generally. The text here establishes contact with a series of investment models developed by the World Bank ("industrial investment programs"). The resulting formats determine optimal capital formation in an industry or an economic sector operating a series of independent activities and when prices of both final goods and resources are subject to market determination so that neither the "cost stream" nor the "income stream" of a single capital formation project is known.

Chapter 6 covers the price formulation of Samuelson's model of spatial equilibrium and of other models dealt with up to this point. There typically exists both a quantity formulation and a price formulation of each model; the first one uses quantity variables as independent variables, the latter price variables as independents. The two formulations are logically equivalent.

Chapter 7 takes the reader on a tour of "goal focusing," a programming approach recently developed by Charnes, Cooper, and their collaborators to deal with cases of multiobjective optimization. In this instance, the goals refer to resource use (target figures on the maximal catch of fish in a lake, say, or on the maximal release into the air of freon from an industrial air-conditioning unit). Goal focusing is a variant of goal programming, permitting the analyst to posit the extremization of an overriding objective such as "efficiency," subject to the secondary requirement that a number of subordinate goals be attained as "closely as possible."

Chapter 7 actually takes us beyond the neoclassical world and permits the analysis of external economies such as those caused by pollution and other damage to the environment (negative external economies).

Chapter 8 breaks away even more definitely from the neoclassical system, rescinding the assumption that markets always clear and that market prices are equilibrium prices. Following the spirit of modern disequilibrium theory, this chapter investigates the nature of rigidities—rigid prices and rigid wages. If the price of a consumer good is prevented from rising, either because there is government price control (like rent control) or because market prices are sticky upward in the short run, there may develop an excess demand for the good, an ex ante market gap between desired purchases and desired supply. If the wages of some category of wage earners fails to fall, either because there is minimum wage legislation or because wage earners refuse to accept work below their reservation wage, there may develop an excess supply of labor, an ex ante unemployment gap. Mathematical programming makes possible the determination of the numerical magnitude of such ex ante gaps.

Chapter 9 outlines the use of chance-constrained programming to deal with the presence of uncertainty in activity analysis and activity networks. Technological uncertainty and the development of new techniques of production, distribution, and marketing will in the setting of activity analysis take the form of uncertain input and output coefficients. When the logistics process is portrayed as a generalized network, the same kind of uncertainty will appear as uncertain amplification/attenuation factors along each link.

The approach of chance-constrained programming permits constraints to be violated, but not more often than in some preassigned frequency of all cases. For instance, production of some final good is to be programmed so that output will cover the demand in at least 95 percent of all cases. In other words, the optimal solution will reflect a standard mode of operation that will occur in most cases. The program does not deal with exceptional cases when the unit output coefficients turn out to be too small. That is, chance-constrained programming does not specify all possible "states of the world" or the possible recourse that would be taken in the event of an extreme outcome (such as importing the shortfalls from abroad).

The chapter ends with some suggestions that innovations and technological change essentially can be viewed as occurring in response to perceived reductions of the uncertainty surrounding new activities not yet operated, and/or in response to an increased willingness of the planner to accept risk.

Chapter 10 returns to saddle-point theory: the analysis of two-person infinite games. In an infinite game, each player may choose from a continuum of alternatives, rather than from among a finite number of moves. For instance, one player is to choose a point along one side of a square, and the other player is to choose a point along the other side. A play then is a single point inside (or on the border of) the square. Assuming that the payoff function is concave-convex (so that a saddle point exists), the minimax theorem for such a game states that the optimal probabilistic strategy of each player actually is a "pure" (deterministic) strategy: the play indicated by the saddle point.

This theorem, which has been known for more than twenty years, has some rather intriguing consequences which economists do not seem to have explored. It means that virtually every single deterministic model of production or distribution in a logistics system alternatively can be looked upon as the quantity solution to an infinite game where one player (the quantity player) controls all quantity variables (such as production, the employment of inputs, shipments, etc.) and the other player is a fictitious price player (the market) that sets prices. The chapter—and the book—ends with some tentative remarks about the nature of dealers (market specialists), who in many ways perform the role of the fictitious price player.

Each chapter contains stylized numerical examples, including programming formulation, numerical solution, and a discussion of the solution. The exercises are intended as illustrations of the more general presentation in the main text; the student is encouraged to program them using some suitable nonlinear code and to solve them using a computer.

At the end of each chapter Bibliographic Notes sketch the origins and subsequent developments of the ideas covered in the main text. There is a list of references to each chapter.

NOTES

1. Early examples of the transportation problem were given by Koopmans [12], Hitchcock [10], and Kantorovich [11]. The standard reference to activity analysis is Koopmans [13].

2. Samuelson [20]. For further comments on this work, see the bibliographic notes to chap. 3. The standard reference work on spatial equilibrium is Takayama and Judge [22].

3. Charnes and Cooper [2] (see also [3], chap. 17). In subsequent work (together with M. H. Miller [5]), Charnes and Cooper also demonstrated how the warehouse problem becomes modified in the presence of borrowing and lending and liquidity constraints (so that there are inventories of both commodities and "money").

4. Morgenstern and Thompson [19], p. 12.

5. References to the numerous works by Charnes and Cooper will be provided in the chapters to follow, as these various techniques and other relevant subject matters are encountered. See also Charnes and Cooper [3]. The original reference for goal programming is Charnes, Cooper, and Ferguson [4]. (Additional references to goal programming and goal focusing will be given in chap. 7.) The original reference for chance-constrained programming is Charnes, Cooper, and Symonds [6]. (For additional references, see chap. 9.)

6. A systematic presentation of the analytical framework of the Stockholm school was given in Lindahl [16]. This work gives references to the various authors active in the school during the 1920s and 1930s. For Svennilson and Faxén, see [21] and [8], respectively.

7. See Drèze [7] and the references cited therein.

8. Kornai [14]. This work was written while Kornai was still active in the United States; returning to Hungary, Kornai was later able to develop his ideas further with special reference to the problems of a centrally planned economy.

9. The GAMS language was originally described in Meeraus [18]. For further references to GAMS and other software packages (such as MINOS and GRG2), see the bibliographic notes to chap. 3.

10. See chap. 3, Sec. 3.4.

11. Mathiesen [17]. See the discussion in chap. 3, sec. 3.4.

12. This definition of equilibrium goes back at least to Hayek [9].

13. See Kozmetsky [15].

REFERENCES

[1.1] Cahn, A. S. "The Warehouse Problem," *Bulletin of the American Mathematical Society,* 54 (Oct. 1948): 1073.

[1.2] Charnes, A. and W. W. Cooper. "Generalizations of the Warehousing Model," *Operational Research Quarterly,* 6/4 (Dec. 1955): 131-172.

[1.3] Charnes, A. and W. W. Cooper. *Management Models and Industrial Applications of Linear Programming.* 2 vols. New York: Wiley. 1961.

[1.4] Charnes, A., W. W. Cooper and R. O. Ferguson. "Optimal Estimation of Executive Compensation by Linear Programming," *Management Science* 1, (Jan. 1955): 138-151.

[1.5] Charnes, A., W. W. Cooper and M. Miller. "Applications of Linear Programming to Financial Budgeting and the Costing of Funds," *Journal of Business of the University of Chicago* 32/1 (Jan. 1959): 20-46.

[1.6] Charnes, A., W. W. Cooper, and G. H. Symonds. "Cost Horizons and Certainty Equivalents: An Approach to Stochastic Programming of Heating Oil," *Management Science* 4 (Apr. 1958): 235-263.

[1.7] Drèze, J. H. "Existence of an Exchange Equilibrium under Price Rigidities," *International Economic Review* 16/2 (June 1975): 301-320.

[1.8] Faxén, Karl-Olof. *Monetary and Fiscal Policy under Uncertainty.* Uppsala: Almqvist and Wiksell, 1957.

[1.9]   Hayek, F. A. "Price Expectations, Monetary Disturbances and Malinvestments." In *Readings in Business Cycle Theory*, ed. American Economic Association. London: Allen and Unwin, 1950.

[1.10]   Hitchcock, F. L. "The Distribution of a Product from Several Sources to Numerous Localities," *Journal of Mathematics and Physics* 20, (1941): 224-230.

[1.11]   Kantorovich, L. V. *Matematicheskie Metody Organizatii i Planirovania Proizvodstva* (Mathematical Methods in the Organization and Planning of Production). Leningrad: Izdanie Leningradskogo Gosudarstvenpogo Universiteta, 1939.

[1.12]   Koopmans, T. C. "Optimum Utilization of the Transportation System," *Proceedings of the International Statistical Conferences* Vol. 5, Washington, D. C., 1947 (repr. suppl. to *Econometrica* 17 [July 1949]: 136–46).

[1.13]   Koopmans, T. C.(ed.) *Activity Analysis of Allocation and Production.* Cowles Commission Monograph, no. 13. New York: Wiley, 1951.

[1.14]   Kornai, J. *Anti-Equilibrium.* Amsterdam: North-Holland, 1971.

[1.15]   Kozmetsky, G. *Transformational Management.* Cambridge, Mass.: Ballinger, 1985.

[1.16]   Lindahl, E. *Studies in Money and Capital.* London: Allen and Unwin, 1939.

[1.17]   Mathiesen, L. "Computational Experience in Solving Equilibrium Models by a Sequence of Linear Complementarity Problems," *Operations Research* 33/6 (Nov.–Dec. 1985): 1225-1250.

[1.18]   Meeraus, A. "An Algebraic Approach to Modeling," *Journal of Dynamics and Control* 5 (1983): 81-108.

[1.19]   Morgenstern, O. and G. L. Thompson. *Mathematical Theory of Expanding and Contracting Economies.* Lexington, Mass.: D.C. Heath, 1976.

[1.20]   Samuelson, P. "Spatial Price Equilibrium and Linear Programming," *American Economic Review* 42 (1952): 283-303.

[1.21]   Svennilson, T. *Ekonomisk Planering* (Economic Planning), Uppsala: Almqvist and Wiksell, 1938.

[1.22]   Takayama, T. and G. G. Judge. *Spatial and Temporal Price and Allocation Models.* Amsterdam: North-Holland, 1971.

2

Some Elements of Saddle-Point Theory

W. W. Cooper
Sten Thore

To an economist, one of the attractive aspects of mathematical optimization is that it provides access to the Lagrange multipliers, which can be used to accord economic meaning to the constraints. The resulting multiplier values become "dual" variables, which can be interpreted as "shadow prices" to serve as evaluators of the constraints. When a constraint in the direct problem takes the form of a market balance condition relating demand to supply, the Lagrange multiplier may be interpreted as the corresponding economic price in the sense of the "opportunity cost" associated with altering this balance condition to some other level. This, in turn, provides information for guiding alterations in supply and/or demand and correcting imperfections that may be present in market structures.

To deal with systems of inequalities, as we shall do, it will be necessary to extend these Lagrange multipliers by means of the Kuhn–Tucker theorem, which plays a central role in mathematical programming. For this theorem a saddle-point problem is formulated and solved in a manner that provides access simultaneously to the optimal values of the direct program variables, such as the amounts to be produced and sold, and the optimal values of the multipliers.

Much of market economics is concerned with groups of persons exhibiting a common orientation. Producers try to maximize the profits to be obtained by supplying a certain good or service while consumers seek to minimize the cost of acquiring the same good or service. Both groups search for markets where a "best" price may be secured. The resulting behavior may then take a form which can be represented as a "saddle-point" with coordinates that result in values that are simultaneously maximal for one group and minimal for the other.

2.1.   SADDLE-POINTS: DEFINITIONS

Consider the problem

$$(2.1) \quad \max_{x} \quad \min_{y} \quad F(x,y)$$

subject to $x \in X, y \in Y$

The unknowns are the N-component vector $x = [x_n]$, $n = 1, 2, \ldots, N$ and the M-component vector $y = [y_m]$, $m = 1, 2, \ldots, M$. The known and given objective function $F(x,y)$ is real-valued and continuous. Further, the objective function is concave in x for $x \in X$ and it is convex in y for $y \in Y$ where $x \in X$ means the collection of N-vectors x which are in the set X while $y \in Y$ is the collection of M-vectors y which are in the set Y.

The sets X and Y are assumed to be nonempty, convex, closed, and bounded so that, geometrically interpreted, the vectors x and y have the following properties: (1) there is at least one vector x in X and one vector y in Y; (2) given two vectors $x_1, x_2 \in X$, then all $x = \gamma x_1 + (1 - \gamma)x_2$ are also in X for any $0 \leq \gamma \leq 1$; and, similarly, given any $y_1, y_2 \in Y$ then $y = \lambda y_1 + (1 - \lambda)y_2$ are also in Y for all $0 \leq \lambda \leq 1$; (3) the boundary points are in the sets X and Y; and (4) the coordinate values of the boundary points are always finite.

Program (2.1) is said to be biextremal because it involves the extremals of maximization over x and minimization over y. That is, the objective involves securing extremals (highest and lowest values) of $F(x,y)$ by selecting the vector pair (x,y) from the collection of $x \in X$ and $y \in Y$ which are simultaneously maximal for x and minimal for y. Given the preceding assumptions, these points exist so that these maxima and minima exist and are attainable. They are not necessarily unique, however, which means that a different x and y may give the same "best" values to $F(x,y)$.

The point (x^*,y^*) is said to be a saddle-point for $F(x,y)$ if

$$(2.2) \qquad F(x,y^*) \leq F(x^*,y^*) \text{ for all } x \in X$$

$$F(x^*,y^*) \leq F(x^*,y) \text{ for all } y \in Y,$$

which can be combined in the single expression

(2.3) $F(x,y^*) \leq F(x^*,y^*) \leq F(x^*,y)$ *for all* $x \in X,\ y \in Y$

Figure 2.1 is illustrative. Here the diagram is restricted to the non-negative orthant $x \geq 0,\ y \geq 0$ so that the components of x and y, respectively, are all constrained to be non-negative. These components may also be regarded geometrically as coordinates of points x and y in the positive orthant as shown in figure 2.1.

Figure 2.1.   A Saddle-Point

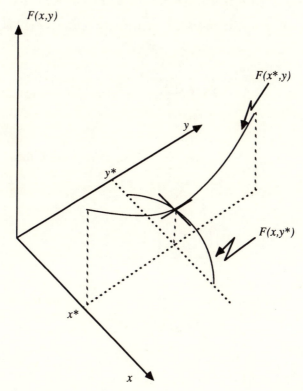

When the function $F(x,y)$ is concave in x, then for any prescribed y we will have the kind of situation described in figure 2.2 for any choice of $0 \leq \gamma \leq 1$. Linear interpolation between $F(x_1)$ and $F(x_2)$ produces a value

(2.4) $\gamma F(x_1) + (1 - \gamma)\, F(x_2) \leq F(\gamma x_1 + (1 - \gamma)x_2) = F(\hat{x})$

for all $\hat{x} = \gamma x_1 + (1 - \gamma)x_2$ and for any $0 \leq \gamma \leq 1$. That is, the thus interpolated value $\gamma F(x_1) + (1 - \gamma)F(x_2)$ never lies above the value of $F(\hat{x})$ for any $0 \leq \gamma \leq 1$.

In similar fashion, the assumption that $F(x,y)$ is convex in y is illustrated in figure 2.3. Here, for any fixed x we have

$$(2.5) \qquad \lambda F(y_1) + (1 - \lambda) F(y_2) \geq F(\lambda y_1 + (1 - \lambda)y_2) = F(\hat{y})$$

for all $0 \leq \lambda \leq 1$, so that the interpolated value obtained from $\lambda F(y_1) + (1 - \lambda) F(y_2)$ will never lie below the value of the function $F(\hat{y})$ at any point on its graph.

Figure 2.2.   Concavity

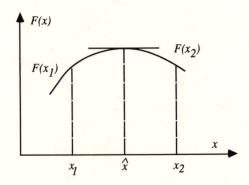

Figure 2.3.   Convexity

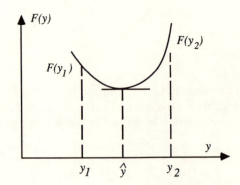

The saddle-point condition (2.3) can now be interpreted as follows. When the value $y = y^*$ is chosen for the minimizing variable, the choices for the maximizing variable x are confined to the section of the three-dimensional surface that is represented by the curve for $F(x,y^*)$ in figure 2.1. When x^* is chosen for the maximizing variable, the choices for the minimizing variable y are confined to the curve for $F(x^*,y)$. For the saddle-point situation represented in figure 2.1 the point (x^*,y^*) is simultaneously maximal for x and minimal for y. That is, (x^*, y^*) is a saddle-point.

If the saddle-point (2.1) exists, the order of the two operators max and min can be reversed and

$$(2.6) \qquad \max_{x} \ \min_{y} \ F(x,y) = \min_{y} \ \max_{x} \ F(x,y)$$

The following simple proof is adapted from J. von Neumann and O. Morgenstern.[1] First, note that it will always be true that

$$(2.7) \qquad \max_{x} \ \min_{y} \ F(x,y) \leq \min_{y} \ \max_{x} \ F(x,y)$$

By definition of the min operator, $\min_y F(x_0,y) \leq F(x_0,y)$ for any fixed $x = x_0$. In particular, choosing $y = y_0$, $\min_y F(x_0,y) \leq F(x_0,y_0)$. Similarly, by the definition of the max operator $F(x,y_0) \leq \max_x F(x,y_0)$ and, in particular, $F(x_0,y_0) \leq \max_x F(x,y_0)$. Hence, by combination $\min_y F(x_0,y) \leq \max_x F(x,y_0)$. In particular, choosing x_0 so that the left-hand side of the latter inequality becomes as large as possible and choosing y_0 so that the right-hand side becomes as small as possible, the same inequality must still hold, which gives (2.7).

Second, note that (2.2) yields

$$(2.8) \qquad \max_{x} F(x,y^*) = F(x^*,y^*)$$

$$\min_{y} F(x^*,y) = F(x^*,y^*)$$

Since

(2.9) $\min_{y} \ \max_{x} \ F(x,y) \leq \max_{y} \ F(x,y^*)$

$\min_{y} \ F(x^*,y) \leq \max_{x} \ \min_{y} \ F(x,y)$

the combination of (2.8) and (2.9) shows that

(2.10) $\min_{y} \ \max_{x} \ F(x,y) \leq \max_{x} \ \min_{y} \ F(x,y)$

Comparing (2.7) and (2.10), the result as desired in (2.6) follows. *Q.E.D.*

This proof depends upon the assumed existence of the indicated saddle-point but does not provide the conditions needed to ensure this existence. Such conditions will shortly be supplied in forms that can be accorded meaningful economic interpretations. Before taking up this topic in the next (and following) sections, however, we need to note that a saddle-point for $F(x,y)$ need not be unique and it need not appear entirely in the positive orthant.

Methods for dealing with the latter problem will be introduced in the next section. The problem of lack of uniqueness can be avoided by assuming that the objective function $F(x,y)$ is *strictly* concave in x (the maximizing argument) and *strictly* convex in y (the minimizing argument). The concept of strict concavity can be illustrated by reference to figure 2.2 where, as can be seen, the equality allowed in (2.4) can hold only at the end points where $\gamma = 0$ or $\gamma = 1$. For all other cases the inequality is strict so that $\gamma F(x_1) + (1 - \gamma)F(x_2) < F(x_2)$ for all $0 < \gamma < 1$. Similarly, the property of strict convexity is illustrated in figure 2.3, where, as can be seen, the equality allowed by (2.5) can hold only at the end points where $\gamma = 0$ or $\gamma = 1$. In all other cases $\gamma F(y_1) + (1 - \gamma)F(y_2) > F(y)$ for any $0 < \gamma < 1$.

Interpreting the function in figure 2.2 to represent $F(x,\bar{y})$ for a fixed value $y = \bar{y}$ it is seen that $F(x,y)$ is strictly concave in x. Interpreting the function in figure 2.3 to represent the behavior of $F(x,y)$ whenever x is fixed we see that $F(x,y)$ is strictly convex in y.

We shall generally assume that our functions $F(x,y)$ are strictly concave in x and strictly convex in y except in situations where alternate saddle-point values (or alternate optima) are of economic interest.

2.2. THE KUHN–TUCKER SADDLE-POINT THEOREM

We now turn to the Kuhn–Tucker theorem to obtain a unifying basis for the developments that we shall use in the chapters that follow. Formal statements of that theorem with accompanying mathematical proofs are available in a variety of papers and texts, beginning with the original paper by H. Kuhn and A. W. Tucker. (See reference [7] at the end of the chapter.) We shall use only parts of that theorem in which the functions behave in a manner analogous to the $F(x,y)$ shown in figure 2.1. The constraint sets are taken to be the entire non-negative orthant; that is, the set X is identified with all $x \geq 0$ and Y with all $y \geq 0$, where these vectors and sets are interpreted as points in a real space with a finite number of dimensions (N and M, respectively). These constraint sets, although convex, are not bounded and closed, so that we shall need to add conditions, as we shall do, when these latter properties are also needed.

We have already assumed that the function $F(x,y)$ is continuous and that it is concave in x and convex in y. Now, let $F(x,y)$ also be differentiable, by which we mean that (x,y) has a derivative at every point of interest. Then one version of the Kuhn–Tucker theorem which is pertinent to this book can be stated in the following form:

Theorem 2.1.   (Kuhn–Tucker)   The function $F(x,y)$ has a saddle-point and a corresponding saddle value at x^*,y^* if and only if the following conditions are satisfied:

$$(2.11) \qquad \frac{\partial F(x^*,y^*)}{\partial x} \leq 0 \ , \ x^{*T} \frac{\partial F(x^*,y^*)}{\partial x} = 0 \ , x^* \geq 0$$

$$(2.12) \qquad \frac{\partial F(x^*,y^*)}{\partial y} \geq 0 \ , \ y^{*T} \frac{\partial F(x^*,y^*)}{\partial y} = 0 \ , y^* \geq 0$$

where $\partial F(x^*,y^*)/\partial x$ is the partial derivative with respect to x and $\partial F(x^*,y^*)/\partial y$ is the partial derivative with respect to y, both evaluated at (x^*,y^*).[2]

These symbols are to be interpreted from right to left as follows. The symbols x^* and y^* in (2.11) and (2.12) respectively are N-vectors $x^* = [x_n^*]$, $n = 1, 2, \ldots , N$ and M-vectors $y^* = [y_m^*]$, $m = 1, 2, \ldots , M$, evaluated at points x^* and y^*, with components or coordinates, which we write in extended form as follows:

$$(2.13) \qquad x^* = \begin{bmatrix} x_1^* \\ x_2^* \\ \cdot \\ \cdot \\ x_n^* \\ \cdot \\ \cdot \\ \cdot \\ x_N^* \end{bmatrix} , y^* = \begin{bmatrix} y_1^* \\ y_2^* \\ \cdot \\ \cdot \\ y_m^* \\ \cdot \\ \cdot \\ \cdot \\ y_M^* \end{bmatrix}$$

These vectors are column vectors and their transposes, represented as x^{*T} and y^{*T}, respectively, are therefore row vectors. The conditions $x^* \geq 0$ and $y^* \geq 0$ means that none of the components of either vector are negative and, of course, the same condition holds for their transposes, x^{*T} and y^{*T}.

The symbols $\partial F(x^*,y^*)/\partial x$ and $\partial F(x^*,y^*)/\partial y$ in (2.11) and (2.12) are defined as follows:

$$(2.14) \qquad \frac{\partial F(x^*,y^*)}{\partial x} = \begin{bmatrix} \dfrac{\partial F(x^*,y^*)}{\partial x_1} \\ \dfrac{\partial F(x^*,y^*)}{\partial x_2} \\ \cdot \\ \cdot \\ \dfrac{\partial F(x^*,y^*)}{\partial x_n} \\ \cdot \\ \cdot \\ \dfrac{\partial F(x^*,y^*)}{\partial x_N} \end{bmatrix} ; \quad \frac{\partial F(x^*,y^*)}{\partial y} = \begin{bmatrix} \dfrac{\partial F(x^*,y^*)}{\partial y_1} \\ \dfrac{\partial F(x^*,y^*)}{\partial y_2} \\ \cdot \\ \cdot \\ \dfrac{\partial F(x^*,y^*)}{\partial y_m} \\ \cdot \\ \cdot \\ \dfrac{\partial F(x^*,y^*)}{\partial y_M} \end{bmatrix}$$

Thus to say that $\partial F(x^*,y^*)/\partial x$ is the partial derivative of $F(x^*,y^*)$ with respect to the N-vector x means that to obtain the resulting vector of derivatives, the function $F(x^*,y^*)$ is differentiated partially with respect to each of the components of x and these derivatives are evaluated at the point (x^*,y^*) to obtain the vector of derivatives for the individual variables as shown for $\partial F(x^*,y^*)/\partial x$ in (2.14). The vector $\partial F(x^*,y^*)/\partial y$ is similarly defined for the partial derivative of $F(x^*,y^*)$ with respect to the components of the M-vector y shown on the right in (2.14).

Using this definition we have for the central term in (2.11),

$$(2.15) \quad x^{*T} \frac{\partial F(x^*,y^*)}{\partial x} = x_1^* \frac{\partial F(x^*,y^*)}{\partial x_1} + x_2^* \frac{\partial F(x^*,y^*)}{\partial x_2}$$

$$+ \ldots + x_n^* \frac{\partial F(x^*,y^*)}{\partial x_n} + \ldots x_N^* \frac{\partial F(x^*,y^*)}{\partial x_N} = 0$$

and similarly for (2.12)

$$(2.16) \quad y^{*T} \frac{\partial F(x^*,y^*)}{\partial y} = y_1^* \frac{\partial F(x^*,y^*)}{\partial y_1} + y_2^* \frac{\partial F(x^*,y^*)}{\partial y_2} +$$

$$\ldots + y_m^* \frac{\partial F(x^*,y^*)}{\partial y_m} + \ldots y_M^* \frac{\partial F(x^*,y^*)}{\partial y_M} = 0$$

We can render these more compactly as

$$x^{*T} \frac{\partial F}{\partial x} = \sum_{n=1}^{n=N} x_n^* \frac{\partial F}{\partial x_n} = 0$$

(2.17)

$$y^{*T} \frac{\partial F}{\partial y} = \sum_{m=1}^{m=M} y_m^* \frac{\partial F}{\partial y_m} = 0$$

where it is understood that these derivatives are all evaluated at (x^*,y^*).

The conditions

$$(2.18) \qquad \frac{\partial F(x^*,y^*)}{\partial x} = \frac{\partial F}{\partial x} \leq 0$$

and

$$\frac{\partial F(x^*,y^*)}{\partial y} = \frac{\partial F}{\partial y} \geq 0$$

mean that none of the components of $\partial F/\partial x$ is positive and none of the components of $\partial F/\partial y$ is negative.

The meaning of these conditions for the saddle-point properties of (x^*,y^*) may be illustrated by reference to figures 2.1 and 2.4 as follows. If the max $F(x,y^*) = F(x^*,y^*)$ occurs inside the positive orthant then all of the component derivatives as defined in (2.14) will be zero. That is, we shall have $\partial F/\partial x_n = 0$ for all $n = 1, 2, \ldots, N$ components of $\partial F/\partial x$ at (x^*,y^*). Suppose, however, that the maximum occurs in a position like the one shown in figure 2.4. Since the constraints require $x^* \geq 0$ the component of x associated with the horizontal line is not in the set of admissible solutions. Thus for this component, say x_n, we will have $x_n^* = 0$, and $\partial F(x^*,y^*)/\partial x_n < 0$. Combining these last two conditions we will have $x_n^* \partial F/\partial x_n = 0$, as the applicable saddle-point condition in (2.17).

Figure 2.4.   The Kuhn–Tucker Theorem on a Boundary

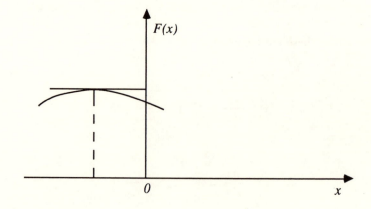

The same line of reasoning applies in the case of y^*. Either y_m^* is on or outside the boundary of the set of admissible solutions, in which case $y_m^* = 0$ is applicable, or else it is in the interior of the set in which case

$\partial F(x^*,y^*)/\partial y_m = 0$. Hence $y_m{}^* \ \partial F/\partial y_m = 0$ which extends to

$$\Sigma_m y_m{}^* \ \frac{\partial F}{\partial y_m} = 0 \text{ with } \partial F/\partial y_m > 0 \text{ when } y_m{}^* \text{ is not in the positive orthant,}$$

and $\partial F/\partial y_m = 0$ when $y_m{}^*$ is in the positive orthant.

From what has just been said it is clear that the conditions of theorem 2.1 are satisfied when (x^*,y^*) is a saddle-point. In other words, these are necessary conditions, which means they will be satisfied when (x^*,y^*) is a saddle-point. It therefore remains only to be shown that they are sufficient so that when these conditions are satisfied at some point (x^*,y^*) this will be a saddle-point.

In general, sufficiency requires the following additional condition:

(2.19)

$$F(x,y^*) \leq F(x^*,y^*) + \sum_{n=1}^{n=N} \frac{\partial F(x^*,y^*)}{\partial x_n} (x_n - x_n{}^*)$$

$$F(x^*,y) \geq F(x^*,y^*) + \sum_{m=1}^{m=M} \frac{\partial F(x^*,y^*)}{\partial y_m} (y_m - y_m{}^*)$$

These expressions may be thought of as a generalization of the usual point-slope formula expression for the tangent planes at (x^*,y^*). Generally referred to as expressions for "supports" or "supporting hyperplanes," the first expression in (2.19) asserts that $F(x,y^*)$ cannot lie above the tangent (supporting) hyperplane through (x^*,y^*). The second expression similarly asserts that $F(x^*,y)$ cannot lie below the supporting hyperplane through (x^*,y^*).

The first condition in (2.19) is satisfied for functions which are concave and differentiable. Since we are assuming that $F(x,y)$ is concave in x as well as differentiable, we therefore need only show that application of (2.11) yields the saddle-point property for (x^*,y^*).

By virtue of the first expression in (2.19) we have, for sufficiency,

$$F(x,y^*) \leq F(x^*,y^*) + x^T \frac{\partial F(x^*,y^*)}{\partial x} - x^{*T} \frac{\partial F(x^*,y^*)}{\partial x}$$

and therefore

(2.20) $F(x,y^*) \leq F(x^*,y^*)$

since $x^{*T} \partial F(x^*,y^*)/\partial x = 0$ and $x^T \partial F(x^*,y^*)/\partial x \leq 0$ by the conditions in (2.11).

Observing that we are assuming that $F(x^*,y)$ is convex in y, we proceed in analogous fashion to obtain

$$(2.21) \qquad F(x^*,y) \geq F(x^*,y^*)$$

Combining (2.20) and (2.21), we have

$$(2.22) \qquad F(x,y^*) \leq F(x^*,y^*) \leq F(x^*,y)$$

Thus the saddle-point property (2.3) is obtained. Hence (2.11) and (2.12) as given in theorem 2.1 are sufficient as well as necessary for (x^*,y^*) to be a saddle-point when $F(x,y)$ has the indicated concavity, convexity, and differentiability properties.

It should be noted that theorem 2.1 extends to vector-valued functions, although we have assumed that $F(x,y)$ is only single-valued in the above development. Unless otherwise noted, however, we shall proceed with the assumptions we now make, namely, $F(x,y)$ is single-valued and strictly concave in x and strictly convex in y, and is differentiable in both x and y. We also assume that solutions exist in which the indicated minimum and maximum values are actually attained in problems we shall be considering.

Figure 2.5 demonstrates the situation when a saddle-point occurs at a point like $(x^*, \hat{y})$ which is outside the positive orthant. The condition $y \geq 0$ precludes attainment of the value $F(x^*,\hat{y})$. The saddle-point satisfying the non-negativity requirement thus occurs at $F(x^*,y^*)$. Although $F(x^*,\hat{y}) < F(x^*,y^*)$ the lowest attainable value occurs when x^* is selected at (x^*,y^*) since the constraints preclude the choice of $(x^*,\hat{y})$. The thus-constrained value, as illustrated in the diagram, satisfies (2.22) as required for a saddle-point at (x^*,y^*) when the variables are constrained to be non-negative.

2.3. THE KUHN–TUCKER THEOREM: NONLINEAR PROGRAMMING

We move on to the aspects of nonlinear programming which form the main subject of our investigatons. As before, our purpose is not to be as general as possible, but rather to sketch the mathematical foundations for some types of mathematical programming problems that we will repeatedly encounter in subsequent economic applications. In most cases, these problems will involve maximizing a concave, mathematically well-behaved function over a linear constraint set and/or minimizing a convex function over a linear constraint set.

Figure 2.5. A Boundary Saddle-Point

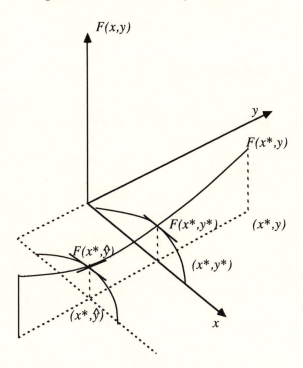

Our problems will generally be of a form like the following: Let $f(x)$ be a concave, continuous, and differentiable function defined for all $x \geq 0$ where x is a vector of dimension N and $x \geq 0$ means that all components are non-negative. The nonlinear programming problem to be considered is the following:

(2.23)   *max f(x)*

subject to $Ax \leq b, x \geq 0$

where A is a matrix of constants $A = [a_{mn}]$ $(m = 1, 2,. . ., M;$ $n = 1, 2, . . .,$ $N)$ and b is a vector of constants $b = [b_m]$ $(m = 1, 2, . . ., M)$.[3] The set of admissible solutions $Ax \le b, x \ge 0$ is assumed to be nonempty, bounded, closed, and convex.

We now utilize the Kuhn–Tucker theorem for which we introduce the vector of Lagrange multipliers or dual variables $y = [y_m]$ $(m = 1, 2, . . .,$ $M)$ constrained to be non-negative in the Lagrangean

$$(2.24) \qquad L(x,y) = f(x) + y^T (b - Ax)$$

and consider the biextremal problem

$$(2.25) \qquad \max_x \ \min_y f(x) + y^T (b - Ax) = \max_x \ \min_y L(x,y)$$

subject to $x \ge 0$, $y \ge 0$

The next theorem provides the motivation for forming the Lagrangean:

Theorem 2.2. Kuhn–Tucker Equivalence Theorem. The N-vector x^* is an optimal solution to the nonlinear programming problem (2.23) if and only if there exists a non-negative M-vector of Lagrange multipliers $y^* = [y_m^*]$ such that (x^*,y^*) is a saddle-point to the biextremal problem (2.25).

The reader should note that this theorem assumes an especially simple and attractive form here since the treatment is limited to nonlinear programming problems with a linear constraint set. The Kuhn–Tucker equivalence theorem tells us that solving the nonlinear programming problem (2.23) and the saddle-point problem (2.25) are mathematically equivalent. This greatly widens the scope of the potential economic applications and helps to explain why we have devoted so much attention to saddle-point characterizations and analyses.

The proof of the "if" part of theorem 2.2 is provided below.

Assume that (x^*,y^*) is a saddle-point to (2.25). Then, by definition,

(2.26) $f(x) + y^{*T} (b - Ax) \leq f(x^*) + y^{*T} (b - Ax^*)$ *for all* $x \geq 0$

(2.27) $f(x^*) + y^{*T} (b - Ax^*) \leq f(x^*) + y^T (b - Ax^*)$ *for all* $y \geq 0$

It is convenient to look at the second of these two equations first. It reduces to

(2.28) $y^{*T} (b - Ax^*) \leq y^T (b - Ax^*)$ *for all* $y \geq 0$

Choosing the components of y arbitrarily large, it follows that $b - Ax^*$ must be non-negative. Choosing $y = 0$, it follows that $y^{*T}(b - Ax^*)$ is nonpositive. Since the vector y itself is non-negative, one concludes that $y^{*T}(b - Ax^*)$ must in fact equal zero.

The inequality (2.26) now reads

(2.29) $f(x) + y^{*T} (b - Ax) \leq f(x^*)$ *for all* $x \geq 0$

which implies

(2.30) $f(x^*) \geq f(x)$

for all x that satisfy $b - Ax \geq 0, x \geq 0$.

In other words, x^* is an optimal solution to (2.23).

Turning to the "only if" part of theorem 2.2, it is instructive first to say a few words about the classical method of Lagrange multipliers. This method applies to the case when all constraints are equality constraints and when the unknowns are unrestricted in sign, that is, when program (2.23) simply reads *max f(x)* subject to $Ax = b$, *x* unrestricted in sign. For the classical method, one defines a vector of Lagrange multipliers y and forms the Lagrangean expression $f(x) + y^T (b - Ax)$. Next, one determines the extreme points of this expression by forming all partial derivatives of the Lagrangean, both with respect to the x variables and the y variables, and putting all these partial derivatives equal to zero.

The underlying reason why the classical method works is that the function $f(x) + y^T(b - Ax)$ has a saddle-point. More precisely, x^* solves the problem *max f(x)* subject to $Ax = b$, x unrestricted in sign, if and only if there exists a vector y^* such that (x^*, y^*) is a saddle-point to $f(x) + y^T(b - Ax)$.

These observations can be taken as a starting point for designing a proof of the "only if" part of theorem 2.2. The extensions of the classical method of Lagrange multipliers may be introduced in two steps, first retaining the assumptions that all constraints are equality constraints but requiring the unknowns to be non-negative, and finally also dealing with inequality constraints.

Rather than going through the details of this reasoning here, we have opted for an exposition of the material in the reverse order, so that we present the most general case right from the start; we shall in a moment proceed to narrow down the mathematical treatment to the special cases dealing with equality constraints or variables unrestricted in sign. The last and final result (theorem 2.5) recovers the classical method of Lagrange multipliers. That is, whereas it is possible to synthesize a proof of the "only if" part of theorem 2.2 by presenting the material in the present section in exactly the opposite order, working backward from the particular to the general, we have opted rather to present to the reader the most general case up front, and its specializations afterward.

We now associate the following assumptions with (2.25) which provides access to theorem 2.1. The objective function $L(x,y) = f(x) + y^T(b - Ax)$ is continuously differentiable. Furthermore, $L(x,y)$ is concave in x and it is convex in y (actually, L is linear in y). Restating theorem 2.1 for the case of the present application, we have the following:

Theorem 2.3. The Lagrangean $L(x,y)$ in (2.24) has a saddle-point solution with non-negative components at (x^*, y^*) and a saddle value of $L(x^*, y^*)$ if and only if the following conditions are satisfied

$$(2.31) \quad \frac{\partial L(x^*, y^*)}{\partial x_n} = \frac{\partial f(x^*)}{\partial x_n} - \sum_{m=1}^{m=M} y_m^* a_{mn} \leq 0, \quad n = 1, \ldots, N$$

$$(2.32) \quad x_n^* \frac{\partial L(x^*, y^*)}{\partial x_n} = x_n^* \left(\frac{\partial f(x^*)}{\partial x_n} - \sum_{m=1}^{m=M} y_m^* a_{mn} \right) = 0, \, n = 1, 2, \ldots, N$$

(2.33) $\qquad x_n^* \geq 0,\ n = 1,\ ,\ldots, N$

(2.34) $\qquad \dfrac{\partial L(x^*,y^*)}{\partial y_m} = b_m - \displaystyle\sum_{n=1}^{n=N} a_{mn} x_n^* \geq 0,\quad m = 1, 2, \ldots, M$

(2.35) $\quad y_m^* \dfrac{\partial L(x^*,y^*)}{\partial y_m} = y_m^* \left(b_m - \displaystyle\sum_{n=1}^{n=N} a_{mn} x_n^*\right) = 0,$

$\qquad m = 1, 2, \ldots, M$

(2.36) $\qquad y_m^* \geq 0,\ m = 1, \ldots, M$

where $\partial f(x^*)/\partial x_n$ is the partial derivative of $f(x)$ with respect to x_n, evaluated at the point x^*.

The equality conditions (2.32) and (2.35) establish the following complementary slackness condition:

Theorem 2.4. Complementary Slackness. At an optimum, either the dual variable y_m^* obtained from the Lagrangean or the slack in the corresponding direct constraint associated with $b_m - \Sigma_n a_{mn} x_n^*$ must be zero. Similarly, either the direct variable x_n^* or the slack in the corresponding Kuhn–Tucker condition amounting to $\partial f(x^*)/\partial x_n - \Sigma_m y_m^* a_{mn}$ must be zero.

In economic applications we shall often use relations like $\Sigma_n a_{mn} x_n \leq b_m$ to indicate a market constraint, with b_m denoting the supply of some good m and $\Sigma_n a_{mn} x_n$ the total demand for the same good. The Lagrange multiplier y_m^* can be interpreted as the economic price of good m. Complementary slackness then states that if the optimal demand is strictly less than the supply $\Sigma a_{mn} x_n^* < b_m$, then the economic price $y_m^* = 0$ (the good is a so-called free good). Conversely, if the economic price is positive, $y_m^* > 0$, demand must equal supply $\Sigma_n a_{mn} x_n^* = b_m$.

The above statements are all in terms of inequalities in the constraint set $Ax \leq b$. This does not involve any real restriction, however, since equalities rather than inequalities can be handled in the following fashion. Suppose that the first inequality actually holds as an equality

$$(2.37) \qquad \sum_{n=1}^{n=N} a_{1n} x_n = b_1$$

Replace it with the following two inequalities.

$$(2.38) \qquad \sum_{n=1}^{n=N} a_{1n} x_n \leq b_1$$

$$(2.39) \qquad \sum_{n=1}^{n=N} - a_{1n} x_n \leq - b_1$$

since $\sum_n a_{1n} x_n = b_1$ if and only if these two inequalities are *both* satisfied. The Kuhn–Tucker conditions can then be written as before where the multiplier associated with (2.38) is represented as $y_1^+ \geq 0$ and the multiplier associated with (2.39) as $y_1^- \geq 0$.

The Lagrangean is now represented as

$$(2.40) \qquad L(x,y) = f(x_1, x_2, \ldots, x_n, \ldots, x_N) +$$

$$+ y_1^+ \left(b_1 - \sum_{n=1}^{n=M} a_{1n} x_n \right) + y_1^- \left(-b_1 + \sum_{n=1}^{n=M} a_{1n} x_n \right) +$$

$$+ \sum_{m=2}^{m=M} y_m \left(b_m - \sum_{n=1}^{n=M} a_{mn} x_n \right)$$

and the Kuhn–Tucker conditions introduced in theorem 2.3 then read

$$(2.41) \qquad \frac{\partial f(x^*)}{\partial x_n} - (y_1^{+*} - y_1^{-*}) a_{1n} - \sum_{m=2}^{m=M} y_m^* a_{mn} \leq 0,$$

$$n = 1, 2, \ldots, N$$

$$(2.42) \qquad x_n^* \left(\frac{\partial f(x^*)}{\partial x_n} - (y_1^{+*} - y_1^{-*}) a_{1n} - \sum_{m=2}^{m=M} y_m^* a_{mn} \right) = 0,$$

$$n = 1, 2, \ldots, N$$

$$(2.43) \qquad x_n^* \geq 0, \, n = 1, 2, \ldots, N$$

$$(2.44) \qquad b_1 - \sum_{n=1}^{n=N} a_{1n} x_n^* \geq 0$$

$$(2.45) \qquad -b_1 + \sum_{n=1}^{n=N} a_{1n} x_n^* \geq 0$$

$$(2.46) \qquad y_1^{+*} \left(b_1 - \sum_{n=1}^{n=N} a_{1n} x_n^* \right) = 0$$

$$(2.47) \qquad y_1^{-*} \left(-b_1 + \sum_{n=1}^{n=N} a_{1n} x_n^* \right) = 0$$

(2.48) $y_1^{+*}, y_1^{-*} \geq 0$

(2.49) $b_m - \sum\limits_{n=1}^{n=N} a_{mn} x_n^* \geq 0, \ m = 2, 3, \ldots, M$

(2.50) $y_m^* (b_m - \sum\limits_{n=1}^{n=N} a_{mn} x_n^*) = 0, \ m = 2, 3, \ldots, M$

(2.51) $y_m^* \geq 0, \ m = 2, 3, \ldots, M$

Noting that (2.46–47) can be condensed into $(y_1^{+*} - y_1^{-*})(b_1 - \Sigma a_{1n} x_n^*) = 0$, we see that the resulting system of conditions is actually identical to what one would get using the single equality (2.37) rather than the pair (2.38–39) and ascribing to it the Lagrange multiplier $y_1^+ - y_1^-$. In fact, defining $y_1 = y_1^+ - y_1^-$ we see that y_1 is not restricted in sign when it serves as the Lagrange multiplier for (2.37) which is the equation equivalent of the two inequalties in (2.38) and (2.39). We thus arrive at this simple rule: An equality appearing in the constraint set is dealt with in the same manner as the inequality constraints in (2.23) except that its Lagrange multiplier is unrestricted in sign.

This is the applicable rule for the conditions (2.35) and (2.36) in theorem 2.3 when y_m^* is associated with an equality that is not constrained in sign. Turning to (2.32) and (2.33), exactly the same reasoning applies to x_n^* when the derivative of the Lagrangean with respect to x_n is to be satisfied as an equality. That is, we replace this equality with two inequalities which are equivalent to the original equality and assign a variable $x_n^{+*} \geq 0$ to one inequality and a variable $x_m^{-*} \geq 0$ to the other inequality. Proceeding as before we thus obtain access to the same simple rule by putting $x_n^* = x_n^{+*} - x_n^{-*}$ so that x_n, a variable that is not constrained in sign, is associated with an equality condition in (2.31).

Proceeding to the generalization implied by these remarks, we have the following:

Theorem 2.5. Ordinary Lagrangean. The ordinary Lagrangean, which is formed only from equations $Ax = b$ with variables that are not restricted in sign, can be accorded the form (2.25) with the inequality conditions $x \geq 0, y \geq 0$ omitted.

It thus has a saddle-point solution *(x*, y*)* with these inequality conditions omitted in theorem 2.2 and the conditions $\partial L(x^*,y^*)/\partial x \leq 0$ and $\partial L(x^*,y^*)\partial y \geq 0$ replaced by $\partial L(x^*,y^*)/\partial x = 0$ and $\partial L(x^*,y^*)/\partial y = 0$, respectively.

Evidently the Kuhn–Tucker conditions greatly extend classical Lagrangean analyses without losing any of their results. Note, for instance, that the results of the latter analyses always satisfy the conditions of complementary slackness as given in theorem 2.4 since the equality conditions which are classically assumed in Lagrangean developments imply that all the corresponding slack variables vanish.

Exercise 2.1

In a market for a single commodity, the demand price function and the supply price function are, respectively,

demand: $P(x_d) = a_{11} + a_{12} x_d$
supply: $Q(x_s) = a_{21} + a_{22} x_s$

Now consider the problem of determining market equilibrium conditions when P, the demand price, is stated as the above (linear) function of the quantity demanded, x_d, and Q the supply price, is similarly stated as a function of x_s, the quantity to be supplied.

This problem can be solved by geometric inspection. It is of some interest for the further developments in this book, however, to note that a market problem of this type can also be represented as the optimal solution to a mathematical program. To see this, form the economic potential function calculated as the area under the demand curve minus the area under the supply curve, namely,

$$\int P(x_d)dx_d - \int Q(x_s)dx_s \equiv a_{11}x_d + 0.5a_{12}x_d^2 - a_{21}x_s - 0.5a_{22}x_s^2$$

where $\int$ is the indefinite integral sign. We omit the constants associated with these indefinite integrals since they do not enter into the solutions to be considered in the following programming problem:

$$max \; a_{11}x_d + 0.5a_{12}x_d^2 - a_{21}x_s - 0.5a_{22}x_s^2$$

subject to

$$x_d - x_s \leq 0, \; x_d, \; x_s \geq 0$$

which mathematically models the following problem: Maximize the economic potenial defined a moment ago subject to the following conditions (1) the quantity demanded cannot exceed the quantity supplied, and (2) neither the quantity demanded nor the quantity supplied can be negative.

Denoting the Lagrange multiplier of the supply constraint by p, the corresponding saddle-point problem is

$$\max_{x} \min_{p} \; a_{11}x_d + 0.5a_{12}x_d^2 - a_{21}x_s - 0.5a_{22}x_s^2 + p(-x_d + x_s)$$

where $x = (x_d, x_s)$.

The Kuhn–Tucker conditions read (see theorem 2.3):

$$p^* \geq a_{11} + a_{12}x_d^* = P_d(x_d^*)$$

$$x_d^*(p^* - a_{11} - a_{12}x_d^*) = 0$$

$$-p^* \geq -a_{21} - a_{22}x_s^* = -Q_s(x_s^*)$$

$$x_s^*(-p^* + a_{21} + a_{22}x_s^*) = 0$$

$$x_d^*, x_s^* \geq 0$$

and also

$$-x_d^* + x_s^* \geq 0$$

$$p^*(x_d^* - x_s^*) = 0$$

$$p^* \geq 0$$

Interpreting p^* (the optimal value of the Lagrange multiplier) as the market price, the following results are obtained at the optimum (which is a saddle-point):

(1) The demand price does not exceed the market price. If a positive amount x_d^* is demanded, the demand price will actually equal the market price: $a_{11} + a_{12} x_d^* = p^*$.
(2) The supply price does not fall short of the market price. If a positive amount x_s^* is supplied, the supply price will actually equal the market price: $a_{21} + a_{22}x_s^* = p^*$.
(3) Demand cannot exceed supply. If a positive price p^* is established in the market, demand will actually equal supply: $x_d^* = x_s^*$.

The procedures illustrated in this small example will be elaborated in the chapters to follow and will be extended along both the spatial and the vertical dimensions for economic activities.

2.4. LINEAR PROGRAMMING

We now show how the Kuhn–Tucker theorem may be used to develop the duality theory of linear programming. Consider

$$(2.52) \qquad max \quad c^T x$$
$$\text{subject to } Ax \leq b,\, x \geq 0$$

This is the standard maximization formulation of a linear programming problem in which c^T is a $1 \times N$ vector of constants and x is a $N \times 1$ vector of variables to be determined under the indicated constraints in (2.52). In addition to nonnegativity on all components of x there are M other constraints generated from the $N \times M$ matrix of constants A and the $M \times 1$ vector of constants b. The constraints in (2.52) are thus

$$(2.53) \qquad \sum_{n=1}^{n=N} a_{mn} x_n \leq b_m$$

for each $m = 1, 2, \ldots, M$.

We now introduce a vector of Lagrange multipliers y and reformulate the above as the following saddle-point problem:

$$(2.54) \qquad \max_{x \geq 0} \quad \min_{y \geq 0} \quad L(x,y) = c^T x + y^T (b - Ax)$$

This function is concave in x and convex in y and hence fits the assumptions we have been making. It is also differentiable and so we can apply the Kuhn–Tucker conditions in the following form:

$$(2.55) \qquad \frac{\partial L}{\partial x_n} = c_n - \sum_{m=1}^{m=M} y_m^* a_{mn} \leq 0,\, n = 1, 2, \ldots, N$$

$$(2.56) \quad x_n^* \frac{\partial L}{\partial x_n} = x_n^*(c_n - \sum_{m=1}^{m=M} y_m^* a_{mn}) = 0,$$

$$n = 1, 2, \ldots, N$$

$$(2.57) \quad x_n^* \geq 0, n = 1, 2, \ldots, N$$

and also

$$(2.58) \quad \frac{\partial L}{\partial y_m} = b_m - \sum_{n=1}^{n=N} a_{mn} x_n^* \geq 0, m = 1, 2, \ldots, M$$

$$(2.59) \quad y_m^* \frac{\partial L}{\partial y_m} = y_m^*(b_m - \sum_{n=1}^{n=N} a_{mn} x_n^*) = 0,$$

$$m = 1, 2, \ldots, M$$

$$(2.60) \quad y_m^* \geq 0, m = 1, 2, \ldots, M$$

Notice that the latter group of constraints (2.58–2.60) reproduces the constraints of the original problem, and adds the conditions of complementary slackness to each of these constraints. As to the interpretation of the first group of constraints (2.55–2.57) consider the following new linear programming problem formed from the same data as in (2.52):

$$(2.61) \quad min \sum_{m=1}^{m=M} y_m b_m$$

subject to
$$\sum_{m=1}^{m=M} y_m a_{mn} \geq c_n, n = 1, 2, \ldots, N$$

$$y_m \geq 0, m = 1, 2, \ldots, M$$

Introducing a vector of Lagrangean multipliers x, we are led to consider the saddle-point problem

$$(2.62) \qquad \min_{y \geq 0} \quad \max_{x \geq 0} \quad L(y,x) = y^T b + x^T (c - A^T y)$$

Writing the Kuhn–Tucker conditions to this new saddle-point problem, we recover exactly the same set of conditions (2.55–2.60). In particular conditions (2.55–2.57) now recoup the constraints of the new problem (2.61) and its corresponding conditions of complementary slackness.

The problems (2.52) and (2.61) are said to be dual to each other.

Thus by means of the Kuhn–Tucker conditions with accompanying interpretations we have been able to discover another problem (2.61), which can be represented in the following manner:

$$(2.63) \qquad \min y^T b$$

subject to $y^T A \geq c^T , y^T \geq 0$

Problem (2.63) is dual to (2.52).

We also have the following very important duality theorem of linear programming as first formulated by Kuhn and Tucker in association with D. Gale, see reference [3] at the end of the chapter.

Theorem 2.6. Duality Theorem of Linear Programming. Let (x^*,y^*) be the saddle-point to program (2.54). Then y^* is an optimal solution to the dual program (2.61), and x^* is an optimal solution to (2.52) with $c^T x^* = y^{*T} b$ (i.e., the optimal value of the direct program equals the optimal value of the dual program).

Proof: We assume as usual that the constraint sets are not empty and that they are convex and closed and bounded. Then since (x^*, y^*) is a saddle-point as obtained from (2.54), the Kuhn–Tucker conditions may be applied as in (2.55–2.60) to obtain values y^* and x^* which are optimal, respectively, for (2.61) and (2.52).

Using (2.59) and summing on m we obtain

$$(2.64) \qquad \sum_{m=1}^{M} y_m^* \, b_m = \sum_{m=1}^{M} \sum_{n=1}^{N} y_m^* \, a_{mn} x_n^*$$

Similarly, using (2.56) and summing on n we obtain

$$(2.65) \qquad \sum_{n=1}^{N} c_n x_n^* = \sum_{m=1}^{M} \sum_{n=1}^{N} y_m^* \, a_{mn} x_n^*$$

and therefore $\sum_m y_m^* \, b_m = \sum_n c_n x_n^*$, as asserted in Theorem 2.6, when y^* and x^* are optimal solutions. *Q.E.D.*

We further have

Theorem 2.7. Duality Theorem of Linear Programming (Weak Form). For any x and y which satisfy the constraints in (2.52) and (2.61), respectively, we have $c^T x \leq y^T b$. That is, all y^T satisfying the constraints of (2.61) will yield a functional value $y^T b$ at least as great as the value that can be secured for $c^T x$ from any x satisfying the constraints of (2.52).

Proof: Consider any solutions y^T and x which satisfy the constraints of (2.61) and (2.52). Applied to (2.61) we then have $y^T A x \geq c^T x$ and applied to (2.52) we have $y^T A x \leq y^T b$ so that

$$(2.66) \qquad c^T x \leq y^T A x \leq y^T b$$

as claimed in the theorem. *Q.E.D.*

Still other extensions of the very sharp and powerful duality theorem for linear programming can be made to situations in which the constraints of one problem or the other cannot be satisfied or in which one problem or the other may have an infinite (unbounded) value possible for the objective function.[4] Throughout this book, as already noted, we assume that such situations are not present. Thus on the assumption that the constraint sets in (2.52) and (2.61) are consistent, we can collect all of the above results together and write

$$(2.67) \qquad c^T x \leq c^T x^* = y^{*T} A x^* = y^{*T} b \leq y^T b$$

when these x and y values satisfy the constraints of (2.52) and (2.61) respectively.

2.5. THE THEORY OF GAMES

We have seen how a problem involving maximization only, as in (2.52), can be recast in a form that provides access to the Kuhn–Tucker theorem for saddle-point problems. In the process of applying this theorem, we discovered an associated dual minimization problem (2.61) with the property that the optimal values of the two problems are equal.

Now we proceed in an opposite direction and show how the Kuhn–Tucker theorem may be used to replace one saddle-point problem with two similar optimization problems. For this development we use an example from the theory of games or, in particular, the theory of zero-sum two-person games in a manner that provides firm contact with the foregoing results in linear programming. These two apparently separate disciplines (i.e., linear programming and the theory of games) are thus joined together so that either may be used, as desired, to interpret, enrich, or provide solution methods for the other.

To introduce pertinent concepts from the theory of zero-sum two-person games, we begin with the graphic example in figure 2.6. This graph is referred to as a game tree and represents the game of matching pennies as follows: A player designated as $\mathcal{P}_1$ is positioned at the bottom node where he is to choose a branch labeled H or T to correspond to a choice of "heads" or "tails," respectively. This choice by $\mathcal{P}_1$ is not revealed to the opposing player (labeled $\mathcal{P}_2$), who is positioned at a node in the tree according to the H or T branch selected by $\mathcal{P}_1$. Not knowing the latter's choice, $\mathcal{P}_2$ knows only that he is in the "information set" represented by the broken lines enclosing both of the nodes at which he might be positioned. Thus this information set represents the state of knowledge for $\mathcal{P}_2$ when he is to make his *H* or *T* choice so that, as represented, P_2 will know only that he is in this set and not the node in this set where he might have been positioned by P_1's choice.

Figure 2.6.   A Game Tree for Matching Pennies

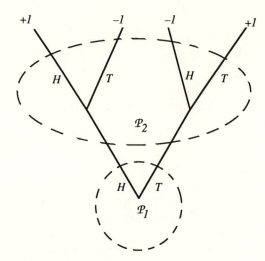

Source: Charnes and Cooper [2], p. 714.

Tracing the paths from an initial node at the bottom of this game tree to a node at the top produces a possible set of choices for P_1 and P_2 and a payoff value as indicated by the amount shown at each terminus at the top of the tree. Thus if the path is *H–H* or *T–T* the value 1 means that P_1 receives one penny as the "matching player." If the path is *H–T* or *T–H* then P_1 receives –1 which means that P_1 must pay one cent to P_2. The game is zero-sum in either case: What one person gains the other loses, in precisely the same amount.[5]

The above represents this game in "extensive form" because it provides extensive detail on all aspects of each move in the game. For many purposes it is preferable to represent the same game in an alternative form such the one in figure 2.7 which is said to represent this game in "normal form."

Each row and column pair in figure 2.7 represents a "pure strategy" choice and the amounts in the cells represent the payoffs for each such pair. Referring first to the rows, the intended meaning of this representation is that P_1 may choose one of two pure strategies such as "always choose H" or "always choose T" in repeated plays of this game. Siminarly, P_2 may choose a pure strategy like "always choose T." With the two pure strategies of "always choose H" by P_1 and "always choose T" by P_2 the amount indicated in the upper right-hand corner of the matrix represents the resulting payoff; the payoffs for any of the other strategy pairs are similarly located in the table.

Figure 2.7. The Matching Pennies Game in Normal Form

	H	T
H	1	-1
T	-1	1

Pure strategies are not the only possible choices, of course, and the theory of games really had its origin as a mathematical discipline when in 1926 John von Neumann introduced the concept of a mixed strategy.[6] To understand this concept, we jump forward and extend the 2 x 2 array of figure 2.7. For this extension we imagine an M x N matrix with elements a_{mn}, $m = 1, 2, \ldots, M$, $n = 1, 2, \ldots, N$, that represents the payoff values when P_1 chooses row m and P_2 chooses column n. If $a_{mn} > 0$, then the payment is from P_2 to P_1; if $a_{mn} < 0$, then the payoff is from P_1 to P_2 with the game being zero-sum, as before, in an evident extension of the conventions used for figure 2.7.

Instead of confining the choices to pure strategies like "always choose row m," we may also allow P_1 to choose row m a proportion of the time $p_m \geq 0$, which together with $\Sigma_m \, p_m = 1$ represents all such choice possibilities. This generalization moves the choices to mixed as well as pure strategy possibilities for P_1. Evidently the choice $p_m = 1$, which corresponds to the choice "always choose row m," continues to be admissible, as before, and this pure strategy choice also continues to be available in those cases where it is "best" for P_1. More generally, the problem for P_1 is to choose the best component values for the vector p with components p_m which satisfy $p_m \geq 0$ and $\Sigma_m \, p_m = 1$. Notice that when this is done then a further advantage occurs to P_1 if he chooses these optimum $p_m = p_m{}^*$ values from a corresponding probability distribution. Even if P_2 discovers P_1's strategy, he will still not know the choice that will actually be made in any play of the game. Indeed, P_1 will himself not know this choice until after drawing from the appropriate probability distribution, that is, a probability distribution which corresponds to these same $p_m{}^*$ values for designating which choices are to be made among the rows $m = 1, 2, \ldots, M$ on each play of the game.

In a similar way we arrive at a situation in which P_2 effects his choices subject to the condition $q_n \geq 0$, $\Sigma_n q_n = 1$, which is also used to identify a probability distribution to be used with the thus chosen strategy. We can therefore formulate the problem of optimal strategy choices for both players in the following terms. P_1 seeks to maximize the expected value of the game and P_2 seeks to minimize its expected value defined by

$$(2.68) \qquad v = \sum_{m=1}^{m=M} \sum_{n=1}^{n=N} p_m\, a_{mn}\, q_n$$

where

$$p_m, q_n \geq 0, \quad \sum_{m=1}^{m=M} p_m = \sum_{n=1}^{n=N} q_n = 1$$

and the optimal solution $v = v^*$ is called the "value of the game."

Notice that both players know the payoff elements in the game and the information sets and strategies available to each other. If each assumes that the other player is optimizing (minimizing or maximizing) in a manner opposite to his own then the problem of choosing an optimal strategy may be formulated as one or the other of the following biextremal problems:

$$(2.69) \qquad \min_{q} \ \max_{p} \ \sum_{m=1}^{m=M} \sum_{n=1}^{n=N} p_m\, a_{mn}\, q_n$$

subject to

$$\sum_{m=1}^{m=M} p_m = 1$$

$$\sum_{n=1}^{n=N} q_n = 1$$

$$p_m \geq 0, m = 1, 2, \ldots, M$$

$$q_n \geq 0, n = 1, 2, \ldots, N$$

and

(2.70)
$$\max_{q} \min_{p} \sum_{m=1}^{m=M} \sum_{n=1}^{n=N} p_m a_{mn} q_n$$

subject to

$$\sum_{m=1}^{m=M} p_m = 1$$

$$\sum_{n=1}^{n=N} q_n = 1$$

$$p_m \geq 0, m = 1, 2, \ldots, M$$

$$q_n \geq 0, n = 1, 2, \ldots, N$$

Here the payoff elements are the constants a_{mn} obtained from the matrix of the game in normal form, as already discussed, and represented in the functional, and the vectors p and q with components p_m and q_n, respectively, represent the strategy choices available to the two players. The terms "biextremal" and "biextremization" refer to the fact that each player is "extremizing" (optimizing) with the objective in (2.69) said to be a "minimax objective" in contrast to (2.70) in which the objective is stated in terms of a "maximin" problem.

In the minimax interpretation, $\mathcal{P}_1$ chooses p to maximize the value of v, as defined in (2.69), and $\mathcal{P}_2$ chooses q to minimize this same value. For maximin the process is reversed. As will be shown in what follows, by using the Kuhn–Tucker conditions, we have

$$(2.71) \qquad \min_{q} \max_{p} \sum_{m=1}^{m=M} \sum_{n=1}^{n=N} p_m a_{mn} q_n$$

$$= \sum_{m=1}^{m=M} \sum_{n=1}^{n=N} p_m^* a_{mn} q_n^*$$

$$= \max_{p} \min_{q} \sum_{m=1}^{m=M} \sum_{n=1}^{n=N} p_m a_{mn} q_n$$

This is the so-called minimax theorem of John von Neumann which, mathematically speaking, asserts that the same result will be achieved without respect to the order in which the extremizations (max and min) are taken. Furthermore, we will also have

$$(2.72) \qquad \sum_{m=1}^{m=M} \sum_{n=1}^{n=N} p_m a_{mn} q_n^* \leq$$

$$\sum_{m=1}^{m=M} \sum_{n=1}^{n=N} p_m^* a_{mn} q_n^* \leq \sum_{m=1}^{m=M} \sum_{n=1}^{n=N} p_m^* a_{mn} q_n$$

which is to say that the solution is at a saddle-point. Finally, as will also be seen, solutions to (2.69) and (2.70) always exist and are finite.

In order to provide the desired characterizations and proofs, we form the Lagrangean corresponding to (2.69):

$$(2.73) \quad \sum_{m=1}^{m=M} \sum_{n=1}^{n=N} p_m a_{mn} q_n + \lambda (1 - \sum_{m=1}^{m=M} p_m) +$$

$$+ \mu (1 - \sum_{n=1}^{n=N} q_n)$$

where λ and μ are Lagrange multipliers which, because they are associated with the equation conditions in (2.69), are not constrained in sign.

Now consider the saddle-point problem

$$(2.74) \quad \begin{array}{c} max \\ p, \mu \end{array} \begin{array}{c} min \\ q, \lambda \end{array} \sum_{m=1}^{m=M} \sum_{n=1}^{n=N} p_m a_{mn} q_n +$$

$$+ \lambda (1 - \sum_{m=1}^{m=M} p_m) + \mu (1 - \sum_{n=1}^{n=N} q_n)$$

subject to $p_m \geq 0$, $m = 1, 2, \ldots, M$, $q_n \geq 0$, $n = 1, 2, \ldots, N$

λ, μ unrestricted in sign

We now apply the Kuhn–Tucker saddle-point theorem. The conditions listed in that theorem as conditions (2.11) and (2.12) here read as follows:

$$(2.75) \quad \sum_{n=1}^{n=N} a_{mn} q_n^* - \lambda^* \leq 0, \, m = 1, 2, \ldots, M$$

$$p_m^* \sum_{n=1}^{n=N} a_{mn} q_n^* - p_m^* \lambda^* = 0, \, m = 1, 2, \ldots, M$$

$$1 - \sum_{n=1}^{n=N} q_n{}^* = 0$$

$$p_m{}^* \geq 0, m = 1, 2, \ldots, M$$

λ^* unrestricted in sign

and also

(2.76)
$$\sum_{m=1}^{m=M} p_m{}^* a_{mn} - \mu^* \geq 0, n = 1, 2, \ldots, N$$

$$q_n{}^* \sum_{m=1}^{m=M} p_m{}^* a_{mn} - q_n{}^* \mu^* = 0, n = 1, 2, \ldots, N$$

$$1 - \sum_{m=1}^{m=M} p_m{}^* = 0$$

$$q_n{}^* \geq 0, n = 1, 2, \ldots, N$$

μ^* unrestricted in sign

Note that summing on m in the second member of the constraint set in (2.75) gives

(2.77)
$$\sum_{m=1}^{m=M} \sum_{n=1}^{n=N} p_m{}^* a_{mn} q_n{}^* = \lambda^* \sum_{m=1}^{m=M} p_m{}^* = \lambda^*$$

since $\sum p_m{}^* = 1$, as given in (2.69). Similarly employing the second member of (2.76)

$$(2.78) \quad \sum_{m=1}^{m=M} \sum_{n=1}^{n=N} p_m{}^* a_{mn} q_n{}^* = \mu^* \sum_{n=1}^{n=N} q_n{}^* = \mu^*$$

so that $\lambda^* = \mu^* = v^*$, where v^* is the value of the game as defined in (2.68).

As was done when dealing with linear programming theory of duality, we interpret (2.75) as being the Kuhn–Tucker conditions formed from the Lagrangean for one problem, and interpret (2.76) as being the Kuhn–Tucker conditions for the Lagrangean for the dual problem. This pair of problems, one called the direct problem and the other called the dual problem, is

$$(2.79) \qquad \min \lambda \qquad\qquad\qquad \max \mu$$

subject to $\qquad\qquad\qquad$ subject to

$$\sum_{n=1}^{n=N} a_{mn} q_n \le \lambda \qquad\qquad \sum_{m=1}^{m=M} p_m a_{mn} \ge \mu$$

for $m = 1, 2, \ldots, M$ $\qquad\qquad$ for $n = 1, 2, \ldots, N$

$$\sum_{n=1}^{n=N} q_n = 1 \qquad\qquad\qquad \sum_{m=1}^{m=M} p_m = 1$$

$q_n \ge 0, n = 1, 2, \ldots, N \qquad\qquad p_m \ge 0, m = 1, 2, \ldots, M$

$\lambda \ge 0 \qquad\qquad\qquad\qquad\qquad \mu \ge 0$

Inspection shows that the solution sets for both problems are nonempty. We can now reason as follows to obtain a saddle-point characterization. The dual pair of linear programs (2.79) has an optimal solution, say $(p^*, \mu^*; q^*, \lambda^*)$. Hence the same point $(p^*, \mu^*; q^*, \lambda^*)$ is also a solution to conditions (2.75–76). The Kuhn–Tucker saddle-point theorem, then tells us that program (2.74) has a saddle-point. In other words,

$$(2.80) \quad \sum_{m=1}^{m=M} \sum_{n=1}^{n=N} p_m a_{mn} q_n{}^* + \lambda^* (1 - \sum_{m=1}^{m=M} p_m) + \mu (1 - \sum_{n=1}^{n=N} q_n{}^*) \le$$

$$\sum_{m=1}^{m=M} \sum_{n=1}^{n=N} p_m^* a_{mn} q_n^* + \lambda^*(1- \sum_{m=1}^{m=M} p_m^*) + \mu^*(1- \sum_{n=1}^{n=N} q_n^*) \le$$

$$\sum_{m=1}^{m=M} \sum_{n=1}^{n=N} p_m^* a_{mn} q_n + \lambda(1 - \sum_{m=1}^{m=M} p_m^*) + \mu^*(1 - \sum_{n=1}^{n=N} q_n)$$

for all $p_m \ge 0$, $m = 1, 2, \ldots, M$, $\mu \ge 0$; $q_n \ge 0$, $n = 1, 2, \ldots, N$, $\lambda \ge 0$.

Since also

(2.81) $$\sum_{m=1}^{m=M} p_m^* = 1 \text{ and } \sum_{n=1}^{n=N} q_n^* = 1$$

the relations (2.80) reduce to

(2.82) $$\sum_{m=1}^{m=M} \sum_{n=1}^{n=N} p_m a_{mn} q_n^* \le \sum_{m=1}^{m=M} \sum_{n=1}^{n=N} p_m^* a_{mn} q_n^* \le$$

$$\sum_{m=1}^{m=M} \sum_{n=1}^{n=N} p_m^* a_{mn} q_n$$

which forms a saddle-point at (p^*, q^*).

Turning from (2.69) to (2.70), the same set of Kuhn–Tucker relations would be obtained in the form of (2.75) and (2.76) when solving (2.70). Hence the optimal solution for (2.69) is also optimal for (2.70) and preceding arguments need not be repeated to show that the minimax theorem as given in (2.71) is true.

To illustrate what has just been done, we return to the game of matching pennies represented in figure 2.6 and utilize (2.79) to obtain the following formulations:

(2.83)   min λ max μ
            subject to   subject to

$$q_1 - q_2 \leq \lambda \qquad\qquad p_1 - p_2 \geq \mu$$
$$-q_1 + q_2 \leq \lambda \qquad\qquad -p_1 + p_2 \geq \mu$$
$$q_1 + q_2 = 1 \qquad\qquad p_1 + p_2 = 1$$
$$q_1, \quad q_2 \geq 0 \qquad\qquad p_1, \quad p_2 \geq 0.$$

Inspecting these two problems, it is clear that $\lambda = 0$ is feasible for one problem and $\mu = 0$ is feasible for the other. Hence via the duality theory of linear programming these solutions are optimal with $\lambda^* = \mu^* = 0$. It follows that we must have $q_1^* \leq q_2^*$ and $q_2^* \leq q_1^*$ which can only be satisfied with $q_1^* = q_2^*$. Because $q_1^* + q_2^* = 1$, this mean that the optimal solution is $q_1^* = q_2^* = 1/2$. By similar reasoning we obtain $p_1^* = p_2^* = 1/2$. Thus, from this analysis we find that the optimal solution for both players is a mixed strategy in which each tosses a fair coin (or utilizes some similar probability device) and then chooses H or T according to what is indicated by the outcome of the toss. This results in a "fair" game since $v^* = 0$ and neither player can expect to win or lose anything in continuing plays of the game if he plays according to his optimal mixed strategy.

In this particular case the solutions were fairly easy to achieve for each of the linear programming problems needed to solve the game of matching pennies. Generally formal algorithms will be needed. Game theory has not been concerned with developing efficient algorithms and has occupied itself mainly with extensions of the basic theory and a rich array of accompanying interpretations. Linear programming, on the other hand, has emphasized algorithmic developments which, starting with the simplex method, have achieved great efficiency and the power to deal with large, complex problems.

Via the connections that have just been established, access is provided to both disciplines when one of them is used. Thus the richness of interpretations from game theory can be imported into mathematical programming via this route or, conversely, the computational power of linear programming can be brought to bear on game theoretic formulations and applications. Indeed, the simplex method of linear programming applied to either member of (2.79) also yields an optimal solution to the other member of this pair without any extra effort (see, e.g., chap. 6 and 19 in [2]). This is to say that an optimizing solution to *one* linear programming problem in (2.79) also solves the bilinear minimax and maximin problems that are formalized in (2.69) and (2.70).

As a byproduct of the above development, we might underscore the fact that a solution to only one problem in linear programming thus solves a pair of nonlinear problems in the theory of games. This is accomplished by means of a solution method (the simplex method) and an accompanying set of theories such as the duality theory of linear programming and the Kuhn–Tucker theorems of nonlinear programming. These and further such possibilities will be explained in the chapters that follow.

Let us return to the concept of a fair game that was mentioned when the value $v^* = 0$ was obtained for the game of matching pennies. Tossing a fair coin and paying off in equal positive or negative amounts according to how the coin lands also yields a fair game. The latter is a game in the classical gambling sense in that it does not admit of different strategy choices and hence can be dealt with by classical (passive) probability theory and without recourse to the more general notion of a strategy. Matching pennies, by contrast, involves *two* players with opposing objectives and so fairness is defined by reference to optimizing choices by *both* players. In this manner the theory of games generalizes classical concepts of rationality and extends them so that they are applicable to multiperson games, not necessarily zero-sum, in which players may both compete and cooperate with each other in numerous ways.

One other point might be made that is sometimes overlooked. The theory of games is just what the name says it is. That is, the theory is applicable to any game without respect to the tendencies, habits or skills of particular players. If the latter aspects are a concern, then an extension along lines suggested by A. Charnes (see [1]) might be used by adjoining constraints that reflect known tendencies or habits of the players. We can briefly indicate what is involved by extending (2.69) to the following

(2.84)
$$\min_{q} \max_{p} \sum_{m=1}^{m=M} \sum_{n=1}^{n=N} p_m a_{mn} q_n$$

subject to

$$\sum_{m=1}^{m=M} p_m = 1$$

$$\sum_{n=1}^{n=N} q_n = 1$$

with p_m, $q_n \geq 0$, as before, and also

$$
(2.85) \quad \sum_{m=1}^{m=M} p_m d_{ms} \geq d_s, \ s \in S
$$

$$
\sum_{n=1}^{n=N} b_{rn} q_n \leq b_r, \ r \in R
$$

where $s \in S$ means the indices s in the set S and $r \in R$ means the indices r in the set R.

The additional constraints in (2.85) represent tendencies of the two players in the following way. The first set of constraints associated with the set S represents known tendencies of $\mathcal{P}_1$ with respect to playing subsets of the rows available to him while the second set represents tendencies by $\mathcal{P}_2$ that are reflected in the subset of columns associated with the set R.

The complete theory for this constrained game formulation along with associated ideas for evaluating concepts such as strategic information on each player's tendencies are set forth on pp. 774–75 and 798–804 in A. Charnes and W. W. Cooper [2]. Here we will only note that the following formulation makes it possible to achieve these same results via the Kuhn–Tucker theorem.

We form the Lagrangean for (2.84) and (2.85):

$$
(2.86) \quad \sum_{m=1}^{m=M} \sum_{n=1}^{n=N} p_m a_{mn} q_n + \lambda \left(1 - \sum_{m=1}^{m=M} p_m \right) + \mu \left(1 - \sum_{n=1}^{n=N} q_n \right) +
$$

$$
+ \sum_{s \in S} x_s \left(d_s - \sum_{m=1}^{m=M} p_m d_{ms} \right) - \sum_{r \in R} w_r \left(b_r - \sum_{n=1}^{n=N} b_{rn} q_n \right)
$$

Carrying through the necessary operations and reasoning like before from the Kuhn–Tucker conditions derived directly from (2.86) produces the following pair of linear programming problems:

$$
(2.87) \quad min \ \lambda + \sum_{s \in S} d_s x_s \qquad max \ \mu + \sum_{r \in R} w_r b_r
$$

subject to   subject to

$$\sum_{n=1}^{n=N} a_{mn}q_n - \lambda + \sum_{s \in S} d_{ms}x_s \le 0$$

$$\sum_{m=1}^{m=M} p_m a_{mn} - \mu + \sum_{r \in R} w_r b_{rn} \ge 0$$

for $m = 1, 2,..., M$ for $n = 1, 2,..., N$

$$\sum_{n=1}^{n=N} q_n = 1$$

$$\sum_{m=1}^{m=M} p_m = 1$$

$q_n \ge 0, n = 1, 2, \ldots, N$ $p_m \ge 0, m = 1, 2, \ldots, M$

$\lambda \ge 0, x_s \ge 0, s \in S$ $\mu \ge 0, w_r \ge 0, r \in R$

Evidently we again have a pair of linear programming problems and if we assume the solution sets are not empty—a required assumption of consistency in this case—we still have a game theoretic setting in which constraints on the opposing player (e.g., due to habits of play) are taken into account in arriving at optimal strategies.

This is as far as we shall carry this exercise. As already shown, however, the Kuhn–Tucker theorem admits of very far-ranging and flexible uses, and we will therefore be able to use it repeatedly to unify our approaches for dealing with the economic problems that are formulated and addressed in the remainder of this book.

NOTES

1. See von Neumann and Morgenstern [9], Sec. 13.4.

2. The zero in the first and third member of (2.11) is a vector, the so-called null vector, with all components equal to zero. The 0 in the second member of (2.11) is the ordinary scalar zero. When the context is clear, as in the present case, we shall not introduce special notation to effect these distinctions explicitly.

3. Program (2.23) is an instance of maximizing a concave function on a convex set. Unfortunately, some authors call this "concave programming," others call it "convex programming." The issue can be avoided entirely by using the term "nonlinear programming".

4. For a proof by means of what are called simplex classification representations, see [2], p. 190.

5. Note, however, that this does not mean that the utilities of the two players are the same. Consequently, in utility terms one may receive more than the other in each case.

6. Von Neumann [8].

BIBLIOGRAPHIC NOTES

Section 2.1 discusses fundamental concepts but does not deal with existence. It should be noted, however, that the assumptions presented in the text (the objective function being continuous and concave-convex, and each constraint set being convex, closed, and bounded) are sufficient to guarantee the existence of a saddle-point. This result follows from von Neumann's famous minimax theorem (see [8] and [9]).

The original reference to the Kuhn-Tucker theorem is [7]. The formulation of the saddle-point theorem (2.1) emerges as a special case of Kuhn and Tucker [7], pp. 482–83. The "if" part of theorem 2.1, stating that the Kuhn–Tucker conditions are a necessary characterization of a saddle point, does not require the objective function to be globally concave-convex. The "only if" part of the same theorem, stating that the Kuhn–Tucker conditions are sufficient for x^*, y^* to be a saddle-point, needs the assumption that $F(x,y^*)$ is globally located not above the gradient through y^* and that $F(x^*,y)$ is globally located not below the gradient through x^*. These latter properties hold, of course, if F is concave-convex (see Charnes and Cooper [2], pp. 405–6).

Theorem 2.2, relating a nonlinear programming problem to the task of finding the saddle-point of the corresponding Lagrangean, is presented in many textbooks as the Kuhn–Tucker theorem (see, e.g., Intriligator [5], sec. 4.3). The "if" part of the theorem does not require differentiability (an elementary proof was supplied by Uzawa [11]).

For the formalities of the proof of the "only if" part of theorem 2.2, following the route indicated in the main text (generalizing the classical method of Lagrange multipliers by steps) see, e.g., Hadley [4], chap. 6. Assuming that the theory of linear programming is already known to the reader, the proof used in Charnes and Cooper [2], pp. 390–93 is attractive.

These proofs all assume differentiability. If differentiability is rescinded, one may follow the approach used in Karlin [6] and Uzawa [11] (see also Intriligator [5]).

If the constraint set in the original nonlinear programming problem is convex but not necessarily linear, the Kuhn–Tucker equivalence theorem requires that the constraints satisfy a constraint qualification condition (there must exist an interior point in the constraint set). The fact that the constraint qualification conditon can be dispensed with entirely in the case of linear constraints was pointed out by Karlin ([6], see his theorem 7.1.2).

REFERENCES

[2.1]   Charnes, A. "Constrained Games and Linear Programming," *Proceedings of the National Academy of Sciences* 39 (1953): 639–41.

[2.2]   Charnes, A. and W. W. Cooper. *Management Models and Industrial Applications of Linear Programming* 2 vols. New York: Wiley, 1951.

[2.3]   Gale, D., H. W. Kuhn, and A. W. Tucker. "Linear Programming and the Theory of Games." In *Activity Analysis of Production and Allocation*, eds. T. C. Koopmans. Cowles Commission Monograph, no. 13. New York: Wiley, 1951.

[2.4]   Hadley, G. *Nonlinear and Dynamic Programming.* Reading, Mass.: Addison-Wesley, 1964.

[2.5]   Intriligator, M.D. *Mathematical Optimization and Economic Theory.* Englewood Cliffs, N.J.: Prentice-Hall, 1971.

[2.6]   Karlin, S. *Mathematical Methods and Theory in Games, Programming and Economics.* Vol. 1. New York: McGraw-Hill, 1960.

[2.7]   Kuhn, H. W., and A. W. Tucker. "Nonlinear Programming." In *Proceedings of the Second Berkeley Symposium on Mathematical Statistics and Probability*, ed. J. Neyman. Berkeley, Calif.: University of California Press, 1951.

[2.8]   Neumann, J. von. "Zur Theorie der Gesellschaftsspiele," *Matematische Annalen* 100 (1926): 295–320.

[2.9]   Neumann, J. von, and O. Morgenstern. *Theory of Games and Economic Behavior*, 3d ed. Princeton, N. J.: Princeton University Press, 1953.

[2.10]   Nikaido, H. "On von Neumann's Minimax Theorem," *Pacific Journal of Mathematics* 4/1 (1954): 65–72.

[2.11]   Uzawa, H. "The Kuhn–Tucker Theorem in Concave Programming." In *Studies in Linear and Nonlinear Programming*, eds. K. J. Arrow, L. Hurwicz, and H. Uzawa. Stanford, Calif.: Stanford Univ. Press, 1958.

3

The Spatial Dimension

Every student of economics knows that equilibrium in a market is established at the point where the demand curve intersects the supply curve. But how do we find equilibrium prices and quantities in *two* geographically separated markets for the same good, with given and known unit transportation costs? That problem was posed and solved by P. A. Samuelson [27] in a paper that was to give rise to an entire body of analysis. In this chapter, Samuelson's original contribution and material directly related to it will be reviewed.

Samuelson limits his treatment to an analysis of spatial equilibrium for a single commodity. The demand in each region depends upon the price in the same region. The supply in each region is either fixed, or it depends on the price. The prices of all other commodities are frozen and kept outside the analysis; the model thus is a case of partial equilibrium (for this term, see sec. 1.3). The production process is not spelled out explicitly but is subsumed behind the supply curve in each region.

Consider the supply point in each region as a separate "origin." Consider each demand point as a "destination." The problem at hand can then be viewed as a specimen of the transportation problem (see sec. 1.1) being imbedded in a setting with a price-sensitive supply at each origin and a price-sensitive demand at each destination.

In order to solve the problem of spatial equilibrium, Samuelson adduces an economic potential function which is designed to reach a peak at the desired equilibrium point. More specifically, the potential function is chosen so that when the Kuhn–Tucker conditions of the resulting nonlinear optimization problem are written down, they will retrieve the desired market clearing conditions characterizing equilibrium. So, the economic potential function is simply a mathematical artifact employed in order to enable the analyst to use mathematical optimization methods to solve the given equilibrium problem.   Samuelson insists that no economic interpretation be given to the potential function itself. (As we shall show, the potential function is actually a utility function, albeit of a quite particular mathematical form.)

Earlier economists had no way of solving equilibrium problems other than equating demand and supply in each market. There would be one such equality for each market. Eventually, economists were to learn how to solve such systems of market equations by fixed-point methods. (For the theoretical developments, see Arrow and Debreu [1]; for the numerical treatment, see Scarf and Hansen [29].) Samuelson uses mathematical optimization as an alternative approach. To be sure, all models of partial equilibrium cannot be solved by optimization. For this, they need to be "integrable" so that the economic potential function exists. All economic equilibrium problems encountered in the present volume are assumed to be integrable so that they can be solved by optimization.

Recently, yet a third approach to the solution of economic equilibrium (partial or general equilibrium) has become practical: the so-called complementarity methods. Although these methods lie outside the purview of the present volume, they are of considerable interest since they provide an avenue for the analysis and numerical solution of nonintegrable equilibrium systems as well. The scope of the models to be discussed below thus actually transcends the limits set by the formal assumptions.

SYMBOLS USED IN CHAPTER 3

$h, k \in H$	regions
$i, j \in I$	goods
G	graph
x_h, x_{hi}	quantity demanded
w_h, w_{hi}	quantity supplied
ξ_h, η_h	variables of integration
p_h, p_{hi}	price
p_h^D, p_h^S	demand price, supply price
$D_h(p_h), D_{hi}(p_{hi})$	demand function
$S_h(p_h), S_{hi}(p_{hi})$	supply function
$P_h(x_h), P_{hi}(x_h)$	demand price function
$Q_h(x_h), Q_{hi}(x_h)$	supply price function
t_{hk}	quantity transported from region h to region k
c_{hk}	unit transportation cost for transportation from region h to region k
M	incidence matrix

α, β coefficients of linear demand price function, as in $\alpha_h - \beta_h x_h$

γ, δ coefficients of linear supply price function, as in $\gamma_h + \delta_h w_h$

3.1. SAMUELSON'S MODEL OF SPATIAL EQUILIBRIUM, 1

Consider the following simple spatial market system. There are several geographical regions $h \in H$ (H is the set of all regions while h indexes the individual regions belonging to this set). A single commodity is demanded in each region. Let the demand function in each region be $x_h = D_h(p_h)$, $h \in H$, here x_h denotes the quantity of the commodity demanded in region h and p_h its local price (the price may vary from location to location due to transportation costs). This is referred to as a "partial demand" function, meaning that the prices of all other goods and consumer income in each region are supposed to be given and held constant.

Under suitable regularity conditions the demand functions can be inverted to yield the corresponding demand price functions $P_h(x_h)$, $h \in H$, where the demand price $P_h(x_h)$ is the highest price that consumers are willing to pay for the quantity x_h. We assume that these functions are positive, differentiable, and nonincreasing on the domain of non-negative quantities $x_h \geq 0$.

There are a number of supply depots, say one in each region $h \in H$. (The concept of a "region" may be used in a flexible manner. For instance, in a study of the mining and distribution of coal, it may be convenient to consider a single mine or mining field as a separate "region"; there may be no demand inside the region itself.) The quantities available at the depots are supposed to be fixed and known. They may be represented by the symbols w_h, $h \in H$.

Let the quantity of the good transported from region h to region k be t_{hk}. Denoting the unit transportation costs between these regions by c_{hk}, total transportation costs are obtained by summing the expression $c_{hk} t_{hk}$ over all regions $h, k \in H$.

In principle, it is assumed that a transportation route exists leading directly from any region h to any other region k for all $h, k \in H$. In many applications, this assumption will not be fulfilled, as only a limited number of railway connections exist, only a few oil pipelines have been constructed, and so forth. With some ingenuity, however—as Phileas Fogg amply demonstrated in *Around the World in Eighty Days*—transportation from h to k can usually be arranged, but at a high cost. In any case, we assume that solutions for all the unknowns t_{hk} exist, $h, k \in H$, but some of the corresponding unit transportation costs c_{hk} may be equal to some very large positive number. For most problem solvers (who are not ready to spend an entire fortune on the task of finding suitable transportation) the optimization procedure to be considered will then drive those t_{hk}s which have a high unit cost down to zero. (The alternative approach is to lay down in advance the network of available transportation routes. See sec. 3.3 below.)

The problem at hand is to determine the spatial allocation of the good and the consumer prices that will be charged in the various regions.

In order to prepare for the analysis, form the following economic potential function in each region:

(3.1) $$\int_{x_{h0}}^{x_h} P_h(\xi_h)d\xi_h = \int P_h(x_h)dx_h$$

The economic potential function is an indefinite integral. In the detailed notation on the left-hand side, the symbol ξ_h is used as the variable of integration. The lower limit of the integration x_{h0} is an arbitrary initial point. The upper limit is x_h. The notation on the right-hand side is the common one of an indefinite integral, using the same symbol for both the variable of integration and for the upper limit of the integral. (The use of an indefinite integral thus involves the presence of an arbitrary integration constant. This will cause no complications in the subsequent development; the optimization to be undertaken is not affected by the presence of an arbitrary constant term in the optimand.)

The potential (3.1) may be interpreted geometrically as the area between the demand curve and the horizontal axis to the left of point x_h. (We shall develop this geometric interpretation further in sec. 3.2, see fig. 3.2.)

Remember that we assumed that the demand price function $P_h(x_h)$ is nonincreasing. The derivative of the expression (3.1) of the second order with respect to x_h is nonpositive. It follows that the potential function is concave.

Now we use the potential function (3.1) to form the programming problem

(3.2) $$max \sum_{h \in H} \int P_h(x_h)dx_h - \sum_{k \in H} \sum_{h \in H} c_{hk}t_{hk}$$

subject to

$$x_h - \sum_{k \in H} (t_{kh} - t_{hk}) \le w_h$$

$x_h, t_{hk} \geq 0$

$h,k \in H$

As can be seen, the objective function in (3.2) is formed by summing the potentials (3.1) in each region and deducting total transportation costs. We shall later—using a term of Samuelson's—refer to the objective function as "net social payoff."

There is one constraint in each region: the local demand in the region cannot exceed the local supply augmented by the net inflows from other regions. The symbol t_{kh} represents inflows or "in-shipments" from region k to region h; summing over all regions k one finds total in-shipments into region h. Similarly, the symbol t_{hk} represents outflows or "out-shipments" from region h to region k; summing over k one finds total out-shipments from region h. The difference between these two sums is net in-shipments into region h.

Program (3.2) is an instance of nonlinear programming in which the objective function is concave; the constraints are linear; and the solution set is non-empty and bounded for any $w_h \geq 0$.

We now solve and interpret this problem using the Kuhn–Tucker analysis from chapter 2. Proceeding as in section 2.3, form the Lagrangean

$$(3.3) \qquad \sum_{h \in H} \int P_h(x_h)dx_h - \sum_{h \in H} \sum_{k \in H} c_{hk}t_{hk}$$

$$+ \sum_{h \in H} p_h(w_h - x_h + \sum_{k \in H} (t_{kh} - t_{hk}))$$

where p_h is the Lagrange multiplier for the hth constraint. These multipliers are non-negative and we interpret the optimal p_h^* as the market price of the commodity, charged for delivery at the supplier's depot in region h.

Partial differentiation of the Lagrangean (3.3) now yields the Kuhn–Tucker conditions listed in theorem 2.3. The following conditions must then hold at any optimum:

(i)   There is equilibrium in each regional market for the good. There is a pair of Kuhn–Tucker conditions stating

(3.4) $x_h^* - \sum_{k \in H} (t_{kh}^* - t_{hk}^*) \leq w_h$

$p_h^*(x_h^* - \sum_{k \in H} (t_{kh}^* - t_{hk}^*) - w_h) = 0;$

$h \in H$

The standard case assumed in economic theory is that a positive price will be quoted. The market must then clear, that is, total demand equals total supply (local supply plus net in-shipments). But it is also possible that some supply is left unsold in the market (an excess supply); the market price must then fall to zero.

(ii)   Regional prices can differ at most by the unit cost of shipping the good from one region to another. A shipper can therefore never make a profit by transporting the good between regions; the best he can do is to break even. The relevant Kuhn–Tucker conditions are

(3.5) $-p_h^* + p_k^* \leq c_{hk}$

$t_{hk}^*(-p_h^* + p_k^* - c_{hk}) = 0;$

$h, k \in H$

A shipper contemplating the transportation of the good from region h to region k will compare the appreciation of value $p_k^* - p_h^*$ with the unit transportation cost c_{hk}. If the increase in market value does not cover the transportation cost, the shipment will not pay for itself. Indeed, conditions (3.5) state that regional prices can differ at most by the unit transportation cost. If positive shipments take place, the price differential assumes this maximum value, that is, if $t_{hk}^* > 0$ then $p_k^* - p_h^* = c_{hk}$ by virtue of the above conditions.

(iii) The consumers in each region are adjusted to equilibrium in the sense that:

(3.6) $p_h^* \geq P_h(x_h^*)$

$x_h^*(p_h^* - P_h(x_h^*)) = 0;$

$h \in H$

As long as a positive quantity is demanded $x_h^* > 0$, the market price will equal the demand price $p_h^* = P_h(x_h^*)$. But in degenerate situations we may have $p_h^* > P_h(x_h^*)$ in which case the market price exceeds the demand price and the second condition above then implies $x_h^* = 0$ and demand must then have dropped to zero. (Remember that as long as the market price is positive, the market must clear, so that local supply plus net in-shipments must then also equal zero.)

Exercise 3.1

For the purpose of marketing industrial air-conditioning equipment in the United States, the country is divided into two geographical areas: the North and the South. The demand price functions in the two regions are, respectively,

$$p_N = 12{,}000 - 2.0x_N$$

$$p_S = 18{,}000 - 3.5x_S$$

The total U.S. market is served by three plants, the output capacity of which are 4,000, 2,800 and 1,800 units per week, respectively. The unit transportation costs (in dollars) from each plant to each demand region are as follows:

	North	South
Plant #1	800	200
Plant #2	400	200
Plant #3	100	500

Write an extremal formulation which will solve for the distribution of output from each plant to the consumer regions.

Solution: For the purpose of forming the economic potential function, first integrate the two demand price functions (suppressing the integration constants):

$$\int (12{,}000 - 2.0x_N)dx_N = 12{,}000x_N - x_N^2$$

$$\int (18,000 - 3.5x_S)dx_S = 18,000x_S - 1.75x_S^2$$

The net potential is obtained as the sum of these two integrals, deducting total transportation cost:

$$12,000x_N - x_N^2 + 18,000x_S - 1.75x_S^2 - 800t_{1N} - 200t_{1S}$$

$$- 400t_{2N} - 200t_{2S} - 100t_{3N} - 500t_{3S}$$

Program (3.2) requires us to maximize this potential subject to a market constraint in each region. For the purpose of the analysis, consider each plant and each consumer market as a separate geographical entity. There are then five "regions" in the model. In two regions there is demand but no supply depot; the in-shipments must cover the local demand:

$$x_N - t_{1N} - t_{2N} - t_{3N} \leq 0$$

$$x_S - t_{1S} - t_{2S} - t_{3S} \leq 0$$

In the remaining three regions there is a single supply depot but no demand; the out-shipments cannot exceed the local supply:

$$t_{1N} + t_{1S} \leq 4,000$$

$$t_{2N} + t_{2S} \leq 2,800$$

$$t_{3N} + t_{3S} \leq 1,800$$

Finally, all unknowns must be non-negative.

The optimal solution is illustrated in figure 3.1. The optimal demand for air-conditioning equipment in the North is 4,345.5; in the South it is 4,254.5. The demand is met by shipments in the following fashion: Plant #1 ships all of its output to the South. Plant #2 ships the quantity 2,545.5 to the North and 254.5 to the South. Plant #3 ships all of its output to the North (notice the low unit transportation cost).

The lower panel illustrates the equilibrium prices. Prices at the three plants are \$2,909.1, \$2,909.1 and \$3,209.1, respectively. Prices in the two consumer regions are $p_N = \$3,309.1$ and $p_S = \$3,109.1$. Note that the price increase from plant to consumer district always equals the unit transportation cost. (The price increase along routes which are not utilized is less than the unit transportation cost.)

Figure 3.1. Optimal Solution to Exercise 3.1

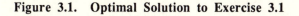

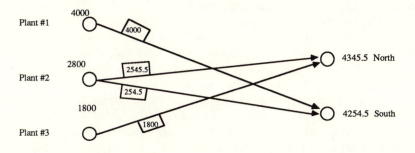

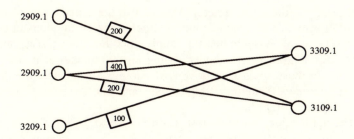

Upper Panel: Quantity solution. Optimal demands are listed at the respective markets, on the right. Flags indicate optimal shipments from plants to markets.

Lower Panel: Price solution. Implied unit costs at plant doors listed on the the left, equilibrium prices in markets on the right. Flags indicate unit transportation costs.

Finally, we note that the demand price in each consumer region equals the market price:

$$p_N = 12,000 - 2.0 \times 4,354.5 = \$3,309.2$$

$$p_X = 18,000 - 3.5 \times 4,254.5 = \$3,309.3$$

(There are some rounding errors because all figures have been rounded off to one decimal point.) So, the consumers in each region are adjusted to equilibrium.

3.2. SAMUELSON'S MODEL OF SPATIAL EQUILIBRIUM, 2

Up to this point we have allowed demand to vary while fixing supply at some known level. Following Samuelson, we now relax the latter condition to account for price sensitivity of supplies as well. Geometrically, we can imagine several diagrams, one for each region. There is a local demand curve and a local supply curve in each region. The local demand can be met by local supply, or by supplies shipped in from other regions (which shifts the supply curve to the right). The task is to determine the equilibrium quantity and price in each region, and the routing of the good from exporting regions to importing regions.

Let the partial demand function and the partial supply function in each region be $x_h = D_h(p_h)$ and $w_h = S_h(p_h)$, respectively, where $h \in H$ indexes the region to be considered. The prices of all other goods and consumer income in each region are supposed to be constant and given. Assuming all demand and supply functions are invertible, we form the demand price functions $p_h^D = P_h(x_h)$ and the supply price functions $p_h^S = Q_h(w_h)$, respectively, $h \in H$. (To avoid misunderstanding, different notations are necessary for the demand price and the supply price.) Assume that the demand price functions $P_h(x_h)$ are positive, differentiable and nonincreasing on the domain of non-negative quantities. Assume that the supply price functions $Q_h(w_h)$ are non-negative, differentiable, and nondecreasing on the domain of non-negative quantities. In most applications, we shall simply assume that the demand curves are downward-sloping straight lines, and that the supply curves are upward-sloping straight lines.

The application that will most readily come to the mind of the reader may be some consumer good being distributed to meet consumer demand at a number of given locations. But the good does not need to be a consumer good. It can also be a producer good, like steel or cotton. The demand functions are then no longer directly generated by some underlying utility theory for the consumers at each location, but will rather reflect the optimal production plans of the various users of the producer good.

Now we extend the economic potential function in each region to the following form:

$$(3.7) \qquad \int_{w_{h0}}^{w_h} P_h(\xi_h)d\xi_h - \int_{w_{h0}}^{w_h} Q_h(\eta_h)d\eta_h =$$

$$= \int P_h(x_h)dx_h - \int Q_h(w_h)dw_h$$

In the extended notation above, the symbol ξ_h is used as the variable of integration for the integration of the demand price function and the symbol η_h as the variable of integration for the integration of the supply price function. The lower limits of integration, x_{h0} and w_{h0}, respectively, are two arbitrary initial points. In the abbreviated notation on the second line, the common notation of indefinite integrals has been used.

In the previous section we encountered the first term of the potential function (3.7). Putting the lower limit equal to zero $x_{h0} = 0$, it can be interpreted as the size of the area between the demand curve and the horizontal axis to the left of point x_h (see the shaded area in fig. 3.2, left panel). It represents the total expenditure which the consumers would be willing to incur if the good were sold to them incrementally, unit by unit. As the diagram makes clear, this total expenditure consists of two parts: actual cash expenditure obtained as p_h^D times x_h (the bottom rectangle) and consumers' surplus (the top triangle).

Figure 3.2. Economic Potential Functions by Region

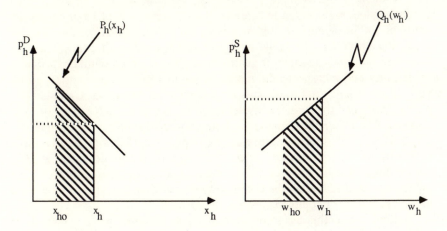

The second and negative term of the potential may also readily be accorded an economic interpretation. Putting the lower limit equal to zero $w_{h0} = 0$, it is the area between the supply curve and the horizontal axis to the left of point w_h (see fig. 3.2, right-hand side panel). It is the total incremental revenue that suppliers would obtain if they were to sell the good incrementally, unit by unit. It equals supplier revenue calculated as p_h^S times w_h (the area of the entire rectangle) minus producers' surplus (in the present instance one should perhaps more aptly use the term "suppliers' surplus").

We shall in general in this book elect to consider these potential functions as purely mathematical artifacts, formed for operational purposes only. As discussed in sec. 3.4, however, the potential (3.7) actually is an instance of a utility function, albeit of a quite restricted mathematical form. The first term of (3.7) then denotes the "utility" of an imaginary composite consumer residing in region h purchasing the quantity x_h, and the second term of (3.7) the "disutility" of an imaginary composite owner of supplies residing in region h supplying the quantity w_h.

Yet another interpretation is sometimes possible. If the good under consideration is a produced good (rather than a natural resource or labor), the supply price function $Q_h(w_h)$ may in the common manner be identified with a marginal cost—the marginal cost of the producers at location h. For instance, the supply price function of oil, or coal, is the same as the marginal cost of this source of energy. The integrated supply price function then simply equals total costs.

It may even be possible to accord a similar interpretation to the integrated demand price function. If the good is a producer good, that is, demanded by producers as an input into a production process, one may be able to identify the demand price $P_h(x_h)$ with the value of the marginal product of the producers at location h. The demand price of labor equals the value of the marginal product of labor. At least in principle, the demand price of coal equals the value of the marginal product of coal. (This last statement requires a number of qualifications having to do with the difficulty of defining and measuring the marginal product of an input demanded by very different industrial users, such as electric utilities, railways, and heating plants, and when these different users also may have several ranges of joint outputs.) The integrated demand price function then equals total revenue.

(If both of these interpretations apply, for both the supply price functions and for the demand price functions, the economic potential [3.7] comes out as the increase of value that occurs as one passes from the the the input costs incurred when the commodity in question is being manufactured to the value of the outputs that eventually result.)

Remember the assumption that each demand price function is nonincreasing and that each supply price function is nondecreasing. The partial derivative of the expression (3.7) of the second order with respect to x_h is non-positive. The partial derivative of the second order with respect to w_h is also non-positive. Hence, the potential function (3.7) is concave.

Consider now the program

$$(3.8) \qquad max \sum_{h \in H} \{ \int P_h(x_h)dx_h - \int Q_h(w_h)dw_h \} - \sum_{h \in H} \sum_{k \in H} c_{hk} t_{hk}$$

subject to

$$x_h - w_h - \sum_{k \in H} (t_{kh} - t_{hk}) \leq 0$$

$$x_h, w_h, t_{hk} \geq 0$$

$$h, k \in H$$

Samuelson called the maximand "net social payoff." It is calculated by summing the potential function (3.7) over all regions and deducting total transportation costs. Samuelson admonishes his readers not to read any economic significance into the concept:

> An economist looking at these figures would naturally think of some kind of consumer's surplus concept. . . However, the name consumer's surplus has all kinds of strange connotations in economics. To avoid these and to underline the completely artificial nature of my procedure, I shall simply define a net social pay-off function. (*op. cit.*, p. 288)

Program (3.7) is again an instance of convex programming with linear constraints. The objective function is concave. If the demand and supply functions are linear, the objective function is quadratic.

Once more we use Kuhn–Tucker analysis, with p_h denoting the Lagrange multipliers which are all non-negative, $h \in H$. We interpret the optimal $p_h{}^*$ as the market price of the good charged in region h. The following conditions are to be satisfied at the optimum point (indicated by an asterisk):

(i)   There is equilibrium in each regional market for the good. This requirement follows from inspection of the following pair of conditions:

(3.9) $$x_h{}^* - w_h{}^* - \sum_{k \in H} (t_{kh}{}^* - t_{hk}{}^*) \leq 0,$$

$$p_h{}^*(x_h{}^* - w_h{}^* - \sum_{k \in H} (t_{kh}{}^* - t_{hk}{}^*)) = 0;$$

$$h \in H$$

The standard case is that the market price p_h^* in region h is positive, in which case the market in the region must clear. But the possibility of an unsold excess supply also exists; in that case the price must drop to zero.

(ii)   Regional prices can differ at most by the unit cost of shipping the good from one region to another. A shipper can therefore never make a profit by transporting the good between regions; the best he can do is to break even. (If he were to suffer a loss, the transportation would not take place.)

For one finds

(3.10) $-p_h^* + p_k^* \leq c_{hk}$

$t_{hk}^*(-p_h^* + p_k^* - c_{hk}) = 0,$

$h, k \in H$

If a positive quantity is transported, the price differential equals the unit transportation cost. But if the price differential is less than the unit transportation cost, no shipments will occur between the two regions.
(We have here recovered condition [3.5] above.)

(iii)   Finally, the Kuhn–Tucker conditions tie the market price both to the demand price and the supply price:

(3.11) $p_h^* \geq P_h(x_h^*), \, x_h^*(p_h^* - P_h(x_h^*)) = 0$

$p_h^* \leq Q_h(w_h^*), \, w_h^*(p_h^* - Q_h(w_h^*)) = 0$

$h \in H$

In the standard case, both equilibrium demand and equilibrium supply in a region are positive. The market price, the demand price, and the supply price are then all equal to each other. But degenerate cases are possible. The demand price may fall short of the market price; if so, demand equals zero. The supply price may exceed the market price; in this situation supply equals zero.

It should of course be no surprise that the Kuhn–Tucker conditions spell out a number of economic properties that we would like to associate with equilibrium, such as market clearing and that regional price differences are exhausted by costs. The economic potential function and program (3.8) were constructed precisely so that they would give rise to these conditions. The reader is asked to remember that the totality of the Kuhn–Tucker conditions is mathematically equivalent to the extremal formulation. To be specific: The point $(x^*, w^*, t^*; p^*)$ satisfies conditions (3.9–11) if and only if x^*, w^*, t^* is an optimal solution to program (3.8) and p^* is the optimal vector of corresponding Lagrange multipliers (refer to theorems 2.2–3 in the preceding chap.). So, from a purely logical point of view we have just converted one mathematical characterization of equilibrium into another equivalent one.

This conversion is a rather remarkable mathematical achievement. The equilibrium conditions (3.9–11) taken by themselves constitute a specimen of a category of mathematical problems that are in general quite difficult to deal with. They form a so-called complementarity problem. The general analysis of such problems falls outside the scope of the present volume and we are therefore not able here to pursue these contacts further. In the present case, we have been able to convert the complementarity problem into an equivalent mathematical programming problem, the solution of which is quite routine. This programming problem is constructed as a mathematical artifact, and is designed to peak at the desired solution point of equilibrium.

From a numerical point of view, the conversion of the given complementarity problem to an extremal formulation permits immediate numerical solution using a standard nonlinear programming computer code.

Exercise 3.2

In a study of the production and distribution of milk, a state has been divided into three regions: the mountains $(h = 1)$, the plains $(h = 2)$, and the coast $(h = 3)$. The supply price functions (in dollars) are, respectively,

$$Q_1(w_1) = 100 + 4w_1$$

$$Q_2(w_2) = 250 + 2w_2$$

$$Q_3(w_3) = 300 + 1.5w_3$$

The supplies w_1, w_2 and w_3 are measured in thousands of gallons per day.

There are two large cities in the state $(h = 4$ and $h = 5)$. The distances (in miles) from the production regions (counted from the supply points) to the cities are as follows:

	City 1	City 2
Mountains	20	80
Plains	60	120
Coast	200	10

The transportation cost is $0.01 per thousands of gallons per mile, in any direction. The demand price functions (in dollars) in the two cities are, respectively,

$$P_4(x_4) = 425 - x_4$$

$$P_5(x_5) = 500 - 1.5x_5$$

The demands x_4 and x_5 are also measured in thousands of gallons per day.

Write an extremal formulation which will solve for the distribution of milk to the two cities, and for the pricing of milk.

Solution. The economic potential function is formed by adding the following three terms:
The integrated demand price functions

$$425x_4 - 0.5(x_4)^2 + 500x_5 - 0.75(x_5)^2$$

minus the integrated supply price functions

$$100w_1 + 2(w_1)^2 + 250w_2 + (w_2)^2 + 300w_3 + 0.75(w_3)^2$$

minus total transportation costs

$$0.2t_{14} + 0.8t_{15} + 0.6t_{24} + 1.2t_{25} + 2.0t_{34} + 0.1t_{35}$$

Proceeding as in (3.8), we should maximize the potential function subject to market conditions in each production region

$$t_{14} + t_{15} - w_1 \leq 0$$

$$t_{24} + t_{25} - w_2 \leq 0$$

$$t_{34} + t_{35} - w_3 \leq 0$$

and a market condition in each consuming region (city):

$$x_4 - t_{14} - t_{24} - t_{34} \leq 0$$

$$x_5 - t_{15} - t_{25} - t_{35} \leq 0$$

All unknowns must be non-negatives.

The optimal solution is illustrated in figure 3.3. The optimal demand for milk in city #1 is 65.66 thousands of gallons per day; in city #2 it is 93.38. In order to satisfy this demand, all milk from the plains is shipped to city #1, and all milk from the coast is shipped to city #2. The remaining demand in the two cities is covered by shipments from the mountains.

Figure 3.3. Optimal Solution to Exercise 3.2

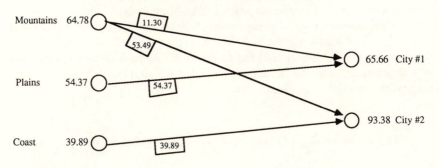

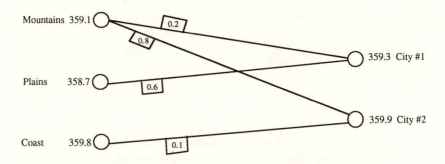

Upper panel: Quantity solution. Optimal supplies are listed on the left, optimal demands on the right. Flags indicate optimal shipments.

Lower panel: Price solution. Equilibrium prices at supply centers are listed on the left; equilibrium consumer prices on the right. Flags indicate unit transportation costs.

The lower panel illustrates optimal prices in dollars per thousands of gallons. The price differential along any route along which milk is shipped equals the unit transportation cost.

As an example of spatial equilibrium, consider the following so-called generalized transportation model.   Assume that the regions can be partitioned into two distinct groups, to be referred to as "origins" and "destinations."   At each origin, there is a supply price function but no demand.   At each destination, there is a demand price function but no supply.   Directed transportation routes link each origin with each destination.

At no region is there both a supply price function and a demand price function.   Neither are there regions lacking both supply and demand (such regions would serve the sole purpose of trans-shipments).

With some change of notation, let there be $h = 1,2,\ldots, H$ origins and $k = 1,2,\ldots,K$ destinations.   At each origin h, there is a supply w_h forthcoming (to be determined) but no demand.   At each destination k, there is a demand x_h (also to be determined) but no supply.   The generalized transportation model then reads

$$(3.12) \quad \max \sum_{k \in K} \int P_k(x_k)dx_k - \sum_{h \in H} \int Q_h(w_h)dw_h - \sum_{h \in H} \sum_{k \in K} c_{hk}t_{hk}$$

subject to

$$x_k - \sum_{h \in H} t_{hk} \leq 0, \, k \in K$$

$$- w_h + \sum_{k \in K} t_{hk} \leq 0, \, h \in H$$

$$x_k, w_h, t_{hk} \geq 0, \, h \in H, \, k \in K$$

Actually, we have already encountered a generalized transportation model. The milk example in exercise 3.2 is a specimen of this model type.

If the supply curve at each origin is vertical (i.e., a fixed and known supply) and if the demand curve at each destination is likewise vertical (a fixed and known demand), program (3.12) simplifies into the well-known transportation problem (for a discussion of the setting of this problem, see sec. 1.1; for references, see chap. 1, n. 1). Using the letter w_h to denote the fixed supply at the origin h and the letter x_h to denote the fixed demand at destination k, it reads

$$(3.13) \qquad \min \sum_{h \in H} \sum_{k \in K} c_{hk}t_{hk}$$

subject to

$$\sum_{h \in H} t_{hk} \geq x_k$$

$$\sum_{k \in K} t_{hk} \leq w_h$$

$$t_{hk} \geq 0,$$

$$h \in H, k \in K$$

This is a simple linear programming problem involving only the shipments t_{hk} as unknowns.

So, Samuelson's model of spatial equilibrium can be transformed into the transportation problem when the regional demand and supply curves are all vertical. Conversely, we may look upon Samuelson's model as a mathematical generalization which extends the transportation problem to price-sensitive demands and supplies rather than fixed demands and fixed supplies.

Winding up our discussion of Samuelson's model of spatial equilibrium, note that if the supply in one or several regions is fixed and given (i.e., the supply curve is vertical) rather than price-sensitive, the area below those supply curves vanishes and the program (3.8) becomes (3.2). Similar simplifications occur if the demand in one or several regions is fixed and given (the demand curve is vertical).

Another kind of simplification occurs when a good is supplied in some regions at a fixed and known price, or when it can be sold at some demand points at a fixed and known price. Such instances may be encountered quite often in partial analysis, when the model builder may decide to treat many supply sources or demand outlets as being outside the current model-building effort, treating the supply prices and the demand prices in these regions as exogenous. What this in effect amounts to is to assume that the supply curve of each exogenous supply and the demand curve of each exogenous demand are horizontal. The area beneath a horizontal supply curve equals the cost of that supply. The area under a horizontal demand curve equals the consumer expenditure on the good. The optimization procedure (3.8) then is to deduct the cost of fixed-price supplies from the objective function, and to add the revenue at fixed-price outlets to it.

3.3. SPATIAL NETWORKS

The models outlined in this chapter can be usefully represented as a network. A network consists of nodes and connecting links (or "arcs"). It is adapted to our purposes by letting each region be represented as a separate node and allowing the transportation of goods from one region to another to be represented by a connecting link between them.

The reader has already encountered some simple examples of networks in the numerical exercises (see figs. 3.1 and 3.3). A slightly more elaborate illustration is found in figure 3.4, which depicts a network with six regions represented as nodes $h = 1,2,3,4,5,6$. A good is produced locally in regions 5 and 6 and the resulting supplies in amounts w_5 and w_6 are entered as influxes into the network as indicated by the large inward pointing arrows at these nodes. The links between node pairs provide the available transportation routes. All routes are "directed," which means that flows can occur only in the directions indicated by the arrows. Note that if transportation were available between two nodes in both directions, two directed links should be entered, one in each direction for the node pair. The good is sold to consumers located in regions 1 and 2. The demands x_1 and x_2 are entered as effluxes from the network as shown by the large outward-pointing arrows at these nodes. At a node of trans-shipment—such as nodes 3 and 4—there is neither an influx nor an efflux.

Figure 3.4.   A Prototype Network

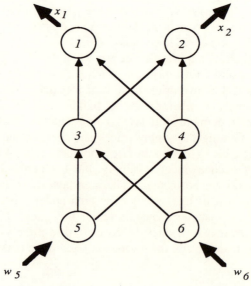

There are in principle two different ways to provide a mathematical specification of the layout of the network. One is to assume formally (as we have done in our treatment of Samuelson's model of spatial equilibrium) that there exists links leading from all other nodes into a given node; and, also, that there are links that lead from a given node to every other node. We may then assign a very large positive unit transportation cost c_{hk} to those links that do not exist in the actual network. The other is to eliminate nonexistent routes from consideration right from the start, putting the flows along such routes equal to zero. Only routes exhibited in the network can be assigned positive flow (the alternative that we are currently pursuing). Evidently, flows along nonexistent routes will be zero in either case.

We now turn to the algebraic representation of the corresponding network graph. The configuration of nodes and links in the network can be described by its incidence matrix arranged as follows. The matrix has one row for each node and one column for each link in the network. The elements of the matrix are entered columnwise as follows: each column corresponds to a link in which a minus 1 is entered in the row for the node on which the tail is incident, and a plus 1 in the row for the node on which the head of the arrow is incident. These are the only two nonzero entries in that column. All other entries are zero.

In the figure 3.4 there are six nodes and eight direct links. The links may be indicated by the notation $(6,3),(6,4),(5,3),(5,4),(4,1),$ $(4,2),(3,1),(3,2)$. The incidence matrix then is

$$
(3.14) \quad M = \begin{array}{c} \\ 1 \\ 2 \\ 3 \\ 4 \\ 5 \\ 6 \end{array}
\begin{array}{cccccccc}
(6,3) & (6,4) & (5,3) & (5,4) & (4,1) & (4,2) & (3,1) & (3,2) \\
\left[\begin{array}{cccccccc}
0 & 0 & 0 & 0 & +1 & 0 & +1 & 0 \\
0 & 0 & 0 & 0 & 0 & +1 & 0 & +1 \\
+1 & 0 & +1 & 0 & 0 & 0 & -1 & -1 \\
0 & +1 & 0 & +1 & -1 & -1 & 0 & 0 \\
0 & 0 & -1 & -1 & 0 & 0 & 0 & 0 \\
-1 & -1 & 0 & 0 & 0 & 0 & 0 & 0
\end{array}\right]
\end{array}
$$

In the common fashion of matrix notation, the elements of the incidence matrix M are exhibited inside two brackets. For the purpose of identification, the nodes are listed in the rim to the left and the links along the top.

Note that each column has exactly two nonzero entries consisting of a -1 and a $+1$.

The vector of influxes and effluxes is

$$(3.15) \qquad x - w = \begin{bmatrix} x_1 \\ x_2 \\ 0 \\ 0 \\ -w_5 \\ -w_6 \end{bmatrix}$$

This vector has one element for each node. The elements are entered as follows: for any influx, enter the amount with a negative sign; for any efflux, enter the amount with a positive sign; in the absence of influx or efflux (a trans-shipment node), enter zero.

The vector of unknown flows over the network is

$$(3.16) \qquad t = \begin{bmatrix} t_{63} \\ t_{64} \\ t_{53} \\ t_{54} \\ t_{41} \\ t_{42} \\ t_{31} \\ t_{32} \end{bmatrix}$$

It has one entry for each link featured in figure 3.4.

The Kirchhoff flow conservation conditions for networks require the sum of all flows entering a given node to equal the sum of all flows leaving the same node. In vector notation

$$(3.17) \qquad Mt = x - w$$

The conditions constitute a system of linear equations in the unknown flows over each link in the network. The vector of these unknowns appears on the left-hand side of the system, premultiplied by the incidence matrix M. The right-hand side is the vector of influxes and effluxes.

Carrying out the indicated multiplication of matrices, one obtains

$$\begin{array}{rcl} t_{41} + t_{31} & = & x_1 \\ t_{42} + t_{32} & = & x_2 \\ t_{63} + t_{53} - t_{31} - t_{32} & = & 0 \\ t_{64} + t_{54} - t_{41} - t_{42} & = & 0 \\ - t_{53} - t_{54} & = & - w_5 \\ - t_{63} - t_{64} & = & - w_6 \end{array}$$

(3.18)

The condition of unidirectional flow is represented by constraining all variables to be non-negative, that is, we require

$$t_{63}, t_{64}, t_{53}, t_{54}, t_{41}, t_{42}, t_{31}, t_{32} \geq 0$$

Now consistency requires that the sum of all influxes must equal the sum of all effluxes. Adding all equations (3.18) together

(3.19) $0 = x_1 + x_2 - w_5 - w_6$

Hence if $x_1 + x_2 \neq w_5 + w_6$ the system will not have any solution.

This consequence of the Kirchhoff conditions does not really limit us to cases in which total demand equals total supply as in (3.19). In case we want to permit the possibility of excess supplies we can easily do this by replacing system (3.17) by

(3.20) $Mt \geq x - w$

At each node, the slack is associated with an excess accumulation of the good (arising from local supply and/or from in-shipments into the node) above the requirements (local demand and/or out-shipments).

The spatial equilibrium network model for the above example can then be obtained from the following formulation:

(3.21) $max \int P_1(x_1)dx_1 + \int P_2(x_2)dx_2 - \int Q_5(w_5)dw_5 - \int Q_6(w_6)dw_6$

$-c_{63}t_{63} - c_{64}t_{64} - c_{53}t_{53} - c_{54}t_{54} - c_{41}t_{41} - c_{42}t_{42} - c_{31}t_{31} - c_{32}t_{32}$

subject to

$$x - w - Mt \leq 0$$

$$x, t \geq 0$$

Turning to the case of any spatial network with a graph G, the general programming format is

(3.22) $\max \sum\limits_{h \in H} \{ \int P_h(x_h)dx_h - \int Q_h(w_h)dw_h \} - \sum\limits_{(h,k) \in G} c_{hk}t_{hk}$

subject to

$$x - w - Mt \leq 0$$

$$x, w, t \geq 0$$

where x_h is the efflux at node h (if there is no efflux from node h, x_h is put equal to zero), w_h is the influx into node h (if there is no influx, w_h is put equal to zero) and $(h,k) \in G$ refers to the set of all links (h,k) that are in the network graph G.

If the graph G contains all possible links (h,k), $h,k \in H$, program (3.22) is identical to program (3.8).

Exercise 3.3

The following stylized example from reference [7] refers to the supply of workers with different educational and vocational backgrounds, and the determination of optimal retraining paths in a network representing all possible career choices.

The nodes of the network (fig. 3.5) represent various stages of education and acquired abilities, as follows:

Node 1:   High school completed with some vocational training in secretarial tasks

Node 2:   High school completed with some vocational training in mechanical subjects

Node 3:   Junior college or community college, liberal arts majors

Node 4:   Junior college or community college, science majors

Node 5:   Social worker

Node 6: Computer programmer
Node 7: Engineer

The links of the network represent avenues of possible training and advancement. The "flow" along each link represents the number of workers that undertake a given training program. The figure attached to each link is the "unit transportation cost," that is, the cost of engaging in a training program that makes the transit possible. In the diagram, this cost is measured in thousands of dollars.

The supply of workers at each node is sensitive to wages; the supply wage functions are as follows

Node 1: $p_1 = 0.00022 \, w_1^2$
Node 2: $p_2 = 0.00017 \, w_2^2$
Node 3: $--$
Node 4: $--$
Node 5: $p_5 = 0.00033 \, w_5^2$
Node 6: $p_6 = 0.00052 \, w_6^2$
Node 7: $p_7 = 0.00132 \, w_7^2$

where w_i is the local supply of workers at node i. The demand for workers, on the other hand, is supposed to be fixed and known, reflecting the particular needs of industry. The demands at the seven nodes are, respectively, *300, 250, 0, 0, 200, 200,* and *150* workers.

Figure 3.5. Retraining Paths in a Network

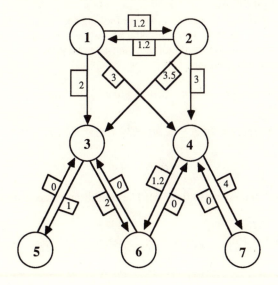

Provide an extremal formulation that will permit the determination of the optimal retraining paths in the network and the equilibrium wages at each node.

   Solution: First form an economic potential function integrating each supply wage function, adding these integrals all together, and also adding total retraining costs. Denoting the number of workers transiting from node i to node j by t_{ij}, the potential function reads

$$1/3\,(0.00022w_1{}^3 + 0.00017w_2{}^3 + 0.00033w_5{}^3 + 0.00052w_6{}^3$$

$$+ 0.00132w_7{}^3) + 1.2t_{12} + 2t_{13} + 3t_{14} + 1.2t_{21} + 3.5t_{23} + 3t_{24}$$

$$+ t_{35} + 2t_{36} + 1.2t_{46} + 4t_{47}$$

The Kirchhoff flow conservation conditions are

$w_1 - t_{12} - t_{13} - t_{14} + t_{21}$					$\geq\ 300$
$w_2 + t_{12}$	$- t_{21} - t_{23} - t_{24}$				$\geq\ 250$
t_{13}	$+ t_{23}$	$- t_{35} - t_{36}$		$+ t_{53} + t_{63}$	$\geq\ 0$
t_{14}	$+ t_{24}$		$- t_{46} - t_{47}$	$+ t_{64} + t_{74}$	$\geq\ 0$
w_5		$+ t_{35}$	$- t_{53}$		$\geq\ 200$
w_6		$+ t_{36} + t_{46}$	$- t_{63} - t_{64}$		$\geq\ 200$
w_7			$+ t_{47}$	$- t_{74}$	$\geq\ 150$

(The inequality signs allow for the possibility of an excess supply of labor—unemployment—at each node.)

   The extremal formulation that we are looking for requires the minimization of the economic potential function stated subject to the listed Kirchhoff conservation conditions and the conditions that all unknowns be non-negative.

   The optimal solution is

$$w_1{}^* = 270.4,\ w_2{}^* = 295.9,\quad w_5{}^* = 219.4, w_6{}^* = 185.5, w_7{}^* = 128.8$$

$$t_{21}{}^* = 29.6, t_{24}{}^* = 16.3,\quad t_{36}{}^* = 19.4, t_{47}{}^* = 21.2,$$

$$t_{53}{}^* = 19.4, t_{64}{}^* = 4.9$$

and all other $t_{hk}{}^* = 0$ (see also fig. 3.6). The equilibrium wages are

$$p_1{}^* = 16.1,\quad p_2{}^* = 14.9,\quad p_3{}^* = 15.9,\quad p_4{}^* = 17.9,$$

$$p_5{}^* = 15.9,\quad p_6{}^* = 17.9,\quad p_7{}^* = 21.9,$$

Note that the following condition is satisfied along each link along which there is a positive flow: the wage at the originating node plus the retraining cost equals the node at the destination node.

Figure 3.6.   Optimal Solution to Exercise 3.3

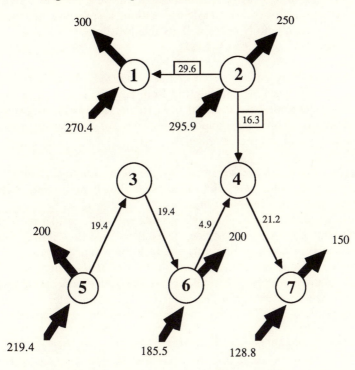

Note: Influxes into nodes indicate labor supply, effluxes indicate labor demand. Flags indicate number of workers retrained. All quantities are in thousands of workers.

Glassey's Lemma

In a lemma, formulated in 1978, Glassey provides an elegant characterization of the structure of an optimal spatial network. For this lemma we need the following concepts from the theory of graphs. (For further material on the theory of graphs, the reader may consult Vajda [39], chap. 4).

Chain—A succession of links without a gap between them.

Tree—A particular graph which has the property that each node can be reached from any other via a chain of links (traversed in any direction) between them, and which has no loop, that is, no chain from any node back to itself. An example of a tree is shown in figure 3.6.

Spanning tree—A tree that is incident on every node in a given graph. As a general proposition, a spanning tree in a graph with N nodes will involve N-1 links.

Forest—A collection of trees.

A graph may be connected or not connected. In a connected graph it is possible, starting out from any given node, to reach any other node by a chain of links (traversed in any direction). A tree is a connected graph. A forest is not connected; it is a collection of connected graphs.

Thus prepared, we are ready to consider Glassey's lemma, which simply states that *the trade routes of positive flow in an optimal solution to the spatial network problem form a forest.*

As an illustration of Glassey's lemma, we may consider the retraining network (fig. 3.6) again. The trade routes of positive flow form a tree. The forest consists of a single tree. Imagine now some adjustment of the data of the problem, which might easily lead to the link *(6.4)* dropping out of the optimal solution entirely. The trade routes of positive flow would then form two trees, one incident upon the nodes *1,2,4,7* and a second tree incident upon the nodes *5,3,6.* This time, the forest would consist of two trees.

Proof: Consider program (3.22), which states the general spatial network problem. Now suppose in an optimal solution we find a subset of *K* regions connected by *K* or more trade routes (links) over which positive trade flow occurs. Then there must be a subset of these links that form a loop. Next superimpose a trade flow around this loop in a direction opposite to at least one of the preexisting optimal flows. The effects of this operation at a node *h* located along the path of the counterflow will be to decrease by the same amount both the in-shipments into node *h* along the direction of the counterflow, and the out-shipments from it along the same direction. But neither the influx w_h* nor the efflux x_h* into node *h* will be disturbed.

As an illustration of this part of the argument, turn to figure 3.7. Panel A shows a subset of the network consisting of four regions *(h = 1,2,3,4)* connected by four trade routes over which positive trade flow occurs. These optimal flows form a loop. The magnitude of the optimal flows are $t_{12}*$, $t_{32}*$, $t_{34}*$ and $t_{41}*$, respectively. Next, a trade flow directed clockwise around the loop and equal to *a* is superimposed upon the earlier optimal solution (see panel B).

Inspecting program (3.22), we see that each constraint will still remain satisfied, so that we have actually generated a new "feasible" solution. Furthermore, the integrals in the objective function remain unchanged, but total transportation costs have been reduced. The value of the objective function has increased.

Figure 3.7. Proof of Glassey's Lemma

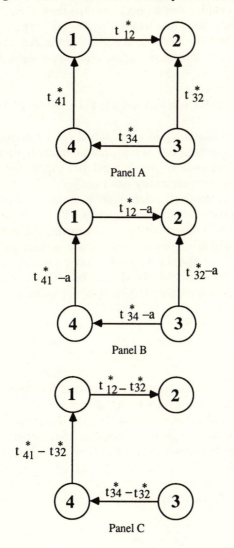

Panel A

Panel B

Panel C

Now increase the amount of the counterflow until it cancels at least one of the preexisting flows in the loop. In this fashion, any loops in the structure of an optimal trade flow pattern can be eliminated.

The procedure is illustrated in panel *C*. The amount of the counterflow has now been increased and equals x_{32}^*. The flow from node 3 to node 2 then becomes exactly offset and vanishes.

In conclusion, the optimal solution flow cannot include a loop. The remaining structure is a collection of trees.

Glassey concludes that an equilibrium solution exists in which the set of *H* regions is partitioned into trading "coalitions." The regions within each coalition trade only with each other, and the set of links with positive trade flow within each coalition forms a spanning tree for the coalition.

3.4. AN EXTENSION BY TAKAYAMA AND JUDGE

Samuelson's spatial equilibrium model can be extended to the case of several consumer goods, if one is prepared to accept quite severe restrictions on the mathematical form of the demand and supply functions (and hence ultimately on the underlying utility functions).

The crucial matter is the definition of the economic potential function to be used as a maximand. This time, let x_h denote a vector of quantities of consumer goods purchased by the consumers in region *h*. The list of consumer goods will be indicated by a second subscript $i \in I$. The list is not exhaustive; rather, we should think of a few related consumer goods, say, some related agricultural products. Let p_h be a vector of prices of the same goods. The demand functions for each good are written

$$(3.23) \qquad D_{hi}(p_h), \ i \in I$$

for each region $h \in H$. These are partial demand functions with the quantity of each good represented as a function of the vector of prices in the same region. The prices of all other goods (beyond the list $i \in I$), and the income of the consumers in each region, are supposed to be constant and given.

Inverting, let the demand price functions in each region h be

$$(3.24) \qquad P_{hi}(x_h), \ i \in I$$

For each region, these functions assign a set of demand prices to each point in the quantity space. Assume that they are positive and differentiable on the domain of non-negative quantities.

In order to indicate the nature of the difficulties that we are about to encounter, it is instructive first to take a look at the case of linear demand price functions, say

$$(3.25) \qquad P_{hi}(x_h) = \alpha_{hi} - \sum_{j \in I} \beta_{hij} x_{hj}, \ i \in I$$

where the α_hs and the β_hs are given and known non-negative constants. A typical cross-coefficient β_{hij}, where j is not equal to i, shows how the demand price for good i depends upon the quantity of another good j (such interdependence occurs if the two goods are complemenary or if they are competing with each other). We now need to assume that these cross-coefficients in each region are all symmetric in the sense that

$$(3.26) \qquad \beta_{hij} = \beta_{hji}$$

for all $i, j \in I$.

To see what is involved, note that if the demand price function (3.25) had been written as a linear expression in the logarithms of both prices and quantities (rather than the prices and quantities themselves), each cross-coefficient would equal the inverted value of a cross-elasticity. So, in this sense, our cross-coefficients are related to cross-elasticities. Of course, it is well known that cross-elasticities for many pairs of goods are *not* symmetric (butter and margarine, beef and pork, etc.).

In any applied situation, the demand price functions (3.25) would presumably have to be estimated by econometric techniques. It is perfectly possible to arrange the statistical estimation so that the symmetry condition (3.26) is fulfilled a priori. But this is just to sweep the dust under the carpet—the substance of the economic assumption is still very much there.

Accepting symmetry, it is possible to integrate all demand price functions in region h to obtain

$$(3.27) \qquad \sum_{i \in I} (\alpha_{hi} x_{hi} - 0.5 \sum_{j \in I} \beta_{hij} x_{hi} x_{hj})$$

The process of integration involved is the one of forming a line integral. To check that (3.27) indeed constitutes the end result of the integration of the demand price functions, the reader may differentiate again; forming the partial derivative of (3.27) with respect to x_{hi}, one gets

$$(3.28) \qquad \alpha_{hi} - 0.5 \sum_{j \in I} (\beta_{hij} + \beta_{hji}) x_{hj}$$

which by (3.26) collapses into the expression (3.25).

Incidentally, forming the partial derivative of (3.27) of the second order, differentiating first with respect to x_{hi} and then with respect to x_{hj}, one simply gets $-\beta_{hij}$. Changing the order of differentiation, differentiating first with respect to x_{hj} and then with respect to x_{hi}, one gets $-\beta_{hji}$. These two derivatives of the second order must be equal, as indeed they are as long as the symmetry condition (3.26) is being upheld.

Proceeding now in a similar fashion on the supply side, write the supply price functions in each region:

$$(3.29) \qquad Q_{hi}(w_h), \ i \in I$$

In each region, these functions assign a set of supply prices to each point in the quantity space. Assume that they are positive and differentiable on the domain of non-negative quantities. Specifically, consider the case of linear supply price functions

$$(3.30) \qquad Q_{hi}(w_{hi}) = \gamma_{hi} + \sum_{j \in I} \delta_{hij} w_{hj}, \ i \in I$$

where the γ_hs and the δ_hs are given and known. The cross-coefficient δ_{hij} (where j is not equal to i) shows how the supply price for good i depends upon the quantity of another good j. Suppose that the cross-coefficients are symmetric

$$(3.31) \qquad \delta_{hij} = \delta_{hji}$$

for all $i,j = 1,2, \ldots, I$. It is then possible to integrate the supply price functions (3.30).

The generalization of Samuelson's model of spatial equilibrium is now immediate. Following Takayama and Judge, form the program

$$(3.32) \quad max \sum_{h \in H} \sum_{i \in I} (\alpha_{hi} x_{hi} - 0.5 \sum_{j \in I} \beta_{hij} x_{hi} x_{hj})$$

$$- \sum_{h \in H} (\gamma_{hi} w_{hi} + 0.5 \sum_{j \in I} \delta_{hij} w_{hi} w_{hj})$$

$$- \sum_{h \in H} \sum_{k \in H} \sum_{i \in I} c_{hki} t_{hki}$$

subject to

$$x_{hi} - w_{hi} - \sum_{k \in H} (t_{khi} - t_{hki}) \leq 0$$

$$x_{hi}, w_{hi}, t_{hki} \geq 0$$

$$h, k \in H, i \in I$$

The maximand is a generalized version of Samuelson's net social payoff, extended to the case of many goods. Takayama and Judge call it "quasi-welfare." It is still obtained by adding all integrated demand functions, subtracting all integrated supply functions, and finally subtracting all transportation costs.

The assumption that the two matrices $\beta_h = [\beta_{hij}]$ and $\delta_h = [\delta_{hij}]$ are symmetric implies that the demand and supply functions are integrable. If the matrices are not symmetric, the functions are nonintegrable, the economic potential function does not exist, and the entire approach (3.32) breaks down.

Expressions like

$$(3.33) \quad \sum_{i \in I} \sum_{j \in I} \beta_{hij} x_{hi} x_{hj} \text{ and } \sum_{i \in I} \sum_{j \in I} \delta_{hij} w_{hi} w_{hj}$$

are called quadratic forms. We need to assume that these two quadratic forms are both positive semidefinite, by which is meant that the two double sums are non-negative for every demand point x_{hi}, $i \in I$ and every supply point w_{hi}, $i \in I$, and that there exists a demand point not identically equal to zero which renders the first double sum in (3.33) equal to zero, and that there exists a supply point not identically equal to zero which renders the second double sum equal to zero.

The two matrices $[\beta_{hij}]$ and $[\delta_{hij}]$ themselves are then said to be positive semidefinite.

There is an elementary theorem for quadratic forms which states that a positive semidefinite quadratic form is a convex function (for proof, see, e.g., Hadley [12], chap. 3). Inspecting the objective function of program (3.32), we see that the only quadratic terms appearing in the objective function are the two double sums (3.33) with a minus sign. All the other terms are linear. Hence, the objective function is concave.

So, proceeding on the assumption of symmetry (which sees to it that the objective function exists) and the assumption that the quadratic forms (3.33) are both positive semidefinite (which sees to it that the objective function is concave), we are now ready to deal with the nonlinear programming problem (3.32).

There is one market constraint for each good in each region. It states that the local supply plus net in-shipments must suffice to cover local demand.

Denote the Lagrange multiplier of each such market constraint by p_{hi}, $h \in H$, $i \in I$. They are all non-negative. We shall interpret the optimal p_{hi}^* as the market price in region h of good i. Using the Kuhn–Tucker theory, the following conditions must be satisfied at the optimum point:

(i)   There is equilibrium in each regional market for each good.

       For one finds

$$(3.34) \qquad x_{hi}^* - w_{hi}^* - \sum_{k \in H} (t_{khi}^* - t_{hki}^*) \leq 0$$

$$p_{hi}^*(x_{hi}^* - w_{hi}^* - \sum_{k \in H} (t_{khi}^* - t_{hki}^*)) = 0$$

(ii)   The price appreciation along a transportation link can never exceed the unit transportation cost. If positive transportation along the link takes place, the price appreciation equals the transportation cost. But if the price appreciation falls short of the transportation cost, no shipments along the link occur.

For one finds:

(3.35) $-p_{hi}{}^* + p_{ki}{}^* \leq c_{hki}$

$t_{hki}{}^* (-p_{hi}{}^* + p_{ki}{}^* - c_{hki}) = 0$

(iii)   The market price for any good cannot fall short of the demand price, and it cannot exceed the supply price. If the demand is positive, the market price equals the demand price; if the supply is positive, the market price equals the supply price.

For one gets

(3.36) $p_{hi}{}^* \geq \alpha_{hi} - \sum_{j \in I} \beta_{hij} x_{hj}{}^*$

$x_{hi}{}^* (p_{hi}{}^* - \alpha_{hi} + \sum_{j \in I} \beta_{hij} x_{hj}{}^*) = 0$

$p_{hi}{}^* \leq \gamma_{hi} + \sum_{j \in I} \delta_{hij} w_{hj}{}^*$

$w_{hi}{}^*(p_{hi}{}^* - \gamma_{hi} - \sum_{j \in I} \delta_{hij} w_{hj}{}^*) = 0$

$i \in I, h \in H$

Obviously, these conditions generalize the results already obtained in section 3.2 (which dealt with the case of a single commodity only).

The conditions provide an exhaustive listing of the characteristics of the optimal solution, in the sense that they are logically equivalent to the programming formulation itself. (Any non-negative vectors x^*, w^*, t^* that together with the non-negative vector p^* satisfies the conditions [3.34–36] must be an optimal solution to program [3.32]).

So, what have we accomplished?   Unfortunately, not much. Ironically, perhaps the most important lesson to be drawn from Takayama and Judge's extension is that in most real situations Samuelson's analysis of spatial equilibrium does not extend to the case of several commodities. Only in the event of symmetric demand price coefficients and supply price coefficients is such generalization possible.   Real-world applications involving symmetric coefficients seem to be quite rare.

The treatment of the nonintegrable case falls outside the scope of this volume. However, the following comments may be helpful. Considering the economic interpretation of the optimum conditions (3.34–36), it will be natural still to insist that these conditions be satisfied. In other words, the "solution" to the nonintegrable case will be defined as a combination of quantity variables x_{hi}^*, t_{khi}^*, and w_{hi}^* and price variables p_{hi}^* that satisfy conditions (3.34–36).

One then faces a set of conditions that look precisely like the Kuhn–Tucker conditions, only the underlying concave function does not exist. Nor, then, does the saddle function of the Kuhn–Tucker theorem exist.

A system of inequalities of this kind is a specimen of a complementarity problem. The problem may still have a well-defined solution, but it cannot be obtained through optimization. Instead, special complementarity methods have to be used (see the bibliographic notes).

To conclude the present section we shall offer some remarks concerning the possibility of carrying through the Takayama–Judge analysis using the general notations (3.24) and (3.29) rather than the linear expressions (3.25) and (3.30).

The question of integrability is still the crux of the matter. This time, we ask if the integrals

$$(3.37a) \qquad \int \sum_{i \in I} P_{hi}(x_h)dx_{hi} = \int_{C_{1h}} \sum_{i \in I} P_{hi}(\xi_h)d\xi_{hi}$$

$$(3.37b) \qquad \int \sum_{i \in I} Q_{hi}(w_h)dw_{hi} = \int_{C_{2h}} \sum_{i \in I} Q_{hi}(\eta_h)d\eta_{hi}$$

exist. These integrals are so-called line integrals. The path of integration for the first integral is some path C_{1h} in the demand space in region h; it runs from some fixed arbitrary point to x_h. The path of integration for the second integral is some path C_{2h} in the supply space in the same region; it runs from some arbitrary initial point to w_h.

The reader who would like to review some basic material regarding line integrals is referred to a mathematics text (e.g., Courant and John [6], chap.1). The definition of the line integrals requires that

(3.38a)
$$\frac{\partial P_{hi}\,(x_h)}{\partial x_{hj}} = \frac{\partial P_{hj}\,(x_h)}{\partial x_{hi}}$$

(3.38b)
$$\frac{\partial Q_{hi}\,(x_h)}{\partial w_{hj}} = \frac{\partial Q_{hj}\,(x_h)}{\partial w_{hi}}$$

for all $i,j \in I$. This is the generalized version of the symmetry condition already encountered in (3.26) and (3.31). If it is fulfilled, the line integrals (3.37) have a value which is independent of the paths C_{1h} and C_{2h}. The value of each line integral depends only upon the end point of that path. The conditions (3.38) are usually referred to as the conditions of integrability or of path independency.

Thus prepared, form the economic potential function

(3.39)
$$\int \sum_{i \in I} P_{hi}(x_h)dx_{hi} - \int \sum_{i \in I} Q_{hi}(w_h)dw_{hi}$$

$$- \sum_{h \in H} \sum_{k \in H} \sum_{i \in I} c_{hki} t_{hki}$$

We have already assumed that the two matrices

(3.40a)
$$\left[\frac{\partial P_{hi}\,(x_h)}{\partial x_{hj}} \right]$$

(3.40b)
$$\left[\frac{\partial Q_{hi}\,(w_h)}{\partial w_{hj}} \right]$$

are symmetric. Hence, the two line integrals appearing in the economic potential function (3.39) are well defined and path-independent.

Note that the matrix (3.40a) is actually the matrix of partial derivatives of the second order of the line integral (3.37a). Such a matrix is called a Hessian matrix. There is a fundamental theorem for a twice differentiable function which states that the function is concave if and only if its Hessian is negative semidefinite for all possible values of the unknowns. (On this point, the reader is referred again to the text by Courant and John [6].) The theorem is a generalization to many dimensions of the proposition that a function of a single variable is concave if and only if its second derivative is nonpositive. In order to ensure that the potential function (3.39) is concave, we therefore additionally need to assume that the matrix (3.40a) is negative semidefinite, and that (3.40b) is positive semidefinite. (The case of linear demand functions [3.25] and linear supply functions [3.30] discussed a moment ago can be analyzed using the terms now mentioned. The Hessian to [3.27] is simply $[-\beta_{hij}]$. The Hessian to the integrated supply function is $[\delta_{hij}]$.)

The conditions now listed are quite restrictive. In order to understand their implications, we may ask what conditions they place on the underlying utility functions which presumably generate the demand price functions and the supply price functions in the first place. The answer is provided by the following.

> ***Theorem 3.1.*** Let the (ordinal) utility function defining the demand price functions (3.24) in region h be $U_h(x_h)$. Then $U_h(x_h)$ must be a monotonic transformation of the line integral (3.37a).

There is a similar theorem for the (dis)utility function defining the supply price functions.

So, in the sense of the theorem, the line integral (3.37a) actually is the underlying utility function and the integral (3.37b) is the underlying disutility function.

The proof of the theorem rests upon the fact that the tangent plane to the hypersurface defined by the line integral (3.37a) coincides with the tangent plane to the utility function. (The two planes have proportional directional elements.) Hence, the function (3.37a) and $U_h(x_h)$ have identical indifference maps. The one function must be a monotonic transformation of the other (Thore [35]).

BIBLIOGRAPHIC NOTES

Rereading Samuelson's pioneering contribution [27] today, one can only admire the clarity and farsightedness of this piece. It was published at a time when even basic issues regarding linear programming were not yet settled.

Samuelson showed how a class of equilibrium problems can be converted into extremal problems to be solved by optimization methods. But in the early 1950s the time was not yet ripe to translate those theoretical results into empirical work.

In the late 1950s, several algorithms for the solution of the quadratic programming problem were proposed, and in 1959 Wolfe published the well-known simplex method for quadratic programming. The building blocks were then in place for actual empirical estimation of Samuelson's model of spatial equilibrium.

The task was taken up by the research team of Takayama and Judge at the University of Illinois (see their three papers—[30], [31], [32]—published in 1964 and their subsequent monograph [33] published in 1971).

In the 1960s, quadratic programming still offered considerable computational challenges. Takayama and Judge [30] proposed a primal-dual formulation of the quadratic programming problem that was used in several early studies of agricultural commodities (see Sazaki [28]; Lee and Seaver [18]; and Zusman, Melamed and Katzir [40]). A few applications in the field of energy economics (Uri [37], [38]) were also quite successful.

Early large-scale applications, such as the study of multilevel planning in Mexico (Goreux and Manne [11]) were solved numerically by replacing the quadratic objective function by a piecewise linear approximation and then employing a standard linear programming code.

In 1978 two general-purpose nonlinear programming codes became available: *MINOS* (see Murtagh and Saunders [22]) and *GRG* (see Lasdon and Waren [17]). The numerical exercises in the present volume were solved using *GAMS* (General Algebraic Modeling System, see Meeraus [21]; and Brooke, Kendrick, and Meeraus [2]). There is now no need for the economist to bother at all about the algorithmic aspects of medium-sized applications. In the case of very large applications, there may still be a need for special algorithms which exploit the mathematical structure of the particular application at hand (see, e.g., Glassey [10]; Pang and Lin [25]).

In the treatment of spatial equilibrium in the main text, it is assumed that unit transportation costs are fixed and given. For an extension of nonconstant unit transportation costs, see Florian and Los [8].

The development of the generalized transportation problem belongs to Rowse [26].

The concepts of network theory reviewed in section 3.3 are standard (see, e.g., Charnes and Cooper [4]). For Glassey's lemma, see Glassey [10]. Example 3.3 is brought from Faxén and Thore [7].

It is assumed in section 3.3 that each link in the graph of the network represents a separate transportation connection. Building on the work by Florian and Los [8], recent literature has extended this analysis to the case when a number of alternate shipping "routes" are available between each pair of nodes, each route consisting of a series of joined links. For instance, in the case of a network of airline passenger traffic, a passenger may be able to choose between a number of different routes between each node-pair (see Tobin and Friesz [36]; Harker and Friesz [14]).

The treatment of several commodities in section 3.4 is based upon Takayama and Judge [31]. As explained, the integrability condition places quite stringent conditions on the mathematical form of the demand price functions (and on the supply price functions). For an investigation of the restrictions thereby implicitly placed on the underlying utility function, see Thore [35].

In order to deal with the nonintegrable case, Takayama and Judge [33] developed a "self dual" quadratic programming approach, maximizing "net social monetary gain." In this formulation, however, feasibility and optimality are equivalent, so that the objective function is, from a computational point of view, redundant (see Carey [3]). Instead, one is left with a so-called (linear or nonlinear) complementarity problem (see Takayama and Uri [34]).

The analysis of complementarity problems falls outside the scope of the present volume. The following brief comments may, however, be helpful. Recall that the ultimate rationale for the formation of the economic potential function employed in the various programming formulations was provided by the Kuhn–Tucker conditions characterizing the obtained optimum, which spelled out the properties of the desired market equilibrium. In the sense of the Kuhn–Tucker equivalence theorem (theorem 2.2), the original nonlinear programming problem and the set of all Kuhn–Tucker conditions are mathematically equivalent. The Kuhn–Tucker conditions to any nonlinear mathematical programming problem can be viewed as a specimen of a complementarity problem.

As long as there is integrability, one will naturally opt to deal with this complementarity problem via the route of integrating the demand price functions and the supply price functions, forming the economic potential function and solving the programming problem obtained. When integrability does not obtain, one is left with the original set of equilibrium conditions. For numerical solution, one would instead turn to complementarity methods.

There has recently been considerable progress in the numerical solution of nonlinear complementarity problems; in particular, reference may be made to Mathiesen [20], who solves such problems as a sequence of linear complementarity problems. Work is currently underway to develop various software packages based upon Mathiesen's algorithm. Thus, in the near future, economists may no longer find nonintegrability to offer any particular numerical difficulties.

A few other techniques are also available to deal with the nonintegrable case. One is the method of variational inequalities, originally introduced as a tool for the study of partial differential equations but later adapted to spatial price equilibrium problems by Florian and Los [8]. See Pang [24], Kyparisis [16], and the review article of Nagurney [23]. Under the hands of Nagurney, this approach is currently under additional rapid development.

Finally, conventional fixed point methods may also be used to deal with the nonintegrable case (MacKinnon [19]).

REFERENCES

[3.1]   Arrow, K. J. and G. Debreu. "Existence of Equilibrium for a Competitive Economy," *Econometrica* 22/3 (1954): 265–90.

[3.2]   Brooke, A., D. Kendrick, and A. Meeraus. *GAMS: A User's Guide.* Redwood City, Calif.: Scientific Press, 1988.

[3.3]   Carey, M. "Integrability and Mathematical Programming Models: A Survey and A Parametric Approach," *Econometrica,* 45/8, (Nov. 1977): 1957–76.

[3.4]   Charnes, A., and W. W. Cooper. "Some Network Characterization for Mathematical Programming and Accounting Approaches to Planning and Control," *Accounting Review* (Jan. 1967): 24–52.

[3.5]   Charnes, A., and W. W. Cooper. *Management Models and Industrial Applications of Linear Programming.* 2 vols. New York: Wiley, 1961.

[3.6]   Courant, R., and F. John. *Introduction to Calculus and Analysis.* Vol. 20 New York: Wiley, 1974.

[3.7]   Faxén, K.O., and S. Thore. "Retraining in an Interdependent System of Labor Markets: Network Analysis," *European Journal of Operational Research,* 44(1990): 349–56.

[3.8]   Florian, M., and M. Los. "A New Look at Static Spatial Price Equilibrium Models," *Regional Science and Urban Economics* 12 (1982): 579–97.

[3.9]   Friesz, T. L., R. L. Tobin, T. E. Smith and P. T. Harker. "A Nonlinear Complementarity Formulation and Solution Procedure for the General Derived Demand Network Equilibrium Problem," *Journal of Regional Science* 23 (1983): 337–59.

[3.10]   Glassey, C. R. "A Quadratic Network Optimization Model for Equilibrium Single Commodity Trade Flows," *Mathematical Programming* 14 (1978): 98–107.

[3.11]   Goreux, L., and A. Manne. *Multilevel Planning: Case Studies in Mexico.* Amsterdam: North-Holland, 1973.

[3.12]   Hadley, G. *Nonlinear and Dynamic Programming.* Reading, Mass: Addison-Wesley, 1964.

[3.13]   Harker, P. T., ed. *Spatial Price Equilibrium: Advances in Theory, Computation and Applications.* New York: Springer, 1985.

[3.14]   Harker, P. T., and T. L. Friesz. "The Use of Equilibrium Network Models in Logistics—With Applications to the U.S. Coal Industry," *Transportation Research* 19B/5, (1985): 457–70.

[3.15]   Judge G. G., and T. Takayama, eds. *Studies in Economic Planning over Space and Time.* Amsterdam: North-Holland, 1973.

[3.16]   Kyparisis, J. "Sensitivity Analysis Framework For Variational Inequalities," *Mathematical Programming* 38 (1987): 203–13.

[3.17]   Lasdon, L. S., and A. D. Waren. "Generalized Reduced Gradient Software for Linearly and Nonlinearly Constrained Problems," in *Design and Implementation of Optimization Software*, ed. H. Greenberg, Amsterdam: Sijthoff and Nordhoff, 1978.

[3.18]   Lee, T. C., and S. K. Seaver. "A Positive Model of Spatial Equilibrium with Special Reference to the Broiler Markets." In [3.15].

[3.19]   MacKinnon, G. G. "A Technique for the Solution of Spatial Equilibrium Models," *Journal of Regional Science* 16 (1976): 293–307.

[3.20]   Mathiesen, L. "Computational Experience in Solving Equilibrium Models by a Sequence of Linear Complementarity Problems," *Operations Research*, 33/6, (Nov.–Dec. 1985): 1225–50.

[3.21]   Meeraus, A. "An Algebraic Approach to Modeling," *Journal of Dynamics and Control* 5 (1983): 81-108.

[3.22]   Murtaugh, B. A., and M. A. Saunders. "Large-Scale Linearly Constrained Optimization," *Mathematical Programming* 14 (1978): 41–72.

[3.23]   Nagurney, A. "Competitive Equilibrium Problems, Variational Inequalities, and Regional Science," *Journal of Regional Science* 27 (1987): 503–17.

[3.24]   Pang, J. S. "Solution of the General Multicommodity Spatial Equilibrium Problem by Variational and Complementarity Methods," *Journal of Regional Science* 24/3 (1984): 403–14.

[3.25]   Pang, J. S., and Y. Lin. "A Dual Conjugate Gradient Method for the Single-Commodity Spatial Price Equilibrium Problem." In [3.13].

[3.26]   Rowse, John. "Solving the Generalized Transportation Problem," *Regional Science and Urban Economics* 11 (1981): 57–68.

[3.27]   Samuelson, P. A. "Spatial Price Equilibrium and Linear Programming," *The American Economic Review* 42 (1952): 283–303.

[3.28] Sazaki, K. "Spatial Equilibrium Analysis of Livestock Products in Eastern Japan." In [3.15].

[3.29] Scarf, H. E., with T. Hansen. *Computation of Economic Equilibrium*. New Haven: Yale University Press, 1973.

[3.30] Takayama, T., and G. G. Judge. "Spatial Equilibrium and Quadratic Programming," *Journal of Farm Economics* 46 (1964): 67–93.

[3.31] Takayama, T., and G. G. Judge. "Equilibrium Among Spatially Separated Markets: A Reformulation," *Econometrica* 32/4 (Oct. 1964): 510–24.

[3.32] Takayama, T. and G. G. Judge. "An Interregional Activity Analysis Model of the Agricultural Sector," *Journal of Farm Economics*, 46 (May 1964): 349-365.

[3.33] Takayama, T., and G. G. Judge. *Spatial and Temporal Price and Allocation Models*. Amsterdam: North-Holland, 1971.

[3.34] Takayama, T., and N. Uri. "A Note on Spatial and Temporal Price and Allocation Modeling. Quadratic Programming or Linear Complementarity Programming?" *Regional Science and Urban Economics* 13 (1983): 455–70.

[3.35] Thore, S. "Hotelling Utility Functions." In *Foundations of Utility and Risk Theory with Applications,* eds. B. P. Stigum and F. Wenstop. Dordrecht: D. Reidel, 1983.

[3.36] Tobin, R. L., and T. L. Friesz. "Formulating and Solving the Derived Demand Network Equilibrium Problem in Terms of Arc Variables," *Journal of Regional Science* 23 (1983): 187–98.

[3.37] Uri, N. D. *Towards An Efficient Allocation of Electric Energy*. Lexington, Mass: D. C. Heath & Co. 1975.

[3.38] Uri, N. D. "A Spatial Equilibrium Analysis of Electrical Energy Pricing and Allocation," *American Journal of Agricultural Economics* (Nov. 1976): 653–62.

[3.39] Vajda, S. *Mathematical Programming*. Reading, Mass: Addison-Wesley, 1961.

[3.40] Zusman, P., A. Melamed and I. Katzir, "A Spatial Analysis of the EEC Trade Policies in the Market for Winter Oranges." In [3.15].

4

The Vertical Dimension

Economists often use the term "vertical" to refer to the production chain that converts resources into intermediate products and, ultimately, into consumer goods. For instance, vertical integration occurs when a shipowner buys a shipyard or when a newspaper buys a paper mill. Quite generally, we shall here use the term "vertical dimension" to refer to the logistics processes that antecede the production or distribution of any economic good or service.

This book deals with partial economic theory. It is not our intent to trace the antecedents of every single component of the final product, or of every former intermediate state that this product assumed as it traveled along the vertical production chain. Those inputs into the production processes left out of the current discussion—exogenous inputs—are assumed to be available in the marketplace as required, at fixed and given prices. Those manufactured inputs that we do want to investigate further are seen as the outputs of underlying production processes which in their turn may have employed both exogenous and endogenous inputs. In this fashion it must be possible to unravel the entire production chain so that, ultimately, we are brought back entirely to the use of exogenous inputs and to the supply of resources like labor and land.

The present chapter surveys a series of programming models that can be used to analyze the flow of one or several related goods and services along a vertical chain of production and distribution. Along such a chain, there is (or there can be imagined to exist) a series of markets at the successive steps of production. Typically, the optimal solution to the programming problem to be formulated will deliver information about quantities of outputs obtained, the particular production processes to be chosen, and the required inputs at each production step. The Lagrange multipliers will deliver information about the equilibrium prices that will clear all markets.

To make these ideas specific, consider the commercial breeding of mink, the mink fur industry, and the marketing of mink coats and mink fur. Mink breeders buy large quantities of fish meal, which is the staple diet of the mink. The model builder now has to make the decision whether he wants to take the fish meal industry as exogenous to the model—in which case the price of fish meal will be taken as a given datum—or whether he wants to roll back the explanation even further to include an account of the optimal production of fish meal as well. In the latter case, the equilibrium price of fish meal is an unknown, to be determined.

The analytical tools to be used are borrowed from activity analysis, which was developed by T. Koopmans in 1951. Production is modeled through elementary processes called "activities," each of which can be run at any non-negative "level" or "intensity." The quantities of inputs required per unit level of operation (the input coefficients) and the quantities of outputs obtained per unit level of operation (the output coefficients) are fixed and known. In the space of all outputs and all inputs, a single activity can be illustrated by a ray through the origin. Selecting some point on the ray, the distance from the origin indicates the level of operation of the activity. In general, several activities will be operated at the same time; the total outputs produced and the total inputs required are obtained by simply adding the outputs and inputs, respectively, for each of the activities at the particular levels chosen.

In the standard format of activity analysis, goods and services are divided into three classes: primary, intermediate, and final. Primary goods are the original inputs like land, mineral resources, capital, and available workforce. Final goods are produced by combinations of primary and intermediate goods and then delivered to cover final demand (consumption, government demand, investment demand, or exports). Intermediate goods are outputs which, in turn, serve as inputs which are used in the production of final goods. Unlike final goods, which have value per se, all intermediate goods have value only insofar as they can be used (along with other inputs) in the production of final goods. Koopmans assumed that the supplies of all primary goods are fixed and given. (There is a given "endowment" of each primary good.) The set of feasible combinations of final goods is then a polyhedral convex set. The set of extremal points of this set is the production frontier. Figure 4.1 may serve as a reference to illustrate these fundamental concepts. There are two final goods, x_1 and x_2. The convex set O-E_1-E_2-E_3-E_4-E_5-E_6-O is the set of feasible combinations of final goods that can be attained (the production possibility region). The line segments O-E_1-E_2-E_3-E_4-E_5-E_6-O constitute the production frontier.

A vector of final goods x is said to be efficient, in the sense of Koopmans, if and only if there is no other vector x' available with the property $x' \geq x$, $x' \neq x$. That is, no component of x' is less than the corresponding component of x, and at least one component of x' exceeds its correspond in x. The set of all efficient points is a subset of the production frontier. Referring again to figure 4.1, the set of all efficient points consists of the line segments E_2-E_3-E_4-E_5. Note that points E_1 and E_6 are not efficient.

Figure 4.1. Fundamental Efficiency Concepts

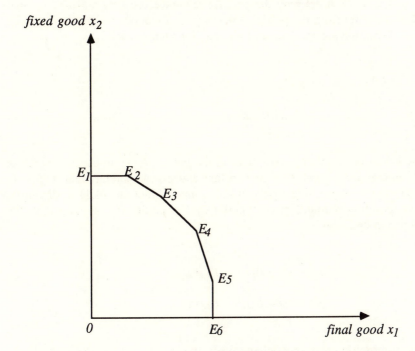

Which one of all efficient points will actually be chosen? In a market economy, that decision is made by consumers on the basis of the prices of the consumer goods, their income, and their preferences. If the space (x_1,x_2) as illustrated in figure 4.1 provides an exhaustive representation of all consumer goods and services, one can imagine an ordinal preference field and a map of indifference curves located in the orthant $x_1,x_2 \geq 0$. The point along the production frontier which yields the highest level of preference would be the point actually chosen. Under weak regularity conditions placed on the mathematical form of the indifference map, this optimal point is efficient.

In a partial economic world these propositions require some elaboration. The preference field *(x₁,x₂)* in figure 4.1 is now well defined only with reference to a given and constant vector of all other goods and services to be taken as exogenous. For instance, letting x_1 = number of ladies' full-length mink coats and x_2 = number of ladies' mink jackets, mink fur caps, and other mink fur apparel, an indifference curve would trace the combinations of these two product categories that would leave the consumer indifferent, assuming that the demand for all other clothes, and all other consumer goods and services was kept given and fixed.

Rather than defining the partial preference ordering a priori, we shall opt to start out from the partial demand price functions themselves (see sec. 3.4). Write the partial demand functions for each good:

(4.1) $$x_1 = D_1(p_1,p_2)$$

$$x_2 = D_2(p_1,p_2)$$

The prices of all other goods (beyond the list $i = 1,2$) and the income of the consumers are supposed to be constant and given. Under weak regularity conditions it is possible to invert the demand functions (4.1) to obtain the corresponding demand price functions. For simplicity, assume that they happen to be linear

(4.2) $$p_1 = \alpha_1 - \beta_{11}x_1 - \beta_{12}x_2$$

$$p_2 = \alpha_2 - \beta_{21}x_1 - b_{22}x_2$$

with symmetric cross-coefficients $\beta_{12} = \beta_{21}$.

In the numerical applications, we shall usually make even more stringent assumptions, such as positing that the cross-coefficient $\beta_{12} = \beta_{21}$ vanishes so that the demand price of each good depends only upon the quantity bought of the same good. As discussed in section 3.4, the requirement of integrability will under all circumstances lay down quite severe restrictions on the mathematical form of the underlying utility function.

(Assumptions—and quite substantive assumptions at that—about the mathematical form of the underlying utility function cannot be avoided. The alternative approach would be to postulate a priori the existence of a partial utility function $U(x_1,x_2)$. In order to make this approach operational one would need to estimate the utility function from empirical data. Such estimation requires assumptions about the mathematical form of the function U.)

Next, adopting the procedures that we have already encountered in the analysis of Samuelson's model of spatial equilibrium (see the analysis of several consumer goods in section 3.4), integrate the demand price functions to form total social payoff:

$$(4.3) \qquad \alpha_1 x_1 + \alpha_2 x_2 - 0.5\beta_{11}x_1^2 - \beta_{12}x_1 x_2 - 0.5\beta_{11}x_2^2$$

Thus prepared, maximize the economic potential function (4.3) subject to the constraints that the output point (x_1, x_2) be feasible (i.e., that it belongs to the set O-E_1-E_2-E_3-E_4-E_5-E_6-O). The optimal solution is the point that consumers will actually choose. It will be efficient.

SYMBOLS USED IN CHAPTER 4

$h, k \in H$	regions
$i \in I$	final goods
$j, k \in J$	intermediate goods
$r \in R$	resources
$m \in M$	activities
G	graph
P as superscript	primary goods (resources)
I as superscript	intermediate goods
F as superscript	final goods
$A^P = [a_{rm}^P]$, $A^I = [a_{jm}^I]$	matrix of input coefficients
$B^I = [b_{jm}^I]$, $B^F = [b_{im}^F]$	matrix of output coefficients
z_m	level of operation of activity m
x_i, x_{hi}	quantity demanded of final good i
w_r, w_{hr}	quantity supplied of resource r
p_i, p_{hi}	price of final good i
q_r, q_{hr}	price of resource r
$D_i(p)$, $D_{hi}(p_h)$	demand function for final good i
$S_r(q)$, $S_{hr}(q_h)$	supply function for resource r
$P_i(x_i)$, $P_{hi}(x_{hi})$	demand price function for final good i
$Q_r(w_r)$, $Q_{hr}(w_{hr})$	supply price function for resource r

$\bar{z}_m$	capacity level of activity m
$u^F{}_i$, $u^F{}_{hi}$, $u^F{}_{ki}$	Lagrange multiplier of market balance for final good i
$u^I{}_j$, $u^I{}_{hj}$	Lagrange multiplier of market balance for intermediate good j
$u^P{}_r$, $u^P{}_{hr}$	Lagrange multiplier of market balance for resource r
s_m, s_{hm}	Lagrange multiplier of capacity condition for activity m
δ_{jk}	amplification factor along link in generalized network
t_{jk}, t_{hk}, t_{hki}	quantity shipped along link
c_{jk}, c_{hk}, c_{hki}	unit transportation cost along link
M	incidence matrix

4.1   A SAMUELSON TYPE FORMULATION OF A PARTIAL ACTIVITY ANALYSIS MODEL

For a brief review of elementary concepts in standard activity analysis, turn to figures 4.2 and 4.3. The diagrams illustrate the case of two inputs and two outputs. Each activity is represented by a ray through the origin. Activity 1 requires a_{11} units of input 1 and a_{21} units of input 2 when operated at unit level. If the activity is operated at twice that level, it requires twice as many inputs. In other words, any one ray is followed outward from the origin as intensity is increased. The input requirements to variations in scale are constant. The corresponding output situation is represented in the lower figure. The same activity produces b_{11} units of output 1 and b_{21} units of output 2. If it is operated at twice that level, it produces twice as many outputs so there are also constant output returns to scale.

Activity 2 requires a_{12} units of input 1 and a_{22} units of input 2 when operated at unit level. It then produces b_{12} units of output 1 and b_{22} units of output 2.

Let activity 1 be operated at level z_1 and activity 2 at level z_2. The total combination of inputs required is then $(a_{11}z_1 + a_{12}z_2, a_{21}z_1 + a_{22}z_2)$; the total combination of outputs obtained is $(b_{11}z_1 + b_{12}z_2, b_{21}z_1 + b_{22}z_2)$.

To see what is meant by this we may refer to the two solid lines shown in figures 4.2 and 4.3. The lower solid line in figure 4.2 connects all input combinations which are characterized by the condition that the sum of the two activities equals unity, $z_1 + z_2 = 1$. The profile of this line is convex toward the origin. The upper solid profile in the same diagram interconnects all output combinations for which $z_1 + z_2 = 2$. This profile is also convex toward the origin. The upper profile may be obtained from the lower one by radial expansion from the origin in the fixed ratio 2:1.

Figure 4.2.   Activity Analysis—Inputs

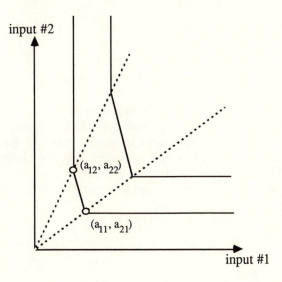

Figure 4.3.   Activity Analysis—Outputs

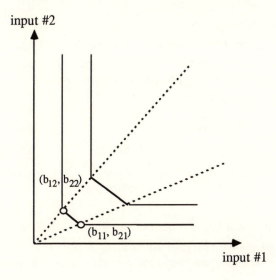

In the formal analysis to follow, three categories of goods and services are distinguished: primary goods and services (resources), intermediate goods and services which are produced at earlier stages of the production chain and then entirely used up at some later stage of the production chain; and final goods and services (consumer goods and services). Let

$M = \{M\}$ the set of individual activities available
$R = \{r\}$ the set of primary goods and services
$J = \{j\}$ the set of intermediate goods and services
$I = \{i\}$ the set of final goods and services

In the particular activity analysis model to be developed, the set I should include all final goods and services which are obtained from the activities that are being subjected to study, whether endogenous or exogenous. The set J should include all intermediate goods that are required as inputs to the same activities. The set R should include all primary goods and services that are required as inputs at some stage of the production chain.

Define the matrices of input coefficients

$$AP = [a^P_{rm}] \quad (r \in R, \, m \in M)$$

$$AI = [a^I_{jm}] \quad (j \in J, \, m \in M)$$

where a^P_{rm} is the quantity of resource r which is used and a^I_{jm} is the quantity of intermediate good j which is used when activity m is operated at unit level. Similarly, define the matrices of output coefficients

$$BI = [b^I_{jm}] \quad (j \in J, \, m \in M)$$

$$BF = [b^F_{im}\} \quad (i \in I, m \in M)$$

where b^I_{jm} is the quantity of intermediate good j obtained and b^F_{im} is the quantity of final good i obtained when activity m is operated at unit level. The input coefficients and the output coefficients are all non-negative constants.

Denote the vector of variable activity levels to be determined by $z = [z_m]$ $(m \in M)$. Each element is required to be non-negative. The vector of inputs of primary goods and services is then $A^P z$. The vector of inputs of intermediate goods is $A^I z$. The vector of outputs of intermediate goods is $B^I z$. The vector of outputs of final goods and services is $B^F z$.

In many applications, the level of operation of any given activity will be limited by existing production facilities. For instance, the production of a given mink farm may be limited by the number of breeding animals, the size of the farm and its capital equipment, and so on. The operations of an advertising agency may be limited by its location, the availability of skilled copywriters, its existing goodwill, its capitalization, and so on. Mathematically, this may be represented as

$$(4.4) \qquad z \leq \bar{z}$$

where $\bar{z} = [\bar{z}_m]$, $m \in M$ is a vector of given non-negative numbers. For simplicity, we have here assumed that every single activity has an upper bound. Even if a particular activity is not limited by a capacity constraint, relation (4.4) can always formally be satisfied by choosing for the activity a sufficiently large positive number as its upper bound.

In chapter 3 we analyzed the spatial flow of one or several commodities from a number of origins to a number of destinations. The transportation system was imbedded inside a framework of price-sensitive supplies at each origin and price-sensitive demands at each destination. We showed how it is possible to solve for the optimal flows by maximizing an economic potential function, originally proposed by Samuelson. The task confronting us here is not dissimilar. This time we are analyzing a flow along the vertical dimension of one or several related commodities through an activity analysis model. Each resource is an "origin" and each final good or service is a "destination." We propose to imbed the activity format inside a setting of price-sensitive supplies at each origin (read: of each resource) and of price-sensitive demands at each destination (read: for each final good or service). We shall accomplish this by maximizing an economic potential function, analogous to the one used by Samuelson.

Let the partial demand functions for all final goods and services under consideration be

$$(4.5) \qquad x_i = D_i(p), \ i \in I$$

where $x = [x_i]$, $i \in I$ is the vector of quantities of final goods and services bought by the consumers, and $p = [p_i]$ is the vector of prices. The prices of all other goods (beyond the set I) and the income of the consumers are supposed to be constant and given. Under weak regularity conditions it is possible to invert the demand functions (4.5) to obtain the corresponding demand price functions. To simplify matters, we shall limit the treatment in the present chapter to the case when the demand price for a good depends only upon the quantity consumed of the same good (the goods are "independent"). The demand price functions may then be written

$$(4.6) \qquad p_i = P_i(x_i), \, i \in I$$

It is assumed that these demand price functions are all positive, differentiable and nonincreasing on the domain of non-negative quantities.

The supply functions for all resources appearing in the model are

$$(4.7) \qquad w_r = S_r(q), \, r \in R$$

where $w = [w_r]$, $r \in R$ is the vector of quantities of resources employed, and $q = [q_r]$ is the vector of resource prices. Inverting (4.7), one obtains the corresponding supply price functions. The resources are also supposed to be "independent" so that the supply price functions can be written

$$(4.8) \qquad q_r = Q_r(w_r), \, r \in R$$

It is assumed that the supply price functions are all positive, differentiable, and nondecreasing on the domain of non-negative quantities.

The economic potential function to be formed (social pay-off), arising from both the purchases of final goods and services and from the supplies of resources is defined as the algebraic sum of integrals

$$(4.9) \qquad \sum_{i \in I} \int P_i(x_i) dx_i - \sum_{r \in R} \int Q_r(w_r) dw_r$$

Purchases of final goods and services yield non-negative social pay-off. Supplies of resources yield nonpositive pay-off.

Under the assumptions made concerning the properties of the demand price functions and the supply price functions, the expression (4.9) is a concave function.

The assumptions about independency are more restrictive than necessary. It would be easy to extend the analysis to deal with linear demand price functions and linear supply price functions, permitting the demand price of each consumer good to depend upon the quantities of other goods consumed as well, and permitting the supply price of each resource to depend upon the quantities of other resources supplied as well. In order to ensure integrability, the cross-coefficients would have to be assumed to be symmetric, both on the demand side and on the supply side (see the discussion in sec. 3.4 and the simple example relations [4.2] above). Even more general forms of the demand price functions and the supply price functions are possible (see sec. 3.4).

Now consider the programming model

$$(4.10) \qquad max \quad \sum_{i \in I} \int P_i(x_i)dx_i - \sum_{r \in R} \int Q_r(w_r)dw_r$$

$$\text{subject to} \quad x - B^F z \leq 0$$

$$A^I z - B^I z = 0$$

$$A^P z - w \leq 0$$

$$z \leq \bar{z}$$

$$x,z,w \geq 0$$

In plain words, the objective of program (4.10) is to maximize the total economic potential arising in the system. There are four sets of constraints. The first set states that the output of each final good or service must suffice to cover the demand for it. The second set of constraints states that the input requirement of each intermediate good must precisely equal the output of it. (Indeed, this equality may be taken as the very definition of an intermediate good.) The third set of constraints states that the input requirement of each resource must not exceed the supply of it. Finally, the fourth set of constraints spells out the capacity constraints, one for each activity of operation.

The maximand in (4.10) is concave; the constraint set is linear.

Denote the vectors of Lagrange multipliers that can be assigned to the four sets of constraints by

$$u^F = [u_i^F] \qquad i \in I$$

$$u^I = [u_j^I] \qquad j \in J$$

$$u^P = [u_r^P] \qquad r \in R$$

$$s = [s_m] \qquad m \in M$$

They are all non-negative except the u_j^I which are unrestricted in sign. We interpret the optimal $u^{F*} = [u_i^{F*}]$ as a vector of market prices of the final goods and services $i \in I$, the optimal $u^{I*} = [u_j^I]$ as a vector of market prices of the intermediate goods $j \in J$, and the optimal $u^{P*} = [u_r^{P*}]$ as a vector of market prices of the resources $r \in R$. Also, we interpret $s* = [s*_m]$ as a vector of imputed unit charges to be assessed whenever an activity m hits its upper bound $\bar{z}_m, m \in M$.

The Kuhn–Tucker conditions stipulate the following for optimum (denoted by an asterisk):

(i)   There is equilibrium in all markets (final, intermediate, and primary).

The standard case is that each market clears. Intermediate markets always clear (by definition). Clearing must also occur for final and primary markets, if the market price is positive. But it may happen that one is left with an excess supply in a final or primary market. The price must then have fallen to zero.

For one gets

$$(4.11) \qquad x_i* - \sum_{m \in M} b_{im}^F z_m* \leq 0, \ u_i^{F*} \ (x_i* - \sum_{m \in M} b_{im}^F z_m*) = 0, \ i \in I$$

$$A^I z* - B^I z* = 0$$

$$\sum_{m \in M} a^P_{rm} \, z_m^* - w_r^* \le 0, \, u_r^{P*} \left(\sum_{m \in M} a^P_{rm} \, z_m^* - w_r^* \right) = 0, \, r \in R$$

(ii) The demand price for a final good or service cannot exceed the market price. If a positive quantity of the good is purchased, the demand price equals the market price. But if the demand price does fall short of the market price, the good is not bought.

Also, the supply price of a resource cannot fall short of the market price. If a positive quantity of the resource is supplied, the supply price equals the market price. But if the supply price does exceed the market price, the resource is not offered on the market.

These somewhat roundabout conditions can be summed up under the simple statement that all consumers of final goods and services and all suppliers of resources must be "adjusted to equilibrium."

The conditions now mentioned are contained in

(4.12) $\quad u_i^{F*} \ge P_i(x_i^*), \, x_i^*(u_i^{F*} - P_i(x_i^*)) = 0, \, i \in I$

$\quad -u_r^{P*} \ge -Q_r(w_r^*), \, w_r^*(-u_r^{P*} + Q_r(w_r^*)) = 0, \, r \in R$

(iii) The imputed profit of operating any activity is nonpositive. For the purpose of the calculation of the imputed profit, the possible charges for hitting the capacity limits of activities have to be included among the costs. If the activity is operated, the profit vanishes. But if the profit is negative, the activity is not operated.

These standard conditions are spelled out by the relations

(4.13) $\quad -\sum_{i \in I} u_i^{F*} b^F_{im} + \sum_{j \in J} u_j^{I*} (a^I_{jm} - b^I_{jm}) + \sum_{r \in R} u_r^{P*} a^P_{rm}$

$\quad + s_m^* \ge 0, \, m \in M$

$$z_m*(- \sum_{i \in I} u_i^{F*} b_{im}^F + \sum_{j \in J} u_j^{I*} (a_{jm}^I - b_{jm}^I)$$

$$+ \sum_{r \in R} u_r^{P*} a_{rm}^P + s_m*) = 0, \quad m \in M$$

The gross returns from operating any activity m equals the sum of the value of final goods and services and the value of intermediate outputs. The cost arising from the operation of activity m is given as the sum of the cost of intermediate inputs, the cost of final inputs, and the possible cost charge for hitting the capacity limit.

The conditions (4.13) may be written in the simplified form

Cash profit from operating activity $m \leq$ imputed charge s_m*,

z_m^* (cash profit from operating activity m − imputed charge s_m*) = 0,

$m \in M$

Remember that the charge s_m* is an imputed assessment, calculated by the analyst. There is no cash counterpart to this charge. The difference between the cash profit and the imputed cost charge may be referred to as the "imputed profit." Hence,

Imputed profit from operating activity $m \leq 0$,

z_m* times the imputed profit from operating activity $m = 0$,

$m \in M$

which yields the conditions spelled out in (iii) above.

So, activity analysis is perfectly compatible with positive cash profits. As we shall now show, cash profits typically arise when activities are operated at their capacity levels.

(iv)   The level of operation of any activity cannot exceed its capacity limit. If a positive capacity charge is assessed, the activity is operated at its capacity. But if the activity is operated below its capacity limit, no charge is assessed.

The Kuhn–Tucker conditions are

$$(4.14) \qquad z_m{}^* \leq \overline{z}_m, \, s_m{}^* \, (\overline{z}_m - z_m{}^*) = 0, \, m \in M$$

The stated conditions (iv) follow from the fact that $s_m{}^* > 0$ implies that $z_m{}^* = \overline{z}_m$, that is, the activity is operated at its capacity. Further, if $z_m{}^* < \overline{z}_m$ one concludes that $s_m{}^* = 0$.

Returning for a moment to (4.13), one sees that if the cash profit is positive, it follows a fortiori that $s_m{}^*$ is also positive. Looking at (4.14), one concludes that $z_m{}^* = \overline{z}_m$. In other words, a positive cash profit may be viewed as a signal indicating that an activity is operated at its capacity level.

In some applications of activity analysis, one may want to include lower limits on activities rather than upper capacity bounds. Such a lower limit may indicate a social concern that some minimum level of operation be maintained. An example may be the operation of a day care center for the children of employees. We will not carry out the formalities of the mathematical analysis here, but the reader will readily understand that in this case an activity may actually generate a cash loss. A cash loss signals that an activity is operated at its lower threshold level.

There is a rather interesting "global" equilibrium condition that follows as a consequence of the Kuhn–Tucker conditions. Use all the equalities appearing in (4.11–14); elementary substitution of variables yields

$$(4.15) \qquad \sum_{i \in I} P_i(x_i{}^*)x_i{}^* = \sum_{r \in R} Q_r(w_r{}^*)w_r{}^* + \sum_{m \in M} s_m{}^* \overline{z}_m$$

In other words, total consumer expenditure equals total resource income plus total imputed capacity charges. Or, since total imputed capacity charges equal cash profits, we see that each dollar of consumer expenditure eventually ends up as income, either in the pockets of the resource owners or as cash profit.

Exercise 4.1

In a study of the home security industry, the following activities are discerned:

Patrolling security guards *(m = 1)*

Manufacture and installation of sound detection systems *(m = 2)*

Manufacture and installation of movement detection systems *(m = 3)*

Monitoring of sound detection systems *(m = 4)*

Monitoring of movement detection systems *(m = 5)*

There are three primary goods used as inputs:

Security guards *(r = 1)*

Technicians and engineers *(r = 2)*

Electronic support systems (telephone switchboards, sensors, wiring, etc.)
(r = 3)

Note that the electronic support systems are here treated as a primary input, although in a more extensive modeling effort it may rather be desired to treat such support systems as an intermediate good, rolling back the level of explanation to the supply of chips, metals, and so on.

The labor inputs *(r = 1* and *2)* are measured in thousands of manhours per week. The electronic support systems employed are measured by a volume index.

The unit requirements of each activity are listed in table 4.1. The dimensions of each input coefficient is a quantity per unit level of operation of the activity.

There are two intermediate goods—sound detection systems *(j = 1)* and movement detection systems *(j = 2)*, both measured by the number of units manufactured and installed.

The top box of coefficients in table 4.1 is the matrix A^P. The lower box is the matrix A^I.

Table 4.1. Unit Input Requirements

	m = 1	m = 2	m = 3	m = 4	m = 5
r = 1	3.5	0.0	0.0	0.3	0.3
r = 2	0.0	5.0	4.5	0.0	0.0
r = 3	2.0	8.0	9.0	0.0	0.0
j = 1	0.0	0.0	0.0	1.0	0.0
j = 2	0.0	0.0	0.0	0.0	1.0

In this simple example, each activity has a single output. The unit level of operation of an activity is defined as the level which generates one unit of output. The unit outputs of each activity are listed in table 4.1. There are two categories of final services:

surveillance by patrolling security guards *(i = 1)*

electronic surveillance monitored by guards $(i = 2)$.

The first of these outputs is measured in thousands of customer hours per week, and the second in numbers of installed systems monitored.

Table 4.2. Unit Outputs

	m = 1	m = 2	m = 3	m = 4	m = 5
i = 1	1	0	0	0	0
i = 2	0	0	0	1	1
j = 1	0	1	0	0	0
j = 2	0	0	1	0	0

The top box of coefficients in table 4.2 is the matrix B^F. The bottom box is B^I.

The demand price functions for the two outputs are (in thousands of dollars):

$$i = 1: \quad 12 - 0.4x_1$$

$$i = 2: \quad 5 - 0.25x_2$$

where x_1 and x_2 are the quantities of the two final services demanded by the consumers.

There are given and fixed endowments of all listed resources:

Security guards	*100*	thousand manhours per week
Technicians and engineers	*357.5*	thousand manhours per week
Electronic support systems	*227.5*	

The entries constitute the elements of the vector $w = [w_r]$.

Determine the optimal level of operation of each activity, the outputs obtained, and the equilibrium prices in all markets.

Solution: The present example is quite typical of the kind of applications that are here envisioned for partial activity analysis. It is believed that the analytical framework is sufficiently flexible to be able to accommodate a wide range of sector applications, brought from an advanced developed economy.

No attempt is made to track the production chains back to the supplies of natural resources and raw materials such as coal, iron ore, or agricultural land. The production chains are only rolled back sufficiently to provide the kind of detail and background desired for the purpose of the problem at hand. A study of the home security industry naturally would take as given most of the products and services of the modern economy, such as the electronics industry in general and the education and training of engineers.

The concept of endowments is thus one of convenience only, serving to delimit the field of endogenous variables from deeper lying exogenous variables. The vector $w = [w_r]$ lists the variables that are believed to be scarce to the functioning of the sector under investigation as a whole, and the supply of which are here being assumed to be nonsensitive to price (the supply curves are vertical).

In any case, there is no need to insist that the supply of these endowments be fixed and given. As we have shown, we can easily handle the case of supply price-dependent supplies (the mathematical format then requiring the integration of the supply price functions).

The final goods that the security industry delivers are all services. The production and delivery of a wide variety of services has become one of the characteristic traits of the postindustrial economy. The numerical prototype chosen here demonstrates that delivery of services may involve long and complicated production chains.

There are, as it were, two different "techniques" of producing final good $m = 2$, using either sound detection systems or movement detection systems. Both techniques require complicated electronic hardware and some manpower. The consumer cares only about the services that the electronic hardware delivers; the choice of technique will therefore be taken based only upon considerations of comparative costs.

Program (4.10) now reads

$$max\ 12x_1 - 0.2x_1^2 + 15x_2 - 0.125x_2^2$$

subject to

$$
\begin{aligned}
x_1 - z_1 &\le 0 \\
x_2 - z_4 - z_5 &\le 0 \\
-z_2 + z_4 &= 0 \\
-z_3 + z_5 &= 0 \\
3.5z_1 + 0.3z_4 + 0.3z_5 &\le 100 \\
5z_2 + 4.5z_3 &\le 357.5 \\
2z_1 + 8z_2 + 9z_3 &\le 227.5 \\
x, z &\ge 0
\end{aligned}
$$

The optimal solution is

$$x_1^* = 24.126,\ x_2^* = 22.406$$

$$z_1^* = 24.126,\ z_2^* = 22.406,\ z_3^* = 0,\ z_4^* = 22.406,\ z_5^* = 0$$

Only sound detection systems will be manufactured and installed.

The equilibrium prices (obtained from the Lagrange multipliers) are:

$$u_1^{P*} = 0, \qquad u_2^{P*} = 0, \qquad u_3^{P*} = 1.175$$

$$u_1^{I*} = 9.399, \qquad u_2^{I*} = 10{,}573$$

$$u_1^{F*} = 2.350, \qquad u_2^{F*} = 9.399$$

It turns out that there is an excess supply of both manpower resources, and the wages drop to zero. (This is, of course, an eminently unsatisfactory result. Wages in the real world do not drop to zero, even if there is unemployment. In a later chapter, we shall learn how to deal with such situations of disequilibrium, letting the wage rate in the case of unemployment only fall to a lower threshold level.)

Construction of the Locus of Efficient Points of Final Demand: The Charnes–Cooper "Spiral Method"

Following Charnes and Cooper ([2], vol. I, pp. 308–309), we use the following "spiral" method of parametric programming to determine the locus of efficient points of final demand. Denoting the prices of the final services by $p = [p_i]$, $i = 1,2$, program (4.10) reads

$$max \ p_1 x_1 + p_2 x_2$$

subject to

$$
\begin{aligned}
x_1 - z_1 & & & \leq 0 \\
x_2 & & -z_4 - z_5 & \leq 0 \\
& -z_2 & + z_4 & = 0 \\
& -z_3 & + z_5 & = 0 \\
3.5z_1 & & + 0.3z_4 + 0.3z_5 & \leq 100 \\
& 5z_2 + 4.5z_3 & & \leq 357.5 \\
2z_1 + 8z_2 + 9z_3 & & & \leq 227.5 \\
\end{aligned}
$$

$$x, z \geq 0$$

We now undertake a series of numerical experiments, varying the prices p_1 and p_2 parametrically over the interval $p_1, p_2 > 0, 0 > -p_1/p_2 > -\infty$, each time solving the linear program anew and recording the optimal point (x_1^*, x_2^*) (see tab. 4.3).

Table 4.3. Results from Parametric Programming

Numerical Experiment	p_1	p_2	Slope $-p_1/p_2$	x_1^*	x_2^*
#1	1	100	−0.01	0	28.44
#2	1	10	−0.1	0	28.44
#3	1	5	−0.20	0	28.44
#4	10	41	−0.24	0	28.44
#5	10	39	−0.26	26.71	21.76
#6	1	1	−1	26.71	21.76
#7	3	1	−3	26.71	21.76
#8	3.19	1	−3.19	26.71	21.76
#9	3.21	1	−3.21	28.57	0
#10	10	1	−10	28.57	0
#11	100	1	−100	28.57	0

We also plot the result of each experiment in figure 4.4, exhibiting each time both the optimal solution found and the price direction that generated it. As long as the price slope remains fairly flat and less in absolute value than 0.25, the optimal solution is $A = (0, 28.44)$. But as the slope becomes steeper than −0.25, the optimal solution jumps to $B = (26.71, 21.76)$.

Apparently there exists some critical value of p_1/p_2 when the optimal solution flips from point A to point B. It is easy to see that this critical value is

$$-p_1/p_2 = -(28.44 - 21.76)/26.71 = -0.25,$$

that is, the slope of the line AB itself.

Increasing the slope even further, eventually one reaches a new critical value of the slope coefficient, the optimal solution jumping to the point $C = (28.57, 0)$. It is easy to see that this new critical value is

$$-p_1/p_2 = -21.76/(28.57 - 26.71) = -3.20,$$

that is, the slope of the line BC.

The frontier ABC including the end points A and B constitutes the frontier of efficient combinations of outputs. The region $OABC$ is the production possibility region. Among all points in $OABC$, only points along the frontier ABC can be obtained as the optimal solution to the activity analysis program. Points in the production possibility region other than the efficiency points are necessarily suboptimal points. At a suboptimal point it is possible to increase the deliveries of one final good without decreasing the deliveries of the other.

**Figure 4.4.   Generating the Efficiency Frontier
by the Charnes–Cooper Spiral Method**

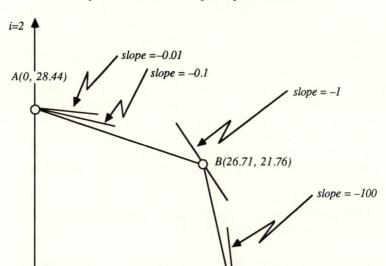

The reader should note that the concepts of a final good and a resource as used in partial activity analysis are only defined in relation to the industry or sector under study. A final good is an ultimate output of the industry or sector. For instance, in a study of the steel industry, one final good may be rolled steel products, another steel wire, and so on. So, a final good is not necessarily a consumer good. Subsequent fabrication, processing, and distribution may be needed before the commodity reaches the ultimate consumer. But these later links of the production chain may in any given modeling effort lie outside the current field of investigation. Hence, they are treated as exogenous.

Similarly, a resource is an ultimate input to the industry or sector being investigated. For instance, a resource in the steel industry may be coal or electricity. What this means is that the study is confined to the productive activities within the steel industry itself, and that the mining and distribution of coal or the generation and transmission of electricity is left outside the current modeling effort and is taken as given.

The demand price functions (4.6) are therefore not necessarily derived from some underlying utility theory of a typical consumer. They may instead reflect the nature of downstream production technologies which are considered exogenous to the current modeling effort.

In the same way, the supply price functions (4.8) may not be derived from some underlying utility theory of a hypothetical resource owner but may reflect the technology of producing the input at an earlier stage of the production chain which we have chosen to treat as exogenous.

We have already pointed out in section 3.2 that when the resource under consideration actually is a produced good, it may sometimes be possible to identify the supply price of the good with its marginal costs and the integrated supply price function with total costs. Similarly, when a final good actually is a producer's good, it may be possible to identify the demand price function with marginal revenue (of those producers buying the good as an input) and the integrated demand price function with their total revenue.

4.2. GENERALIZED NETWORKS OF THE FLOW OF INTERMEDIATE GOODS

The classification of goods and services into primary, intermediate, and final provides a first approximation of the vertical dimension of an industry. Beyond that, an inspection of the particular inputs and outputs of individual activities may reveal that some activities must precede others, and that other activities again may have to be operated at a later stage in time. The unit input coefficients and the unit outputs may imply an ordering of goods and activities in terms of antecedents and postcedents. For instance, if activity #1 uses goods 1 and 2 to produce good 3, and if activity #2 uses goods 2 and 3 to produce good 4, we conclude that goods 1 and 2 must antecede the production of good 3, and that good 3 must antecede good 4. We also conclude that activity #1 must antecede activity #2.

Expanding on this example, we realize that the matrices of input coefficients (A^P, A^I) and of output coefficients (B^I, B^F) contain all the information necessary to establish the complete system of ordering of individual goods and activities throughout the production and distribution processes of the industry under consideration. But it is also clear that the activity analysis format as such is not well suited to display the hierarchy of these antecedents. In order to get a better view of the vertical dimension, we now turn to generalized networks.

At this point the reader is asked to briefly review the material in section 3.3, which provides an account of basic concepts in the mathematical programming of networks. We used the network model to represent the physical transportation of a commodity from one location to another. The packaging, the measures, and the characteristics of the good transported remained the same along the optimal path of transportation, from the supply points (influxes) to the points of ultimate demand (effluxes). Typical applications are coal, oil, and cement. There was no production in this network except for transportation (transportation, after all, in the standard terminology of economics, being a form of production).

In a generalized network, some transformation of the commodity flowing along each link of the network may occur, changing the physical characteristics of the commodity. Mathematically, such change is captured by a factor of attenuation or amplification of the commodity along each link. For instance, in a study of the processing and overseas distribution of orange juice, one particular activity may represent the dehydration of fresh juice to produce orange juice pulp. Suppose that 1 gallon of fresh juice yields 1.5 pounds of pulp. We may represent this particular activity as a link in a generalized network, with the amplification factor 1.5 pounds per gallon.

The format of a generalized network enables us to trace the production chains as an intermediate good travels along the path from the supply of primary goods and services to the distribution of the final consumer good to the supermarket or other sales outlet. These production chains may sometimes span the entire globe. Consider the chain that brought tea leaves harvested in Assam into the tea bag in your morning cup of tea, or coffee beans from Colombia to your cup of decaffeinated coffee.

So, the format that we are about to develop combines two theoretical ideas: activity analysis and generalized networks. The analytical advantage of activity analysis is that it brings into focus the task of designing a plan for the operation of multiple industrial activities in the face of scarce resources. But Koopmans' original format is too general to be able to spell out the various logistic alternatives that available technology offers for the transformation of resources into final goods. This is where the generalized network comes in. It provides the detailed modeling of the successive transformation alternatives and alternative transformation chains that may be used to convert Koopmans' theoretical system into an operational tool of analysis.

Figure 4.5 provides a pictorial representation of a generalized network. In the specimen illustrated, there are six nodes $J = \{1,2,3,4,5,6\}$. Each node represents a possible intermediate state as a good travels along its path from resources to final consumer good. The nodes are interconnected by eight directed links $(6,3)$, $(6,4)$, $(5,3)$, $(5,4)$, $(4,1)$, $(4,2)$, $(3,1)$, and $(3,2)$; the directions indicate possible routes of travel.

We shall find it convenient to use the example exhibited in figure 4.5 for the purpose of the model developments to follow. In any given application, the network must be drawn to correspond to the institutional setting of the problem at hand and its natural delimitations. The exercise following the main text of the present section will provide an example of how the model developments can be adapted to a specific application.

Figure 4.5.   Generalized Network of the
Flow of Intermediate Goods

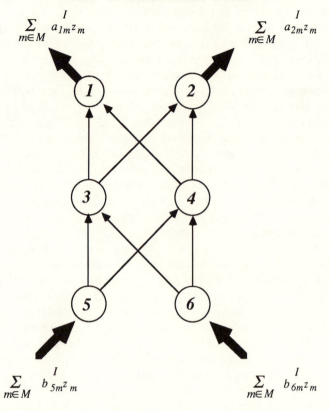

$$\underset{m\in M}{\Sigma}\ ^{I}a_{1m}z_m \qquad\qquad \underset{m\in M}{\Sigma}\ ^{I}a_{2m}z_m$$

$$\underset{m\in M}{\Sigma}\ ^{I}b_{5m}z_m \qquad\qquad \underset{m\in M}{\Sigma}\ ^{I}b_{6m}z_m$$

There are two influxes into the bottom of the network, at nodes 5 and 6, as indicated by the large inward-pointing arrows. Each such influx represents the production of the intermediate good in question, using resources as inputs. There are two effluxes indicated by large outward-pointing arrows: the deliveries of intermediate goods 1 and 2. Each such efflux represents a production process converting these intermediate goods into final goods.

We have already listed the links (j,k) that exist in the network, $j,k \in J$. We use the notation t_{jk} to denote the quantity that travels along the link extending from node j to node k. The dimension or measure of this quantity may be different for each link. We also define amplification factors δ_{jk} for each link (j,k). Sending off a single unit from node j addressed to node k, the quantity δ_{jk} will actually arrive at node k. (There is amplification proper of the flow along the link if $\delta_{jk} > 1$; if $\delta_{jk} < 1$ we should rather speak of attenuation along the link.)

We define the incidence matrix of a generalized network as follows. The matrix has one row for each node and one column for each link in the network. The elements of the matrix are entered columnwise as follows: each column corresponds to a link in which a -1 is entered in the row for the node on which the tail is incident, and a $+\delta_{jk}$ in the row for the node on which the head of the arrow is incident. These are the only two nonzero entries in that column. All other entries are zero.

In figure 4.5, the incidence matrix has six rows and eight columns

(4.16)

$$
M = \begin{array}{c}
 \\
1 \\
2 \\
3 \\
4 \\
5 \\
6
\end{array}
\begin{array}{cccccccc}
(6,3) & (6,4) & (5,3) & (5,4) & (4,1) & (4,2) & (3,1) & (3,2) \\
\left[\begin{array}{cccccccc}
0 & 0 & 0 & 0 & \delta_{41} & 0 & \delta_{31} & 0 \\
0 & 0 & 0 & 0 & 0 & \delta_{42} & 0 & \delta_{32} \\
\delta_{63} & 0 & \delta_{53} & 0 & 0 & 0 & -1 & -1 \\
0 & \delta_{64} & 0 & \delta_{54} & -1 & -1 & 0 & 0 \\
0 & 0 & -1 & -1 & 0 & 0 & 0 & 0 \\
-1 & -1 & 0 & 0 & 0 & 0 & 0 & 0
\end{array}\right]
\end{array}
$$

(For the purpose of identification, the nodes are listed in the rim to the left and the links along the top.)

The vector of influxes and effluxes is written as:

(4.17)

$$
\begin{bmatrix}
efflux\ at\ node\ 1 \\
efflux\ at\ node\ 2 \\
0 \\
0 \\
-influx\ at\ node\ 5 \\
-influx\ at\ node\ 6
\end{bmatrix}
$$

It has one element for each node. The elements are entered as follows: for any influx, enter the amount with a negative sign; for any efflux, enter the amount with a positive sign; in the absence of influx or efflux (a transshipment node), enter zero.

The vector of unknown flows over the network is

$$(4.18) \qquad t = \begin{bmatrix} t_{63} \\ t_{64} \\ t_{53} \\ t_{54} \\ t_{41} \\ t_{42} \\ t_{31} \\ t_{32} \end{bmatrix}$$

It has one entry for each link featured in the network.

The Kirchhoff flow conservation conditions can now be written:

$$(4.19) \qquad Mt = vector\ of\ effluxes\ and\ influxes$$

Carrying out the indicated multiplication of matrices, one obtains

$$\begin{aligned}
\delta_{41}t_{41} + \delta_{31}t_{31} &= efflux\ at\ node\ 1 \\
\delta_{42}t_{42} + \delta_{32}t_{32} &= efflux\ at\ node\ 2 \\
\delta_{63}t_{63} + \delta_{53}t_{53} - t_{31} - t_{32} &= 0 \\
\delta_{64}t_{64} + \delta_{54}t_{54} - t_{41} - t_{42} &= 0 \\
-t_{53} + t_{54} &= -influx\ at\ node\ 5 \\
-t_{63} + t_{64} &= -influx\ at\ node\ 6
\end{aligned}$$

(4.20)

As in a conventional transportation or network problem, we define unit transportation costs c_{jk} for each link (j,k) in the network. These costs may possibly refer to actual physical transportation, but will more generally be taken to refer to all the various processing and manufacturing costs that are incurred when the commodity is converted from intermediate state j to intermediate state k. The standard formulation of a generalized network problem involves the minimization of total transportation and processing costs $\Sigma\, c_{jk}t_{jk}$, where the summation is to be carried out over all links (j,k) in the graph of the network, say graph G. The minimization is to be carried out subject to the constraints that the Kirchhoff flow conservation conditions are to be obeyed at each node, and subject to the condition that all flows be non-negative. Mathematically,

(4.21) $min \sum c_{jk} t_{jk}$
           $(j,k) \in G$

subject to Mt = *vector of effluxes and influxes,*

$t \geq 0$

We now discuss how one may use a generalized network to describe the flow of intermediate commodities in an activity analysis system. That is, we now propose to imbed the generalized network in a setting of activity analysis.

Note that each link in the network represents an individual production activity in the sense of activity analysis. These are very special activities, however. Each activity has only one intermediate good as an input and only one intermediate good as an output. In addition, there may be other inputs the prices of which lie outside the current modeling effort and which are taken as given and known. These are the inputs that go into the cost coefficients c_{jk}.

In order to achieve what is desired, we now need to spell out which additional activities are present in the activity analysis model, converting resources into intermediate goods and converting intermediate goods into final goods. In brief, we need to imbed the generalized network of figure 4.5 into the setting of a complete activity analysis format that covers the entire logistic chain ranging from the use of resources primary goods and services like land and labor to the production and distribution of final goods.

Define the set $M = \{m\}$ as being a listing of all these additional production activities, that is, all activities which are required to model the influxes into the network at nodes 5 and 6 and all activities that are needed to model the further flow of the effluxes from the network.

The generalized network figure 4.5 features the transportation processing activities *(6,3), (6,4), (5,3), (5,4), (4,1), (4,2), (3,1),* and *(3,2).* These activities involve intermediate goods only. In a complete listing of all the activities of the activity analysis format now being developed, there are thus two categories of activities: the set *M* which involves everything in the model that happens before the influxes into the network materialize and after the effluxes from the network are further processed into final goods, and the activities *(j,k)* of the network itself.

Define the matrix of coefficients of primary inputs $AP = [a_{rm}^P]$ $(r \in R,$ $m \in M)$ and the matrix of final outputs $B^F = [b_{im}^F]$ $(i \in I, m \in M)$ as in section 4.1. As before, the expression $A^P z$ then is the vector of primary inputs, and $B^F z$ is the vector of final outputs.

There are six intermediate goods in the model, one intermediate good being associated with each node in the network. The set of intermediate goods is $J = \{1,2,3,4,5,6\}$.

The matrix of coefficients of intermediate inputs $A^I = [a_{jm}^I]$ $(j \in J,$ $m \in M)$ has six rows, one for each node in the network. The expression

$$\sum_{m \in M} a_{jm}^I z_m$$

is the total input of intermediate good j that goes into the activities $m \in M$. In other words, it is the efflux from node j in figure 4.5. The efflux from node 1 is $\sum a_{1m}^I z_m$. The efflux from node 2 is $\sum a_{2m}^I z_m$. There is no efflux from nodes 3, 4, 5, 6.

The matrix of coefficients of intermediate outputs $B^I = [b_{jm}^I]$ $(j \in J,$ $m \in M)$ also has six rows, one for each node in the network. The expression

$$\sum_{m \in M} b_{jm}^I z_m$$

is the total of intermediate good j that leaves the activities $m \in M$. It is the influx into node j in figure 4.5. As shown in the diagram, there is no influx into nodes $1, 2, 3, 4$. The influx into node 5 is $\sum b_{5m}^I z_m$. The influx into node 6 is $\sum b_{6m}^I z_m$..

The Kirchhoff flow conservation conditions (4.19) can then be written

$$(4.22) \qquad Mt = -B^I z + A^I z$$

Apparently, this formulation is general enough to cover any configuration of the network of intermediate goods.

For the entire activity analysis format one then has the nonlinear program (extending our previous formulation program (4.10)):

$$(4.23) \qquad max \sum_{i \in I} \int P_i(x_i)dx_i - \sum_{r \in R} \int Q_r(w_r)dw_r - \sum_{(j,\,k) \in \mathcal{G}} c_{jk}t_{jk}$$

subject to

$$x - B^F z \leq 0$$

$$A^I z - B^I z - Mt = 0$$

$$A^P z - w \leq 0$$

$$z \leq \overline{z}$$

$$x,z,t,w \geq 0$$

In the spirit of Samuelson's original model of spatial equilibrium, the economic potential function appearing in the maximand can be interpreted as net social payoff (or net quasi-welfare, to use the term preferred by Takayama and Judge), the net calculation involving the deduction of all transportation costs arising in the network. There are four sets of constraints. We have encountered these constraints before, and the reader may at this point refer back to our discussion of program (4.10). The only new feature is the particular formulation of the market relations for intermediate goods, which restates the Kirchhoff conditions (4.22).

Define vectors of Lagrange multipliers u^F, u^I, u^P and s as earlier. They are the equilibrium prices of final, intermediate, and primary goods, respectively, and the implied cost charges to be assessed whenever an activity is operated at its capacity level.

The Kuhn–Tucker conditions state the following conditions of equilibrium:

(i) There is equilibrium in all markets (final, intermediate, and primary).

The standard case is that markets clear. But it may also happen that one is left with an excess supply in a final or primary market. The price must then have fallen to zero. For one finds:

(4.24) $x^* - B^F z^* \leq 0, \; u^{F*T}(x^* - B^F z) = o$

$A^I z^* - B^I z^* - M t^* = 0$

$A^P z^* - w^* \leq 0, \; u^{P*T}(A^P z^* - w^*) = 0$

(ii)   All consumers of final goods and services and all suppliers of resources are adjusted to equilibrium.

What this means is that, in the standard case, the demand price of a final good or service equals its market price. This happens when a positive quantity of the good is demanded. Similarly, the supply price of a resource will equal its market price as long as a positive quantity of the good is supplied. But the demand price of a final good may also fall short of the market price; then the good is not bought. The supply price of a resource may exceed the market price; then the resource is not supplied.

These statements follow from the fact that the relevant Kuhn–Tucker conditions recoup (4.12).

(iii) The imputed profit of operating any activity is nonpositive. If the activity is operated, the profit vanishes. But if the profit is negative, the activity is not operated.

In brief, the industry being modeled is "profitless." The calculation of profits involves the assessment of an imputed unit charge s_m^* whenever an activity m is operated at its capacity level.

These results follow from the Kuhn–Tucker conditions in question which retrieve (4.13).

(iv)   Next, there are the capacity constraints for the various activities, and the corresponding relations of complementary slackness involving the imputed capacity charges s_m^*, $m \in M$.

We recover relations (4.14) which state that the level of operation of any activity cannot exceed its capacity limit. When an imputed capacity charge is assessed, the activity is operated at its limit. But if the activity is operated below capacity, there is no charge.

One also concludes that the presence of a positive cash profit signals that an activity is being operated at its capacity level.

(v)   The appreciation in value that occurs when a unit of a commodity is shipped along a link in the network of intermediate goods cannot exceed the transportation cost along the link. If positive shipments do take place along the link, the appreciation in value must be exactly exhausted by the unit transportation cost. But if the appreciation in value falls short of this cost, no shipments take place.

The condition (v) is new and deserves some elaboration. The relevant Kuhn–Tucker conditions read

$$(4.25) \qquad u_j^{I*} - \delta_{jk} u_k^{I*} \geq - c_{jk},$$

$$t_{jk}^*(u_j^{I*} - \delta_{jk} u_k^{I*} + c_{jk}) = 0$$

$$(j,k) \in G$$

Imagine that a hypothetical shipper undertakes the transportation of the intermediate good along the link (j,k) of the graph G. The shipper acquires the commodity at node j at the price u_j^{I*}. During the subsequent transportation along the link, two things happen: (1) An increase in the market price occurs as one passes from node j to node k; upon arrival at node k, the good now sells at the price u_k^{I*}. (2) At the same time an attenuation or amplification of volume occurs along the link. The attenuation or amplification factor is δ_{jk}. Consider the expression $\delta_{jk} u_k^{I*}$. It is the value upon arrival at node k of one unit departing from node j.

The conditions (4.25) then simply relate the appreciation of a good as it is being transported along link (j,k) to the transportation cost. For the purpose of these calculations, the appreciation of the commodity along the link (j,k) is defined as the arrival value at node k of one unit departing from node j minus the departure value of the same unit.

In the case of attenuation along the link $(\delta_{jk} < 1)$, we may say that the value of the surviving volume arriving at node k must cover both the value of the original shipment (the departing volume) and the transportation cost, if the transportation is to be warranted. In the case of amplification $(\delta_{jk} >$

1), the value of the amplified volume arriving at node k must cover both cost components, if the transportation is to be warranted.

A Special Case: Activity Networks

We have developed a programming format that combines conventional activity analysis with generalized networks. The reader should realize that the particular formulation (4.23) may be modified in several ways in order to accommodate different assumptions relating to the nature of the logistics process.

For instance, it may be that some inputs required to operate an activity represented by the link *(j,k)* can indeed be procured at fixed and given prices, so that the costs of these inputs is c_{jk} per unit of operation of the activities, but that there also are other inputs needed which are scarce and available in limited supply only (vertical supply curves). The processing of an intermediate good transforming it from stage (= node) j to stage k may require some specialized labor which is in overall short supply. There will then have to be adjoined to the format (4.23) additional constraints reflecting the market balances for these scarce factors.

In other applications the format (4.23) may appear to be unnecessarily involved, and the posing of the logistics problem may permit some simplification. One such special case, simply to be called "activity networks," will now be briefly outlined.

Assume that all inputs can be split into two categories according to their location along the logistics chain. Inputs in the form of produce, minerals, or industrial subassemblies represent earlier stages of a production chain; during later stages there will be subsequent processing, refining, manufacturing, and distribution before these goods reach the final consumer. The conversion from an earlier stage of this production chain to a subsequent one can be represented by a fixed and given amplification/ attenuation factor. There are also inputs that can be procured at fixed and given prices. Then the entire logistics process, from primary goods to final goods, may be represented as a generalized network.

With some modification of earlier notation, let

$i,j \in I$ = stages of production, whether primary, intermediate, or final

G = graph of network

x_i = final demand of good at stage i

w_i = primary supply of good located at state i

$P_i(x_i)$ = demand price function at stage i

$Q_i(w_i)$ = supply price function at stage i

c_{ij} = unit cost along link (i,j)
t_{ij} = quantity leaving node i en route for node j
δ_{ij} = amplification/attenuation factor along link (i,j)
M = incidence matrix

The two categories of inputs mentioned may then be specified as follows. Inputs of the first category at any node $i \in I$ are the local supplies w_i. The total cost of these supplies can be calculated by integrating marginal costs and are given by expression $\int Q_i(w_i)\, dw_i$. Inputs of the second category at any node j are all flows t_{ij} arriving from other nodes i and flowing into node j, $(i,j) \in G$. The cost of these inputs is $\Sigma_i\, c_{ij}\, t_{ij}$.

The entire model then reads

$$(4.26) \qquad max \sum_{i \in I} \int P_i(x_i) dx_i - \sum_{i \in I} \int Q_i(w_i) dw_i - \sum_{(i,j) \in G} c_{ij} t_{ij}$$

subject to

$$x - w - Mt = 0$$

$$x, t, w \geq 0$$

Note the formal similarity between this program and the spatial network (3.22). Here, however, the nodes represent different stages along the production chain, rather than different regions.

It is left to the reader to check the optimal properties of this program. Suffice it to mention that, denoting the Lagrange multipliers by $u = [u_i]$, the Kuhn–Tucker conditions require that

$$(4.27) \qquad u_i^* - \delta_{ij}\, u_j^* \geq -c_{ij},$$

$$t_{ij}^*(u_i^* - \delta_{ij} u_j^* + c_{ij}) = 0$$

$$(i,j) \in G$$

The appreciation of unit value along link (i,j) cannot exceed the unit cost. If there is a positive flow along the link, the appreciation equals the unit cost.

Exercise 4.2

Countries like Spain and Israel export orange juice all over the world. All orange juice is first pasteurized and dehydrated. The resulting syrup or pulp may be pumped on board specially designed tankers, shipped to the importing country, reconstituted, and distributed to the retail outlets. Or, the pulp may be frozen and distributed as frozen concentrate.[*]

A generalized network will here be employed to illustrate the flow of the product through the orange juice industry in these two countries. The network (fig. 4.6) has six nodes:

$j = 1$ frozen concentrate, retail
$j = 2$ reconstituted juice, retail
$j = 3$ frozen pulp in bulk
$j = 4$ dehydrated pulp in bulk
$j = 5$ orange juice pressed in Spain
$j = 6$ orange juice pressed in Israel

There are five activities:

(6,4)   pasteurization and dehydration of orange juice made from Israel oranges
(5,4)   pasteurization and dehydration of orange juice made from Spanish oranges
(4,3)   the freezing of pulp
(4,2)   shipping pulp, reconstituting the juice, and packaging for retail distribution
(3,1)   shipping frozen concentrate and retail distribution

The flow through the network may be further characterized by the parameters listed in the table below:

Link (j,k)	Attenuation Coefficient δ_{jk}	Unit Variable Cost c_{jk}
(6,4)	0.4	0.2
(5,4)	0.4	0.1
(4,3)	0.98	0.05
(4,2)	1.8	0.3
(3,1)	0.95	0.3

---

[*]For an econometric study of the orange juice industry in the United States, see R. Roll, "Orange Juice and Weather," *American Economic Review* 75/4 (Dec. 1984): 861–80.

**Figure 4.6. Generalized Network Prototype
for Orange Juice Industry**

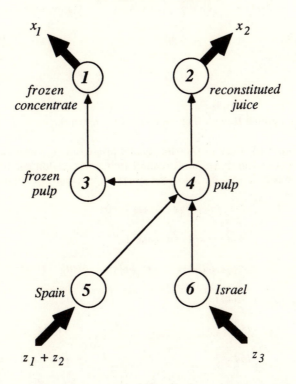

Turning now to consumer demand for frozen concentrate and for reconstituted juice, assume that the demand price functions for these two final goods are (in U. S. dollar equivalents)

$$p_1 = 20 - 0.5x_1$$

$$p_2 = 12 - 0.3x_2$$

where x_1 is the quantity of concentrate bought in thousands of pounds and x_2 is the quantity of reconstituted juice bought, in thousands of gallons.

On the resource side, let us imagine that there are two distinct varieties of Spanish oranges, here to be called "Valencia" and "Murcia." Oranges from Israel will be referred to as "Jaffa." The price that the juice industry has to pay to the orange growers and its production requirement are as follows:

	Price of Harvested Oranges per Pound	Requirement of Harvested Oranges in Pounds per Gallon of Pressed Juice
Valencia	*0.20*	*10*
Murcia	*0.18*	*9*
Jaffa	*0.15*	*12*

Determine the optimal flows along the links of the network.

Solution: In order to prepare for the programming formulation, it may be helpful first to write down the Kirchhoff flow conservation conditions. Using the attenuation coefficients δ_{jk} listed, the system of equations (4.19) now reads

$$0.95 t_{31} = \textit{efflux at node 1}$$

$$1.8\, t_{42} = \textit{efflux at node 2}$$

$$0.4\, t_{64} + 0.4\, t_{54} - t_{42} - t_{43} \qquad = 0$$

$$0.98\, t_{43} - t_{31} \qquad = 0$$

$$-t_{54} \qquad = - \textit{influx at node 5}$$

$$-t_{64} \qquad = - \textit{influx at node 6}$$

The network exhibits only the flow of intermediate goods. In order to form the entire activity analysis model, we need to specify the demand for final goods and the availability of primary goods (resources). The demand for frozen concentrate is x_1, and the demand for reconstituted juice is x_2. (See the broad efflux arrows at nodes 1 and 2 in fig 4.6).

The primary good of the orange juice industry is harvested oranges, delivered to the industry for pressing. The prices of harvested oranges are taken as given and known, that is, as an exogenous variable to the juice industry. The supply curves of primary goods are horizontal. Apparently, there are three different activities available for pressing oranges:

$$m=1 \ \ \textit{pressing Valencia oranges}$$

$$m=2 \ \ \textit{pressing Murcia oranges}$$

$$m=3 \ \ \textit{pressing Jaffa oranges}$$

Using the symbol $z = [z_m]$, $m = 1,2,3$ to denote the vector of levels of operation of these activities, and defining the unit level of operation of each activity as the pressing of one gallon of orange juice, the requirements for juice in

Spain is $z_1 + z_2$, and z_3 in Israel (see the broad influx arrows at nodes 5 and 6 in the diagram).

Using the listed data on the unit yield of the pressing operation, these requirements can be converted into corresponding requirements for harvested oranges. They are:

total requirements of Valencia oranges	*$10z_1$ pounds*
total requirements of Murcia oranges	*$9z_2$ pounds*
total requirements of Jaffa oranges	*$12z_3$ pounds*

Denoting the vector of available harvest by $w = [w_r]$, $r = 1,2,3$, one then has the following market balances for primary goods:

$$10z_1 - w_1 \leq 0$$
$$9z_2 - w_2 \leq 0$$
$$12z_3 - w_3 \leq 0$$

Program (4.26) now reads

$$max \quad 20x_1 - 0.25x_1^2 + 12x_2 - 0.15x_2^2 - 0.20w_1 - 0.18w_2 - 0.15w_3 -$$

$$- 0.2t_{64} - 0.1t_{54} - 0.05t_{43} - 0.3t_{42} - 0.3t_{31}$$

subject to

$$x_1 - 0.95t_{31} \leq 0$$

$$x_2 - 1.8t_{42} \leq 0$$

$$-0.4t_{64} - 0.4t_{54} + t_{42} + t_{43} = 0$$

$$-0.98t_{43} + t_{31} = 0$$

$$-z_1 - z_2 + t_{54} \qquad\qquad = 0$$

$$-z_3 \qquad + t_{64} \qquad\qquad = 0$$

$$10z_1 \qquad\qquad -w_1 \qquad \leq 0$$

$$9z_2 \qquad\qquad -w_2 \qquad \leq 0$$

$$12z_3 \qquad\qquad -w_3 \qquad \leq 0$$

The four first terms of the maximand are the integrated demand price functions. The next three terms are the negative of the integrated supply price functions of primary goods; since the supply curves are vertical we simply get the costs of these primary goods (i.e., the cost of harvested oranges). Finally, all variable costs along the production and distribution paths of the network are also deducted.

The optimal solution is listed below:

$x_1^* = 30.02, w_2^* = 31.48$

$z_1^* = 0$, $z_2^* = 124.35$, $z_3^* = 0$

$t_{64}^* = 0$, $t_{54}^* = 124.35$, $t_{43}^* = 32.25$, $t_{42}^* = 17.49, t_{31}^* = 31.60$

$w_1^* = 0$, $w_2^* = 1,119.12$, $w_3^* = 0$

Only Murcia oranges will be bought. The total requirements of the entire industry is 1,119.12 thousands of pounds. These oranges will deliver 124.35 thousands of gallons of pressed juice which in its turn translates into 49.74 thousands of gallons of pulp. Of this quantity, 32.25 thousands of gallons will be earmarked for retailing as frozen concentrate, and 17.49 thousands of gallons for retailing as reconstituted juice.

On the dual side, one finds the optimal price of Murcia oranges (in U. S. dollar equivalents) equal to 0.18 per pound. This translates into a price of 0.18 x 9 = 1.62 per gallon of pressed juice. Making the pressed juice into concentrate, one has to add the unit cost of 0.1, so that the total cost of pulp is 1.72 per gallon of juice, or 1.72:0.4 = 4.3 per gallon of pulp.

The unit cost of reconstituted juice, at retail, then comes out as (4.3 + 0.3)/1.8 = 2.56 per gallon. Note that this price coincides with the demand price 12 − 0.3 x 31.48 = 2.56.

Looking at the cost of frozen pulp instead, the unit cost is (4.3 + 0.05)/ 0.98 = 4.43 per gallon of frozen pulp in bulk. This translates into a unit cost of (4.43 + 0.3)/ 0.95 = 4.98 per gallon of frozen concentrate sold in retail. This price coincides with the demand price 20 − 0.5 x 30.02 = 4.99.

4.3   THE TAKAYAMA–JUDGE MODEL

The purpose of the models described below is to determine the regional choice of technologies and the regional level of operations in a spatial production and distribution system.

In a study of the U. S. vegetable industry, for instance, the problem is to determine where the cultivation of various kinds of produce will be located, and which cultivation and harvesting methods will be used. Cauliflower can be grown in most parts of the United States if sufficient care is taken. Commercially, however, the growers in California and in the Rio Grande Valley have a comparative advantage relative to growers in most other regions. Further, there exists a range of technologies for growing cauliflower, from the small cauliflower bed of a weekend gardener to large mechanized cauliflower farms. The large commercial growers in California operate at much lower unit costs than a small farmer in the state of New York; they can therefore compete with and undersell the local farmer in the supermarkets in the city of New York even though paying larger transport and/or storage costs.

There are many reasons why cauliflower growers in California have lower unit costs than growers in other parts of the country. The climate is more favorable; farms, warehouses, and distribution systems are more mechanized; and there is an abundance of cheap labor in the form of migrant farm workers from Latin America. Assume that a part of the California harvest is ruined by bad weather; this can be reflected mathematically in a parametric shift in the output coefficients. We would like to find out how this will affect the system of national production and distribution. The California growers cannot maintain their former market shares. The price of cauliflower in the supermarkets in New York will increase and local growers in upstate New York will be able to increase their shipments to the New York supermarkets.

Takayama and Judge demonstrated in 1964 how one can replace the regional supply functions in a spatial equilibrium model with an explicit model of production. In doing so, they joined together Samuelson's model of spatial equilibrium and activity analysis.

Using the same notations and the same assumptions as in section 4.1, assume that the outputs of final goods and services $i \in I$ are demanded in several geographical regions $h \in H$, with the consumers in each region treated as one composite unit. Let the vector $x_h = [x_{hi}]$, $i \in I$ represent the quantities of these goods by the consumers in region h. Assuming that the demand for a consumer good in each region depends only upon the price of the same good in the region, the demand price functions in each region are written

$$P_{hi}(x_{hi}), i \in I$$

for each region $h \in H$. It is assumed that these functions are positive, differentiable, and nonincreasing on the domain of non-negative quantities.

Let the vector $w_h = [w_{hr}]$ represent the supply in region h of primary immobile resources $r \in R$. (The case of mobile resources, such as labor, will be discussed later.) Assuming that the supply of a resource in each region depends only upon the price of the same good in the region, the supply price functions in each region are written as

$$Q_{hr}(w_{hr}), r \in R$$

for each region $h \in H$. These functions are taken to be positive, differentiable and nondecreasing on the domain of non-negative supplies.

The contribution to the economic potential function to be formed arising from both the final demand for goods and services in region h and the supply of resources in the same region is defined as the algebraic sum of integrals

$$(4.28) \qquad \sum_{i \in I} \int P_{hi}(x_{hi})dx_{hi} - \sum_{r \in R} \int Q_{hr}(w_{hr})dw_{hr}$$

What is involved here is a straightforward summation of the economic potential arising from each final demand (positive contribution) and each resource (negative contribution) in each region. Takayama and Judge called the economic potential (4.28) "quasi-welfare."

Note that under the assumptions made, the function (4.28) is continuous and concave.

The assumptions made up to this point are more restrictive than necessary. In their original work Takayama and Judge employed linear demand price functions, permitting the demand price of one consumer good to depend upon the quantities of other goods consumed; in order to ensure integrability, the cross-coefficients were assumed to be symmetric. As we have already explored at some length in section 3.4, even more general forms of demand price functions are possible.

Production is specified by a linear activity analysis model. Define

matrices $A^P = [a^P_{rm}]$, $A^I = [a^I_{jm}]$, $B^I = [b^I_{jm}]]$, $B^F = [b^F_{im}]$ as before. Assume that the list of activities $m \in M$ is an exhaustive enumeration of all technologies regardless of region. The matrices A^P, A^I, B^I, and B^F are then the same in all regions and do not require a region subscript.

Denote the vector of activity levels to be determined in each region by $z_h = [z_{hm}]$, $m \in M$. The vector of inputs of resources in each region is then $A^P z_h$; the vector of inputs of intermediate goods and services is $A^I z_h$. Similarly, the vector of intermediate outputs in region h is $B^I z_h$ and the vector of outputs of final goods and services is $B^F z_h$.

Let $t_{hk} = [t_{hki}]$, $i \in I$ be a vector of consumer goods shipped from region h to region k. Alternatively, we may refer to t_{hk} as a vector of levels of trade activities. A trade activity is operated at unit level when one unit of a commodity is shipped from h to k. The symbol $c_{hk} = [c_{hki}]$, $i \in I$ is used in an analogous manner to denote unit costs for transporting goods from h to k. These transportation costs are assumed to be given and fixed.

Following Takayama and Judge, we now form the mathematical program

$$(4.29) \qquad max \sum_{h \in H} \{ \sum_{i \in I} \int P_{hi}(x_{hi}) dx_{hi} - \sum_{r \in R} \int Q_{hr}(w_{hr}) dw_{hr} \}$$

$$- \sum_{h \in H} \sum_{k \in K} c_{hk}^T t_{hk}$$

subject to

$$x_h - B^F z_h - \sum_{k \in H} (t_{kh} - t_{hk}) \leq 0$$

$$A^I z_h - B^I z_h \qquad\qquad = 0$$

$$A^P z_h - w_h \qquad\qquad \leq 0$$

$$z_h \qquad\qquad\qquad \leq \overline{z}$$

$$x_h, z_h, t_{hk}, w_h \geq 0$$

$$h, k \in H$$

The objective function is net quasi-welfare (calculated net of total transportation costs). There are four sets of constraints for each region. The first set states that the local supply in a region plus net in-shipments from other regions must suffice to cover local demand. The second set of constraints states that the output of each intermediate good must equal the use of it. The third set of constraints states that the local supply of each immobile resource must suffice to cover the local input requirements of it. Finally, there are the capacity constraints.

The maximand is concave. The constraint set is linear.

Define vectors of Lagrange multipliers, say $u_h^F = [u_{hi}^F]$, $i \in I$, $u_h^I = [u_{hj}^I]$, $j \in J$, $u_h^P = [u_{hr}^P]$, $r \in R$ and $s_h = [s_{hm}]$, $m \in M$ respectively. The optimal u_h^{F*} will be interpreted as the vector of equilibrium prices of final goods in region h. It is non-negative. The optimal u_h^{I*} will be interpreted as the vector of equilibrium prices of intermediate goods in region h. Formally, it is unrestricted in sign (the direct constraints are equalities). The optimal u_h^{P*} will be interpreted as the vector of equilibrium prices of resources in region h. It is non-negative. The optimal s_h* is the vector of optimal capacity charges in region h. It is also non-negative.

Once more we list the conditions of equilibrium and equilibrium adjustment, spelled out by the Kuhn–Tucker conditions:

(i)   All regional markets are in equilibrium. This holds for final goods and services, intermediate goods, and resources.

For one gets

(4.30) $$x_h* - B^F z_h* - \sum_{k \in H} (t_{kh}* - t_{hk}*) \leq 0,$$

$$u_h^{F*T} (x_h* - B^F z_h* - \sum_{k \in H} (t_{kh}* - t_{hk}*)) = 0$$

$$A^I z_h* - B^I z_h* = 0$$

$$A^P z_h* - w_h* \leq 0, \; u_h^{P*T} (A^P z_h* - w_h*) = 0$$

The markets for intermediate goods must always clear (by definition). The markets for primary goods and resources will typically also clear; this happens when the equilibrium price is positive. But the possibility of an excess supply also exists; in that case the price drops to zero.

(ii)   The consumers of final goods and services in each region, and the suppliers of resources in each region, are all adjusted to equilibrium.

In the standard case, when some positive quantity of a final good is demanded in a region, the demand price must equal the market price. And when a positive quantity of a resource is supplied, the supply price must equal the market price. But the demand price of a final good may also fall short of the demand price; then the good is not demanded. Similarly, the supply price may exceed the market price; then the good is not supplied. For one gets, in each region

(4.31) $u_{hi}^{F*} \geq P_{hi}(x_{hi}*), \, x_{hi}*(u_{hi}^{F*} - P_{hi}(x_{hi}*)) = 0, \, i \in I, \, h \in H$

$u_{hr}^{P*} \leq Q_{hr}(w_{hr}*), \, w_{hr}*(u_{hr}^{P*} - Q_{hr}(w_{hr}*)) = 0, \, r \in R, \, h \in H$

(iii)   No activity can be operated at a profit. Activities actually in operation break exactly even.

We have already encountered this condition of nonpositive profits a couple of times (see secs. 4.1 and 4.2, above). Now we see that it even applies to the operation of regional activities. As before, the no-profit condition applies to imputed profits, calculated after the deduction of the possible capacity charges s_h*. A positive capacity charge s_h* occurs whenever a regional activity is operated at its capacity limit.

(4.32) $-B^{FT}u_{h}^{F*} + (A^I - B^I)^T u_{h}^{I*} + A^{PT}u_{h}^{P*} + s_{h}^{*} \geq 0$

$z^{*T}(-B^{FT}u_{h}^{F*} + (A^I - B^I)^T u_{h}^{I*} + A^{PT}u_{h}^{P*} + s_{h}^{*}) = 0$

$h \in H$

or, expressed quite simply,

Cash profit from operating activity m in region $h \leq$ imputed charge $s_{hm}*$,

$x_{hm}*$ (cash profit from operating activity m in region h – imputed charge $s_{hm}*$) = 0,

all regions h, all activities m

One concludes that the imputed profit arising from the operation of any regional activity can never be positive. If the activity is operated, the profit vanishes. But if a negative profit were to occur, the activity would not be operated.

(iv)   There is a capacity constraint in each region h for each activity m. If the constraint is nonbinding, the imputed

cost charge $s_{hm}*$ is zero. But when a positive charge is
assessed, the capacity constraint is tight.

For one gets

$$(4.33) \qquad z_h* \leq \overline{z}, s_h^{*T}(z_h* - \overline{z}) = 0, h \in H$$

and if $z_{hm}* < \overline{z}_m$ for some region h and some activity m, then it follows
that $s_{hm}* = 0$, so that the imputed charge is zero. Conversely, if $s_{hm}* > 0$
then necessarily $z_{hm}* = \overline{z}_m$ so that the capacity limit in region h for
activity m must be binding.

(v)   Regional prices of the same final good can differ at most
by the unit cost of shipping the good from one region to
another. If positive shipments occur, the price
differential assumes this maximum.

For one finds

$$(4.34) \qquad -u_{hi}^{F*} + u_{ki}^{F*} \leq c_{hki},$$

$$t_{hki}*(-u_{hi}^{F*} + u_{ki}^{F*} - c_{hki}) = 0,$$

$$i \in I, h, k \in K$$

These conditions are, of course, quite familiar to us by now. We have
encountered them again and again in the analysis of spatial equilibrium.

Exercise 4.3

There are four regions, $h = 1,2,3,4$. Regions 1,2,3 are in the farm belt,
while region 4 is a metropolitan area. The demand price in dollars for milk in the
four areas is given by

$$p_h = 230 - 1.2x_h/N_h, h = 1,2,3,4$$

where x_h is the demand in region h, measured in thousands of kilograms per day
and N_h is the local population in millions of persons, as follows

$[N_h] = (0.1, 0.1, 0.3, 1.2)$

There are two breeds of milk cows, Jerseys and Holsteins. Three resources—fodder $(r = 1)$, labor $(r = 2)$, capital $(r = 3)$—are required to produce milk. A Jersey cow produces 19 kilograms of milk per day; the input requirements of the three resources are 7.4, 2.5, and 30.0 respectively. A Holstein produces 20 kilograms of milk; the input requirements are 8.0, 2.5, and 32.5, respectively.

The total availability of resources in the three farm regions are displayed in the table below

	Region h = 1	Region h = 2	Region h = 3
fodder	*10,000*	*15,000*	*25,000*
labor	*7,500*	*4,000*	*6,000*
capital	*150,000*	*200,000*	*100,000*

Resources are region-specific, that is, they cannot be moved from one region to another in the short run.

The cost of transporting one thousand kilograms of milk from the three farming regions to the metropolitan area are, respectively, $8.00, 12.00, and 9.00.

Solution: Form first the integrated demand price functions for milk:

$$\int (230 - 12\, x_1)\, dx_1 = 230\, x_1 - 6x_1^2$$
$$\int (230 - 12\, x_2)\, dx_2 = 230\, x_2 - 6x_2^2$$
$$\int (230 - 4\, x_3)\, dx_3 = 230\, x_3 - 2x_3^2$$
$$\int (230 - x_4)\, dx_4 = 230\, x_4 - 0.5x_4^2$$

Total net quasi-welfare is formed by adding these four terms together and deducting the transportation costs:

$$8\, t_{14} + 12\, t_{24} + 9\, t_{34}$$

There are two activities: Jerseys $(m = 1)$ and Holsteins $(m = 2)$. The vectors of activity levels in the three regions are

$$z_1 = \begin{bmatrix} z_{11} \\ z_{12} \end{bmatrix} \qquad z_2 = \begin{bmatrix} z_{21} \\ z_{22} \end{bmatrix} \qquad z_3 = \begin{bmatrix} z_{31} \\ z_{32} \end{bmatrix}$$

The matrix of input requirements is

$$A = \begin{bmatrix} 7.4 & 8.0 \\ 2.5 & 2.5 \\ 30.0 & 32.5 \end{bmatrix}$$

and the matrix of output coefficients is

$$B = \begin{bmatrix} 0.019 & 0.020 \end{bmatrix}$$

The extremal formulation requires maximizing net quasi-welfare subject to the market constraints listed below, and subject to the conditions that all unknowns be non-negative.

Milk:
$$x_1 - 0.019\, z_{11} - 0.020\, z_{12} + t_{14} \leq 0$$
$$x_2 - 0.019\, z_{21} - 0.020\, z_{22} + t_{24} \leq 0$$
$$x_3 - 0.019\, z_{31} - 0.020\, z_{32} + t_{34} \leq 0$$
$$x_4 - t_{14} - t_{24} - t_{34} \qquad\qquad \leq 0$$

Fodder:
$$7.4\, z_{11} + 8\, z_{12} \quad \leq \quad 10{,}000$$
$$7.4\, z_{21} + 8\, z_{22} \quad \leq \quad 15{,}000$$
$$7.4\, z_{31} + 8\, z_{32} \quad \leq \quad 25{,}000$$

Labor:
$$2.5\, z_{11} + 2.5\, z_{12} \quad \leq \quad 7{,}500$$
$$2.5\, z_{21} + 2.5\, z_{22} \quad \leq \quad 4{,}000$$
$$2.5\, z_{31} + 2.5\, z_{32} \quad \leq \quad 6{,}000$$

Capital:
$$30\, z_{11} + 32.5\, z_{12} \quad \leq \quad 150{,}000$$
$$30\, z_{21} + 32.5\, z_{22} \quad \leq \quad 200{,}000$$
$$30\, z_{31} + 32.5\, z_{32} \quad \leq \quad 100{,}000$$

The entire program now reads:

$$\max 230\, x_1 - 6\, x_1^2 + 230\, x_2 - 6 x_2^2 + 230\, x_3 - 2\, x_3^2 + 230\, x_4 -$$
$$- 0.5 x_4^2 - 8\, t_{14} - 12\, t_{24} - 9\, t_{34}$$

subject to

$$x_1 - 0.019z_{11} - 0.020z_{12} + t_{14} \leq 0$$

$$x_2 - 0.019z_{21} - 0.020z_{22} + t_{24} \leq 0$$

$$x_3 - 0.019z_{31} - 0.020z_{32} + t_{34} \leq 0$$

$$x_4 - t_{14} - t_{24} - t_{34} \leq 0$$

$$7.4z_{11} + 8z_{12} \leq 10,000$$

$$7.4z_{21} + 8z_{22} \leq 15,000$$

$$7.4z_{31} + 8z_{32} \leq 25,000$$

$$2.5z_{11} + 2.5z_{12} \leq 7,500$$

$$2.5z_{21} + 2.5z_{22} \leq 4,000$$

$$2.5z_{31} + 2.5z_{32} \leq 6,000$$

$$30z_{11} + 32.5z_{12} \leq 150,000$$

$$30z_{21} + 32.5z_{22} \leq 200,000$$

$$30z_{31} + 32.5z_{32} \leq 100,000$$

$$x,t,z \geq 0$$

The optimal production pattern is shown below:

	Jerseys	Holsteins	Total Milk Produced, (in thousands of kg. per day)
Region #1	1,351.4	0	25.67
Region #2	0	1600	32.00
Region #3	0	2400	48.00

Figure 4.7 shows the production and consumption of milk in each region. The shipments from the farm regions to the metropolitan region are 19.02, 25.01, and 27.79, respectively, adding up to a total consumption of 71.83 in the metropolitan region.

The lower panel illustrates the optimal prices of milk in the four regions, which come out as $150.17, $146.17, $149.17, and $158.17, respectively, per thousand kilograms.

The cattle kept in region #1 are Jerseys. The only binding resource constraint in this region is fodder, which is priced at $0.38557. The price of labor and capital in the region have both dropped to zero.

Figure 4.7. The Milk Industry

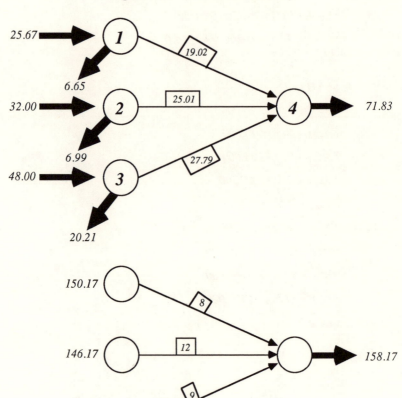

Upper panel: Quantity solution. Production is illustrated as influx into nodes, consumer demand as efflux from nodes. Flags indicate optimal shipments. ***Lower panel:*** Price solution. Flags indicate unit transportation costs.

The cattle kept in regions #2 and 3 are Holsteins. In these two regions, the only binding resource constraint is labor, which is priced at $1.16936 in region 2 and at $1.19336 in region 3. The price of fodder and capital in these regions have dropped to zero.

The net profit per one single cow in each region can be calculated as follows

	Region #1	Regon #2	Region #3
Value of Output	*0.019 x 150.17*	*0.020 x 146.17*	*0.020 x 149.17*
Cost of Fodder	*7.4 x 0.38557*	—	—
Cost of Labor	—	*2.5 x 1.16936*	*2.5 x 1.19336*
Cost of Capital	—	—	—
Net Profit	*0.00001*	*0.0000*	*0.0000*

Decentralization Properties

The programming formulation now discussed seems reasonable provided the entire industry were run by a single corporation, operating both the production facilities at the various locations and the transportation between these locations. But in the real world, the industry is made up of many corporations, each one operating at just a few locations. Who, then, would be the master planner to formulate and solve program (4.29)?

The answer is that the optimal solution derived still is a prescription for the optimal behavior of each participant in the industry, in the sense that if everybody else adheres to that solution then it will also be optimal for any single participant to do so. This holds for each local production manager. It even holds for a hypothetical manager charged with routing transportation.

In order to see this, assume that the optimal solution to program (4.29) has already been established at all locations except at location h; the optimal transportation along all routes has also been established so that the net required out-shipments at location h are known. It only remains to determine consumer demand for final goods, the optimal pattern of production, and the supply of primary goods at location h. Inspecting program (4.29), we see that it boils down to a single location activity-analysis type program, the matematical structure of which is identical to program (4.10).

Arguing along a different track, assume now that the optimal solution to program (4.29) has been established at all locations but let the transportation routing between regions remain to be determined. Inspecting program (4.29) this time, we see that it boils down to a conventional transportation problem with given supplies (the local outputs) and given demands (the local demands).

To conclude, the master program (4.29) defines a totality of individual plans, for individual consumers, production managers, resource owners, and managers of transportation, which have the property that each single such plan defines optimal behavior, given that all the other individual plans are implemented.

Production and Distribution Systems

In order to highlight the flow of final goods from producers to consumers, one may formally treat each plant as a region of its own, a region where there is production but no final demand. Assume that the regions of the Takayama–Judge model are divided into two sets:

regions $h \in H$:   *plants*

regions $k \in K$:   *marketing regions*

In the regions k there is final demand but no production.

Since transportation of output only takes place leaving regions h and arriving at regions k, program (4.29) then takes on the simpler form:

$$(4.35) \quad max \sum_{k \in K} \sum_{i \in I} \int P_{ki}(x_{ki})dx_{ki} - \sum_{h \in H} \sum_{r \in R} \int Q_{hr}(w_{hr})dw_{hr}$$

$$- \sum_{h \in H} \sum_{k \in K} c_{hk}^T t_{hk}$$

subject to

$$x_k - \sum_{h \in H} t_{hk} \leq 0, k \in K$$

$$-B^F z_h + \sum_{k \in K} t_{hk} \leq 0, h \in H$$

$$A^I z_h - B^I z_h = 0, h \in H$$

$$A^P z_h - w_h \leq 0, h \in H$$

$$z_h \leq \bar{z}, h \in H$$

$$x_k \geq 0, k \in K$$

$$z_h, t_{hk}, w_h \geq 0, h \in H, k \in K$$

Program (4.35) can be viewed as a kind of combination of activity analysis and a generalized transportation model.

A well-known problem addressed by program (4.35) is the optimal location of plants designed to service a series of existing marketing areas. On the one hand, factories need to be close to the marketing areas in order to lower the transportation cost from factory to customer. On the other hand, cost considerations also seem to indicate that factories should be located in the vicinity of abundant sources of supply. These considerations may easily pull in different directions, and so the most advantageous location of the factories may be problematic.

So far, we have only allowed for the transportation of final goods in the Takayama–Judge model. The model is easily adapted to deal with the transportation of primary goods as well. With a change of notation, let us now write

regions $h \in H$: *regions of supply*

regions $k \in K$: *plants*

and suppose that there is a local demand x_{ki} for each final good i in each region k. That is, this time we focus the modeling effort on the transportation of resources from the various regions of supply (harvesting regions of various produce, mining areas, etc.) to processing plants. But the transportation from plant to final consumer is shortcircuited, positing a given demand of each final good at the factory doors. Using t to denote quantities of primary goods transported, the model this time reads

$$(4.36) \quad max \sum_{k \in K} \sum_{i \in I} \int P_{ki}(x_{ki})dx_{ki} - \sum_{h \in H} \sum_{r \in R} \int Q_{hr}(w_{hr})dw_{hr}$$

$$- \sum_{h \in H} \sum_{k \in K} c_{hk}^{T} t_{hk}$$

subject to

$$x_k - B^F z_k \leq 0$$

$$A^I z_k - B^I z_k = 0, \ k \in K$$

$$A^P z_k - \sum_{h \in H} t_{hk} \leq 0, \ k \in K$$

$$-w_h + \sum_{k \in K} t_{hk} \leq 0, \, h \in H$$

$$z,t,w \geq 0$$

The reader may easily extend the model even further, allowing for the transportation of both primary goods and final goods at the same time (there would then be three sets of regions: supply regions, plants, and marketing regions). Remembering the analysis in section 4.2, we may construct even more complicated production and distribution systems, involving the transportation of primary goods, a network of production and distribution of intermediate goods, and a final system of distribution of consumer goods.

Exercise 4.4

There are three regions in Honduras where pineapples are grown. The supply price functions for harvested pineapples in the three regions are:

$$q_1 = -20,000 + 5w_1$$
$$q_2 = -5,000 + w_2$$
$$q_3 = -12,000 + 2w_3$$

where the harvest w_h, $h = 1,2,3$ is measured in pounds/day and the supply prices q_h, $h = 1,2,3$ are in \$/pound.

There are two pineapple-canning plants in the country, located on the Gulf of Mexico coastline, each having its own harbor and export dock. Three resources are required to operate a canning plant: harvested pineapples, labor, and capital. Labor is paid \$1.25/hour and capital resources are paid \$0.40/capital hour (horizontal supply curves).

One of the two plants is newer and more capital-intensive than the other. The quantities of the three resources required at this plant to make one case of cans are 0.04 labor hours, 2.00 capital hours, and 16 pounds of pineapple. In the older plant, the corresponding figures are 0.08, 1.20, and 16, respectively.

The unit transportation costs for shipping the freshly harvested pineapples from the growing regions to the two canning plants are as follows (measured in \$/pound):

From Region	To New Plant	To Old Plant
1	0.02	0.04
2	0.015	0.03
3	0.04	0.01

The world price for a case of canned pineapple at the shipping dock is $12.50.

Solve for the supply, distribution, and pricing of harvested pineapples.

Solution: Use the notation

$$h = 1,2,3 \text{ indexes the growing region}$$

$$k = NEW, OLD \text{ indexes processing plant}$$

At plant *NEW* only the new technology is available, operated at, say, level z_{NEW}. (We may quite simply define the unit level of operation as the production of one case of canned pineapple.) At plant *OLD*, only the old technology is available operated at level z_{OLD}. One then gets the program

$$max \; 12.50(z_{NEW}+z_{OLD})+20,000w_1-2.5w_1^2+5,000w_2-0.5w_2^2+12,000w_3$$

$$-w_3^2-1.25(0.04z_{NEW}+.08z_{OLD})-0.40(2.00z_{NEW}+1.20z_{OLD})$$

$$-(0.02t_{1NEW}+0.015t_{2NEW}+0.04t_{3NEW}+0.04t_{1OLD}+0.03t_{2OLD}+0.01t_{3OLD})$$

subject to

$$16z_{NEW} - t_{1NEW} - t_{2NEW} - t_{3NEW} = 0$$

$$16z_{OLD} - t_{1OLD} - t_{2OLD} - t_{3OLD} = 0$$

$$t_{1NEW} + t_{1OLD} - w_1 \leq 0$$

$$t_{2NEW} + t_{2OLD} - w_2 \leq 0$$

$$t_{3NEW} + t_{3OLD} - w_3 \leq 0$$

$$z,t,w \geq 0$$

The optimal solution is illustrated in figure 4.8. The network shows the flow of fresh pineapples from harvesting regions to plants. The supplies in the three harvesting regions are 4000.1, 5000.7, and 6000.4, respectively. The supply in region #1 is shipped to the new plant; it is then operated at the level 4000.1/16=250.0. All supply in regions #2 and #3 is shipped to the old plant; it adds up to 11,001.1. The old plant is operated at the level 11,001.1/16=687.6.

The lower panel illustrates optimal prices. The price of pineapples delivered at the new plant is 0.728; at the old plant it is 0.745. The supply prices that the growers in the three regions receive have been entered in the panel in the left-hand margin. The price appreciation along the utilized transportation routes exactly equals the unit transportation costs.

Figure 4.8.   Optimal Solution to Exercise 4.4

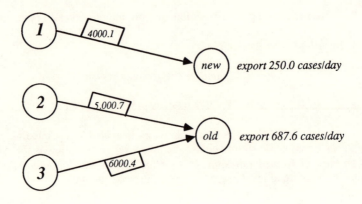

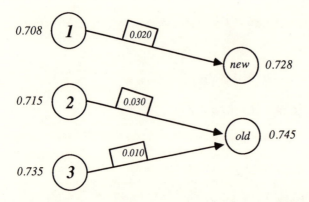

Upper panel: Quantity solution. Flags indicate optimal shipments in pounds/day. ***Lower panel:*** Price solution. Flags indicate unit transportation costs.

Note that the world export price is exactly exhausted by costs in both plants. In the new plant, the price can be broken down as follows:

Cost of fresh pineapples	0.728 x 16	= 11.65
Cost of labor	1.25 x 0.04 =	0.05
Cost of capital	0.40 x 2.00 =	0.80
Sum		12.50

In the old plant, the corresponding calculation is

Cost of pineapples	*0.745 x 16 = 11.92*
Cost of labor	*1.25 x 0.08 = 0.10*
Cost of capital	*0.40 x 1.2 = 0.48*
Sum	*12.50*

BIBLIOGRAPHIC NOTES

Following Koopmans [7], the standard format used to represent the concepts of activity analysis is in terms of topology. In this approach, the purpose of the analysis is to determine that portion of the production possibility frontier which constitutes the loci of efficient points.

As shown by Charnes and Cooper [2], the set of efficient points can alternatively be obtained by solving a parametric linear programming problem, varying the vector of positive prices of final deliveries. This equivalence establishes a bridge which leads from the set theoretic formulation to the formats used in the present chapter.

The origin of regional activity analysis is a 1955 paper by Beckman and Marschak [1]. The details of the model were worked out by Lefeber [9] and Stevens [11]. These authors all followed the Koopmans' original format, assuming a fixed and given supply of primary resources.

An activity in the sense of activity analysis may be operated by a single plant or by many plants in the industry. In so-called project analysis the task is to determine the level of operation of some large industrial project like a hydroelectric power plant or an irrigation project. This is the typical way many lending projects of the World Bank are formulated (see the monograph by Kendrick and Stoutjesdijk [6]).

The use of networks is standard in the literature of production scheduling. The particular formulation used in the main text is one of a so-called generalized network (also called weighted distribution, or machine-loading problem) (see Dantzig [3], chap. 21. For similar developments in spatial equilibrium, see Thore [14].

The Takayama–Judge activity analysis format has found many applications in agricultural economics (see the study of the U. S. apple industry by Fuchs, Farrish, and Bohall [4]). Other agricultural applications concern the dairy industry, wheat, beef, vegetables, and so on. Once the model parameters have been estimated and the model has been solved, it can be used for policy analysis, for example, to explore the effects of changing export or import prices, the sensitivity to wage rate increases, to the introduction of new activities, to new constraints, or to changes of the right-hand side. In each case, the resulting effects can be interpreted as welfare effects and assessed by computing the net change of the maximand.

Larger studies, involving the entire agricultural area, have been reported for a number of developing countries, such as Mexico (see Goreux and Manne [5]), Tunisia, Nicaragua, and Brazil. For a review of these and other applications, see McCarl and Spreen [10].

REFERENCES

[4.1]   Beckman, M. J., and T. Marschak. "An Activity Analysis Approach to Locations Theory." *Kyklos* 8 (1955): 125–45.

[4.2]   Charnes, A., and W. W. Cooper. *Management Models and Industrial Applications of Linear Programming.* Vol. 1. New York: Wiley, 1961.

[4.3]   Dantzig, G. B. *Linear Programming and Extensions.* Princeton: Princeton University Press, 1963.

[4.4]   Fuchs, H. W., R. O. P. Farrish, and R. W. Bohall. "A Model of the U. S. Apple Industry: A Quadratic Interregional Intertemporal Activity Analysis Formulation." *American Journal of Agricultural Economics* 56/4 (Nov. 1974): 739–50.

[4.5]   Goreux, L. M., and A. S. Manne eds., *Multi-level Planning: Case Studies in Mexico.* Amsterdam: North-Holland, 1973.

[4.6]   Kendrick, A. A., and A. J. Stoutjesdijk. *The Planning of Industrial Investment Programs.* Baltimore: Johns Hopkins University Press, 1978.

[4.7]   Koopmans, T. C. *Three Essays on the State of Economic Science.* New York: McGraw-Hill, 1957.

[4.8]   Koopmans, T. C., ed. *Activity Analysis of Allocation and Production.* Cowles Commission Monograph, 13. New York: Wiley, 1951.

[4.9]   Lefeber, L. *Allocation in Space,* Amsterdam: North-Holland, 1958.

[4.10]   McCarl, B. A., and T. H. Spreen. "Price Endogenous Mathematical Programming as a Tool for Sector Analysis," *American Journal of Agricultural Economics,* 62/1 (Feb. 1980): 87–102.

[4.11]   Stevens, B. H. "An Interregional Linear Programming Model," *Journal of Regional Science* 1(1959): 60–98.

[4.12]   Takayama, T., and G. G. Judge. "An Interregional Activity Analysis Model of the Agricultural Sector," *Journal of Farm Economics* 46 (May 1964): 349–65.

[4.13]   Takayama, T., and G. G. Judge. *Spatial and Temporal Price and Allocation Models.* Amsterdam: North-Holland, 1971.

[4.14]   Thore, Sten. "Generalized Network Spatial Equilibrium: The Deterministic and the Chance-Constrained Case," *Papers of the Regional Science Association* 59 (1986): 93–102.

[4.15]   Zusman, P. "The Stability of Interregional Competition and the Programming Approach to the Analysis of Spatial Trade Equilibria," *Metroeconomica* 21 (1969): 45–57.

5

The Time Dimension

In order to investigate how producers and distributors draw up economic plans that allow for economic change, it is desirable to expand the analytical format from simple one-period models (those we have been using up to now) to intertemporal or multiperiod models featuring an explicit account of the time path to be determined of unknowns such as quantities of goods to be produced and their market prices.

The distinction between economic flows and stocks is fundamental to economic analysis. In a one-period model, all stocks are implicitly taken as given and known. When the analytical format is expanded to a multiperiod model, it becomes possible for the analyst to investigate the optimal determination of the stocks themselves over time, such as holdings of inventory capital. The purpose of intertemporal planning is often to obtain a suitable smoothing over time of economic variables, such as the smoothing of purchasing requirements that a producer may obtain by holding inventory of raw materials and spare parts.

One of the earliest programming studies of the optimal smoothing of production, inventories and workforce is that of C. H. Holt, F. Modigliani, J. F. Muth, and H. A. Simon (reference [8]). The objective function in their programming model is the expected costs of a producer over a number of months. The cost components are regular payroll costs, hiring and layoff costs, overtime costs and inventory-connected costs. A quadratic cost function for each such cost component was estimated from empirical data.

There is a vast literature, belonging to the theory of the firm, dealing with optimal inventory and investment decisions. Most of this theory is microtheory, concerned with the drawing up of optimal plans for a producer or a single investor operating in an economic environment where his own decisions do not affect the decisions of other units, and where all prices may be taken as given and known. The smoothing and investment problems that are going to concern us in the present chapter are more complex in that they will be formulated for an entire industry or sector of the economy, so that prices in markets may in general not be taken as known but are to be determined as well.

In brief, the task is to determine the competitive equilibrium time paths of inventories, capital stock, investment rates, output, output prices, inputs and input prices for the industry as a whole and for the component firms. Once such supply variables as inventory holdings and investment behavior have been determined, they will—in conjunction with industry demand—generate equilibrium prices.

The presence of real capital, be it inventory (circulating) capital or fixed capital, is typically reflected in a programming model by a capacity constraint. We have already encountered capacity constraints in the simple transportation model and in conventional network models, presumably reflecting the limited availability of transportation capacity such as trucks or railroad boxcars. Investment in real capital generates added capacity. Mathematically, one can explore the effects of a proposed investment program by recomputing the mathematical program at hand with an expanded capacity constraint. The optimal investment path in the industry can be solved from the program by making the capacity limit in each time period a decision variable, and recognizing the costs of such capacity expansion.

At this point, our text establishes contact with important work carried out by the World Bank on the planning of industrial investment, as applied for instance to the South American fertilizer industry, the Brazilian steel industry, the mechanical engineering industry in Korea, and the Indian electric power sector (for references, see the bibliographic notes at the end of the chapter).

The limitations of the text to follow must be stressed. Sector economic analysis is a young subject of inquiry, and many research tasks in the field cry out for treatment. Essentially, what we shall be able to accomplish is to pursue a few of the approaches that have turned out to be successful for the analysis of the spatial dimension (chap. 3) and the vertical dimension (chap. 4), extending them to an intertemporal setting. Other work will have to wait. In particular, we shall not find space to deal with techniques of smoothing and forecasting economic time series, with linear and nonlinear decision rules, nor with control theory. Important and essential as these and other subject matters are for the analysis of the time dimension, we must here leave them aside.

SYMBOLS USED IN CHAPTER 5

$h \in H$	originating regions
$m \in M$	warehouses (sec. 5.2), activities (sec. 5.4)
$k \in K$	consumer regions
$i \in I$	final goods
$j \in J$	intermediate goods
$r \in R$	resources
$n, v = 1, 2, \ldots, N$	time periods
x_n, x_{kn}, x_{in}	final demand in period n
w_n, w_{hn}, w_{rn}	supply of resources in period n
p_n, p_{in}	price of a final good in period n
q_n, q_{rn}	resource price in period n
$P_n(x_n), P_{kn}(x_{kn})$	demand price function in period n
$Q_n(w_n), Q_{hn}(w_{hn}), Q_{rn}(w_{rn})$	supply price function in period n
t_{hmn}, t_{mkn}	quantity transported from h to m
	(from m to k) in period n
c, c_1, c_m	unit inventory carrying costs
c_2, c_{2n}	unit capacity charge (variable cost portion of capacity or capacity expansion costs)
c_3, c_{3n}	fixed cost portion of capacity expansion costs
σ	capital recovery factor
c_{hm}, c_{mk}	unit transportation costs
δ	attenuation factor
I_n, I_{mn}	inventory in period n
a, b	initial and desired horizon holdings of inventory, respectively
$\bar{I}, \bar{I}_0, \bar{I}_m$	initial inventory capacity
$\Delta \bar{I}_n$	increase of inventory capacity in period n
P as superscript	primary goods (resources)
I as superscript	intermediate goods
F as superscript	final goods
$A^P = [a^P_{rm}], A^I = [a^I_{jm}]$	matrix of input coefficients
$B^I = [b^I_{jm}], B^F = [b^F_{im}]$	matrix of output coefficients
z_{mn}	level of operation of activity m in period n
$\bar{z}_0$	initial operation capacity
$\Delta \bar{z}_n$	increase in operation capacity in period n

$$p_{n,u} \overset{F}{_{in}}$$

Lagrange multiplier of consumer market
balance in period n

$$u_n^I, u_{jn}^I$$

Lagrange multiplier of balance for
intermediate goods in period n

$$u_n^P, u_m^P$$

Lagrange multiplier of resource balance in
period n

s_n

Lagrange multiplier of capacity condition in
period n

5.1. INDUSTRY WAREHOUSING

In the late 1950s, several authors developed the so-called warehouse model (for references, see the bibliographic notes at the end of the chapter). An operator of a warehouse buying and selling some staple commodity faces given and known prices in the marketplace; the task is to determine the optimal time path of purchases and sales, given the maximal storage capacity of the warehouse and unit inventory holding costs.

We now propose to study the corresponding problem for an entire industry. According to the traditional scheme of things, wholesalers would buy a finished product from producers, store it in warehouses, and sell it to retailers. Today the borderline between wholesalers and retailers is often blurred; many producers sell directly to ultimate consumers (through direct mail, for instance). Furthermore, warehousing is just one of the various marketing functions of modern salesmanship; others are advertising, service, repair, and the like. In order to focus on the role of warehousing as such we shall here assume that there are three distinct categories of economic agents in the industry: producers, operators of warehouses, and consumers. When the operators of the warehouses replenish their inventory, purchasing a commodity from producers, they face a given and known supply price function in each time period. When they unload inventory, selling the commodity to consumers, they face a given and known demand price function in each time period. Collectively, the operators have some maximal storage capacity. For simplicity, it is assumed that they all have the same unit inventory holding costs. The task is to determine the optimal time path of purchases and sales for the entire industry.

Inventories establish the physical flow of commodity from one time period to the next—a kind of "transportation" where the inventory is the quantity transported and unit storage costs are the unit transportation costs. Using this simile, we may construct a model of temporal equilibrium for the warehousing operations as a specimen of Samuelson's model of spatial equilibrium. The model takes the form of a network (see sec. 3.3) with one link for each time period. If there are losses of inventory as one passes from one time period to the next (associated with theft, spoilage of perishable goods, etc.), the flow through the network will be subject to attenuation over time. The model is then a generalized network (sec. 4.2).

Let the index $n = 1, 2, \ldots, N$ denote consecutive time periods, with $n = 1$ referring to the first planning period and the end of the last period $n = N$ being the planning horizon. In each time period the producers can either sell their good in the marketplace right away, or they can store it as inventory. Let the magnitude of the inventories at the end of time period n (after current adjustments of the inventory have been made) be I_n, to be balanced over to the time period $n + 1$.

The opening stock on hand at the beginning of the first time period $n = 1$, say $I_0 = a$, and the desired terminal holdings at the planning horizon $n = N$, say $I_N = b$, are both assumed to be given and known.

The warehouse model forms a network as shown in figure 5.1. There is one node for each time period. The good can be "transported" (stocked) from one time period to the next, as indicated by the successive directed horizontal links. The supply w_n is entered as an influx into each node n; in addition, the initial stock on hand at the beginning of the first period is entered as an influx into node 1. The demand x_n is entered as an efflux from each node n; in the terminal period N there is also the efflux b.

Figure 5.1. The Warehouse Model

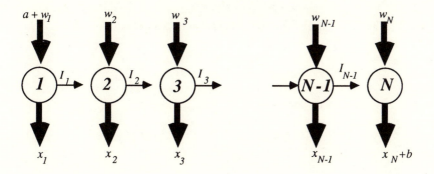

Using the same notation as in earlier chapters, we write the demand price function and the supply price function in each time period $P_n(x_n)$ and $Q_n(w_n)$, respectively. They are both supposed to be non-negative and differentiable; the demand price function is taken to be nonincreasing and the supply price function to be nondecreasing.

The economic potential to be formed (social payoff), arising over the entire planning span from both the demand of consumers and the supply of producers, equals

(5.1)
$$\sum_{n=1}^{n=N} \{\int P_n(x_n)dx_n - \int Q_n(w_n)dw_n\}$$

It is formed by adding the (undiscounted) social payoff in each single time period.

Let the cost of holding one unit of the good in inventory for one time period be c. Total inventory holding costs during the entire time span are then

(5.2)
$$c(a + \sum_{n=1}^{n=N-1} I_n)$$

The warehouse model is then

(5.3)
$$max \sum_{n=1}^{n=N} \{\int P_n(x_n)dx_n - \int Q_n(w_n)dw_n\} - c \sum_{n=1}^{n=N-1} I_n)$$

subject to

$$x_1 - w_1 + I_1 \qquad\qquad = \delta a$$

$$x_2 - w_2 - \delta I_1 + I_2 \qquad = 0$$

$$\cdot$$

$$\cdot$$

$$x_{N-1} - w_{N-1} - \delta I_{N-2} + I_{N-1} = 0$$

$$x_N - w_N - \delta I_{N-1} \qquad = -b$$

$$I_n \leq \overline{T}, \; n = 1,2, \ldots, N-1$$

$$x,w,t \geq 0$$

The Time Dimension 169

The objective function is net social payoff, obtained by deducting total inventory costs from the gross potential (5.1). (The constant ca has been suppressed.)

There is a market constraint in each time period stating that the total availability of the commodity must equal total use. Availability consists of fresh supply w_n bought in period n plus surviving inventory δI_{n-1} becoming available at the beginning of the period. The coefficient δ is the attenuation factor—the percentage inventory survival ratio from one time period to the next. Use consists of current demand x_n and inventories I_n held at the end of the period.

Using the terminology of networks, each market constraint is a Kirchoff condition for the conservation of flow in the corresponding time period.

The warehouse(s) will have some maximal storage capacity. The last set of constraints in program (5.3) allows for such limitations, with $\overline{I}$ denoting the maximal storage capacity of the warehouse(s). For simplicity, the capacity has been assumed to remain constant over time. Alternatively, we might also have assumed that the available capacity increases over time in some known fashion, reflecting some given program of warehouse expansion. (In sec. 5.3 we turn to the case when capacity itself is an unknown to be determined.)

Denote the Lagrange multipliers of the constraints of program (5.3) by p_n, $n = 1,2, \ldots, N$ and s_n, $n = 1,2, \ldots, N-1$, respectively. The p_n are unrestricted in sign; the s_n are non-negative. We interpret the optimal $p^* = [p_n^*]$ as a vector of market prices of the commodity in question in successive time periods n. Further, as we shall see in a moment, the optimal $s^* = [s_n^*]$ may be interpreted as a vector of imputed inventory charges, to be assessed whenever the warehouse is full.

The Kuhn–Tucker conditions characterizing an optimal solution (denoted by an asterisk) are listed below:

(i)   There is equilibrium in the market for the commodity in question in each single time period.

In brief, demand equals supply in each time period. For one gets

$$(5.4) \qquad x_n^* - w_n^* - \delta I_{n-1}^* + I_n^* = 0, \, n = 1,2, \ldots, N$$

taking $I_0^* = a$ and $I_N^* = b$.

(ii)   The demand price of the commodity in any time period cannot exceed the market price. If a positive quantity of the good is purchased, the demand price equals the market price. But if the demand price falls short of the market price, the good is not bought by the consumers in that time period.

Also, the supply price of the good cannot fall short of the market price. If a positive quantity of the good is supplied by the producers, the supply price equals the market price. But if the supply price exceeds the market price, the good is not produced in that time period.

In brief, both the consumers and the producers are adjusted to equilibrium in each time period. For

$$(5.5) \qquad p_n^* \geq P_n(x_n^*), \ x_n^*(p_n^* - P_n(x_n^*)) = 0$$

$$p_n^* \leq Q_n(w_n^*), \ w_n^*(p_n^* - Q_n(w_n^*)) = 0,$$

$$n = 1, \ldots, N$$

(iii)   The inventory position in any time period cannot exceed the capacity limit. If a positive capacity charge is assessed, the warehouse is full. But if the warehouse is less than full, no charge is assessed.

The Kuhn–Tucker conditions are:

$$(5.6) \qquad I_n^* \leq \overline{I}, \ s_n^*(I_n^* - \overline{I}) = 0, \ n = 1, 2, \ldots, N\text{-}1$$

which yields the requirements stated.

(iv)   Keeping one unit of the good in storage from one period to the next, the resulting appreciation in market value cannot exceed the unit storage cost. If positive inventories are held, the appreciation in value must exactly equal these unit storage costs. But if the appreciation in market value during a time period falls short of the storage costs, no inventory will be held.

The appreciation in market value must be calculated net of attenuation losses. Storing one unit of the good from period n to period $n + 1$, the appreciation is obtained as the market value of the surviving fraction of that unit in period $n - 1$ reckoned above its market price in period n. Mathematically, the formula is $\delta p_{n+1}{}^* - p_n{}^*$.

Unit storage costs are obtained as the sum of the direct cash cost c, and the shadow price of the inventory capacity condition—the Lagrange multiplier $s_n{}^*$.

The appreciation can never be greater than the storage cost. No profit can ever occur from the warehousing operations, storing inventory from one time period to a later one. If inventory is carried, the operator of the warehouse breaks even: the appreciation of value is "exhausted" by costs. But if an implied loss from the warehousing operation were to occur, the inventory position would be reduced to zero.

The conditions listed under (iv) are spelled out by

$$(5.7) \qquad \delta p_{n+1}{}^* - p_n{}^* \le c + s_n{}^*, \; I_n{}^*(\delta p_{n+1}{}^* - p_n{}^* - c - s_n{}^*) = 0$$

$$n = 1,2, \ldots, N\text{-}1$$

So, it is perfectly possible that market prices may fall over the time span. Then no inventories will be carried. If prices rise, but by an amount less than c plus the shadow price of the capacitating condition, still no inventories will be carried. Positive inventories are held only when the price rise between two consecutive time periods reaches $c + s_n{}^*$. A more rapid price increase is not possible.

Exercise 5.1

The operator of a warehouse wants to develop a plan for his purchases and sales of a commodity during the next five months, $n = 1,2,3,4,5$. The supply price functions and demand price functions (in dollars) that he expects to face during these months are as follows:

Month n	Supply Price Function	Demand Price Function
1	$-30 + 2w_1$	$40 - 0.75x_1$
2	$-25 + 2w_2$	$42 - 0.75x_2$
3	$-20 + 2w_3$	$44 - 0.75x_3$
4	$-15 + 2w_4$	$46 - 0.75x_4$
5	$-10 + 2w_5$	$48 - 0.75x_5$

Initial inventory on hand is $a = 300$ units. The desired inventory at the planning horizon is $b = 300$ units, that is, the same as the opening inventory. The capacity of the warehouse is 310 units.

The commodity does not deteriorate during storage; the unit storage cost is $0.80 per month.

Determine the optimal purchases and sales, and the resulting optimal time path of inventory holdings.

Solution. Integration and adding all the demand price functions, one gets

$$40x_1 + 42x_2 + 44x_3 + 46x_4 + 48x_5 - 0.375(x_1^2 + x_2^2 + \ldots + x_5^2).$$

Similarly, integrating and adding the supply price functions, one has

$$-30w_1 - 25w_2 - 20w_3 - 15w_4 - 10w_5 + w_1^2 + w_2^2 + w_3^2 + w_4^2 + w_5^2$$

The entire programming model (5.3) then reads

$$max \ 40x_1 + 42x_2 + 44x_3 + 46x_4 + 48x_5 - 0.375(x_1^2 + x_2^2 + \ldots + x_5^2) +$$

$$30w_1 + 25w_2 + 20w_3 + 15w_4 + 10w_5 - (w_1^2 + w_2^2 + \ldots + w_5^2) -$$

$$0.80 \ (I_1 + I_2 + I_3 + I_4)$$

subject to

$$x_1 - w_1 + I_1 = 300$$

$$x_2 - w_2 - I_1 + I_2 = 0$$

$$x_3 - w_3 - I_2 + I_3 = 0$$

$$x_4 - w_4 - I_3 + I_4 = 0$$

$$x_5 - w_5 - I_4 = -300$$

$$I_1, I_2, I_3, I_4 \leq 310$$

$$x, w, I \geq 0$$

The optimal solution is illustrated in figure 5.2. The top panel, drawn in the fashion of figure 5.1, shows the quantity solution. The optimal purchases in month 1 are 27.32; the optimal sales are 20.47. The difference is added to inventory which means that the inventory held at the end of month 1 is 300 + 27.32 − 20.47 = 306.85.

In month 2 the addition to inventory is 25.22 − 22.07 = 3.15, which brings inventory in month 2 up to its capacity limit of 310. In month 3 purchases equal sales—they are both equal to 23.27, and inventory stays at its capacity limit. In month 4, sales exceed purchases which results in a depletion of inventory;

inventory now falls to 310 − 24.47 + 21.32 = 306.85. In month 5, there is a further reduction of inventory to 300, as required.

Figure 5.2.   Optimal Solution to Exercise 5.1

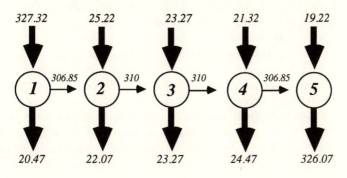

Top panel: Quantity solution. For notation, see fig. 5.1. Horizontal arrows depict inventory holdings. Bottom panel: Price solution. Flags indicate unit storage costs.

The lower panel illustrates the development of the market price. The equilibrium price in month 1 is 24.65. The price in month 2 equals the price in month 1 plus the unit storage cost, adding up to 25.45.

In the passage from month 2 to month 3, two things happen that affect the price in month 3: there is the storage cost of 0.80 and the capacity limit of the warehouse is reached entailing an imputed cost equal to 0.30 (the optimal value of the Lagrange multiplier of the capacity constraint in month 3). So, the equilibrium price in month 3 equals 25.45 + 0.80 + 0.30 = 26.55.

As we have already found, inventory stays at its capacity limit during month 4 as well. The capacity charge happens to be the same, 0.30, and the price in month 4 equals 26.55 + 0.80 + 0.30 = 27.65. The price in month 5, finally, is 27.65 + 0.80 = 28.45.

5.2. A SPATIAL EQUILIBRIUM MODEL OF WAREHOUSING

The discussion in section 5.1 concentrated entirely on the time dimension of the warehousing problem. The problem that we posed and solved concerned the right time to buy and the right time to sell. But in the real world, there is more to warehousing than this. Typically, many warehouses in different locations are available so that the problem is not only *when* to accumulate inventory but also *where* to do so.

Consider the distribution of marketing of brand-name motor oil. The product is manufactured at a number of factories. It is shipped from factories to regional warehouses, stored, and eventually sold to consumers in a number of retail areas. (See fig. 5.3, which features a number of supply points $h \in H$, a number of warehouses $m \in M$, and a number of demand points $k \in K$.) The problem at hand is to determine the optimal routing of the product throughout this spatial distribution system, and the optimal time path of inventories at each warehouse.

Figure 5.3.   A Spatial System of Warehousing

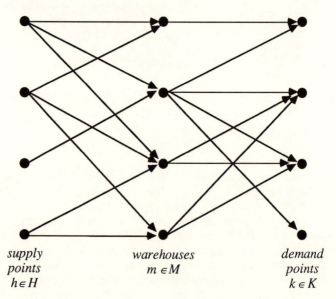

supply	*warehouses*	*demand*
points	$m \in M$	*points*
$h \in H$		$k \in K$

The same kind of problem is encountered in the distribution of furniture, refrigerators, farm equipment, and so on. In some instances, an integrated firm may operate both the factories and the warehouses (as in the case of motor oil). In other cases, large department stores operate the warehouses and the retail outlets (furniture sold by Sears, Montgomery Ward, etc.).

The mathematics to follow necessarily has to become a bit messy, with most variables having subscripts referring to both location and time period. Thus, the consumer demand at a particular demand point k in time period n will be denoted x_{kn}. The demand price function at the same point is written $P_{kn}(x_{kn})$. The supply price function is $Q_{hn}(w_{hn})$. These functions are all assumed to be non-negative and differentiable; the demand price functions are taken to be nonincreasing and the supply price functions to be nondecreasing.

Total gross social payoff over the entire time span $n = 1, 2, \ldots, N$ is calculated as

$$(5.8) \qquad \sum_{n=1}^{n=N} \left\{ \sum_{k \in K} \int P_{kn}(x_{kn}) dx_{kn} - \sum_{h \in H} \int Q_{hn}(w_{hn}) dw_{hn} \right\}$$

In order to form the net social payoff, two types of operating costs have to be deducted: all inventory holding costs and all transportation costs. The unit inventory holding cost at warehouse m will be written c_m. The unit transportation costs of shipping the product in question from supply point h to warehouse m is written c_{hm}, $h \in H$, $m \in M$. The unit transportation cost of shipping the product from warehouse m to demand point k is written c_{mk}, $m \in M$, $k \in K$. For simplicity, all unit costs are assumed to remain constant over time, so that no index denoting the time period is required.

Total inventory holding costs over the time span can then be written

$$(5.9) \qquad \sum_{n=1}^{n=N-1} \sum_{m \in M} c_m I_{mn}$$

where I_{mn} is the amount of inventory at warehouse m held during time period n. The transportation costs relating to shipments from supply points to warehouses are

$$(5.10) \qquad \sum_{n=1}^{n=N} \sum_{h \in H} \sum_{m \in M} c_{hm} t_{hmn}$$

where t_{hmn} is the quantity transported from supply point h to warehouse m in time period n. And the transportation costs relating to the shipments from warehouses to demand points are

$$(5.11) \qquad \sum_{n=1}^{n=N} \sum_{m \in M} \sum_{k \in K} c_{mk} t_{mkn}$$

where t_{mkn} is the quantity transported from warehouse m to demand point k in time period n.

Subtracting the operating costs (5.9–11) from the gross social payoff (5.8), one obtains the economic potential function appearing as maximand in the program below:

$$(5.12) \qquad \max \sum_{n=1}^{n=N} \{ \sum_{k \in K} \int P_{kn}(x_{kn}) dx_{kn} - \sum_{h \in H} \int Q_{hn}(w_{hn}) dw_{hn}$$

$$- \sum_{h \in H} \sum_{m \in M} c_{hm} t_{hmn} - \sum_{m \in M} \sum_{k \in K} c_{mk} t_{mkn} \}$$

$$- \sum_{n=1}^{n=N-1} \sum_{m \in M} c_m I_{mn}$$

subject to

$$- w_{hn} + \sum_{m \in M} t_{hmn} \leq 0, \, h \in H, \, n = 1, 2, \ldots, N$$

$$\sum_{k \in K} t_{mkn} - \sum_{h \in H} t_{hmn} + I_{m,n+1} - \delta I_{m,n} = 0, \, m \in M,$$

$$n = 1, 2, \ldots, N$$

$$x_{kn} - \sum_{m \in M} t_{mkn} \leq 0, \, k \in K, \, n = 1, 2, \ldots, N$$

$$I_{mn} \leq \overline{I}_m, \, m \in M, \, n = 1, 2, \ldots, N-1$$

There are four sets of constraints. The first set spells out the commodity balances at all supply points, stating that the shipments from each supply point cannot exceed the local supply. The second set of constraints spells out the commodity balances at the warehouses, stating that fresh in-shipments to each warehouse plus inventories surviving from the preceding time period must equal current out-shipments from the warehouse plus inventories to be balanced over to the next time period. The third set of constraints are the commodity balances at the demand points, stating that the deliveries at each demand point must suffice to cover the local demand. The fourth set of constraints are the warehouse capacity conditions. $\overline{T}_m$ is the maximal storage capacity of warehouse m.

It is not necessary to repeat the Kuhn–Tucker analysis of program (5.12); the reader may easily check the following Kuhn–Tucker conditions:

(i)   All local markets for the commodity in question will be in equilibrium at all time.

This holds for all supply points, warehouses, and demand points. Starting with any supply point, in the standard case the market price will be positive and the local supply will exactly equal the sum of all out-shipments leaving that point. But there may also occur an excess of local supply above the out-shipments (resulting in an accumulation of inventory at the supply point); in this case the market price must have fallen to zero. At each warehouse, the sum of all in-shipments will exactly equal all out-shipments plus desired inventory buildup. Finally, consider a demand point. In the standard case there will be positive market price and the local sum of all in-shipments equals exactly the local demand. But an excess supply is also possible, in which case the price must have dropped to zero.

(ii)   Both the consumers and the producers are adjusted to equilibrium in the sense of relations (5.5).

(iii)   The inventory position at any warehouse in any time period cannot exceed the capacity limit. If a positive capacity charge is assessed, the warehouse is full. But if there is still storage space available, no charge is assessed.

(iv)   Finally, there is a no-profit condition. It states that no profit can ever occur as a good is being shipped from a supply point to a warehouse, as it is stored, or as it is shipped from a warehouse to a demand point. For the purpose of this condition, the profit from transportation along any link in the network of distribution and storage is calculated as the increase in market price minus the cash shipping cost. The profit from storage is the appreciation in market value calculated net of imputed inventory costs.

Starting with the transportation from a supply point to a warehouse, the Kuhn–Tucker condition states that the appreciation in price cannot exceed the unit shipping cost. If a positive quantity is transported along any particular route, the price appreciation exactly equals the unit cost. At any warehouse, the appreciation of the value of stock from one period to the next equals the market value of the surviving fraction of a unit reckoned above its original market price. This net appreciation cannot exceed the total imputed unit costs consisting of direct inventory cash charges and imputed capacity charges. If there is positive inventory, the net appreciation equals total imputed costs.

The last link of the transportation network is the shipment from a warehouse to a demand point. The Kuhn–Tucker condition states that the appreciation in price along this link cannot exceed the unit shipping cost; if there is a positive shipment, the price appreciation is precisely equal to the unit cost.

5.3. THE OPTIMAL CONSTRUCTION OF NEW WAREHOUSE CAPACITY

Simple textbook models of the investment of the firm are often posed as the problem of installing some piece of real capital which would yield a given and know "income stream" over a number of months or years. The model presumably enables the analyst to compare the expected generated income stream with the cost of capital, and thus to decide if the proposed project is worthwhile.

There are at least three reasons why such a way of posing an investment problem may be too simplified and of little value in a real-life situation. First, the income stream to be generated from any particular investment path over time may not be known but rather be part of the problem at hand. Investment in inventory may not generate any direct income at all. Instead, it may create some more leeway for the operator of the warehouse and some potential for storing a greater surplus of purchases above sales. These purchases and sales are all unknowns, to be determined. Only *after* the solution to the problem has already been computed will it be meaningful to speak about the income stream generated by an expansion of warehouse capacity. Recomputing the warehouse problem under the assumption of an alternative and expanded capacity, one can calculate the additional purchases and sales in each time period that would be warranted, and compute the resulting additional income in each time period.

Second, in any realistic setting of the investment problem the choice is rarely one among a few discrete investment alternatives, such as to buy a machine or not to buy it. Rather, typically, the task to be faced is to determine some optimal time path of capital formation, that is, a problem of accumulation of capital where marginal acquisitions in every single time period have to be evaluated. Also, there may exist alternative capital goods to be considered, each one being associated with its own specific technology of operation and laying down its own characteristic claims on labor, raw materials, and other inputs. These technologies may not be exclusive, so that several different kinds of capital and technologies may actually be operated concurrently. In brief, the choice is one among several interdependent investment processes over time.

To illustrate, an operator may have available some suitable land for the construction of warehouse facilities to store some range of food products. Some of these products must be refrigerated, others need controlled humidity. Arrangements have to be made for the internal transportation of products (fork-trucks, traveling cranes, stacked containers) and for the supervision and management of the warehouse (computerized systems, quality control, and security systems). Some warehouse land and potential warehouse space will presumably be left undeveloped for possible future expansion. None of these decisions can be taken independently; a number of interdependent decision-making problems present themselves.

Third, in industry models such as those that concern us here, prices may not be known but themselves be part of the set of variables to be determined. If the product under consideration is some agricultural product of a fairly perishable nature (most produce), the price of the product *without* inventories may display strong seasonal variation, with the price falling during the harvesting season, reflecting the sudden supplies entering the market at this time. During the off-season, the product may be entirely unavailable or scarce, with high prices. The scenario now indicated is of course the classical case for the operation of a warehouse, the operator of the warehouse buying the produce in question during the harvesting season when price is low and selling it back to the market again when the price is high. The result of such action will be a strengthening of the price during the harvesting season and some easing during the off-season. If one wants to construct a warehousing model for the entire industry that would have some claim to viability also after the warehouse has been constructed and put in operation, one needs to solve for the optimal inventory in each time period in the face of given supply price functions and demand price functions responding in a known manner to the actions of the warehousing operations.

The starting point for the developments to follow is the simple warehousing model in section 5.1 The purpose of the treatment is to replace the simple capacity constraint

(5.13) $I_n \leq \overline{I}$

by some program of warehouse capacity expansion

(5.14) $I_n \leq \overline{I}_0 + \displaystyle\sum_{v=1}^{v=n} \Delta\overline{I}_v$

where the increased capacity in each time period $\Delta\overline{I}_v$ is a decision variable to be determined.

The warehouse model program (5.3) must now be modified in two respects: the constraints (5.13) should be replaced by (5.14), and some cost of warehouse capacity must be introduced, so that it becomes possible to arrive at some optimal tradeoff between the indirect benefits of the additional capacity and its cost.

The subject matter of the cost of capacity requires some elaboration; it will be dealt with in some detail in section 5.4 At the moment we shall simply assume a constant and given cost charge per unit of capacity, say c_2. Also, the inventory charge will be written c_1, rather than just c. To repeat, the new notation is

> c_1 = cost charge per unit of inventory actually stored in the warehouse
> c_2 = cost charge per unit of inventory capacity

If actual inventory is 50 and capacity is 100, the total cost is $50c_1 + 100c_2$.

The distinction between charges on inventory actually on hand and capacity charges clearly is one between variable costs and fixed costs. Actual charges include labor costs, electricity, maintenance, security, and the like. The capacity charge is interest on the financial capital that has been sunk in the warehouse facilities.

The following nonlinear programming model is then obtained:

(5.15) $max \displaystyle\sum_{n=1}^{n=N} \{\int P_n(x_n)dx_n - \int Q_n(w_n)dw_n\}$

$$-c_1 \sum_{n=1}^{n=N-1} I_n - c_2 \sum_{n=1}^{n=N-1} \left(\overline{T}_0 + \sum_{v=1}^{v=n} \Delta \overline{T}_v\right)$$

subject to

$$x_1 - w_1 + I_1 = \delta I_0$$

$$x_2 - w_2 - \delta I_1 + I_2 = 0$$

$$\ldots$$

$$x_{N-1} - w_{N-1} - \delta I_{N-2} + I_{N-1} = 0$$

$$x_N - w_N - \delta I_{N-1} = -I_N$$

$$I_n - \sum_{v=1}^{v=n} \Delta \overline{T}_v \le \overline{T}_0, \, n = 1, 2, \ldots, N-1$$

$$x_n, w_n \ge 0, \, n = 1, 2, \ldots, N, I_n, \Delta \overline{T}_n \ge 0,$$

$$n = 1, 2, \ldots, N-1$$

The Lagrange multipliers are denoted p_n, $n = 1, 2, \ldots, N$ and s_n, $n = 1, 2, \ldots, N-1$ as before. The optimal p_n^* is the price in period n; the optimal s_n^* is the imputed capacity charge in period n, to be applied when the warehouse is filled to capacity (the capacitating condition is tight).

So, there are two kinds of capacity charges in this model: direct cash charges c_2 and imputed charges s_n^*. Clearly, the distinction is essentially one of periodizing because the charge c_2 is fixed and unaltered in all time periods whereas the charge s_n^* is zero when the warehouse is not filled to capacity. A mathematical relation spelling out the precise relationship between the two methods of periodizing capacity charges will be derived in a moment.

The Kuhn–Tucker conditions are listed below. The first four conditions are the same as those listed for program (5.3).

(i) The market for the commodity in question is in equilibrium at all times.

(ii) Both consumers and producers are adjusted to equilibrium.

(iii) Inventory held cannot exceed capacity. If a positive capacity charge is assessed, the warehouse is full. But if there is slack in the capacity constraint, no charge is assessed.

(iv) There is the following no-profit condition for the storage operations. No profit can ever occur if inventory costs are taken to include imputed charges when the warehouse is full. If a positive inventory is held, the operator of the warehouse breaks even.

(v)   The next set of conditions is new. They are

$$(5.16) \qquad s_1{}^* + s_2{}^* + \ldots + s_{N-1}{}^* \leq (N-1)\,c_2,$$

$$\Delta \bar{I}_1{}^*(s_1{}^* + s_2{}^* + \ldots + s_{N-1}{}^* - (N-1)\,c_2) = 0$$

$$s_2{}^* + \ldots + s_{N-1}{}^* \leq (N-2)\,c_2,$$

$$\Delta \bar{I}_2{}^*(s_2{}^* + \ldots + s_{N-1}{}^* - (N-2)c_2) = 0$$

$$\ldots$$

$$s_{N-1}{}^* \leq c_2$$

$$\Delta \bar{I}_{N-1}{}^*(s_{N-1}{}^* - c_2) = 0$$

There is little point in looking at each of these conditions separately. But taken together, they lay down a particular way of periodizing total capacity charges over the planning horizon. Summing all the equalities in (5.16), one sees that the periodizing formula satisfies

$$(5.17) \qquad \sum_{n=1}^{n=N-1} s_n{}^* \sum_{v=1}^{v=n} \Delta \bar{I}_v{}^* = c_2 \sum_{n=1}^{n=N-1} \sum_{v=1}^{v=n} \Delta \bar{I}_v{}^*$$

that is, the total capacity charges over the entire time span are the same, whether one uses the constant cash charge c_2 or the imputed charges $s_n{}^*$.

5.4. THE PLANNING OF INDUSTRIAL INVESTMENT PROJECTS

We have just learned how to allow for the possibility of expanding warehouse capacity in a simple warehouse model. Capacity has become a decision variable rather than a given datum. Clearly, the same analytical approach can be employed in other situations where production or distribution and transportation and marketing decisions are limited by existing capacity. To demonstrate the scope of the approach, we now turn to a conventional intertemporal activity analysis type model. The level of operation of each activity is at all time limited by existing production capacity. Through the installation of new machines and the construction of new production facilities—in brief, through real investment—existing production capacity may be expanded. We formulate a programming model that solves for the optimal production plan in each time period, and for the optimal time path of capacity expansion.

The point of departure is the specimen of the general activity analysis format discussed in section 4.1. Consider a sector of the economy producing a number of related final goods $i \in I$. To simplify matters, we shall assume that the time path of demand for these goods is fixed and known, say $x_n = [x_{in}], n = 1, 2, \ldots, N$.

There are a number of activities available for the production of these goods, say the activities $m \in M$. The vector of activity levels in each time period m is written $z_n = [z_{mn}], n = 1, 2, \ldots, N$. And here we are at the crux of the matter right away, because rather than assuming , as we have before, that these activities are limited by existing capacity.

$$(5.18) \qquad z_n \leq \bar{z}$$

we shall this time allow for the possibility of a program of capacity expansion

$$(5.19) \qquad z_n \leq \bar{z}_0 + \sum_{v=1}^{v=n} \Delta \bar{z}_v$$

where the vector of increased capacity in each time period $\Delta \bar{z}_v$ is a decision variable to be determined.

Using the same notation as in section 4.1, let there be three categories of goods and services

$R = \{r\}$ the set of primary goods and services
$J = \{j\}$ the set of intermediate goods and services
$I = \{i\}$ the set of final goods and services

Define the matrices of input coefficients $A^P = [a^P_{rm}]$ and $A^I = [a^I_{jm}]$ exhibiting the unit requirements of primary goods and intermediate goods, respectively, needed to operate activities at unit level. Similarly, define the matrices of output coefficients $B^I = [b^I_{jm}]$ and $B^F = [b^F_{im}]$ exhibiting the quantities of intermediate goods and final goods obtained, respectively, when activities are operated at unit level. Note that no time index is needed for these coefficients—the coefficients are assumed to remain unchanged over time. (If there is technological change, it would be represented as a switch from one constant technology to another.)

In a series of applied studies, including the fertilizer industry, mechanical engineering, and the production of heavy electrical equipment, the World Bank has pioneered the construction and numerical solution of sectorwide investment planning models. The use of mathematical programming enables the analyst to recognize the interdependence of economic activities and to examine many variants of a given project. The methodology used by the World Bank was summarized in a study by D. A. Kendrick and A. J. Stoutjesdijk [11]. The activity analysis format presented below draws heavily on their formulations.

We shall show how it is possible to imbed an interdependent project evaluation model such as those developed by the World Bank in a partial equilibrium format, where the prices of some or all factors to be used are unknown and are to be determined too. The scope of this category of investment planning models is then greatly enhanced. For a developing country with few primary goods and services (such as skilled labor, electric energy, and financial capital), investment plans would easily go astray were one to base them on the assumption that all primary goods and services can be procured at given and known prices. A project under consideration may use up a sizeable proportion of total national resources, and the realization of the project will then drive up the prices of these scarce resources.

To accomplish what has now been promised, let there be a given and known supply price function, say $Q_{rn}(w_{rn})$ of each primary good r in each time period n. Following the analysis in chapter 4, we assume that the supply price of each primary good depends upon the quantity supplied of the same good only. (If so desired, more general formulations are possible, as long as the supply price functions are integrable.) Assume that each price function is non-negative, differentiable and nondecreasing.

Thus prepared, consider the intertemporal programming model

$$(5.20) \quad min \ \sum_{n=1}^{n=N} \{ \ \sum_{r \in R} \int Q_{rn}(w_{rn})dw_{rn} +$$

$$\sum_{v=1}^{v=n} \sum_{m=1}^{m=M} \sigma_m c_{2m} \Delta \bar{z}_{mv} \}$$

subject to

$$B^F z_n \geq x_n$$

$$- A^I z_n + B^I z_n = 0$$

$$- A^P z_n + w_n \geq 0$$

$$- z_n + \sum_{v=1}^{v=n} \Delta \bar{z}_v \geq - \bar{z}_0$$

$$z_n, w_n, \Delta \bar{z}_n \geq 0, \ n = 1, 2, \ldots, N$$

The maximand is total costs, summed over the entire planning span. There are two cost elements: costs of primary goods and services and capacity charges. The first component is obtained by integrating the supply price functions of all primary goods and services (remember that the supply price is the same as marginal cost; total costs equal integrated marginal costs).

The capacity charges in each time period are formed by multiplying a capacity charge by the amount of capacity held. The method is the same as the one already encountered in the preceding section, dealing with inventory charges. Indeed, one of the "activities" presently under discussion could very well be the operation of a warehouse, with z_{mn} denoting some chosen level of inventories in warehouse m, and $\bar{z}_{mn}$ the warehouse capacity.

Some comments about the formation of capacity charges are in order. They should be calculated as interest costs run up on the total investment sunk in expanding capacity. There are two issues here: the development of a formula that reflects the correct interest charge, and the determination of total investment costs. Kendrick and Stoutjesdijk discuss both issues at some length ([11], pp. 38–59).

The interest charge may be interpreted as a rental payment on the total investment value. The rental payment should be reckoned from the period the capacity in question is installed and placed in operation, and during its entire useful life. There is a simple textbook formula that expresses the required capital recovery factor σ as a function of the discount rate per period, and the useful life of the investment. The formula is actually identical to the one used for computing an annuity with present value equal to unity. For instance, with an expected capacity lifetime equal to ten years and a discount rate of five percent, the capital recovery factor is 0.1295. If the lifetime is 15 years and the discount rate five percent, the factor is 0.0963.

(The formula is $\sigma = r/(1 - (1 + r)exp(-L))$ where r is the discount rate per time interval and L is the useful life of the productive unit. See [11], p. 40.)

The determination of total investment costs is more difficult. There are two cases: economies of scale, when the investment cost function is concave, and diseconomies of scale with a convex cost function. The first case is troublesome, as is the case of economies of scale quite generally in mathematical programming models of production. To see this, note that if one were to insert a strictly concave capacity investment function into program (5.20), the objective function would no longer be convex.

To deal with economies of scale, Kendrick and Stoutjesdijk approximate the concave investment cost function by a linear one, featuring both a fixed cost component and constant unit variable costs. Fixed costs are incurred only if the investment project is actually carried out; the mathematical expression of total investment costs therefore involves a 0–1 variable (taking on the value 1 if the project is carried out and the value 0 if the project is not carried out). The resulting mathematical formulation then is one of programming with 0–1 variables. See below.

The formulation (5.20) represents only a first cut at the problem. Here it is assumed that investment costs are directly proportional to the size of the project. There are then neither economies of scale nor diseconomies of scale. Unit investment costs expanding the capacity of activity m are constant, say $\sigma_m c_{2m}$ when σ_m is the capital recovery factor and c_{2m} is the unit cost in each time period of the life of the investment.

The constraints in program (5.20) are straight-forward. There are market balances for all final, intermediate, and primary goods, and there is a capacitating condition on each activity. Each of the constraints has to hold in each time period.

Three strands of economic modeling are interwoven in program (5.20). First, of course, there is activity analysis, in each time period separately. Second, there is the intellectual heritage of the Samuelson model of spatial equilibrium, utilized for the endogenous determination of prices of all primary goods and services and the formation of partial equilibrium in the markets for them. Third, there is the mathematical programming of independent investment projects and the determination of the optimal time path of productive capacity.

To see how these building blocks fit together, consider the Kuhn–Tucker conditions expressing the mathematical characteristics of optimum. Denoting the Lagrange multipliers $u_n^F = [u_{in}^F]$, $u_n^I = [u_{jn}^I]$, $u_n^P = [u_{rn}^P]$ and $s_n = [s_{mn}]$ respectively, and listing the conditions in the order that has by now become familiar to us, they are:

(i)   The markets for final, intermediate, and primary goods and services are all in equilibrium.

For one gets, in each time period $n = 1, 2, \ldots, N$,

$$(5.21) \qquad B^F z_n^* \geq x_n, \; (u_n^{F*})^T (B^F z_n^* - x_n) = 0$$

$$- A^I z_n^* + B^I z_n^* = 0$$

$$- A^P z_n^* + w_n^* \geq 0, \; (u_n^{P*})^T (-A^P z_n^* + w_n^*) = 0$$

(ii)   The supplies of all primary goods and services are adjusted to equilibrium.

We have used this expression before to describe the conditions

$$(5.22) \qquad u_{rn}^{P*} \leq Q_{rn}(w_{rn}^*), \; w_{rn}^* \, (u_{rn}^{P*} - Q_{rn}(w_{rn}^*)) = 0$$

for all primary goods and services $r \in R$ and all time periods $n = 1, 2, \ldots, N$.

(iii) The level of operation of any activity cannot exceed the installed capacity; if the existing capacity is fully utilized an imputed charge is levied equal to the optimal value of the Lagrange multiplier of the capacitating condition.

Mathematically,

$$(5.23) \qquad -z_n^* + \sum_{v=1}^{v=n} \Delta \bar{z}_v^* \geq -\bar{z}_0,$$

$$(s_n^*)^T \left(-z_n^* + \sum_{v=1}^{v=n} \Delta \bar{z}_v^* + \bar{z}_0 \right) = 0$$

in each time period $n = 1, 2, \ldots, N$.

(iv)   No activity can be operated at a profit. Activities that are operated break even.

In the common manner, the application of this condition requires the imposition of a capacity charge (s_n^*) whenever the capacity limit of an activity is encountered. Mathematically,

$$(5.24) \qquad (B^F)^T u_n^{F*} - (A^I - B^I)^T u_n^{I*} - (A^P)^T u_n^{P*} - s_n^* \leq 0,$$

$$z_n^{*T} \left((B^F)^T u_n^{F*} - (A^I - B^I)^T u_n^{I*} - (A^P)^T u_n^{P*} - s_n^* \right) = 0$$

in all time periods $n = 1, 2, \ldots, N$. Finally,

(v)   There is a set of conditions on the imputed capacity charges. The total imputed capacity charges levied over the entire time span equal total cash charges. But the periodizing of the imputed charges is different.

Writing the relevant Kuhn–Tucker conditions and summing, one finds (just as the summation of (5.16) leads to (5.17)):

$$(5.25) \qquad \sum_{n=1}^{n=N} \sum_{v=1}^{v=n} \sum_{m=1}^{m=M} s_{mn}^* \Delta \bar{z}_{mv}^* =$$

$$\sum_{n=1}^{n=N} \sum_{v=1}^{v=n} \sum_{m=1}^{m=M} \sigma_m c_{2m} \Delta \bar{z}_{mv}^*$$

Economies of scale. The treatment of increasing returns of scale may be briefly indicated as follows. Write total investment costs in period n as

$$(5.26) \qquad c_2 \, \Delta \bar{z}_n + c_3 y_n$$

where, as before, c_2 is a row vector of unit capacity charges and c_3 is a row vector of fixed costs. That is, we now allow for the presence of not only variable costs of capacity expansion—such as the cost of buying new machinery—but also for the presence of fixed costs that are incurred regardless of the magnitude of the capacity expansion. Examples are R&D costs, expenditures incurred in buying patents, the acquisition of land for the construction of new plant—in fact, all cost elements that cannot be directly associated with the scale of operation of the investment. To repeat,

$c_2 = [c_{2m}]$ a row vector of unit capacity expansion charges— the variable cost portion of capacity expansion costs,

$c_3 = [c_{3m}]$ a row vector of fixed capacity expansion costs— the fixed cost portion of capacity expansion costs.

The unknown y_n is a vector of binary setup variables, equal to 1 if some capacity expansion is carried out (the investment project is "set up"), but equal to zero if no new capacity is installed (the investment project is not set up). Mathematically,

$$(5.27) \qquad c_{2m} \, \Delta \bar{z}_{mn} + c_{3m} y_{mn} \begin{cases} = c_{2m} \, \Delta \bar{z}_{mn} + c_{3m} & \text{if } \Delta \bar{z}_{mn} > 0 \\ = 0 & \text{if } \Delta \bar{z}_{mn} = 0 \end{cases}$$

The average cost of expanding the capacity of any activity is now falling (assuming that the fixed cost is positive). There are economies of scale in undertaking a larger investment project rather than a smaller one.

In order to ensure that the setup variables posses the stipulated properties, we adjoin to the relation (5.27) the inequality

$$(5.28) \qquad \Delta \bar{z}_{mn} \leq N_m \, y_{mn}$$

where N_m is the maximal amount of capacity that may be installed in any one period. Just as there are upper limits to current production, there are also upper limits to investment in new capacity. For instance, while the current operations of an airline is limited by the number of aircraft already on hand, the number of new planes that the airline may add to its fleet in any one time period is limited by the production capacity of the aircraft manufacturer. Inspecting (5.28), we see that if the setup variable equals unity, then the investment variable on the left-hand side of the inequality is free to assume its maximal value. But if the setup variable equals zero, (5.28) forces the investment to equal zero as well.

Program (5.20) should now be amended to read

$$(5.29) \qquad min \sum_{n=1}^{n=N} \{ \sum_{r \in R} \int Q_{rn}(w_{rn})dw_{rn}$$

$$+ \sum_{v=1}^{v=n} \sum_{m=1}^{m=M} \sigma_m(c_{2m}\Delta \bar{z}_{mv} + c_{3m}y_{mv})\}$$

subject to

$$B^F z_n \geq x_n$$

$$- A^I z_n + B^I z_n = 0$$

$$- A^P z_n + w_n \geq 0$$

$$- z_n + \sum_{v=1}^{v=n} \Delta \bar{z}_v \geq - \bar{z}_0$$

$$\Delta \bar{z}_{mn} - N_m y_{mn} \leq 0, \; m = 1, 2, ..., M$$

$$z_n, w_n, \Delta \bar{z}_n \geq 0, \; n = 1, 2, ... N$$

$$y_{mn} = 0 \; or \; 1, \; m = 1, ..., M \; and \; n = 1, 2, ..., N$$

It is a nonlinear program with 0–1 variables. With currently available standard software packages (1990), such a program is not easy to solve numerically. The exercise that follows assumes that production costs are linear so that (5.29) boils down to an instance of linear programming with 0–1 variables.

Exercise 5.2

In an agricultural region in Latin America farmers grow corn and wheat. Some land is better suited to grow corn; other land is better suited for wheat. An acre of corn land yields *120* bushels of corn, an acre of wheat land yields *85* bushels of wheat.

Let the cultivation of corn be activity $m = 1$ and the cultivation of wheat be activity $m = 2$. The matrix of output coefficients is

$$B = \begin{bmatrix} 120 & 0 \\ 0 & 85 \end{bmatrix}$$

On the input side, three resources are needed: land, fertilizer, and machinery. The matrix of input coefficients is

$$A = \begin{bmatrix} 1 & 1 \\ 2.5 & 1.75 \\ 0.5 & 0.60 \end{bmatrix}$$

It is assumed that the market prices of resources are given and known. They are $25 an acre, $95 per ton of fertilizer, and $500 per machine day, respectively.

The total acreage of land available in the region is 600 thousand acres of corn land and 1,500 acres of wheat land. (To simplify the calculations, only figures for one representative farm are shown.)

Farmers may put more land under the plough by razing tropical rainforest. The cost of such capacity expansion include the purchase of forest land, the erecting of temporary living quarters for work crews, the burning of trees and underbrush, building access roads, and so on. Let these costs in any one given year n be given by the cost function

$$100 \, \Delta \bar{z}_{mn} + 40{,}000 y_{mn}$$

The variable cost is $100 per acre of land cleared. The fixed cost is $40,000. These parameters of the cost function do not depend upon the intended use of the land, whether for the cultivation of corn $(m = 1)$ or for wheat $(m = 2)$. Fixed costs accrue only if land is cleared $(y_{mn} > 0, m = 1, 2)$. There is no fixed charge if no additional land is cleared $(y_{mn} = 0, m = 1,2)$.

The following information is supplied for the calculation of the capital recovery factor. The discount rate is 10 percent and the expected life of the land clearing project is ten years (many tracts of tropical rain forest may eventually be restored in the future).

Available resources permit no more than 1,000 acres of new land to be cleared in any one time period.

Calculate the optimal land clearing program over the next three years, when the expected consumer demand is given by the data in the table below (in bushels):

	Year 1	Year 2	Year 3
Demand for corn	*50,000*	*80,000*	*100,000*
Demand for wheat	*120,000*	*200,000*	*275,000*

Solution. Turning first to the supply of resources, one finds

$$\sum_{r=1}^{r=3} \int Q_{rn}(w_{rn}) dw_{rn} = [25 \ 95 \ 500] \ A z_n = 512.5 z_{1n} + 491.3 z_{2n}$$

The capital recovery factor comes out as

$$\sigma = 0.10(1-1.10^{-10}) = 0.1627$$

Program (5.20) then reads

$$min \ \sum_{n=1}^{n=3} (1/1.10^n) \ \{512.5 z_{1n} + 491.3 z_{2n} +$$

$$+ \ \sum_{v=1}^{v=n} \sum_{m=1}^{m=2} 0.1627 \ (100 \Delta \bar{z}_{mv} + 40,000 y_{mv})\}$$

subject to

$$120 z_{11} \geq 50,000, \ 85 z_{21} \geq 120,000$$

$$120 z_{12} \geq 80,000, \ 85 z_{22} \geq 200,000$$

$$120 z_{13} \geq 100,000, \ 85 z_{23} \geq 275,000$$

$$z_{11} - \Delta \bar{z}_{11} \leq 600$$

$$z_{21} - \Delta \bar{z}_{21} \leq 1500$$

$$z_{12} - \Delta \bar{z}_{11} - \Delta \bar{z}_{12} \leq 600$$

$$z_{22} - \Delta \bar{z}_{21} - \Delta \bar{z}_{22} \leq 1500$$

$$z_{13} - \Delta \bar{z}_{11} - \Delta \bar{z}_{12} - \Delta \bar{z}_{13} \leq 600$$

$$z_{23} - \Delta \bar{z}_{21} - \Delta \bar{z}_{22} - \Delta \bar{z}_{23} \leq 1500$$

$$\Delta \bar{z}_{mn} - 1{,}000 y_{mn} \leq 0 \text{ for } m = 1{,}2 \text{ and } n = 1{,}2{,}3$$

$$z, \Delta \bar{z} \geq 0, y = 0 \text{ or } 1$$

(The discounting of future costs to the present is optional. It is shown explicitly here. Alternatively, as in (5.20), it may be subsumed in the specification of all future cost items.)

The GAMS software package includes a feature that routinely handles linear programs with 0–1 variables. The optimal solution is exhibited in the table below (rounded to four figures):

	Year n = 1	n = 2	n = 3
Corn—level of operation z_{1n}	416.7	666.7	833.3
Corn—capacity $\bar{z}_{1n}$	600.0	666.7	833.3
Wheat—level of operation z_{2n}	1412	2353	3235
Wheat—capacity $\bar{z}_{2n}$	1500	2353	3235

In period 2 the farmers will clear 66.7 acres of new corn land and 853 acres of wheat land. In period 3 the corresponding figures are 166.7 acres and 882 acres, respectively.

BIBLIOGRAPHIC NOTES

The so-called warehouse model (see Cahn [1]; Dantzig [6]; Charnes and Cooper [2], [3], pp. 562–79) was one of the first model types recognized in linear programming and was studied by a number of authors in the late 1950s. The original formulation assumes fixed and known demand prices and supply prices in all time periods. The nonlinear version in section 5.1 was suggested in Thore [19].

Already Samuelson [17] had noted that the spatial equilibrium model can normally be extended to an intertemporal framework by treating inventory carrying costs as a kind of "transportation" cost from one period to another. In their book [18], Takayama and Judge developed most of their various models both in the spatial dimension and in the time dimension.

Their treatment of inventories was only schematic, however, and allowed for little institutional detail in terms of actual inventory management practices. For some empirical work applying the Takayama and Judge intertemporal framework, see Fuchs, Farrish, and Bohall [7], Kottke [12], and Martin and Zwart [15]. Additional realism was provided by Nagurney and Aaronson [16] who allowed for the presence of backordering. The complete combination of the warehouse model and spatial equilibrium, demonstrated in section 5.2, is new, and so is the material in section 5.3.

The interest at the World Bank in modeling the planning of industrial investment programs can be traced back to an early paper by Chenery [4] and subsequent work by Manne and Markowitz [14] and Kendrick [9]. Recent studies carried out by World Bank staff include Choksi, Meeraus, and Stoutjesdijk [5] (the fertilizer industry), and Kendrick, Meeraus, and Alatorre [10] (the steel industry). The World Bank methodology was outlined in Kendrick and Stoutjesdijk [11].

The idea to construct a partial equilibrium model of industry investment by maximizing an economic potential function tailored after the concept of consumer surplus was used in Lucas and Prescott [13].

REFERENCES

[5.1]   Cahn, A. S. "The Warehouse Problem," *Bulletin of the American Mathematical Society* 54 (Oct. 1948): 1073.

[5.2]   Charnes, A., and W. W. Cooper. "Generalizations of the Warehousing Model," *Operational Research Quarterly* 6 (Dec. 1955): 131–72.

[5.3]   Charnes, A., and W. W. Cooper. *Management Models and Industrial Applications of Linear Programming.* 2 vols. New York: Wiley, 1961.

[5.4]   Chenery, H. B. "The Interdependence of Investment Decisions." In *The Allocation of Economic Resources,* ed. M. Abramovitz. Stanford, Calif.: Stanford University Press, 1959.

[5.5]   Choksi, A. M., A. Meeraus, and A. J. Stoutjesdijk. *The Planning of Investment Programs in the Fertilizer Industry.* Baltimore, Md.: Johns Hopkins University Press, 1980.

[5.6]   Dantzig, G. "Maximization of a Linear Function of Variables Subject to Linear Inequalities." In *Activity Analysis of Production and Allocation,* ed. T. C. Koopmans. New York: Wiley, 1959.

[5.7]   Fuchs, H. W., R. O. P. Farrish, and R. W. Bohall. "A Model of the U. S. Apple Industry: A Quadratic Interregional Intertemporal Activity Analysis Formulation," *American Journal of Agricultural Economics* 56 (1974): 739–50.

[5.8]   Holt, C. H., F. Modigliani, J. F. Muth, and H. A. Simon. *Planning Production, Inventories, and Work Force,* Englewood Cliffs, N. J.: Prentice-Hall, 1960.

[5.9]   Kendrick, D. A. *Programming Investment in the Process Industries: An Approach to Sectoral Planning.* Cambridge, Mass.: M. I. T.., 1967.

[5.10] Kendrick, D. A., A. Meeraus, and J. Alatorre. *The Planning of Investment Programs in the Steel Industry.* Baltimore, Md.,: Johns Hopkins University Press, 1984.

[5.11] Kendrick, D. A., and A. J. Stoutjesdijk. *The Planning of Industrial Investment Programs. A Methodology.* Baltimore, Md.: Johns Hopkins University Press, 1978.

[5.12] Kottke, M. "Spatial, Temporal and Product-use Allocation of Milk in an Imperfectly Competitive Dairy Industry," *American Journal of Agricultural Economics* 52 (1970): 33–40.

[5.13] Lucas, R. E., and E. C. Prescott.   "Investment under Uncertainty," *Econometrica* 39 (Sept. 1971): 659–81.

[5.14] Manne, A. S., and H. M. Markowitz, eds. *Studies in Process Analysis, Economy-wide Production Capabilities.* New York, N.Y.: Wiley, 1963.

[5.15] Martin, L., and A. C. Zwart. "A Spatial and Temporal Model of the North American Pork Sector for the Evaluation of Policy Alternatives," *American Journal of Agricultural Economics* 57 (1975): 55–66.

[5.16] Nagurney, A., and J. Aaronson. "A General Dynamic Spatial Price Equilibrium Model: Formulation, Solution, and Computational Results," *Journal of Computational and Applied Mathematics* 22 (1988): 339–57.

[5.17] Samuelson, P. A. "A Spatial Price Equilibrium and Linear Programming," *American Economic Review* 42 (1952): 283–303.

[5.18] Takayama, T., and G. G. Judge. *Spatial and Temporal price and Allocation Models.* Amsterdam: North-Holland, 1971.

[5.19] Thore, S. "Generalized Network Spatial Equilibrium: The Deterministic and the Chance-Constrained Case," *Papers of the Regional Science Association* 59 (1986): 93–102.

6

Price Formulations

In 1963, V. L. Smith investigating Samuelson's spatial equilibrium model, found that there exists a second optimization program that solves precisely the same system of regional markets. The unknowns in Samuelson's program are all quantities: quantities of some consumer good supplied, quantities transported from one region to another, and quantities demanded. The maximand to be optimized (social payoff) is formed by integrating the inverted demand functions, which are functions of the quantities of consumer goods bought. The market prices do not enter the direct problem; instead they are obtained as the Lagrange multipliers of the physical market balances.

In Smith's alternative formulation, the unknowns of the direct program are all prices—the various regional prices of the good. The optimization is one of minimization rather than maximization. The minimand is formed by integrating the partial direct demand functions, stated as functions of all prices (income is assumed to be fixed and known). There is one constraint for each pair of regions, stating that the price appreciation occurring when the good is transported from one region to another cannot exceed the unit transportation cost. With this formulation, the quantities are obtained as the Lagrange multipliers.

From a mathematical point of view, this result is quite attractive. We are presented with two mathematical programs which are dual to each other—a direct or primal max problem in quantity variables, and a dual min problem in price variables. The Lagrange multipliers of the max program solve the min program, and the Lagrange multipliers of the min program solve the max program. Neither problem requires any information whatsoever on the other problem's optimal solution. In this sense, the two problems are completely separable, and each problem has its own distinct set of variables with its own economic interpretation.

The existence of a pair of dual programs is of fundamental importance in the case of linear programming (see sec. 2.4). When it comes to nonlinear programming, the dual program is typically of a quite complicated mathematical nature involving at least some of the variables of the primal problem. A general analysis of the dual of a nonlinear program falls outside the scope of the present volume. What we are presently dealing with is a special class of nonlinear programs that do possess a dual in completely separate variables.

The advantage of the price formulation is that there is no need to invert the demand functions (to obtain the demand price functions). If the demand functions are linear or constant-elastic, there is no problem in inverting them. But for other, more complicated functional forms inversion may be difficult. On the other hand, the price formulation has its obvious limitations. Capacity limits on output or shipments can be immediately adjoined to the programming format in quantity variables (see chap. 3). It is not immediately clear how such quantity constraints can be handled with the price formulation.

Actually, all programming models of distribution and production discussed up to this point (in chaps. 3, 4 and 5) possess a price equivalent.

It would serve no purpose to run through the entire list of models that we have covered so far, spelling out the price formulation that corresponds to each quantity formulation. Instead, the reader should try to understand the general principle involved in forming the price formulation.

Quantity formulations always deal with the optimization of an economic potential function, subject to a series of linear constraints. The gross potential function is formed by integrating the demand price functions of all demand and the supply price functions of all supply. (The net potential function is formed by deducting the costs of transportation and of exogenous production factors, the prices of which are taken as given and constant.) There is essentially one constraint for each good appearing in the model, stating that the use of that good cannot exceed the available supply. If a good is sold or produced at many locations, there is such a balancing condition at each location.

The price formulation, too, involves the optimization of an economic potential function, subject to a series of linear constraints. This time the potential function is formed by integrating the direct demand functions and the direct supply functions. There is one constraint for each transportation activity or production activity appearing in the model, stating that the operation of the activity cannot yield a profit.

SYMBOLS USED IN CHAPTER 6

$h,k \in H$ regions

t_{hk}	quantity shipped from region h to region k
c_{hk}	unit transportation cost shipping good from region h to region k
$i \in I$	final goods
$j \in J$	intermediate goods
$r \in R$	resources
P as superscript	primary goods (resources)
I as superscript	intermediate goods
F as superscript	final goods

$A^P = [a^P_{rm}], A^I = [a^I_{jm}]$ matrix of input coefficients

$B^I = [b^I_{jm}], B^F = [b^F_{im}]$ matrix of output coefficients

z_m	level of operation of activity m
x_h	quantity demanded
w_h	quantity supplied
p_h, p_k	price
ϕ_h, ψ_h	variables of integration
q_r	price of resource r
$D_h(p_h), D_i(p_i)$	demand function
$S_h(p_h), S_r(q_r)$	supply function
$P_h(x_h)$	demand price function
$Q_h(w_h)$	supply price function
$\bar{z}_m$	capacity level of activity m
u^I_j	Lagrange multiplier of market balance for intermediate good j
s_m	Lagrange multiplier of capacity condition for activity m

6.1. SMITH'S PRICE FORMULATION OF SPATIAL EQUILIBRIUM

Let us return to Samuelson's model of spatial equilibrium for a single good (see sec. 3.2). There are $h \in H$ different regions. The direct demand functions are $D_h(p_h)$, the direct supply functions are $S_h(p_h)$.

As indicated, the direct functions, rather than the demand price functions and the supply price functions, will be used. The regional prices p_h are now the unknowns; the quantities are the dependent variables. It is assumed that $D_h(p_h)$ and $S_h(p_h)$ are both non-negative, and differentiable on the domain of non-negative prices, with the demand functions nonincreasing and the supply functions nondecreasing.

Form the economic potential function in region h

$$(6.1) \quad -\int_{p_{h0}}^{p_h} D_h(\phi_h)d\phi_h + \int_{p_{hl}}^{p_h} S_h(\psi_h)d\psi_h = -\int D_h(p_h)dp_h$$

$$+ \int S_h(p_h)dp_h$$

In the extended notation to the left, the symbol ϕ_h is used as the variable of integration for the integration of the demand function, and the symbol ψ_h as the variable of integration for the integration of the supply function. The lower limits of integration p_{h0} and p_{hl} are two arbitrary initial points. In the abbreviated notation to the right, the common notation of indefinite integrals has been used.

Remembering the assumptions placed on the demand and supply functions, we see that the potential function (6.1) is continuous and convex.

For a geometric illustration of the potential (6.1), turn to figure 6.1. For convenience, the lower limits of the two integrals have been put equal to the same positive number p_{h0}. Observing that both variables of integration are measured along the vertical axis, each integral can be read off the diagram as a surface to the *left* of the schedule in the diagram. The potential equals the shaded area to the left of the supply curve minus the shaded area to the left of the demand curve.

Summing the potential (6.1) over all regions, we form the program

$$(6.2) \quad min \sum_{h \in H} \{-\int D_h(p_h)dp_h + \int S_h(p_h)dp_h\}$$

subject to

$$p_h - p_k \geq -c_{hk}$$

$$p_h \geq 0$$

$$h, k \in H$$

Figure 6.1. The Indirect Potential Function

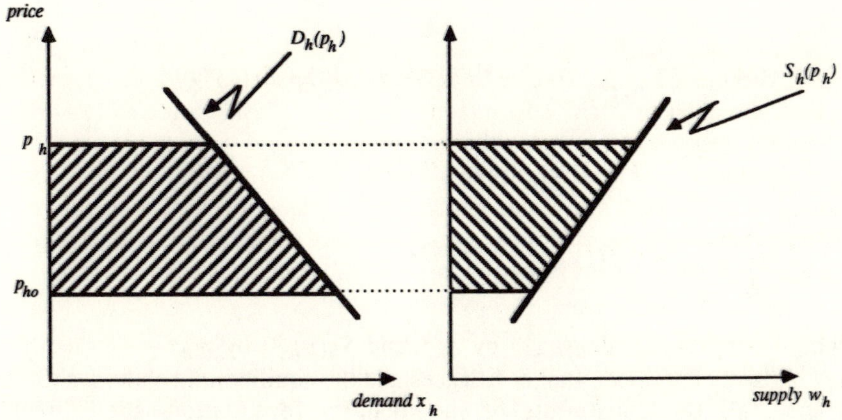

In analogy with Samuelson's terminology, we may refer to the minimand as indirect social payoff. Smith uses the term "virtual economic rent." Takayama and Judge call the same expression "indirect quasi-welfare."

Program (6.2) is an instance of nonlinear programming with linear constraints. (If the demand and supply functions are linear, the minimand is quadratic.) The constraints spell out the requirement that the regional price difference between any two regions cannot exceed the unit cost of shipping the good from one region to another. A hypothetical shipper buying the good in one region, running up transportation costs, and selling the good in another region, cannot make a profit.

Denote the Lagrange multipliers of the constraints by t_{hk}. They are to be nonnegative. Writing down the Kuhn–Tucker conditions, one finds at the point of optimum (indicated by an asterisk):

(6.3) $$p_h{}^* - p_k{}^* \geq -c_{hk}$$

$$t_{hk}{}^* (p_h{}^* - p_k{}^* + c_{hk}) = 0$$

$$h, k \in H$$

Whenever a positive shipment takes place between two regions, the price appreciation reaped by the shipper will be exactly exhausted by his unit transportation cost. If the price appreciation does not cover the unit transportation cost, the shipper will not be able to cover his costs and no transportation will occur. Also,

$$(6.4) \qquad \sum_{k \in H} (t_{hk}^* - t_{kh}^*) \leq -D_h(p_h^*) + S_h(p_h^*)$$

$$p_h^* \left(\sum_{k \in H} (t_{hk}^* - t_{kh}^*) + D_h(p_h^*) - S_h(p_h^*) \right) = 0$$

$$h \in H$$

which—replacing $D_h(p_h^*)$ by x_h^* and $S_h(p_h^*)$ by w_h^*—we readily recognize as the direct market balances and the equilibrium conditions (3.9). Hence, all the constraints of the quantity formulation (the "direct" formulation) program (3.8) and all its attendant Kuhn–Tucker conditions are recovered. The results (i) and (ii) in section 3.2 will therefore hold as before.

The stage is now set for establishing the equivalence of the quantity formulation (3.8) and the price formulation (6.2). The technical tool for the required demonstration is the Kuhn–Tucker equivalence theorem (theorem 2.2). Consider any optimal solution pair to (6.2), say (p^*,t^*) together with $x^* = D(p^*)$ and $w^* = S(p^*)$. As has already been pointed out, the $*$ point satisfies all the Kuhn–Tucker conditions of program (3.8). The saddle-point program corresponding to (3.8) reads

$$(6.5) \qquad \max_{x,w,t} \; \min_{p} \; \sum_{h \in H} \{ \int P_h(x_h)dx_h - \int Q_h(w_h)dw_h \}$$

$$- \sum_{h \in H} \sum_{k \in K} c_{hk}t_{hk} + \sum_{h \in H} p_h(-x_h + w_h + \sum_{k \in K} (t_{kh} - t_{hk}))$$

subject to $x,w,t \geq 0, p \geq 0$

So, we have a point $(x^*,w^*,t^*;p^*)$, a mathematical program—program (3.8)—and a saddle point problem—problem (6.5). We know that the point satisfies all the Kuhn–Tucker conditions of the program. Hence, by theorem 2.3, it is a saddle point to the saddle-point problem. Further, by theorem 2.2, (x^*,w^*,t^*) is an optimal solution to the mathematical program (3.8).

Conversely, consider any optimal solution pair to (3.8), say $(x^\#,w^\#,t^\#;p^\#)$. Starting out from program (3.8) and its accompanying Kuhn–Tucker conditions, one can recover the direct constraints and the Kuhn–

Tucker conditions of the price formulation. The saddle-point program corresponding to (6.2) reads

$$
(6.6) \qquad \underset{t}{max} \quad \underset{p}{min} \; \sum_{h \in H} \{-\textstyle\int D_h(p_h)dp_h + \textstyle\int S_h(p_h)dp_h\}
$$

$$
+ \sum_{h \in H} \sum_{k \in K} t_{hk}(-c_{hk} - p_h + p_k)
$$

subject to $t \geq 0, p \geq 0$

Using theorem 2.3 again, it follows that $(t\#,p\#)$ is a saddle point to (6.6). Hence, by theorem 2.2, $p\#$ is an optimal solution to program (6.2).

In sum, the quantity formulation (3.8) and the price formulation (6.2) are logically equivalent.[1] The two formulations stand in a dual relationship to each other, in the sense explained.

We have just now shown that the two saddle points (6.5) and (6.6) are equivalent. It is of some interest to note that an even stronger proposition holds true: the two saddle *functions* themselves are actually equivalent, and the one can be transformed into the other by a change of variables. To see this, note the rules for partial integration of indefinite integrals:

$$
(6.7) \qquad p_h x_h - \textstyle\int P_h(x_h)dx_h = \textstyle\int D_h(p_h)dp_h
$$

$$
p_h w_h - \textstyle\int Q_h(w_h)dw_h = \textstyle\int S_h(p_h)dp_h
$$

These formulas make it possible to take the step from the saddle function appearing in (6.5) involving the demand price functions and the supply price functions to a corresponding expression involving the direct demand and supply functions instead. Inserting into (6.5), one gets

$$
(6.8) \qquad \sum_{h \in H} \{p_h x_h - \textstyle\int D_h(p_h)dp_h - p_h w_h + \textstyle\int S_h(p_h)dp_h\}
$$

$$
- \sum_{h \in H} \sum_{k \in K} c_{hk} t_{hk} + \sum_{h \in H} p_h(-x_h + w_h + \sum_{k \in K} (t_{kh} - t_{hk}))
$$

Collecting terms, this simplifies to

(6.9) $\sum_{h \in H} \{-\int D_h(p_h)dp_h + \int S_h(p_h)dp_h\}$

$- \sum_{h \in H} \sum_{k \in K} c_{hk}t_{hk} + \sum_{h \in H} p_h \sum_{k \in K} (t_{kh} - t_{hk})$

which is the saddle function appearing in (6.6). *Q.E.D.*

Program (6.2) also covers the degenerate cases when one or several demand curves are vertical or horizontal and/or one or several supply curves are vertical or horizontal. All these various combinations are quite straightforward; here we shall mention only the case of fixed and given supply (vertical supply curves).

Assume that there is a fixed and given supply w_h in each region. The quantity formulation was given as program (3.2). The corresponding price formulation is

(6.10) $min - \sum_{h \in H} \int D_h(p_h)dp_h + \Sigma p_h w_h$

subject to

$p_h - p_k \geq - c_{hk}$

$p_h \geq 0$

$h,k \in H$

The contribution to the potential function from the supply side equals the market value of all the fixed supplies.

Writing all the Kuhn–Tucker conditions and replacing $D_h(p_h^*)$ by x_h^*, one readily retrieves all the constraints of the direct formulation (3.2). Hence, the results (i) and (ii) in section 3.1 hold as before.

Exercise 6.1

Returning to exercise 3.1 involving the marketing of air-conditioning equipment in the United States, let us solve the same problem using the price formulation instead.

The demand functions in the two regions (the North and the South) are, respectively

$$x_N = 6,000 - 0.5p_N$$

$$x_S = 5,143 - 0.2858p_S$$

The potential function this time is formed by adding the following two terms:

- The sum of the integrated demand functions, with a minus sign

$$-(6000p_N - 0.25(p_N)^2 - (5143p_S - 0.1429(p_S)^2)$$

- The sum of the integrated supply functions. Since the supply curves are all vertical (constant available supplies), this amounts to forming—quite simply—the market value of the available supplies (denoting the market price of the output at plant h by p_h, $h = 1,2,3$)

$$4000p_1 + 2800p_2 + 1800p_3$$

Program (6.2) instructs us to minimize the potential now formed subject to a price constraint along each link of the transportation network. Each such price constraint states that the price differential arising along the link cannot exceed the unit transportation cost. The entire program then reads

$$min - (6000\ p_N - 0.25\ p_N^2) - (5143\ p_S - 0.1429\ p_S^2)$$

$$+ 4000p_1 + 2800p_2 + 1800p_3$$

subject to

$$p_1 - p_N \geq -800$$
$$p_2 - p_N \geq -400$$
$$p_3 - p_N \geq -100$$
$$p_1 - p_S \geq -200$$
$$p_2 - p_S \geq -200$$
$$p_3 - p_S \geq -500$$
$$p_N, p_S, p_1, p_2, p_3 \geq 0$$

The optimal solution retrieves the results displayed in figure 3.1.

Several Commodities

The extension to the case of several commodities is immediate. The same kind of reservations, however, must be made that we have already encountered in the case of the quantity formulation: assumptions have to be made which lay down quite severe restrictions on the mathematical form of the demand and supply functions, and hence, ultimately on the underlying utility functions.

We shall only offer a few comments, discussing the general nature of the problem.

Consider a list of consumer goods $i \in I$. Let x_h, w_h, p_h be vectors with as many elements as there are goods. In section 3.4 we employed the demand price functions and the supply price functions for each good. Here we shall instead need the corresponding direct demand functions and supply functions, say

$$(6.11) \qquad D_{hi}(p_h), S_{hi}(p_h), i \in I$$

respectively.

The analysis is all the time partial, in that all prices outside the model, and income, are kept constant.

Passage from the direct to the indirect demand functions and vice versa is a well known procedure.[2] Following Samuelson, it has become common simply to postulate invertibility, rather than spell out some underlying conditions which would see to it that the so-called implicit functions theorem could be applied. It is therefore simply assumed that all direct demand functions and supply functions as given by equation (6.11) exist, are single-valued, and are non-negative and differentiable on the domain of positive prices.

Retaining the assumption that the matrix defined by the elements (3.38a) is symmetric and negative semidefinite, it follows that the matrix

$$(6.12) \qquad \left[\frac{\partial D_{hi}(p_h)}{\partial p_{hj}} \right] \quad (i,j \in I)$$

must also be symmetric and negative semidefinite.[3]

Similarly, retaining the assumption that the matrix defined by the elements (3.38b) is symmetric and positive semidefinite, it follows that the matrix

$$(6.13) \qquad \left[\frac{\partial S_{hi}(p_h)}{\partial p_{hj}} \right] \quad (i, j \in I)$$

is symmetric and positive semidefinite. The contribution to the indirect potential function (indirect social payoff, indirect quasi-welfare) from both demand and supply in region h is defined as

$$(6.14) \qquad -\int \sum_{i \in I} D_{hi}(p_h) dp_{hi} + \int \sum_{i \in I} S_{hi}(p_h) dp_{hi}$$

The assumptions introduced see to it that the two line integrals exist; the entire expression is convex.

As pointed out in section 3.4, direct quasi-welfare is a utility function. In a similar fashion, it can be shown that indirect quasi-welfare is an *indirect* utility function. More precisely, starting out from the quantity formulation and inverting all demand price functions and supply price functions, direct quasi-welfare inverts into the corresponding indirect quasi-welfare. The direct utility function inverts into the corresponding indirect utility function.[4]

6.2. A PRICE FORMULATION OF ACTIVITY ANALYSIS

We turn to the formulation of a logistics system involving the production and marketing of final goods by the use of intermediate goods and primary goods. Section 4.1 outlined a simple programming model of such a system, taking the form of an activity analysis type linear production system embedded in a setting of price-sensitive demand and/or price-sensitive resource supply. Our immediate aim is to furnish the price equivalent of program (4.10).

The task that we face can be characterized in the following general terms. The programming models that were discussed in chapter 4 involved all quantities as unknowns: quantities of final goods produced and demanded, quantities of intermediate goods produced, and quantities of resources employed as inputs. This time, all the unknowns are prices: prices of final goods, intermediate goods, and resources.

The quantity formulations took the form of the maximization of an economic potential function, obtained through the integration of the demand price functions and the supply price functions. The maximization was to be carried out subject to a number of market balancing conditions, essentially stating that the use of an input or an output could never exceed its availability. From time to time we also included capacity constraints, placed on the maximal level of operation of activities.

The price formulations that are our current concern take the form of the minimization of an economic potential function, obtained through the integration of the demand functions and the supply functions. These functions all depend upon prices, so that the potential function itself becomes a function of prices. The minimization of the potential function is to be carried out subject to constraints placed on the various production activities. Each constraint states a kind of no-profit condition: the return obtained from operating any activity at unitary level cannot exceed the costs that are associated with it. As we shall see, these costs consist of both direct cash costs for the purchase of inputs and of imputed cost charges (to be levied when activities reach their capacity level).

The economic potential function of a partial economic model may be referred to as the "driver" of that partial economy. In Smith's formulation of the spatial economy (sec. 6.1), the driver was formed by integrating the demand and supply functions in each region. No contribution per se to the driver occurred as the commodity in question was being transported from a supply point to a demand point. Instead, there was a constraint for each transportation link stating that the shipment along that link taken by itself cannot yield a profit.

As we now turn to the price formulation of an activity analysis type partial economy, we shall find that the driver of the economy is formed by integrating the demand functions of all final goods and the supply functions of all resources. No contribution to the driver will be reckoned as one follows the production chain from primary goods, to intermediate goods, to final goods. Instead, there will be a constraint for each production activity stating that the operation of that activity taken by itself cannot yield a profit.

The driver uses both a carrot and a stick. The role of the carrot is played by final demand, setting up incentives for the delivery of final goods at the demand points. The driver of the price formulation being a potential function to be minimized, final demand provides negative contributions to the potential. The stick is resource supply. It provides positive contributions to the economic potential.

Using the same notation as in chapter 4, let there be $i \in I$ final goods and $r \in R$ resources. The direct demand functions are $D_i(p_i)$, with p_i being the price of final good i. The direct supply functions are $S_r(q_r)$, with q_r being the price of resource r.

As in the preceding chapter, considerably more mathematical generality could be accommodated, permitting, for instance, linear demand and supply functions with nonzero symmetric cross-price coefficients. We have already discussed these generalizations (sec. 3.4) and there is no need to go into these matters again. The demand and supply functions are all supposed to be non-negative and differentiable, with the demand functions nonincreasing and the supply functions nondecreasing.

The driver or economic potential function is formed as

$$(6.15) \qquad - \sum_{i \in I} \int D_i(p_i) dp_i + \sum_{r \in R} \int S_r(q_r) dq_r$$

Additional notation is brought from chapter 4 to account for the productive processes which convert primary goods into intermediate goods and, eventually, into final goods. Let there be $m \in M$ different production activities. There are two A matrices specifying the input requirements of the activities and two B matrices stating the unit outputs. The matrix $A^P = [a^P_{rm}]$ lists in a spread-sheet format the unit requirements of resources. The matrix $A^I = [a^I_{jm}]$ lists the unit requirements of intermediate goods $j \in J$. The matrix $B^F = [b^F_{im}]$ lists the unit outputs of final goods. The matrix $B^I = [b^I_{jm}]$ lists the unit outputs of intermediate goods.

The prices p_i (prices of final goods) and q_r (resource prices) have already been defined. They are the unknowns of the price formulation, to be determined. We also need the prices of intermediate goods, say u^I_j, $j \in J$. And, allowing for the possibility that activities may have upper capacity limits, we shall also need the unit charges s_m. Each such charge is to be applied if the level of operation of an activity m hits its upper limit.

Thus prepared, we are ready to write the entire price formulation of the activity analysis format, obtaining

$$(6.16) \qquad min - \sum_{i \in I} \int D_i(p_i) dp_i + \sum_{r \in R} \int S_r(q_r) dq_r$$

subject to

$$- \sum_{i \in I} b^F_{im} p_i + \sum_{j \in J} (a^I_{jm} - b^I_{jm}) u^I_j + \sum_{r \in R} a^P_{rm} q_r + s_m \geq 0,$$

$$m \in M$$

$$p_i \geq 0, i \in I$$

$$u^I_j \text{ unrestricted in sign, } j \in J$$

$$q_r \geq 0, r \in R$$

$$s_m \geq 0, m \in M$$

As signaled, the constraints state that no activity can be operated at a profit. For the purpose of this profit calculation, the unit costs of operating any activity m consist of both cash costs of inputs used (resources and intermediate goods) and the imputed charge s_m associated with the possible limitation of capacity of the activity.

Program (6.16) is mathematically equivalent to program (4.10). The proof of the equivalence proceeds as before, observing that the two programs have identical Kuhn–Tucker conditions.

Exercise 6.2

In order to illustrate the price models of activity analysis, we return to exercise 4.1 involving a stylized example from the home security industry.

Solving for the demand functions for the two final outputs, one finds

$i = 1$ *(patrolling security guards)*   : $x_1 = 30 - 2.5 p_1$

$i = 2$ *(electronic surveillance)*   : $x_2 = 60 - 4 p_2$

The contribution to the economic potential function to be formed is obtained by integrating the demand functions and changing signs:

$$-30p_1 + 1.25p_1^2 - 60p_2 + 2p_2^2$$

The second contribution to the economic potential function is the sum of the integrated supply functions for primary goods. The primary goods are security guards, technicians and engineers, and electronic support systems. There were fixed and given endowments of each of these; that is, the supply curves are vertical. We then simply form the market value of these endowments (denoting the market prices, to be determined, by q_1, q_2, q_3 respectively):

$$100q_1 + 357.5q_2 + 227.5q_3$$

We are now ready to write the entire mathematical program (6.16). The formation of the mathematical potential function, to be minimized, has already been explained.   There are six constraints, one for each activity $m = 1,2,3,4,5,6$. Each constraint states that the unit return from the operation of the activity cannot exceed its unit costs. These costs involve charges for the use of primary goods (prices q_1, q_2, q_3) and charges for the use of intermediate goods (prices u_1^I, u_2^I).

The program then reads

$$min\ -30p_1 + 1.25\,p_1{}^2 - 60p_2 + 2p_2{}^2 + 100q_1 + 357.5q_2 + 227.5q_3$$

subject to

$$-p_1 + 3.5q_1 + 2q_3 \geq 0$$

$$-u_1^I + 5q_2 + 8q_3 \geq 0$$

$$-u_2^I + 4.5q_2 + 9q_3 \geq 0$$

$$-p_2 + u_1^I + 0.3q_1 \geq 0$$

$$-p_2 + u_2^I + 0.3q_1 \geq 0$$

$$p,q \geq 0, u^I\ unrestricted\ in\ sign$$

Solution gives

$$p_1{}^* = 2.350, p_2{}^* = 9.399$$

$$u_1^{I\,*} = 9.399, u_2^{I\,*} = 10.573$$

$$q_1{}^* = q_2{}^* = 0, q_3{}^* = 1.175$$

which retrieves the results already found in the solution of exercise 4.1. The Lagrange multipliers of the five constraints are, in order:

$$z_1{}^* = 24.126, z_2{}^* = 22.406, z_3{}^* = 0, z_4{}^* = 22.406, z_5{}^* = 0$$

These values also coincide with the numerical results already obtained.

It remains to determine the final outputs.   Inserting into the demand functions one finds

$$x_1^* = 30 - 2.5 \times 2.350 = 24.125$$

$$x_2^* = 60 - 4 \times 9.399 = 22.404$$

as before.

NOTES

1. The proof has been adapted from Takayama and Woodland [13], pp. 895–96.
2. See Samuelson's *Foundations* [7], p. 185; also Samuelson [8], mathematical appendix.
3. Hurwicz [4], p. 178, discusses in some detail issues which I am dealing with rather summarily.
4. See Thore [14].

BIBLIOGRAPHIC NOTES

V. L. Smith [10] was led to his original formulation of the price formulation of spatial equilibrium by a study of the concept of virtual rent. His point of departure is the observation that in a single market the equilibrium price minimizes total virtual rent received by buyers and sellers. According to him, virtual rent is "that 'unearned increment' of two centuries of economic thought, which some have sought to tax and others sought to steal" [10], p. 25).

As in the case of Samuelson's net social payoff, we had better disregard the colorful interpretations that this terminology invites and stick to the notion of a mathematical potential function, formed for operational purposes only. In the main text, we have therefore preferred the more neutral term "indirect payoff."

Smith stated correctly that "the rent minimization problem is the dual of a maximization problem which differs only by a constant from Samuelson's problem" (p. 24). In a paper published one year later, Takayama and Judge [11] reviewed the Samuelson model and gave both the quantity formulation and the corresponding price formulation of it. They pointed out that the price formulation resulted when the domain of the integral of the quantity formulation was converted from the quantity space to the price space. The two formulations were said to be "equivalent" (p. 513).

Six years later, however, Takayama, in a joint paper with Woodland [13], maintained that the equivalence between the quantity and price formulation had only been developed in those earlier works, but was not yet formally established. Takayama and Woodland proceeded to supply the required proof. The heart of the proof is the observation that the two formulations have identical sets of Kuhn–Tucker conditions (p. 895).

Takayama and Woodland also proposed an alternative constructive proof, converting the quantity formulation into the price formulation. Using an early duality theorem by Dorn [2] and Hanson [3], they wrote down a dual problem to the direct quantity formulation. This dual problem involves both direct and dual variables. They thereupon proceeded to purify the obtained result, purging it of the remaining direct variables. After quite extensive developments, they finally ended up minimizing virtual economic rent, subject to the relevant constraints.

Further insight into the relation between the quantity and price formulations emerges when one considers the case of several consumer goods. Net social payoff (or quasi-welfare as Takayama and Judge prefer to call it) then becomes an instance of a particular utility function, and indirect social payoff becomes the corresponding indirect utility function. This observation helps to explain why direct payoff converts into indirect payoff as one switches from quantity to price variables. See Thore [14].

More recently, the relation between the quantity formulation and the price formulation was explored by Carey [1], who actually studied three different formulations. The third, a mixed formulation, is a saddle-point program, involving a maximization over quantity variables and a minimization over price variables. The same line of approach was pursued by Kortanek and Pfouts [5], who also combined their work with some special assumptions concerning the behavioral nature of firms (essentially identifying the supply curve of each firm with its average cost plus a markup plus a market "spread").

Using the price formulation, Silberberg [9] investigated the stability of spatial equilibrium.

An instructive application of the price formulation of the spatial equilibrium model was provided by Martin and Zwart in a study of the North American pork sector [6]. The demand for pork in any region consists of two components: demand for consumption and demand for cold storage stocks. Likewise, the supply of pork consists of two components: supplies of fresh pork and storage supply. The unknowns of the problem are the demand prices and the supply prices. The problem formulation makes use of data on the following transfer costs: transfer costs for shipping fresh pork from a producing region to a consuming region, transfer costs for shipping pork from storage to a consuming region, transfer costs for shipping pork from storage in one region to storage in another region.

REFERENCES

[6.1]   Carey, M. "A Reformulation of Generalized Benefit Maximizing Models." *Series A, Report #206.* Department of Industrial Economics and Business Studies, University of Birmingham, England, Nov. 1976.

[6.2]   Dorn, W. S. "Duality in Quadratic Programming," *Quarterly of Applied Mathematics* 18, (July 1960): 155–62.

[6.3]   Hanson, M. A. "A Duality Theorem in Nonlinear Programming with Nonlinear Constraints," *Australian Journal of Statistics* 3 (1961): 64–72.

[6.4]   Hurwicz, L. "On the Problem of Integrability of Demand Functions." In *Preferences, Utility and Demand*, eds. J. S. Chipman et al. New York: Jovanovich, 1971.

[6.5]   Kortanek, K. O., and R. W. Pfouts. "A Biextremal Principle for a Behavioral Theory of the Firm," *Mathematical Modeling* 3 (1982): 573–90.

[6.6]   Martin, L. J., and A.C. Zwart. "A Spatial and Temporal Model of the North American Pork Sector for the Evaluation of Policy Alternatives," *American Journal of Agricultural Economics* 57/1 (Feb. 1975): 55–66.

[6.7]   Samuelson, P. *Foundations of Economic Analysis.* Cambridge, Mass.: Harvard University Press, 1947.

[6.8]   Samuelson, P. "The Problem of Integrability in Utility Theory," *Economica* 17/68 (Nov. 1950): 355–85.

[6.9]   Silberberg, E. "A Theory of Spatially Separate Markets," *International Economic Review* 11/12 (June 1970): 334–48.

[6.10]   Smith, V. L. "Minimization of Economic Rent in Spatial Price Equilibrium," *Review of Economic Studies* (Feb. 1963): 24–31.

[6.11]   Takayama, T., and G. G. Judge. "Equilibrium among Spatially Separated Markets: A Reformulation," *Econometrica* 32/4 (Oct. 1964): 510–24.

[6.12]   Takayama, T., and G. G. Judge. *Spatial and Temporal Price and Allocation Models.* Amsterdam: North-Holland, 1971.

[6.13]   Takayama, T., and A. D. Woodland. "Equivalence of Price and Quantity Formulations of Spatial Equilibrium: Purified Duality in Quadratic and Concave Programming," *Econometrica* 38/6 (Nov. 1970): 889–906.

[6.14]   Thore, S. "Hotelling Utility Functions." In *Foundations of Utility and Risk Theory with Applications,* eds. B. P. Stigum and F. Wenstöp. Dordrecht: D. Reidel, 1983.

7

Resource Management by Goal Focusing

This chapter deals with the management of resources. The aims of such management may be many. There may be a concern with excessive extraction of scarce minerals, crude oil, or ground water. These are depletable and nonreproducible resources. Once the existing deposits have been exhausted, they are gone. Considerations of national security (strategic materials) or economic independence (oil) may suggest that a nation should not dip too deeply into such stocks. Perhaps some buffer should be set aside for possible use in the future.

Ground water is in many instances a public good rather than a private good, and its price (essentially the unit-drilling and pumping cost) may grossly underestimate the true opportunity cost of it to society. A lowering of the water table may occur as the result of excessive use of water; it may also take place as a result of environmental changes prompted by actions of man such as deforestation and urban growth.

Other resources can in principle be restored, such as fish in a lake. But such restoration is costly and it takes time. If the reproducible resource is a private good, such as a salmon river owned by a private land owner, the market price of it should in principle reflect the cost of conservation and prudent management (the market value being equal to the discounted present value of the net income stream yielded by the resource, net income incorporating deductions for the maintenance and reproduction of it). But if the resource is a public good and no ownership of the resource is defined— such as in the case of the air in a big city—there is no market price that can signal the scarcity of the resource. The competitive economy will adjust as if the supplies of it were inexhaustible. One needs to implement a system of local management to protect and to clean up the air in cities or polluted lakes.

The particular formal representation of the management problem to be presented in this chapter is goal focusing. In order to explain this term, it may be helpful first to say a few words about the more conventional concept of goal programming. Goal programming is an optimization technique invented by A. Charnes and W. W. Cooper to handle decision-making situations where a number of conditions characterized as goals are to be met as closely as possible.

Goal programming allows the modeler to deal with "soft" constraints, those which the market does not take into explicit account. These constraints may be violated, but at a cost. The various goals need not be met exactly, but penalties are assigned to deviations from them. The more urgent the goal, the greater the penalty. The penalties assessed may be different for overperformance and underperformance. Consider, for instance, a numerical goal for the annual catch of salmon in a particular river. The concern here may be directed to overfishing the waters, and no penalty may be levied on underfulfillment of the goal. Suppose that we are drawing up a master plan for the annual catch in all rivers in an entire coastal area. Specifying penalties for overfishing that are greater in one river than in another, we implicitly establish a hierarchical ranking of priorities.

Conventional goal programming proceeds through the direct minimization of all penalties thus established. If the minimand can be brought down to zero, all constraints can be met and no penalty arises in the system. But if such an outcome is not possible, the goal-programming format will instead look for some optimal tradeoff among violations of different constraints in order to make the total penalty as low as possible.

The companion approach of goal focusing (the term was first used in Charnes et al. [8]) applies when the formulation of the goals is attached to a prior mathematical program existing in its own right but where it is now desired to temper the objective of that program, requiring the solution values to come as close as possible to the goals. The objective function of the goal-focusing program equals the objective of the prior (nongoaled) program adjusted by the sum of all penalties. That is, while the prior objective (market efficiency, say) is still sought so long as the goals so permit, one introduces the possibility of a tradeoff if all goals cannot be realized exactly, trading off some efficiency against penalties.

The technique of goal focusing may then be employed to temper the optimal solutions of the various mathematical programs presented in this volume, looking for the possibility of establishing some tradeoff between the conventional partial equilibrium solution and the possible fulfillment of one or several resource goals.

In both goal programming and goal focusing, a problem that presents itself in practical application is one of implementation: once having found an optimal solution to the goaling program, how do we actually implement it? This problem arises in particular when goals are attached to variables that are not directly controlled by the policy maker who formulates the goals.

An important point of the treatment to follow is to demonstrate, and to illustrate, the general proposition that for a wide class of goal-focusing models, it is possible to implement the optimal solution by a suitable system of Pigou taxes and unit subsidies. A Pigou tax (see Pigou [12]) is an excise tax levied on the purchase of any good or service, such as the excise tax on gasoline that is levied in most states in the United States. The unit subsidies that are being referred to here would be direct cash contributions paid by the government to the purchaser of a resource—a negative Pigou tax. The tax introduces a wedge between the price the purchaser pays and the price that the resource owner collects. The unit subsidy introduces a wedge between the same two prices in the opposite direction. So, the proposition is that by suitable correction of the free prices being established in the marketplace it would be possible to simulate the presence of the goals in the sense that the optimal solution to the goal-focusing model would also be an efficient point without reference to the goals in an alternative partial economy with suitably distorted prices.

The obvious application of these results is a planning situation where the policy maker is a branch of local or central government for which the introduction of Pigou taxes or subsidies is a viable alternative of actual implementation. But, in addition, even in cases where the policy-maker does not contemplate any interference with the workings of the free markets or is in no position to make any such attempt, it is felt that the results to follow are instructive in making clear the logical connection between goaling and the price system, and the demonstration that for a wide class of goal-focusing models what the goaling essentially accomplishes is to modify the existing price system.

SYMBOLS USED IN CHAPTER 7

$h \in H$	originating regions
$k \in K$	destination regions
$i \in I$	final goods
$j \in J$	intermediate goods
$r \in R$	resources
$m \in M$	activities
x_k, x_i	demand
w_h, w_r	supply
$Q_h(w_h), Q_r(w_r)$	supply price function
t_{hk}	quantity transported from origin h to destination k
c_{hk}	unit transportation cost
p_k, q_h	price at destination k and origin h, respectively

$w_h\#, w_r\#$	supply goal
d_h, d_r	underperformance relative to goal (deficiency)
e_h, e_r	overperformance relative to goal (excess)
M_h, M_r	penalty for underperformance
N_h, N_r	penalty for overperformance
P as superscript	primary goods (resources)
I as superscript	intermediate goods
F as superscript	final goods

$A^P = [a^P_{rm}], A^I = [a^I_{jm}]$ matrix of input coefficients

$B^I = [b^I_{jm}], B^F = [b^F_{im}]$ matrix of output coefficients

z_m	level of operation of activity m
u^F_i	Lagrange multiplier of consumer demand balance
u^I_j	Lagrange multiplier of balance for intermediate good
u^P_r	Lagrange multiplier of resource balance
s_h, s_r	Lagrange multiplier of goaling relation (if positive, a Pigou subsidy; if negative, a Pigou tax)

7.1. A TRANSPORTATION TYPE MODEL WITH GOALS AT ALL ORIGINS

Although they have many virtues, the neoclassical models of economics do not portray the social complexities of the modern world sufficiently for use in many contexts. Production decisions and supply decisions are not made in a social vacuum. In addition to operating costs, economic decision makers today are faced with many considerations, including health, environment, technology, the media, public opinion, government bureaucrats, and so on. Often such considerations can be formalized in terms of goals which are to be used to influence or direct the behavior of individual consumers, producers, and resource owners.

For a clarification of the concept of a goal, turn to figure 7.1 which illustrates the local supply curve for some commodity in amount w_h in region h, $h \in H$. The supply curve shows the supply price as an upward sloping function $Q_h(w_h)$ of the quantity w_h supplied. If the price is low, supply will be low. If the price is higher, a greater supply will be forthcoming.

Figure 7.1. A Regional Supply Goal

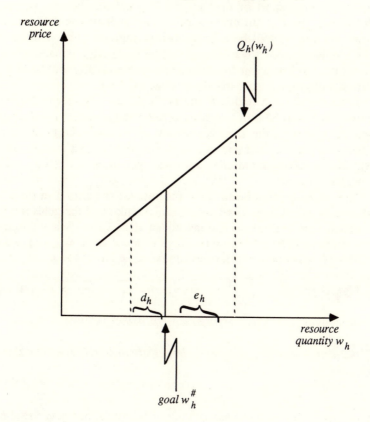

Suppose now that it is possible to encapsulate other considerations regarding the supply of w_h in a single numerical goal $w_h^\#$, as illustrated by the vertical line. The goal is set as a desirable target. Exact realization is not necessary. Deviations from the goal are permitted, both in the negative direction (an underfulfillment or deficiency denoted as d_h) and in the positive direction (an overfulfillment or excess denoted as e_h). Mathematically, any actual supply value w_h can then be expressed in terms of the goal, say w_h, via

$$(7.1) \qquad w_h + d_h - e_h = w_h^\#$$

where d_h and e_h are both non-negative and $d_h e_h = 0$, that is at least one of the two deviations must equal zero.

Deviations from the goal are associated with penalties. Let the unit penalty for falling short of the goal be M_h and the the unit penalty for overfulfillment be N_h. In many applications, at least one of the two unit penalties M_h and N_h will be a large positive number. For instance in the case of supply of ground water there will be some large penalty to be paid for overwithdrawal of water from the aquifer. No penalty will be levied for withdrawals of ground water that falls below the goal.

Total penalties in region h amount to $M_h d_h + N_h e_h$ and not both of these two terms will be different from zero. Total penalties in all regions is obtained by summing the same expression over all h. The greater the unit penalties in a region, the more urgent is the goal for that region. In other words, the relative magnitudes of these penalties reflect the relative priorities of the goals.

The penalties may be cardinal magnitudes (measured in dollars and cents), or they may be specified as an ordinal ranking of the goals by the use of so-called non-Archimedean transcendentals. To see what this means, consider this example: There are two regions $h = 1$ and $h = 2$, and two goals $w_1\#$ and $w_2\#$. Assume that priorities can be ranked as follows:

highest priority	*no underperformance relative to goal $w_1\#$*
next highest priority	*no overperformance relative to goal $w_1\#$*
third priority	*no underperformance relative to goal $w_2\#$*
fourth priority	*no overperformance relative to goal $w_2\#$*

In order to establish this ordinal ranking of priorities, one may use the non-Archimedean transcendentals $M_1 > N_1 > M_2 > N_2$, meaning that no positive multiple k of any N_2 can give $kN_2 \geq M_2$, and so on (see pp. 316–317 in [1]). Numerically, one may provisionally use large penalties such as $M_1 = 4,444$, $N_1 = 3,333$, $M_2 = 2,222$ *and* $N_2 = 1,111$, provided one checks afterward to see whether the numerical solutions that these numbers generate have the desired properties (i.e., that the goals are satisfied in order of their priorities, so that a goal of a higher priority always takes precedence over a goal with a lower priority, and the achievement of a higher-priority goal is never "contaminated" by the possibility of achieving a lower-priority goal).

For an example of regional supply goals, reference may be made to a model of the lumber industry ranging from the supply of felled logs to the deliveries at sawmills. The supply price curve of logs in each region h, as illustrated in figure 7.1, will depend upon the age and size of trees, the methods and costs of felling trees, the value of the land, the cost of replanting, and other factors. In the common fashion, the supply price can be identified with the marginal cost of supplied and felled logs.

The transportation of logs to sawmills may be by truck, rail, or water. If there are several sawmills, a choice has to be made about the routing of the logs from each forest region. This choice will be influenced by the geographical orientation of railway connections and waterways. Existing facilities and the capacity of the waterways may lay down upper limits on the quantities of timber that may be transported along each transportation link.

The equilibrium solution (i.e., in the absence of goals) to the regional supply and distribution system indicated can be obtained by applying the methods of spatial equilibrium which are now familiar to us. There are two categories of nodes or regions: forest regions and sawmills. The forest regions are origins with local supply but no local demand. The sawmills are destinations with local demand but no local supply. (For analytical purposes, any sawmill located in a forest region will be kept apart from it as a separate entity.) This supply and distribution system is then of the transportation model type (see sec. 3.2).

Actually, at the origin, supply is price-dependent so that the model is one of generalized transportation. But to simplify matters, the demand at each destination will be assumed to be given and known. Using k to index the sawmills, $k \in K$, the demand for logs at sawmill k will be written as x_k. The equilibrium model would then be (cf. program [3.12])

(7.2)
$$\min \sum_{h \in H} \int Q_h(w_h)dw_h + \sum_{h \in H} \sum_{k \in K} c_{hk}t_{hk}$$

subject to

$$\sum_{h \in H} t_{hk} \geq x_k, \ k \in K$$

$$w_h - \sum_{k \in K} t_{hk} \geq 0, \ h \in H$$

$$w_h, t_{hk} \geq 0, \ h \in H, \ k \in K$$

The potential function featured in the minimand simply equals the sum of all supply costs (obtained through the integration of marginal costs) and all transportation costs. The first set of constraints states that the deliveries at each sawmill must cover the local demand. The second set of constraints states that the quantity of logs shipped from each logging region cannot exceed the local supply.

(One may also adjoin a capacitating condition on the quantity t_{hk} shipped along each link *(h,k)*. The treatment is straightforward and need not delay us.)

We now proceed to show how it is possible to temper the equilibrium supplies of resources w_h^* in each region that can be obtained from model (7.2) by the introduction of a goal-focusing mechanism aimed at the possible realization of the goal $w_h\#$ in each region. The reason may be a wish to express various environmental goals, such as conservation of flora and fauna in various logging regions, the prevention of erosion of soil, or even the maintenance of current climatic conditions. The forest in question may be located in Africa, being a sanctuary for wildlife or serving as a buffer against the advances of the desert. It may be located in the Amazons, where rapid deforestation might prompt periodic floodings of the Amazon River and the destruction of precarious ecological balances. It may be a redwood forest in California, which provides opportunities for hiking and tourist life in nearby residential areas.

In the particular application now envisaged, there would presumably be zero penalties for underfulfillments of the goals, that is, all $M_h = 0$. The relative penalties to be levied on overfulfillments—N_h—would reflect the relative priorities of limiting the logging activities in the various regions.

A policy maker has formulated a supply target or supply goal $w_h\#$ for each region, as illustrated in figure 7.1, and an ordinal ranking of the priorities of these goals as expressed by the penalties M_h and N_h. Consider the goal-focusing program

(7.3)
$$min \sum_{h \in H} \int Q_h(w_h)dw_h + \sum_{h \in H} (M_h d_h + N_h e_h)$$

$$+ \sum_{h \in H} \sum_{k \in K} c_{hk} t_{hk}$$

subject to

$$\sum_{h \in H} t_{hk} \geq x_k, \, k \in K$$

$$w_h - \sum_{k \in K} t_{hk} \geq 0, \, h \in H$$

$$w_h + d_h - e_h = w_h\#, \, h \in H$$

$$w_h, t_{hk}, d_h, e_h \geq 0, \, h \in H, \, k \in K$$

The minimand this time includes a collection of penalty costs. There also is an additional set of constraints—the definitions of the supply goals $w_h\#$ brought from equation (7.1).

As long as there is some deviation from the goals, the presence of the penalty terms will lower the optimal value of the maximand. The program will search out a combination of deviations which makes the net value of the program as small as possible.

Note that it is not necessary to introduce the requirement $d_h e_h = 0$ explicitly; it will be automatically satisfied at the point of solution. For assume, per contra, that both d_h and e_h were positive and satisfied (7.1) for any h. It would then be possible to shave off some small positive constant from each of d_h and e_h and still satisfy this constraint without altering any other variable in the program. Such a change would decrease the value of the minimand by reducing $M_h d_h + N_h e_h$ since each of these terms involves only non-negative values. Indeed, one would be able to continue this procedure until one of the two deviations were reduced to zero.

Now we turn to the dual variables. Denote the Lagrange multipliers of the first set of constraints by p_k, $k \in K$. They are non-negative. Let the optimal $p_k = p_k^*$ be interpreted as the market price of logs at sawmill k. The Lagrange multipliers of the second set of constraints will be written q_h, $h \in H$. These multipliers are also non-negative. The optimal $q_h = q_h^*$ can be interpreted as the market price of logs quoted in forest region h.

The Lagrange multiplier of the goaling relation will be denoted s_h. It is the purpose of much of the discussion to follow to make clear the meaning of the optimal $s_h = s_h^*$. It may be positive, zero, or negative.

The optimal solution to program (7.3) represents an allocation where the producers are holding back the local supply wherever it would otherwise exceed the local goal. But they will step up the local supply wherever it would otherwise fall short of the local goal.

To formalize these propositions, turn to the Kuhn–Tucker conditions. Denoting optimum values by an asterisk (*), these conditions are as follows.

(i)   There will be equilibrium in the local market for the commodity at each demand point (destination). Further, under a suitable pricing system, there could be equilibrium in the local market at each supply point (origin).

The condition for the market formation at each destination is straightforward and follows from inspection of the pair of conditions

$$(7.4) \qquad \sum_{h \in H} t_{hk}^* \geq x_k, \; p_k^*(\sum_{h \in H} t_{hk}^* - x_k) = 0, \; k \in K$$

The condition for the market formation at each origin, however, is treacherous. Formally, it looks innocent enough:

$$(7.5) \qquad w_h^* - \sum_{k \in K} t_{hk}^* \geq 0, \, q_h^*(w_h^* - \sum_{k \in K} t_{hk}^*) = 0, \, h \in H$$

This would seem to imply that the price q_h^* can serve as an equilibrium price in the market at origin h. Indeed, that is how we have defined market equilibrium and the clearing of a market over and over again. If the price is positive, the market clears. If there is an excess supply in the local market, the price drops to zero.

In the present instance, however, additional considerations arise. Will the suppliers in region h want to supply the quantity w_h^* by their own free will, or is this something that the policy maker overseeing the goaling mechanism will coerce them to do? Equilibrium, after all, is something that should be established by market forces rather than through the intervention of a policy administrator or regulator.

(ii)   The appreciation in value that occurs as the commodity is being transported from a supply point to a demand point cannot exceed the unit transportation cost. If a positive quantity is being transported, the appreciation in value equals the unit transportation cost. But if the appreciation does not cover the unit transportation cost, no shipments will take place along that link.

For one finds

$$(7.6) \qquad p_k^* - q_h^* \leq c_{hk}, \, t_{hk}^*(p_k^* - q_h^* - c_{hk}) = 0, \, h \in H, \, k \in K$$

We recognize the standard proposition in spatial equilibrium that no hypothetical shipper can ever make a profit along any link of a transportation system. But consider the next condition:

(iii)   At each supply point, the market price cannot exceed the supply price $Q_h(w_h^*)$ minus the value of the Lagrange multiplier s_h^* of the goaling relation. If the good is supplied at all, the market price must equal this adjusted value.

For one gets

(7.7) $q_h{}^* + s_h{}^* \leq Q_h(w_h{}^*), \; w_h{}^*(q_h{}^* + s_h{}^* - Q_h(w_h{}^*)) = 0, \, h \in H$

The multiplier $s_h{}^*$ is further explicated by the conditions

(iv)   If the optimal supply in region h falls short of the goal, so that the deviation $d_h{}^*$ is positive, the multiplier $s_h{}^*$ equals M_h. If the optimal supply exceeds the goal, so that the deviation $e_h{}^*$ is positive, the multiplier $s_h{}^*$ equals $-N_h$. If the optimal supply coincides with the goal, the multiplier $s_h{}^*$ may take on some numerical value (positive, zero, or negative) that lies between these two extremes.

Mathematically,

(7.8) $s_h{}^* \leq M_h, \; d_h{}^*(s_h{}^* - M_h) = 0, \, h \in H$

(7.9) $-s_h{}^* \leq N_h, \; e_h{}^*(-s_h{}^* - N_h) = 0, \, h \in H$

So, we see that the multiplier $s_h{}^*$ must always fall in the interval $-N_h \leq s_h{}^* \leq M_h$. If the optimal supply in region h falls short of the goal (but still is positive), the multiplier falls at the upper end point of that interval. If the optimal supply exceeds the goal (but still is positive), the multiplier falls at the lower end point of the interval. The multiplier is then negative (the penalties M_h and N_h are always non-negative, of course).

Taking conditions (iii) and (iv) together, we see that if the optimal supply in region h falls short of the goal (but still is positive), the market price falls short of the supply price by the amount of the penalty M_h. If the optimal supply exceeds the goal, the market price exceeds the supply price by the amount of the penalty N_h.

This means that suppliers are required to adjust their supply price in region h by the amount of the shadow price associated with the goal in that region. If the optimal supply in region h falls short of the goal, the adjustment involves reducing the supply price by the amount of the unit penalty for underfulfillment. The supply curve is shifted downward and this, ceteris paribus, tends to stimulate supply. If, on the other hand, the optimal supply in region h exceeds the goal, the adjustment means adding to the supply price the amount of the unit penalty for overshooting. In this case, the supply curve is shifted upward and this, ceteris paribus, tends to reduce supply. In either case, the adjusted supply price is $Q_h(w_h{}^*) - s_h{}^*$.

There are several ways of characterizing this adjustment. One is that suppliers voluntarily correct their supply prices. The supply price is the lowest price that a supplier requires in order to induce him to supply a given quantity. The correction would, of course, interfere with his underlying profit considerations. If the correction is positive, it means that he would require a higher price for supplying the same quantity.

In the case of the logging industry, forest owners may voluntarily increase their supply price in forest regions where they feel that the existing forest is being harvested too fast. In other words, forest owners may withhold supply in regions where they feel that there would otherwise be an exploitation of the existing resources.

Under this interpretation, the penalties for deviations from the goals are in the nature of psychological costs which reflect the voluntary preferences of the suppliers and which cause them to depart from the neoclassical supply curves. We have shown just now that such considerations may alternatively be replaced by a system of psychological corrections of the supply prices in various regions.

But in the real world it may not always be possible to rely on voluntary cooperation. Some branch of local or central government may decide to enforce the goals and to levy cash penalties for deviations from them. The required corrections of the supply prices can then be carried out by levying an excise tax (a Pigou tax, after Pigou [12]) to be paid by the supplier of the resource, or paying a unit subsidy to him. The required value of this correction is obtained as the optimal value s_h^* of the Lagrange multiplier of the goaling relation. If the multiplier is negative, it is an excise tax. If the multiplier is positive, it is a unit subsidy.

To see this, note that the expression $q_h^* + s_h^*$ will then denote the market price of the resource in region h *after* the addition of a possible subsidy or the deduction of a possible tax. It is the unit sales return that the resource owner will actually put into his pockets. Conditions (7.7) now state that the resource owner under this hypothetical regime actually would be adjusted to equilibrium. The net price calculated after subsidies and taxes cannot exceed the supply price. If a positive quantity is supplied, the net price equals the supply price.

So, there is equilibrium at all locations after all, at both all supply points and all demand points. But the price that actually accomplishes this equilibrium is not a free market price. It is a manipulated price that involves a discrepancy between the price that the resource owner gets and the price that a purchaser of those resources pays. A wedge has been driven between those two prices. That wedge is the unit subsidy or the tax.

It should be pointed out that in general the optimal Pigou taxes are not cardinally determined. As stated in condition (iv) above, in the case that the optimal supply of a resource exceeds the goal, the Pigou tax will equal the non-Archimedean transcendental associated with overfulfillment of this goal.

In the case that the optimal supply falls short of the goal, the tax equals the transcendental associated with underfulfillment of the goal. One may speculate that perhaps there will exist an optimal ordinal system of Pigou taxes that solves the general model (7.3).[1]

Exercise 7.1

Strip mining of coal occurs in four regions A, B, C, D in a state. The supply price functions are, respectively (in dollars per thousand ton),

$$Q_A(w_A) = -10 + 1.8\,w_A$$

$$Q_B(w_B) = -8 + 2.0\,w_B$$

$$Q_C(w_C) = -4 + 1.6\,w_C$$

$$Q_D(w_D) = -8 + 1.8\,w_D$$

where w_h is the quantity mined in region h, measured in thousand tons, $h = A,B,C,D$. Once mined, the coal is transported by rail to two large electric utilities K and L. The demand for coal at these locations is $x_K = 40$ *and* $s_L = 48$ thousand tons.

The distances (in miles) between mines and utilities are as follows:

	To Utility K	To Utility L
From mines in region A	*600*	*1000*
From mines in region B	*1000*	*800*
From mines in region C	*200*	*1500*
From mines in region D	*500*	*750*

Railway costs are $.002 per thousand ton mile.

There is some concern in all four regions about the effects of strip mining on the environment. An environmental study has resulted in the formulation of the following supply goals, in thousand tons:

Region A	*11.5*
Region B	*20*
Region C	*40*
Region D	*16*

A supply in a region that is equal to or less than the stated goal is believed to have no long-term detrimental effects on the environment. But supply in excess of the goal is to be avoided, if possible.

(Notice that the goals add up to 87.5, which is slightly less than total demand 88. Hence, it is not possible to satisfy all goals at the same time.)

There is general agreement that the top priority must be to meet the goal in region C. But there are some different opinions about the relative urgency of the other goals, and a policy maker decides to consider two alternative priority rankings:

	Policy Alternative (a)	Policy Alternative (b)
1st priority	*region C*	*region C*
2nd priority	*region D*	*region D*
3rd priority	*region A*	*region B*
4th priority	*region B*	*region A*

Formulate a goal-focusing model for both policy alternatives and solve it.

Solution: Integrating each supply price function and adding, one finds total supply costs

$$-10w_A + 0.9w_A{}^2 - 8w_B + w_B{}^2 - 4w_C + 0.8w_C{}^2 - 8w_D + 0.9w_D{}^2$$

Total transportation costs are

$$1.2t_{AK} + 2t_{BK} + 0.4t_{CK} + t_{DK} + 2t_{AL} + 1.6t_{BL} + 3t_{CL} + 1.5t_{DL}$$

No penalties will be associated with undersupply d_h below the stated goals. But there are positive penalties for oversupply e_h, $h = A,B,C,D$. We may then use the following large numbers for the penalties N_h of the two policy alternatives (chosen to reflect the relative priorities laid down):

Alternative (a)	Alternative (b)
$N_C = 888$	$N_C = 888$
$N_D = 666$	$N_D = 666$
$N_A = 444$	$N_B = 444$
$N_B = 222$	$N_A = 222$

Dealing first with policy alternative (a), total penalties are

$$444e_A + 222e_B + 888e_C + 666e_D$$

Turning to the constraints, there are two demand balances, one at each electric utility:

$$t_{AK} + t_{BK} + t_{CK} + t_{DK} \geq 40$$

$$t_{AL} + t_{BL} + t_{CL} + t_{DL} \geq 48$$

Next, there are four supply balances, one at each mine:

$$w_A - t_{AK} - t_{AL} \geq 0$$

$$w_B - t_{BK} - t_{BL} \geq 0$$

$$w_C - t_{CK} - t_{CL} \geq 0$$

$$w_D - t_{DK} - t_{DL} \geq 0$$

Finally, there are the goal definitions

$$w_A + d_A - e_A = 11.5$$

$$w_B + d_B - e_B = 20$$

$$w_C + d_C - e_C = 40$$

$$w_D + d_D - e_D = 16$$

Bringing all the elements of the programming model together, we thus arrive at the goal focusing program:

$$min - 10w_A + 0.9w_A^2 - 8w_B + w_B^2 - 4w_C + 0.8w_C^2 - 8w_D + 0.9w_D^2 +$$

$$1.2t_{AK} + 2t_{BK} + 0.4t_{CK} + t_{DK} + 2t_{AL} + 1.6t_{BL} + 3t_{CL} + 1.5t_{DL} +$$

$$444e_A + 222e_B + 888e_C + 666e_D$$

subject to

$$
\begin{array}{ll}
t_{AK} + t_{BK} + t_{CK} + t_{DK} & \geq 40 \\
t_{AL} + t_{BL} + t_{CL} + t_{DL} & \geq 48 \\
w_A - t_{AK} - t_{AL} & \geq 0 \\
w_B - t_{BK} - t_{BL} & \geq 0 \\
w_C - t_{CK} - t_{CL} & \geq 0 \\
w_D - t_{DK} - t_{DL} & \geq 0 \\
w_A + d_A - e_A & = 11.5 \\
w_B + d_B - e_B & = 20
\end{array}
$$

$$w_C + d_C - e_C \qquad\qquad = 40$$

$$w_D + d_D - e_D \qquad\qquad = 16$$

$$w,t,d,e \geq 0$$

In order to prepare for the discussion of the goal-focusing program and its solution, we shall first briefly present the optimal solution to the corresponding generalized transportation problem *without* goals. Replace for a moment the unit penalties *(444,222,888,666)* by *(0,0,0,0)* to obtain the optimal solution

$$w_A^* = 23.1, w_B^* = 20.0, w_C^* = 22.7, w_D^* = 22.2$$

$$t_{AK}^* = 17.3, t_{AL}^* = 5.8, t_{BL}^* = 20.0, t_{CK}^* = 22.7, t_{DL}^* = 22.2$$

with the shipments along all other links being equal to zero. The corresponding equilibrium prices are

$$p_K^* = 32.7, p_L^* = 33.5$$

$$q_A^* = 31.5, q_B^* = 31.9, q_C^* = 32.3, q_D^* = 32.0$$

Note that the implied appreciation of value along any link that is actually used for transportation equals the unit transportation cost.

In order to approach the given goal-focusing problem step by step, we next turn to a slightly modified version where it would be possible to satisfy all the goals without penalty.

This time restore the unit penalties *(444,222,888,666)* but change the goals to, say

$$w_A\# = 16$$

$$w_B\# = 20$$

$$w_C\# = 40$$

$$w_D\# = 16$$

These goals add up to 92, which exceeds total demand *(40 + 48 = 88)*. As we now proceed to show, the four goals may then be satisfied without penalties. For the optimal solution would then be

$$w_A^* = 16, w_B^* = 20, w_C^* = 36, w_D^* = 16$$

$$t_{AK}^* = 4, t_{AL}^* = 12, t_{BL}^* = 20, t_{CK}^* = 36, t_{DL}^* = 16$$

with all other shipments equal to zero. As seen, these supplies in no case exceed the desired goals. However, at origin C, the supply falls short of the goal by 4,000 tons. This does not matter, since a shortfall relative to the goal does not call for a penalty.

The solution prices are:

Demand prices at destinations: $p_K^* = 54.0, p_L^* = 54.8$

Market prices at origins: $q_A^* = 52.8, q_B^* = 53.2, q_C^* = 53.6, q_D^* = 53.3$

The market prices at the various origins (mines) are not necessarily the same as the supply prices. In order to implement the optimum solution, it may be necessary to apply a Pigou tax levied on the supplies at the various locations. The magnitude of the tax is

$$-s_A^* = 34.0, -s_B^* = 21.2, -s_C^* = 0, -s_D^* = 32.5$$

so that the supply price *plus* the Pigou tax equals the market price:

Supply Price	Pigou Tax	Market Price
$A: -10 + 1.8w_A^* = 18.8$	34.0	52.8
$B: -8 + 2.0w_B^* = 32.0$	21.2	53.2
$C: -4 + 1.6w_C^* = 53.6$	0	53.6
$D: -8 + 1.8w_D^* = 20.8$	32.5	53.3

The Pigou tax raises the market price at an origin above the supply price, and has the effect of inhibiting supply so that it stays within the postulated goal limit. No tax is needed at origin C, since the supply—even without a tax—falls clear of the goal.

Notice that in cases like the one just now demonstrated, when all penalties can be brought down to zero, the soft constraints of goal programming actually can be replaced by hard constraints which may not be violated. In the particular numerical example discussed just now, the goal-programming feature could have been replaced by the hard constraints:

$$w_A \le 16$$

$$w_B \le 20$$

$$w_C \le 40$$

$$w_D \le 16$$

At the point of optimum, the first, second, and fourth of these constraints would have been binding. But the third constraint would have been slack.

(As a general proposition, it is easy to show that if it is possible to drive all goal deviations down to zero so that all goals can be attained simultaneously, the goal-programming/goal-focusing approach is identical to a system of hard constraints which may not be violated. The dual of each goaling relation then coincides with the dual of the corresponding hard constraint. It does not depend upon the relative or absolute magnitude of the penalties used.)

We are now ready to solve the numerical problem at hand. Because the supply goals together fall short of total demand it is not possible to satisfy all goals at the same time. It is not possible to replace the soft constraints of goal programming by hard constraints. Some penalties will have to be incurred, and the purpose of the goal-programming problem is to establish a tradeoff among the penalties involved resulting from violation of the goals at different origins. The relative ranking of the various unit penalties now comes into play, and the goal program will naturally look for possibilities of avoiding more costly deviations, instead accepting deviations where the penalty is smaller.

The optimal solution is

$$w_A{}^* = 11.5, w_B{}^* = 20.5, w_C{}^* = 40, w_D{}^* = 16$$

$$t_{AL}{}^* = 11.5, t_{BL}{}^* = 20.5, t_{CK}{}^* = 40, t_{DL}{}^* = 16$$

and all other shipments equal to zero.

The solution prices are

Demand prices at destinations: $p_K{}^* = 255.8, p_L{}^* = 256.6$

Market prices at origins: $q_A{}^* = 254.6, q_B{}^* = 255.0, q_C{}^* = 255.4,$

$$q_D{}^* = 255.1$$

The Pigou taxes are

$$-s_A{}^* = 243.9, -s_B{}^* = 222.0, -s_C{}^* = 195.4, -s_D{}^* = 234.3$$

At each origin, the supply price plus the Pigou tax equals the market price:

Supply Price	Pigou Tax	Market Price
$A: -10 + 1.8w_A{}^* = 10.7$	243.9	254.6
$B: -8 + 2.0w_B{}^* = 33.0$	222.0	255.0
$C: -4 + 1.6w_C{}^* = 60.0$	195.4	255.4
$D: -8 + 1.8w_D{}^* = 20.8$	234.3	255.1

The optimal solution is illustrated in figure 7.2. It turns out that the goals in region A, C, and D can be met, but that the quantity mined in region B exceeds the set goal by 0.5 thousand tons. Some penalty therefore has to be accepted at the point of the optimal solution.

(Note that the Pigou tax depends upon the penalty choice 222 used for region B where the goal violation occurs.)

Figure 7.2.   Optimal Solution to Exercise 7.1

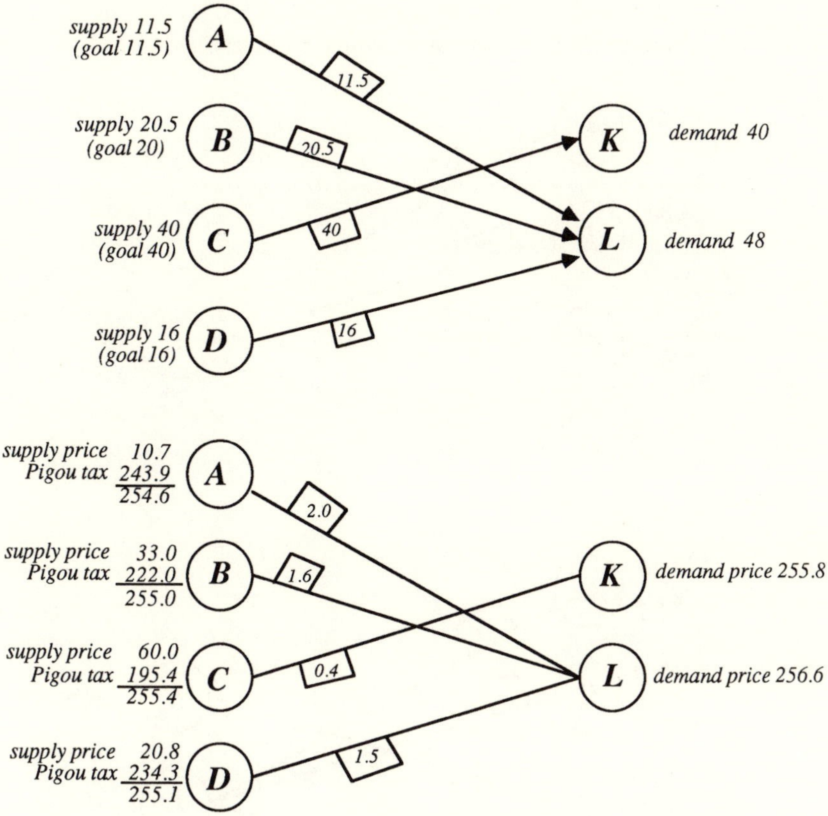

Note: Goals are ranked in the following order: C, D, A, B. Upper panel: Quantity solution. Flags indicate quantities shipped. Lower panel: Price solution. Flags indicate unit transportation costs.

The lower panel in figure 7.2 shows the formation of prices. The market price in each mining region is obtained as the sum of the supply price and the Pigou tax. The Pigou tax in region B (the region where the goal violation occurs) equals \$222 (i.e., it equals the unit penalty). The Pigou taxes in the other regions fall short of the unit penalties.

Turning to policy alternative (b), let the total penalties this time be given by the expression

$$222e_A + 444e_B + 888e_C + 666e_D$$

Reformulating the goal-focusing program, one obtains the optimal solution illustrated in figure 7.3. Now the goals in regions B, C, and D are met but the mining in region A exceeds the goal by 0.5 thousand tons.

Figure 7.3.   Optimal Solution to Exercise 7.1

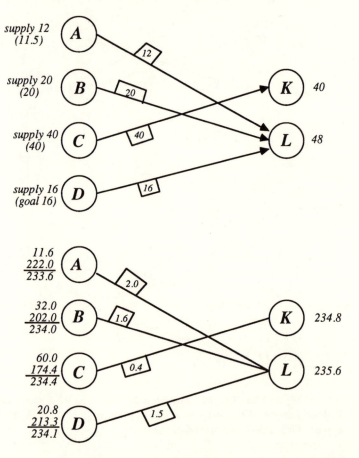

Note: Goals are ranked in the following order C, D, B, A. Upper panel: Quantity solution. Flags indicate quantities shipped. Lower panel: Price solution. Flags indicate unit transportation costs.

The Pigou tax equals the unit penalty in region A. In the other regions it falls short of the unit penalties.

So, switching the priorities does indeed result in a switching of the optimal solutions. Each time, the optimal solution satisfied the more urgent goals and chooses to take an unavoidable penalty in the region where the unit penalty is smallest. (This result seems natural enough. Unfortunately, however, it does not hold as a general mathematical proposition. It is easy to construct numerical examples where the optimal solution involves the use of other penalties than just the smallest ones.)

7.2. ACTIVITY ANALYSIS WITH RESOURCE GOALS

The competitive market system makes the use of resources respond to the tastes and even the whims of consumers. It is the beauty of this system that logistics chains can be set up and maintained, spanning half the globe, to serve the consumer. And all along these chains, producers and distributors find it useful to contribute freely and willingly to the collective enterprise.

But there is an obvious danger, when the mind of the consumer is so far separated from the world of the producers who tap the ultimate resources. The longer the chains, the more insulated will the consumer be from the implications of the use of resources. The consumer who buys a coat with fur trim does not see the clubbing of baby seals on the ice outside Newfoundland.

We have in the preceding section studied the problem of resource management in a conventional transportation type model where each origin was identified as a resource supply point. Now we shall let the transportation of the commodity extend through the dimension of a vertical production chain instead, tracing production back through a series of intermediate products to the use of primary products (resources). This time, the logistics chain is even longer and more tenuous. Through a series of linked markets, the invisible hand will communicate the desires of the consumers and ultimately lay down its claims on the available supplies of resources.

As a particular application, consider the fisheries industry in a maritime nation such as Iceland, Norway, or the Philippines. The resources of the industry, say $r \in R$, are various species of fish, like cod, herring, and so on. The supply of each resource is the annual catch w_r, measured in thousands of metric tons.

A master plan for the industry would involve goals for the use of each resource, say

$$(7.10) \qquad w_r + d_r - e_r = w_r{}^\#$$

where $w_r\#$ is the target utilization of resource r, d_r the possible underachievement compared to the set goal, and e_r is the possible excess above the goal.

The goals may be formulated in terms of target figures for the annual catch of each species of fish. Such targets could, for instance, be developed by an advisory body representing both the interests of the owners of the fishing fleet and marine biologists assessing the viability of the existing stock of fish and its conditions of propagation, maintenance, and growth. The target catch must be large enough to provide industry interests with an adequate income and to meet the demand of consumers; on the other hand, the catch must be kept within limits so that the existing stock of fish is not depleted.

Different targets may be set for the catch during different periods of the fishing season (protecting the spawning and maturing of young fish), in different coastal and ocean waters; the targets may also involve considerations of different kinds of fishing operations (different kinds of nets, trawlers, and so on), the manning of the fishing fleet, the running of facilities on land including freezing operations, and the distribution of fish.

The deviations d_r and e_r are both non-negative. They must satisfy $d_r e_r = 0$, that is, at least one of the two deviations must equal zero.

The list of resources $r \in R$ includes labor, fishing vessels, and on-shore capital installations. There may be targets associated with the use of these resources too, such as some desired employment in the fisheries industry, both on the fishing vessels and on land.

Let the unit penalty for falling short of the goal for the utilization of resource r be M_r, and the unit penalty for overfulfillment be N_r. Total penalties levied on resource r are then $M_r d_r + N_r e_r$.

The penalties may be fines meted out and assessed by a directorate of fisheries, or they may just be ordinal numbers reflecting the relative urgency of the goals in the minds of the planners.

A problem of the real world that we cannot deal with is the fact that different policy makers may entertain different opinions about the relative urgency of the various targets involved. The technique of goal focusing involves no prescription for how such a consensus can be found. The entire political problem of arriving at a consensus must therefore here be put aside. We simply postulate the results of this political process.

The penalty M_r measures the relative urgency that the utilization of resource r not fall short of the set goal. The penalty N_r measures the relative urgency that the utilization not exceed the goal.

If there is some resource r for which a goal has not been set, we may formally put the goal equal to some arbitrary number and levy the penalties $M_r = N_r = 0$ for deviations from it.

The fisheries industry may conveniently be defined as the catching, processing, and distribution of fish products including live and frozen fish,

fish products for the food industry, fish meal, and fish oil. Several of these production and distribution chains are quite long, ranging over a series of consecutive production and transportation activities such as freezing, storage, cleaning, the making of fillets, cooking, salting or curing, packaging, and distribution.

Let there be $m \in M$ individual industrial activities in the industry. Use the symbol z_m to denote the unit level of operation of activity m. Some of these activities will involve the use of primary *(P)* resources w_r, converting them into intermediate *(I)* goods $j \in J$. Other activities convert resources and intermediate goods into other intermediate goods. Finally, some activities convert primary and intermediate goods into final *(F)* goods, say various consumer goods $i \in I$.

Using the same notation as in chapter 5, define the matrix of input coefficients $A^P = [a^P_{rm}]$. The element a^P_{rm} denotes the quantity of resource r required to operate activity m at unit level. Also, define the matrix of input coefficients of intermediate inputs $A^I = [a^I_{jm}]$. The element a^I_{jm} is the quantity of intermediate good j required to operate activity m at unit level.

Turning to the output side, define the matrix of coefficients of outputs of intermediate goods $B^I = [b^I_{jm}]$, where the element b^I_{jm} is the quantity of intermediate good j obtained when activity m is operated at unit level. Also, we need the matrix of coefficients of outputs of final goods $B^F = [b^F_{im}]$, with b^F_{im} being the quantity of final good i obtained when activity m is operated at unit level.

The activity analysis format sets up a linear relationship between the vector of resource use $w = [w_r]$ and the vector of consumer demand $x = [x_i]$. These technical relationships cannot be influenced by the goaling process. Once a certain vector of resources w has been established, whether through the invisible hand of the market or through the coercion of policy makers, it is a matter of a simple linear transformation to compute the resulting vector of final demand x that it can sustain.

What the planners can do, however, is to steer supply (the catch) itself, the vector w. If such control turns out to interfere with the market mechanism, the supply price of each resource $Q_r(w_r)$ will no longer coincide with the market price. The resource owners will no longer be adjusted to equilibrium.

Consider now the goal-focusing model

(7.11) $min \ \sum_{r \in R} \int Q_r(w_r)dw_r + \sum_{r \in R} (M_r d_r + N_r e_r)$

subject to

$$\sum_{m \in M} b^F_{im} z_m \geq x_i, \ i \in I$$

$$\sum_{m \in M} b^I_{jm} z_m - \sum_{m \in M} a^I_{jm} z_m = 0, \ j \in J$$

$$w_r - \sum_{m \in M} a^P_{rm} z_m \geq 0, \ r \in R$$

$$w_r + d_r - e_r = w_r\#, \ r \in R$$

$$w_r, d_r, e_r \geq 0, \ r \in R, \ z_m \geq 0, \ m \in M$$

The objective function has been formed as the sum of total supply costs and all penalties. The cost of each resource r is obtained through the integration of the supply price function (marginal cost function) $Q_r(w_r)$. There are four sets of constraints. The first three are standard for the linear activity analysis format: constraints stating that the output of each final good must suffice to cover the demand for it; that the output of any intermediate good must equal the use of it; and that the total use of any resource cannot exceed the supply of it. The fourth set of constraints simply defines the supply goals (7.10).

Without the goal-focusing mechanism, program (7.11) would simply minimize total resource costs for an activity analysis type partial economy with given and known demands for all final goods. The goaling mechanism provides a tradeoff between resource costs and penalties, seeking an optimal solution that comes as close to the formulated goals as possible.

In the usual manner of goal programming and as explained in section 7.1, it is not necessary to introduce the requirements $d_r e_r = 0, \ r \in R$ explicitly; they will automatically be satisfied at the point of optimum.

In order to prepare for the use of the Kuhn–Tucker theorem, we introduce notation on the dual side of the program as follows. Let the Lagrange multipliers of the first set of constraints be u^F_i, $i \in I$. The optimal $u^F_i = u^{F*}_i$ may be interpreted as the market price of consumer good i. It is non-negative. The Lagrange multipliers of the second set of constraints are u_j^I, $j \in J$. The optimal u_j^{I*} is the market price of intermediate product j. It is unrestricted in sign. The Lagrange multipliers of the third set of constraints are u_r^P, $r \in R$. The optimal u_r^{P*} is the market price of resource r. It is non-negative.

The Lagrange multiplier of the goaling relation will be s_r, $r \in R$. It is unrestricted in sign. The meaning of this multiplier will become clear in a moment.

(i)   All markets (final, intermediate, and primary markets) clear.

The conditions for final and intermediate goods are straightforward, reading,

$$(7.12) \qquad \sum_{m \in M} b_{im}^F z_m^* - x_i \geq 0, \, u_i^{F*} \, (b_{im}^F z_m^* - x_i) = 0, \, i \in I$$

$$(7.13) \qquad B^I z^* - A^I z^* = 0$$

The conditions for the resource markets, however, require careful interpretation. They are

$$(7.14) \qquad w_r^* - \sum_{m \in M} a_{rm}^P z_m^* \geq 0, \, u_r^{P*} \, (w_r^* - \sum_{m \in M} a_{rm}^P z_m^*) = 0, \, r \in R$$

Formally, this looks like an ordinary market-clearing condition. If the resource price is positive, the market clears. But there may also occur an excess supply; in that case the price drops to zero.

The difficulty posed by conditions (7.14) is, as we shall see immediately, that the resource owners will in general not be adjusted to equilibrium at the resource prices u_r^{P*}. Supposing that these prices be established in the marketplace, the resource owners would in general not be willing to supply the amounts w_r^*. So, it is not immediately obvious how the conditions (7.14) could be sustained in a free market situation. In order to sustain them, one would somehow need to suspend the supply price functions and replace them by the optimal amounts w_r* of the goal-focusing program.

(ii)   The imputed profit of operating any activity is nonpositive.   If the activity is operated, the profit vanishes.   But if the profit is negative, the activity is not operated.

Mathematically, one gets

$$(7.15) \quad \sum_{i \in I} u_i^{F*} b_{im}^F + \sum_{j \in J} u_j^{I*} (b_{jm}^I - a_{jm}^I) - \sum_{r \in R} u_r^{P*} a_{rm}^P \leq 0,$$

$$z_m^* \left(\sum_{i \in I} u_i^{F*} b_{im}^F + \sum_{j \in J} u_j^{I*} (b_{jm}^I - a_{jm}^I) - \sum_{r \in R} u_r^{P*} a_{rm}^P \right)$$

$$= 0, m \in M$$

This is the standard no-profit condition of activity analysis.

As written here, the no-profit condition actually states that the cash profit resulting from the operation of any activity must vanish.   This strong condition emerges because the z_m variables denoting the levels of operation to be determined can be varied freely.   If one or several z_m are capacitated, attaining some upper capacity limits, however, a positive cash profit will occur.   If there are lower limits, loss may be incurred.   (These matters were discussed in some detail in sec. 4.1, and it is not necessary to repeat that analysis here.)

Computing the optimal value of the Lagrange multiplier of such capacitating constraints, and imputing a unit cost charge equal to the Lagrange multiplier whenever a capacitating limit is encountered, one would restore the optimal condition of no-profits, only this time it would refer to imputed profits, calculated as cash profits minus imputed charges.

(iii)   For each resource, the market price cannot exceed the supply price $Q_r(w_r*)$ minus the value of the Lagrange multiplier s_r* of the goaling relation.   If the resource is supplied at all, the market price must equal this adjusted value.

For the corresponding Kuhn–Tucker conditions are

(7.16) $u_r^{P*} + s_r^* \le Q_r(w_r^*), w_r^*(u_r^{P*} + s_r^* - Q_r(w_r^*)) = 0, r \in R$

Further,

(iv)   If the optimal use of a particular resource r falls short of the goal so that the deviation d_r^* is positive, the corrected resource price equals $Q_r(w_r^*) - M_r$. In this case there is a negative correction equal to the amount of the unit penalty of underuse. The supply curve is lowered, and this, taken by itself, will tend to stimulate supply.

On the other hand, if the optimal resource use exceeds the goal so that e_r^* is positive, the corrected resource price is $Q_r(w_r^*) + N_r$. This time there is a positive correction equal to the penalty of overuse. The supply curve is shifted upward which tends to induce producers to economize on the use of the resource.

These conditions are spelled out by

(7.17) $s_r^* \le M_r, d_r^*(s_r^* - M_r) = 0, r \in R$

$-s_r^* \le N_r, e_r^*(-s_r^* - N_r) = 0, r \in R$

To see what this all means, consider first the case when the supply goal falls short of the free market solution, so that the suppliers are required to hold back some portion of the supply that they would otherwise prefer to launch on the market. Since the supply price curve has a positive inclination and the supply price falls with decreasing supply, the supply price will then fall short of the market price. The suppliers are not adjusted to equilibrium.

On the price side the desired goaling may be effected by lowering the supply price so that it falls sufficiently below the market price. One way to accomplish this is to introduce a Pigou tax levied on the supply of each resource and equal to the optimal value $-s_r^*$ of the negative of the dual of the goaling relation. The net price of a resource that the suppliers will put in their pockets after the payment of the tax is then the market price minus the Pigou tax. With this net take-home pay, the suppliers are again adjusted.

On the other hand, if the purpose of the goaling is to enhance supply, some mechanism has to be found to make suppliers require a greater supply price than the one that would be obtained in a free market solution. This may be accomplished through the vehicle of a unit subsidy. Setting the subsidy equal to s_r^*, the suppliers are adjusted to equilibrium.

The Pigou tax can never exceed the unit penalty to be levied on overshooting the goal. If it is not possible to drive down the supply of some resource r into equality with the set goal so that a positive excess e_r* occurs, the Pigou tax must in fact equal the unit penalty for such overshooting. Nor can the unit subsidy ever exceed the unit penalty for performance that falls short of the set goal. If it is not possible to push the supply of some resource r into equality with the set goal, so that some positive deficiency d_r* is left unattained, the subsidy must equal the unit penalty for such underperformance.

Exercise 7.2

Whaling occurs in two regions in the Antarctic. The distances (in miles) from hunting regions to ports are as follows:

	From Port A	From Port B
From Region #1	*2,000*	*1,750*
From Region #2	*3,000*	*2,500*

The transportation costs are $0.001 per mile and thousand pounds of processed whale meat.

There are two types of whaling boats, whalers and factory ships, each having its own specialized gear and equipment. Both types of boats process and freeze the catch onboard.

The input requirements per thousand pounds of whale meat are shown in the table below:

	Whalers	Factory Ships
Capital	*0.8*	*1.2*
Fuel	*1.0*	*0.5*
Labor	*1.0*	*0.8*

Region #1 is closer to both ports, but has been more heavily fished in the past, and greater efforts and more time have to be spent to catch a whale in this region. This is reflected in the unit costs per thousand pounds of whale meat, which are

	Region #1	Region #2
Capital	*$ 6.00*	*$ 5.00*
Fuel	*10.00*	*9.00*
Labor	*5.00*	*4.00*

The total demand for whale meat is 30,000 pounds in port A and 60,000 pounds in port B.

Environmental groups are concerned about the possible extinction of whales. A government agency has formulated goals for the total catch, amounting to 43,750 pounds in each hunting region.

The model-builder wants to consider two options: (1) the environmental concern is more urgent in region #1 than in region #2; therefore it is suggested to use penalties equal to $999 and $666 per thousand pounds caught above the set targets, in the two regions, respectively; (2) it is more important to conserve the whale in region #2 and the unit penalties should be set at $666 and $999, respectively.

Determine the optimal catch, the optimal distribution, and optimal prices.

Solution: Denote the catch by whalers and factory ships in the two regions by z_{h1} and z_{h2}, respectively, $h = 1,2$. The catch is measured in thousands of pounds of processed meat.

The total cost components are then as follows:

Capital costs:	$6(0.8z_{11} + 1.2z_{12}) + 5(0.8z_{21} + 1.2z_{22})$
Fuel costs:	$10(z_{11} + 0.5z_{12}) + 9(z_{21} + 0.5z_{22})$
Labor costs:	$5(z_{11} + 0.8z_{12}) + 4(z_{21} + 0.8z_{22})$
Transportation costs:	$2t_{1A} + 1.75t_{1B} + 3t_{2A} + 2.5t_{2B}$

Penalties (starting with option (i) mentioned in the text): $999e_1 + 666e_2$

The goal program will minimize total costs now formed subject to three sets of constraints, namely, first, that the demand at each port should be covered:

$$t_{1A} + t_{2A} \geq 30$$

$$t_{1B} + t_{2B} \geq 60$$

Second, the shipments from each hunting region cannot exceed the total volume of meat processed and frozen in the region:

$$z_{11} + z_{12} - t_{1A} - t_{1B} \geq 0$$

$$z_{21} + z_{22} - t_{2A} - t_{2B} \geq 0$$

Third, the definition of each goal:

$$z_{11} + z_{12} + d_1 - e_1 = 43.75$$

$$z_{21} + z_{22} + d_2 - e_2 = 43.75$$

Finally, all unknowns are non-negative.
Bringing together the entire program, we have

$$min\ 6(0.8z_{11} + 1.2z_{12}) + 5(0.8z_{21} + 1.2z_{22})$$
$$+ 10(z_{11} + 0.5z_{12}) + 9(z_{21} + 0.5z_{22}) + 5(z_{11} + 0.8z_{12})$$
$$+ 4(z_{21} + 0.8z_{22}) + 2t_{1A} + 1.75t_{1B} + 3t_{2A} + 2.5t_{2B}$$
$$+ 999e_1 + 666e_2$$

subject to

$$t_{1A} + t_{2A} \geq 30$$
$$t_{1B} + t_{2B} \geq 60$$
$$z_{11} + z_{12} - t_{1A} - t_{1B} \geq 0$$
$$z_{21} + z_{22} - t_{2A} - t_{2B} \geq 0$$
$$z_{11} + z_{12} + d_1 - e_1 = 43.75$$
$$z_{21} + z_{22} + d_2 - e_2 = 43.75$$
$$z,t,d,e \geq 0$$

The optimal solution in case (i) is illustrated in Figure 7.4. It turns out that factory ships should be used in both hunting regions, but no whalers. The optimal volume of processed and frozen whale meat in region #1 is 43,750; of this 30,000 is transported to port A and the remainder (13,750) to port B. The optimal volume of processed and frozen whale meat in region #2 is 46,250, all of which is shipped to port B.

The total catch in region #1 thus is kept within the desired limit. But the catch in region #2 exceeds the stipulated goal by 2,500 pounds. Penalties for this overhunting have to be paid in the program. The unit penalty in this region is $666. So, the most urgent goal has been met, but it was not possible at the same time to meet the goal with the second highest priority; it is being violated by the amount of 2,500. The total penalties assessed then are 2,500 x 666.

The optimal prices are illustrated in the lower panel in the figure. The price of processed and frozen whale meat calculated at the two hunting fields is 680.45 and 679.70, respectively. Adding in the unit transportation costs, the delivery prices in the two ports come out to be 682.45 and 682.20, respectively.

The optimal prices arise as follows. At the optimal solution, the goal laid down in region #2 is violated. The unit penalty is 666; hence, the price of whale meat in region #2 can be calculated as the sum of all input costs *plus* the penalty (the Pigou "tax"). The input costs, using factory ships in region #2 are

Capital	*5.00 x 1.2 = 6.00*
Fuel	*9.00 x 0.5 = 4.50*
Labor	*4.00 x 0.8 = 3.20*
Sum	*13.70*

The unit penalty is 666. The total price, including the penalty, then becomes 13.70 + 666.00 = 679.70.

Figure 7.4. Optimal Solution to Exercise 7.2

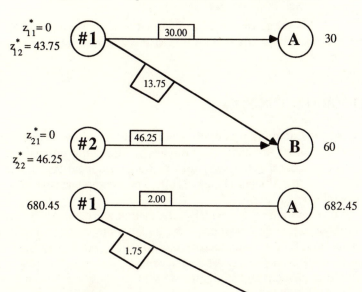

Upper panel: Quantity solution, in thousands of pounds. Flags indicate optimal shipments. **Lower panel:** Price solution. Flags indicate unit transportation costs.

Even if the penalty is formally levied on the operators of the vessels, we see that the *incidence* of the penalty is different: it is just passed on to the ensuing links in the entire distribution network. Ultimately the consumer pays all accumulated unit costs.

It is instructive to compare the solution now discussed with the corresponding solution to case (ii). The priorities have now been switched, and region #2 is considered to be the more sensitive one. The optimal solution still involves only factory ships, but the amount of whale meat processed in region #1 is this time increased up 46,250. Of this, 30,000 is shipped to port A and 16,250 is shipped to port B. The amount of whale meat processed in region #2 can then be lowered to 43,750, which is shipped to B.

The total catch in region #2 is now kept within the desired limit. But this time there is overhunting in region #1 instead. The additional 2,500 pounds required to fill consumer demand are obtained in region #1 rather than in region #2.

NOTE

1.   This suggestion must be credited to G. L.Thompson. Research in these matters is currently underway. Also see comments in the numerical exercise below.

BIBLIOGRAPHIC NOTES

Goal programming was developed by Charnes, Cooper, and Ferguson [3] in 1955 in order to handle the problem of estimating optimal executive compensation under a variety of policy and organizational constraints. (See further Charnes and Cooper [1], pp. 210ff. For a comprehensive survey, see Charnes and Cooper [2].)

Goal programming is a widely used method for dealing with problems of multiple objective optimization when the latter are stated as goals. Later, other techniques of multiobjective optimization were suggested in the operations research literature. The advantage of goal programming is that it is simple to implement and straightforward in its interpretation. It is ideally suited to handle situations where the decision maker considers an entire hierarchy of goals. The ranking (the relative priority) of the goals is then established through the numerical values of the penalties levied on deviations from the goals.

In the modern world, the decision-making problem of consumers and managers is complex, involving choices between conflicting objectives. Goal programming offers an opportunity to breathe new realism into the formalism of neoclassical theory by replacing models of single-objective optimization by an analysis of the possible optimal attainment of a hierarchy of goals.

Applications include land-use economics (Ryan [13]), manpower planning (Charnes, Cooper, and Niehaus [4], [5], and planning models for the social, demographic, and economic development of an entire country (Charnes, Kirby, and Walters [10]). For a goal programming study of activity analysis, see Charnes, Duffuaa, and Al-Saffar [9].

Ryan showed how it was possible to establish the optimal solution of land use, and thus to simulate the workings of the goaling formulation, by a system of property taxes and unit subsidies. The taxes and the subsidies were obtained as the evaluators (dual variables) of the goaling relations.

A systematic treatment of the possibility of establishing the optimal solution to goal programming and goal focusing by means of Pigou taxes is provided in [11].

The technique of goal focusing was developed in three publications involving Charnes and Cooper as principal authors (see [6], [7], and [8]). The concept of goal focusing is directly tied to efficiency, in that "goal focusing seeks the closest 'efficient point' instead of only the 'closest point' to the specified goals" ([7], p. 436). In [8], efficiency was defined with respect to a system of household production technologies. Efficiency in [7] related to maximal economy to be attained in a system of intergenerational transfers of income (such as social security).

REFERENCES

[7.1]   Charnes, A. A. and W. W. Cooper. *Management Models and Industrial Applications of Linear Programming*. New York: Wiley, New York, 1961.

[7.2]   Charnes, A., and W. W. Cooper. "Goal Programming and Multiple Objective Optimizations," *European Journal of Operational Research* 1 (1977): 39–54.

[7.3]   Charnes, A., W. W. Cooper, and R. O. Ferguson. "Optimal Estimation of Executive Compensation by Linear Programming," *Management Science* (Jan. 1955): 138–51.

[7.4]   Charnes, A., W. W. Cooper, and R. J. Niehaus. *Studies in Manpower Planning*. Washington, D.C.: Office of Civilian Manpower Management, 1972.

[7.5]   Charnes, A., W.W. Cooper and R.J. Niehaus, "Dynamic Multiattribute Models for Mixed Manpower Systems," *Naval Research Logistics Quarterly* (June 1975): 205–20.

[7.6]   Charnes, A., W. W. Cooper, J. J. Rousseau and A. Schinnar. "A Goal Focusing Extension for Intergenerational Transfer of Income." In *Production of Well-Being*, ed. N. E. Terleckyj. Washington, D. C.: National Planning Association, 1981.

[7.7]   Charnes, A., W. W. Cooper, J. J. Rousseau, and A. Schinnar. "A Goal Focusing Approach to Analysis of Intergenerational Transfers of Income," *International Journal of Systems Sciences* 17/3 (1986): 433–46.

[7.8]   Charnes, A., W. W. Cooper, A. P. Schinnar, and N. E. Terleckyj. "A Goal Focusing Approach to Analysis of Trade-Offs among Household Production Outputs," *American Statistical Association 1979 Proceedings of the Social Statistics Section*, pp. 194–99.

[7.9]   Charnes, A., S. Duffuaa, and A. Al-Saffar. "A Dynamic Goal Programming Model for Planning Food Self-sufficiency in the Middle East," *Applied Mathematical Modelling* 13 (Feb. 1989): 86–93.

[7.10]   Charnes, A., M. J. L. Kirby, and A. S. Walters. "Horizon Models for Social Development," *Management Science* 17/4 (Dec. 1970): B165–B177.

[7.11]   Charnes, A., and S. Thore. "Goal Focusing by Pigou Taxes and Subsidies," forthcoming.

[7.12]   Pigou, A. C. *The Economics of Welfare.* 4th ed. London: Macmillan, 1952.

[7.13]   Ryan, M. J. "A Goal Programming Approach to Land Use Economics, Planning and Regulation", Ph.D. Thesis, University of Texas at Austin, 1974.

8

Rigid Prices and/or Rigid Wages

Up to this point, we have dealt rather superficially with the concept of economic markets and the formation of equilibrium. The standard assumption has been that markets are free and unconstrained so that they will clear at all times, that is,

demand ≤ supply, price (demand – supply) = 0

If the mathematical solution to the model yields a positive price, demand must equal supply. If demand deviates from supply, the price must have dropped to zero.

Disequilibrium occurs when the price is rigid or constrained so that the market is prevented from clearing. Demand can then deviate from supply even at a positive market price. As empirical illustrations one may cite rent control, continuing unemployment, and government stockpiling of excess agricultural produce.

Consider the latter case. Suppose that the Department of Agriculture imposes a minimum price on wheat. If there is a bumper crop, the government buys the excess supply rather than allowing wheat prices to fall. Now, is there really disequilibrium in this market? Would it perhaps not be more correct to say that the private demand *plus* government demand exactly matches supply, and that the result of the price support program is that equilibrium is established at the minimum price? In order to answer this question, it is important to remember the difference between ex ante plans and ex post realizations with possible discrepancies between plans and actual outcomes. In equilibrium, all economic agents realize their plans and the ex ante concepts become identical with ex post concepts (planned demand = actual purchases; planned supply = actual deliveries).[1] But when a market is in disequilibrium, not all agents can realize their plans. At an enforced minimum price, the total wheat that farmers want to sell in the market may exceed the consumers' desired purchases. There is then an excess supply in the market that the consumers do not want to buy. This ex ante dilemma is resolved by the government stepping in ex post, absorbing the surplus in the market. The total quantity purchased in the market equals the quantity sold ex post; the ex ante market gap has been wiped out by the government stepping into the market ex post.

Rigidities may be introduced into a market from the outside in the form of government price controls or they may arise internally as consumers and producers fail to respond or respond only slowly to changing market conditions.

In particular, rigidities in the labor markets have been much discussed by economists. As is well known, there is no consensus among economists about the nature of unemployment. The new classical macroeconomists argue that wages are flexible and that labor markets are always cleared. According to this school of thought, there exists no involuntary unemployment. We do not share this view. To us, involuntary unemployment is an empirical fact that needs to be explained. Nominal wages sometimes fail to fall to the level where markets would be cleared. Nominal wages are "sticky downwards."

Several economic theories are able to produce such rigidities in labor markets. For good recent surveys, see C. L. Schultze [15] and R. M. Solow [17]. A common denominator for much of this theoretical thinking is the emphasis on the existence of so-called implicit contracts between employers and employees. During an act of employment, an association of some duration is set up between the employer and the employee and both parties have some interest in the continuitity of this relation. Workers acquire nontransferable, firm-specific skills and knowledge about the nonwage attributes of a job through experience on that job. Transition, search and moving costs are incurred by both workers and employers when the association is broken.

Within the framework of a conventional model of comparative statics with full certainty, such wage rigidity takes the form of a wage floor, beneath which the wage cannot fall.

The production and distribution models that have occupied us so far will presently be extended to the case of disequilibrium caused by direct controls or rigidities. It will be seen that the mathematical procedures that we are now familiar with transcend equilibrium and extend to disequilibrium situations as well.

The obvious and direct way of dealing with price constraints is to write the price formulation of the programming model of the production and distribution system under consideration, and to adjoin the price constraints to it.

In many applications, it is desired to adhere throughout to the quantity formulation. How is it then possible to account for the presence of price constraints? As we have seen, each price in the quantity formulation can be obtained as the optimal value of the Lagrange multiplier of the corresponding market restriction. Mathematically, the presence of price constraints means that the optimization problem includes constraints on both the direct and the dual variables.

Fortunately, there exists a simple programming procedure that is capable of handling the situation. A simple modification of the quantity formulation takes care of the presence of upper and lower limits on one or several prices.

In order to illustrate further the scope of the disequilibrium methods, we shall discuss Koopmans' activity analysis in the presence of price constraints in the markets for primary goods. The supply of each primary good may be responsive to its price and the supply curve forward-sloping so that a higher price of the good calls forth a greater supply. The market price of the primary good, however, will be taken to be sticky downward, by which is meant that there exists a price floor below which the price cannot fall.

Rigidities in the labor markets have already been mentioned. The markets of many other production factors may be rigid too, in particular the markets for real capital. Markets for existing real capital (such as furnaces in the steel industry or shipyards in the shipbuilding industry) are typically both thin (there are few transactions) and shallow (there is a large spread between the asked price and the bid price). In the face of weakening demand and falling prices of real capital, neoclassical adjustment would require managers to sell off some portion of their stock of real capital. They would realize some portion of the capital losses that have been suffered. But in the real world, managers have a psychological resistance against realizing capital losses. The market price of existing furnaces or shipyards is sticky downward. At the ruling price, there will instead develop some unused capacity (excess supply of capital).

The study of disequilibrium in economics goes back to work carried out by Swedish economists in the 1920s (Lindahl [9]); this work has recently experienced a renaissance in the hands of modern mathematical economists belonging to the French school led by Drèze [5], Malinvaud [10] and others. Here, we shall touch only indirectly upon these and similar works. Our attention will be limited to the study of ex ante market gaps (excess demand or excess supply, as the case may be) rather than a full-fledged dynamic analysis over time.

SYMBOLS USED IN CHAPTER 8

$h, k \in H$	regions
$i \in I$	final goods and services
$r \in R$	resources
$m \in M$	activities
x_h	demand
w_h, w_r	supply
p_h, p_i	price of consumer good
$\underline{p}_h, \overline{p}_h$	lower and upper bound on price of consumer good
$D_h(p_h), S_h(p_h)$	demand and supply functions, respectively
$P_h(x_h), Q_h(w_h)$	demand price function, supply price function
t_{hk}	quantity transported from region h to region k
c_{hk}	unit transportation cost
d_h, d_r	excess supply
e_h, e_r	excess demand
$A = [a_{rm}]$	matrix of input coefficients
$B = [b_{im}]$	matrix of output coefficients
z_m	level of operation of activity m
$\overline{z}_m$	upper limit on level of operations
z_{dm}	excess capacity of activity m
q_r	Lagrange multiplier of resource balance
$\underline{q}_r, \overline{q}_r,$	lower and upper bound on resource price
s_m	Lagrange multiplier of capacitating condition

8.1   SPATIAL DISEQUILIBRIUM: A PRICE FORMULATION

Price rigidities and controls may distort the allocative efficiency of the market system. When the invisible hand of Adam Smith works, a high price accompanied by excess demand indicates a shortage; it will stimulate an increased supply. A low price accompanied by excess supply indicates a glut; it will discourage supply. But when prices are rigid and no longer respond to the market mechanism, they will in general transmit distorted information. A minimum price may prevent a local price from falling and will thus mask the need to cut supply; a maximum price may prevent a local price from rising and will mask the need to increase supply.

For an introductory diagrammatical discussion of this subject, turn to figures 8.1 and 8.2. They illustrate the market behavior for some hypothetical good in two different regions $h = 1,2$. With no trade between the regions (autarchy), and no impediments to equilibrium, a low price would have been established in region #1 and a considerably higher price in region #2. With trade and with no hindrance to free market formation, the price gap would be equal to the unit transportation cost of sending goods from region #1 to region #2.

In figure 8.1 it is assumed that a minimum price is established in region #1 which lifts the price in the region above the equilibrium level. The disequilibrium solution can then be constructed diagrammatically in the following fashion. The price in region #2 must equal $\underline{p}_1 + c_{12}$, where c_{12} is the unit cost of shipping goods from region #1 to region #2 (assuming that positive shipments will occur). Since prices are free to move in region #2, a local equilibrium will be established at that price as shown in the right-hand portion of figure 8.1. The total supply curve in region #2 (local supply plus in-shipments) must therefore intersect the demand curve at this price. One can then read the amount of in-shipments into the region from the diagram (the quantity t_{12}). In other words, we now know the amount of shift of the local supply curve to the right. Returning to the corresponding diagram for region #1, the supply curve here must have been shifted by the same amount to the left. The excess supply can be read off the diagram. The end result is quite sensible, of course. The good is shipped out of the region where the price floor has generated a glut and into the region where it has created a shortage.

Figure 8.1. Adjustments in the Face of a Minimum Price

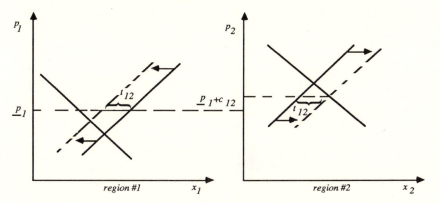

An emerging excess supply is partially wiped out by shipments into the region.

Turn now to figure 8.2. This time a minimum price is established in region #2 . The diagrammatical construction proceeds as before. The price in region #1 will be $\underline{p}_2 - c_{21}$, and it is assumed that prices in the region are free to move to this level. The local demand curve and the total supply curve (local supply minus out-shipments) in region #1 must then intersect at this price, and one can read off the amount of in-shipments into the region from the diagram (the quantity t_{21}). Shifting the local supply curve in region #2 to the right by the same distance, there is an increased excess supply in region #2. On the surface of it, the result seems quite unreasonable. It is bad enough that an original excess supply of goods piled up in region #2 in the face of the minimum price. But with the opening up of interregional trade, even more goods are shipped to region #2, adding to the existing supply there. What is the purpose of rerouting goods which perfectly well could have been sold in region #1 to another region where they will not be sold?

Figure 8.2.   Adjustments in the Face of a Minimum Price

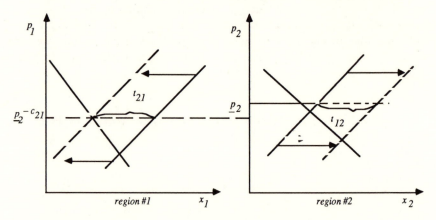

An emerging excess supply is aggravated by shipments into the region.

The answer to this question is that the movement of goods responds to price differentials. The high price in regions #2 attracts goods to the region, regardless of whether they will actually be sold or just stored. The high price in region #2 is a false market signal and it induces false adjustment. The fact that there is already an excess supply in that region does not deter the additional shipments into it.

Thus prepared, we now turn to the general case involving the marketing of a good in a number of regions, say the regions h with h belonging to the set of regions H. The point of departure is the price formulation of spatial equilibrium, outlined in section 6.1. There is a local (partial) demand function $D_h(p_h)$ and a local (partial) supply function $S_h(p_h)$ in each region h. They are non-negative and differentiable, and each demand function is nondecreasing. The price p_h to be quoted in each region h is unknown, to be determined.

The economic potential function to be used is the same as before (to be referred to, if so desired, as indirect social payoff).

$$(8.1) \qquad \sum_{h \in H} \{-\int D_h(p_h)dp_h + \int S_h(p_h)dp_h\}$$

It is formed by summing the negative of all integrated demand functions and summing all integrated supply functions.

In principle, the commodity may be shipped from any one region h to any other region k. The price appreciation resulting from such a shipment equals $p_k - p_h$. A shipper will compare this price appreciation with the attendant unit transportation cost c_{hk}. The conventional no-profit condition reads

$$(8.2) \qquad p_k - p_h \leq c_{hk}, \ h, \ k \in H$$

In addition, let the price in each region be constrained by the presence of an upper limit (a price ceiling) and a lower limit (a price floor):

$$(8.3) \qquad \underline{p}_h \leq p_h \leq \overline{p}_h, \ h \in H$$

As has already been explained at some length, these limits express the idea that prices are rigid and may only vary within some given interval.[2] The origin of such rigidity may be that the price is controlled by government or some other intervening agency, or that prices respond slowly and incompletely to changing conditions.

Price constraints of type (8.3) also arise in the case of goods that are traded internationally; the price of a good that can be produced either domestically or imported from abroad cannot rise above the import price, and the price of a good that can be either sold domestically or exported cannot fall short of the export price. In other words, world market prices set limits on domestic prices.

The entire programming model now reads

$$(8.4) \qquad min \sum_{h \in H} \{-\int D_h(p_h)dp_h + \int S_h(p_h)dp_h\}$$

subject to

$$p_h - p_k \geq -c_{hk}$$

$$p_h \geq \underline{p}_h$$

$$-p_h \geq -\overline{p}_h$$

$$h,k \in H$$

The objective in this program is to maximize total social payoff, net of transportation costs, subject to a market constraint and the indicated supply limitations, in each regions.

Denote the Lagrange multipliers of the three sets of constraints by t_{hk}, d_h, and e_h, respectively. They are to be non-negative.

The Kuhn–Tucker conditions require the following results to hold at a point of optimum:

(i)   If the price ceiling in a region is binding, there will occur an excess demand. If the price floor is binding, there will occur an excess supply. But if the price in a region falls between the ceiling and the floor, the market in that region will be in equilibrium.

For one finds

$$(8.5) \qquad \sum_{k \in H} (t_{hk}^* - t_{kh}^*) + d_h^* - e_h^* = -D_h(p_h^*) + S_h(p_h^*)$$

Hence, the expression $d_h^* - e_h^*$ simply equals supply (local supply plus net in-shipments) minus demand in each region. Indeed, d_h^* is simply the excess supply (if any) in the region, and e_h^* equals the excess demand. To see this, note that

$$(8.6a) \qquad p_h^* \geq \underline{p}_h , d_h^*(p_h^* - \underline{p}_h) = 0, h \in H$$

$$(8.6b) \qquad -p_h{}^* \geq - \overline{P}_h \,, e_h{}^*(-p_h{}^* + \overline{P}_h\,) = 0, h \in H$$

If the price ceiling in a region is binding, then the floor is presumably slack.[3] Equation (8.6a) shows that $d_h{}^* = 0$ and there is a non-negative excess demand in the region equal to $e_h{}^*$. If the price floor is binding, then (8.6b) shows that $e_h{}^* = 0$ and there is a non-negative excess supply in the region equal to $d_h{}^*$. If neither the ceiling nor the floor is binding, both $d_h{}^*$ and $e_h{}^*$ vanish, and there is equilibrium in the region.

Following a long-standing tradition in dynamic economic theory, one might at this point assume that consumers always realize their purchase plans.[4] Any excess demand would then be supplied by running down producer inventories or would be covered by imports. Any excess supply would be stored or exported.

No such assumption about the outcome ex post is made here. Program (8.4) determines quantities and prices ex ante, including the ex ante gaps in those consumer markets where there will be disequilibrium. However, the program does not determine how those gaps will eventually be resolved ex post.

(ii)   If positive shipments of the commodity occur from one region to another, the price appreciation between the two regions must equal the unit shipping cost. But if the price appreciation falls short of the unit shipping cost, no shipments occur.

For one obtains

$$(8.7) \qquad p_h{}^* - p_k{}^* \geq -c_{hk}$$

$$t_{hk}{}^* \,(p_h{}^* - p_k{}^* + c_{hk}) = 0$$

$$h, k \in H$$

8.2 PRICE RIGIDITIES: A QUANTITY FORMULATION

Economists have been slow in analyzing spatial market problems under disequilibrium. One would have thought that analysis of this type would abound, because of examples such as support prices for farmers in agriculture, tiered price structures, and so on. The energy sector would seem to constitute another inviting example, with regulation of natural gas and the like. Finally, there is the analysis of various sectors of the labor market in the face of minimum wages and wage rigidity.

One reason for this lack of application may be that the price formulation is not very helpful for practical work. It is difficult to limit the modeling work to price constraints alone. Often, there are limits on the physical quantities shipped between the various links of the transportation network (sec. 3.3). The price formulation—in equilibrium or in disequilibrium—cannot handle the presence of quantity constraints.

In order to improve this situation, a new quantity formulation of price disequilibrium will be presented here. Starting from Samuelson's model of spatial equilibrium in quantity variables, we shall add quantity unknowns which are designed to produce the desired constraints on the Lagrange multipliers (the regional market prices).

Once again the starting point is Samuelson's simple spatial model of equilibrium as presented in program (3.8). Now, however, that model is to be altered so that the Lagrange multipliers of the market constraints in the various regions—the prices p_h—satisfy the bounding conditions (8.3). In other words, we want to impose a priori constraints which these Lagrange multipliers must meet. If it happens that the bounds on prices remain slack at the point of optimum of program (3.8), the previous solutions will continue to apply and all markets will remain in equilibrium. But if one or several of the bounds (8.3) turn out to be binding, the equilibrium obtained from the unaltered Samuelson model will be violated.

We face a problem of nonlinear programming with constraints on both the direct and the dual side. The obvious mathematical representation of such a problem is as a saddle-point problem with constraints on both the direct (max) side and the dual (min) side. We shall eventually provide such representation. In the meantime, however, there is something much more exciting to show. There actually exists a simple quantity formulation that incorporates the presence of the price bounds directly. How is this possible?

Rather than featuring the postulated price bounds explicitly, we adjust the quantity formulation so that the Kuhn–Tucker conditions deliver the desired price bounds. The first step of the required modification of the quantity formulation should be obvious enough. As stated, the market constraints in each region can no longer be expected to be satisfied exactly; instead, there may occur in each region an excess demand or an excess supply.

Now consider the amended quantity formulation

$$(8.8) \qquad max \sum_{h \in H} \{ \int P_h(x_h)dx_h - \int Q_h(w_h)dw_h + \mathcal{P}_h d_h \, \overline{P}_h \, e_h \}$$

$$- \sum_{h \in H} \sum_{k \, \in \, H} c_{hk} t_{hk}$$

subject to

$$x_h - w_h - \sum_{k \in H}(t_{kh} - t_{hk}) + d_h - e_h = 0$$

$$x_h, w_h, t_{hk}, d_h, e_h \geq 0$$

$$h, k \in H$$

Rather than stating the postulated price constraints explicitly, this program contains two new unknowns, d and e. Inspecting the constraints, we see that d_h denotes a possible excess supply in region h; e_h denotes a possible excess demand. (Note that the optimal d_h^* and e_h^* cannot both be positive at the same time. For, per contra, if that were the case, then it would be possible to increase the value of the maximand by subtracting some small positive constant from them both.)

As we shall see in a moment, the price bounds (8.3) are implied by the Kuhn–Tucker conditions corresponding to the new variables d and e.

The contribution to social payoff in region h now contains an additional nonnegative term representing the value of a possible excess supply, and an additional nonpositive term representing the value of a possible excess demand.

What is the rationale behind those two new terms appearing in the economic potential function? One formal answer is that these are the very terms that are required in order to enable us to recover the bounding conditions (8.3) from the Kuhn–Tucker conditions of program (8.8). So program (8.8) is just a mathematical artifact that happens to produce the desired conditions on the dual side.

A second answer is obtained if one looks at the contribution to the economic potential by demand and supply separately. The contribution from demand in each region is

$$\int P_h(x_h)dx_h - \overline{P}_h \, e_h$$

that is, the part of demand that can actually be met in the market. The value of the excess demand is not included. And the contribution from supply is (the negative of)

$$\int Q_h(w_h)dw_h - \underline{P}_h \, d_h$$

that is, only the part of supply that is actually absorbed in the market is included. The value of the excess supply is not included.

Yet a third answer is that program (8.8) may be looked upon as an instance of goal programming, where each local market may or may not clear, but where the goal has been laid down that the excess demand in each market be zero. A possible underperformance relative to the goal at location h is denoted d_h; a possible overperformance relative to the goal is denoted e_h. (This was indeed the notation used in chap. 7, and the reader should now understand why the same notation has been chosen for the present chapter as well.) The unit penalty to be assessed for underperformance is the price floor $\underline{p}_h$; the penalty for overperformance is the price ceiling $\overline{p}_h$.

Turn now to the solution of program (8.8). Denote the Lagrange multiplier of each constraint by p_h. Let the market price quoted in each region be p_h^* (the asterisk indicates that the value of the multiplier should be calculated at the optimal point).

As we shall see, the Kuhn–Tucker conditions will supply the desired price constraints and other conditions characterizing disequilibrium. Specifically, the following conditions must be satisfied at the point of optimum:

(i)   The market in each region may fail to clear. If the price ceiling in the region is binding, there will occur an excess demand. If the price floor is binding, there will occur an excess supply. But if the price in the region falls between the ceiling and the floor, there will be equilibrium in that region.

For one finds

$$(8.9) \qquad x_h^* - w_h^* - \sum_{k \in H} (t_{kh}^* - t_{hk}^*) + d_h^* - e_h^* = 0, \, h \in H$$

Noting that $x_h^* = D_h(p_h^*)$ and $w_h^* = S_h(p_h^*)$, we have here simply recouped equation (8.5).

Further, there is a set of Kuhn–Tucker conditions recovering relations (8.6a–b) which show that the price constraints (8.3) must indeed be satisfied at the point of optimum, and also that the optimal value d_h^* denotes a possible excess supply and that the optimal e_h^* denotes a possible excess demand.

Next, recovering (8.7),

(ii)   Regional prices can differ at most by the unit cost of shipping the good from one region to another. If positive shipments occur, the price differential assumes this maximum.

Finally, just as in section 3.2:

(iii) In each region consumers and suppliers are all adjusted in the following sense. The demand price cannot exceed the market price. The market price cannot exceed the supply price. If a positive quantity of the good is sold, these three prices are all equal.

For one finds

$$(8.10) \qquad p_h{}^* \geq P_h(x_h{}^*),\ x_h{}^*(p_h{}^* - P_h(x_h{}^*)) = 0,\ h \in H$$

$$- p_h{}^* \geq - Q_h(w_h{}^*),\ w_h{}^*(-p_h{}^* + Q_h(w_h{}^*)) = 0,\ h \in H$$

(If in a region there is a positive demand but the market price falls short of the supply price, there will be no local supply and the demand is entirely covered by net in-shipments. If there is a positive supply but the demand price falls short of the market price, there can be no local demand, and all local supply is shipped out of the region. If both the market price falls short of the supply price and the demand price falls short of the market price, there is neither demand nor supply in the region.)

With some reinterpretation and simplification, program (8.8) may be used to solve for disequilibrium in one single market. Let the index h refer to different individuals present in a marketplace, rather than different regions. Then reinterpret the notation as follows:

x_h *demand of individual h*

w_h *supply of individual h*

Demand and supply are non-negative; if $x_h > 0$ and $w_h = 0$ the individual is a buyer only; if $x_h = 0$ and $w_h > 0$ the individual is a seller only. Further

$P_h(x_h)$ *the demand price function of individual h*

$Q_h(w_h)$ *the supply price function of individual h*

Putting all c_{hk} and all t_{hk} identically equal to zero, program (8.8) will then solve for price disequilibrium in this single market.

Exercise 8.1

The iceberg lettuce growers of California employ migrant farm workers for harvesting purposes. The total demand for labor is 2.0 (measured in tens of thousands of workers).

Migrant farm workers arrive from three different regions; the local supply wage functions are (in thousands of dollars earned by one worker during the harvesting season)

$$Region \#1 \quad 0.9 \, (w_1)^2$$
$$Region \#2 \quad (w_2)^2$$
$$Region \#3 \quad 1.2 \, (w_3)^2$$

where w_h is the quantity of labor supplied in region h. However, if the wage falls below 0.95, the migrant farm workers will withdraw from the market (0.95 is the reservation wage).

Travel costs from each region to the harvesting fields are as follows:

$$From \; region \; \#1 \quad 0.4$$
$$From \; region \; \#2 \quad 0.3$$
$$From \; region \; \#3 \quad 0.5$$

Determine the optimal allocations of workers, the market wage, and the possible unemployment of workers.

Solution. In this simple example, there is no local demand in regions #1–3, only supply. Denoting California as region #4, there is no local supply in region #4, only a vertical demand curve.

Social payoff is formed by adding the integrated demand functions and subtracting the integrated supply functions giving, in the present case, simply

$$-0.3 \, w_1^3 - 0.33 \, w_2^3 - 0.4 \, w_3^3$$

Total transportation costs are $0.4 \, t_{14} + 0.3 \, t_{24} + 0.5 \, t_{34}$. Inserting into program (8.8) one has

$$max \; -0.3 \, w_1^3 - 0.33 \, w_2^3 - 0.4 \, w_3^3 - 0.4 \, t_{14} - 0.3 \, t_{24} - 0.5 \, t_{34} + 0.95 \, d_4$$

subject to

$$-w_1 + t_{14} \leq 0$$
$$-w_2 + t_{24} \leq 0$$
$$-w_3 + t_{34} \leq 0$$
$$2.0 - t_{14} - t_{24} - t_{34} + d_4 = 0$$
$$w_1, w_2, w_3, t_{14}, t_{24}, t_{34}, d_4 \geq 0$$

The possible unemployment in California is denoted d_4. The objective function includes the value of the possible excess supply of labor in California. There is one market constraint for labor in each region.

The numerical solution is exhibited in figure 8.3. The supply of labor from the three regions is 0.782, 0.810, and 0.612, respectively, adding up to a total of 2.204. However, only 2,000 will be employed, and the remainder—0.204—will not be able to find work.

Figure 8.3. Optimal Solution to Exercise 8.1

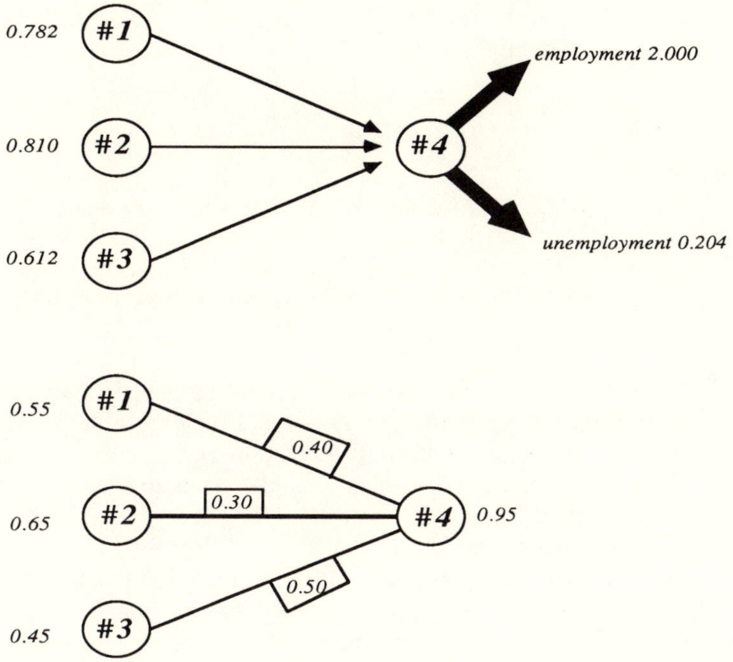

Upper panel: Quantity solution. Lower panel: Price solution.

The solution gross wage is identical with the minimum wage (0.95). The net take-home pay after travel costs is 0.55, 0.65, and 0.45, respectively.

As discussed in section 8.1, the price signals in disequilibrium do not convey correct information about relative scarcities and cause inefficient adjustment. In the present instance, some workers in all three regions are induced to move to California (and to pay the attendant transportation costs) only to find upon arrival that no work is available to them.

It is easy to prove that the price formulation and the quantity formulation of spatial disequilibrium are equivalent.

As in chapter 6, the technical tool for the required demonstration is the Kuhn–Tucker equivalence theorem (theorem 2.2). Consider first an optimal solution pair to (8.4), say $(p^*; t^*, d^*, e^*)$ and define also $x^* = D(p^*)$ and $w^* = S(p^*)$. As pointed out already, the * point satisfies all the Kuhn–Tucker conditions of the quantity formulation (8.8). The saddle-point program corresponding to (8.8) reads

$$(8.11) \quad \max_{x,w,t,d,e} \; \min_{p} \; \sum_{h \in H} \{ \int P_h(x_h)dx_h - \int Q_h(w_h)dw_h + \underline{p}_h d_h $$

$$ - \overline{P}_h \, e_h \} - \sum_{h \in H} \sum_{k \in H} c_{hk} t_{hk} $$

$$ + \sum_{h \in H} p_h(-x_h + w_h + \sum_{k \in H} (t_{kh} - t_{hk}) - d_h + e_h) $$

subject to x, w, t, d, e ≥ 0, p unrestricted in sign

The situation now is that we have a point $(z^*, w^*, t^*, d^*, e^*; \; p^*)$, a mathematical program—program (8.8)—and a saddle-point problem—problem (8.11). The point satisfies all the Kuhn–Tucker conditions of the program. Hence, by theorem 2.3, it is a saddle point to the saddle-point problem. And so, by theorem 2.2, $(x^*, w^*, t^*, d^*, e^*)$ is an optimal solution to the mathematical program (8.8).

Conversely, consider an optimal solution pair to the quantity formulation (8.8), say $(s\#, w\#, t\#, d\#, e\#; p\#)$. Starting from program (8.8) and its accompanying Kuhn–Tucker conditions, we have recovered the direct constraints and the Kuhn–Tucker conditions of the *price* formulation. The saddle-point program corresponding to (8.4) reads

$$(8.12) \quad \max_{t,d,e} \; \min_{p} \; \sum_{h \in H} \{ -\int D_h(p_h)dp_h + S_h(p_h)dp_h \} $$

$$ + \sum_{h \in H} \sum_{k \in H} t_{hk}(-p_h + p_k - c_{hk}) $$

$$ + \sum_{h \in H} \{ d_h(\underline{p}_h - p_h) + e_h(-\overline{P}_h + p_h) \} $$

subject to t,d,e ≥ 0, p unrestricted in sign

Using theorem 2.3, it follows that *(t#, d#, e#; p#)* is a saddle point to (8.12). Hence, by the equivalence theorem, theorem 2.2, *p#* is an optimal solution to program (8.4). In sum, the quantity formulation (8.8) and the price formulation (8.4) are logically equivalent.

As a matter of fact, an even stronger proposition holds true: not only are the two saddle points (8.11) and (8.12) equivalent, but the two saddle functions themselves are actually equivalent, and the one can be transformed into the other by a change of variables (see sec. 6.1).

A Fundamental Saddle-Point Principle

Is it just a mathematical coincidence that there exist two different mathematical programs—the price formulation and the quantity formulation—that are both capable of solving the disequilibrium problem at hand? Or is there some more general mathematical principle at work here?

In order to shed some light on this question, we shall briefly probe a little deeper into the mathematical underpinnings of the two formulations, demonstrating that there exists an underlying simple saddle-point principle from which both formulations flow.

In order to review the argument ab ovo, let us return for a moment to Samuelson's original model of spatial equilibrium, program (3.8). Consider the Lagrangean

$$(8.13) \qquad L(x,w,t) = \sum_{h \in H} \{ \int P_h(x_h)dx_h - \int Q_h(w_h)dw_h \}$$

$$- \sum_{h \in H} \sum_{k \in H} c_{hk}t_{hk} + \sum_{h \in H} p_h(-x_h + w_h + \sum_{k \in H} (t_{kh}-t_{hk}))$$

The saddle-point problem

$$(8.14) \qquad \max_{x,w,t} \quad \min_{p} \quad L(x,w,t) \qquad \text{subject to } x,w,t \geq 0 \text{ and } p \geq 0$$

solves the spatial equilibrium economy.

The equilibrium prices in local markets are found as the optimal values of the Lagrange multipliers p^*.

Now consider the corresponding constrained saddle-point problem, where prices are required a priori to satisfy the constraints (8.3). Consider the constrained saddle-point problem

(8.15) $\underset{x,w,t}{max}$ $\underset{p}{min}$ $L(x,w,t)$

subject to x, w, t ≥ 0 and $\bar{p} \geq p \geq \underline{p}$

This time the Lagrange multipliers are no longer permitted to be varied freely but are required to fall within the specified bounds.

To repeat, program (8.15) is formed by writing the Lagrangean to the given equilibrium problem and modifying it by the additional imposition of the given price bounds. In general, the Lagrange multipliers will then be prevented from assuming their equilibrium values and must instead be determined so that they obey the bounding conditions laid down. The original equilibrium economy is converted into a disequilibrium one.

The formulation (8.15) is the common underlying principle that we have been looking for, and both the price formulation (8.4) *and* the quantity formulation (8.8) follow from this saddle program.

It would take us too far here to establish these equivalences formally; the interested reader may consult the references provided in the bibliographic notes. However, the following general comments may be offered.

First, it has to be established that the saddle-point program (8.15) actually has a saddle point, which is by no means obvious. The Kuhn–Tucker theorem no longer assists us in this matter.

The objective function is continuous and concave-convex. The constraint set on the max side is convex and closed. But it is not necessarily bounded. The constraint set on the min side is convex, closed, and bounded. Does it follow that a saddle point exists? The answer is in the affirmative; the desired result follows from extensions of the von Neumann minimax theorem.[5]

As far as the issue of equivalence, the following results can be established: $(x^*,w^*,t^*;p^*)$ is a saddle point to (8.15) if and only if there exist non-negative d^* and e^* so that $(x^*,w^*,t^*d^*,e^*; p^*)$ is a saddle point to (8.11). The point p^* then solves the price formulation (8.4) and the point (x^*,w^*,t^*,d^*,e^*) solves the quantity formulation (8.8).

So, the biextremal problem (8.15) has two uniextremal equivalents: one maximization problem (8.4) an one minimization problem (8.8). It is no mathematical accident that such equivalence obtains. As shown by A. Charnes [3] and further elaborated by A. Charnes, P. R. Gribik, and K. O. Kortanek [4], when dealing with saddle-point problems that are constrained on both sides, it is the normal state of affairs that the saddle-point problem has two uniextremal equivalents, one max problem and one min problem. Each of these two employs additional variables stemming from the constraints and the objective function of the other. Neither problem requires any information on the other problem's optimal solution. In this sense, the problems are completely separable, and each problem has its own interpretation.

Extensions

The observant reader will immediately see how the disequilibrium format (8.8) can be extended to related spatial models such as those discussed in section 3.3 (spatial networks, the generalized transportation model). Rather than going over the details of the mathematics again, it should suffice here to point out the general principle for converting an equilibrium optimization model to a corresponding optimization model with price rigidities: (1) rewrite the market balances so that they allow for the possibility of both an excess demand and an excess supply in each market at the ruling set of prices to be determined; (2) amend the objective function, adding the value of all excess supply to a maximand and deducting the value of all excess demand (in the case of minimization, the direction of these operations has to be reversed); (3) the new unknown variables representing possible excess supply and excess demand in each market have to be non-negative. The price rigidity conditions are recouped via the Kuhn–Tucker conditions.

8.3 RIGID FACTOR PRICES/WAGES

The disequilibrium techniques surveyed in the present chapter extend to the vertical dimension as well. We may spell out the entire production chain, and still be able to account for the presence of rigid prices. The rigidities may occur at any point along the chain: in the market for one or several consumer goods or intermediate goods, or even in a market for a primary good such as labor. In order to demonstrate how this can be done, we return to the familiar case of Koopmans' activity analysis.

Koopmans assumed that there is a fixed and given endowment of each primary good. In order to spell out the nature of the market formation for these primary goods in the presence of price rigidities, let us replace this assumption by the following two: (1) the supply of each primary good depends upon the price of the same good; let the supply price function of each resource $r \in R$ be $Q_r(w_r)$, where w_r is the supply of the good and Q_r is nondecreasing and differentiable; (2) the market price q_r of each primary good is rigid in the sense that

$$(8.16) \qquad \underline{q}_r \leq q_r \leq \overline{q}_r$$

where $\underline{q}_r$ and $\overline{q}_r$ are given and known lower and upper bounds, respectively.

In the case of labor, the lower bound $\underline{q}_r$ is some threshold level below which employers choose not to offer any employment, and/or below which workers will withdraw from active participation in the labor market. (So, what is at issue here are rigidities of a quite general nature; they do not necessarily have anything at all to do with minimum wage legislation.)

Some studies of rigidities in the labor market employ models of planning under uncertainty (spelling out the idea that firms may be less risk-averse than workers to fluctuations in wages); others draw on developments in economic dynamics (such as search theory) (see the survey articles by Schultze [13] and Solow [15]). Here, our aim is more modest: we simply want to portray the phenomenon of wage rigidities within the framework of a conventional model of comparative statics with full certainty.

For an illustration, turn to figure 8.4. The supply curve of primary good r (some particular category of labor, say) is kinked. It consists of one horizontal segment and one forward-sloping segment. If the demand for the primary good is sufficiently strong, so that the demand curve intersects the supply curve somewhere along the forward-sloping segment, the market will clear and there is equilibrium. But if demand is weaker and the demand curve intersects the supply curve along the horizontal segment, demand may not be sufficient to absorb all the forthcoming supply. The price of the primary good has fallen to its floor $\underline{q}_r$ and there may at that price be present an excess supply in the market that is not to be bought. There is an ex ante market gap between supply demand and supply. The market is in disequilibrium.

Excess supplies of primary goods (such as unemployment) develop because the market price fails to fall. It is rigid. That is how we elect to describe things using the tools of comparative statics. Notice that at this stage of analysis there is provided no explanation why the price is sticky downward. One only asserts that the market formation occurs *as if* the price were sticky. In order to dig deeper, it would be necessary to spell out the institutional characteristics of the market in much greater detail.

Using the same notation as in chapter 4, let there be $m \in M$ activities or productive processes and let $z = [z_m]$ denote the vector of levels of operation of these activities. Activities use primary goods $r \in R$ and transform them into final goods $i \in I$. For our present purposes, it will be sufficient to consider these two categories of goods: primary goods and final goods. The presence of intermediate goods is suppressed. (The reader who so desires should be able to supply any wanted generalizations, drawing upon the developments in chap. 4.) The matrix of input coefficients is $A = [a_{rm}]$, where a_{rm} is the quantity of primary good r required to operate activity m at unit level. The matrix of output coefficients is $B = [b_{im}]$, where b_{im} is the quantity of final good i obtained where activity m is operated at unit level. The vector of inputs is Az; the vector of outputs is Bz.

Figure 8.4.   Rigid Factor Prices

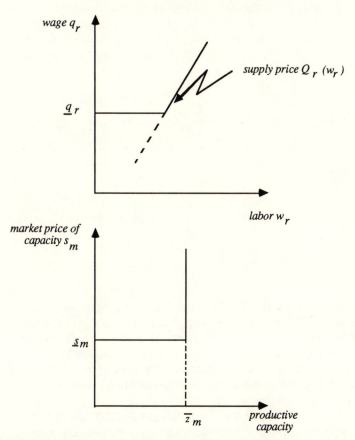

Upper panel: Rigid wages. Lower panel: Rigid market price of productive capacity.

The vector of excess demand for primary goods (demand minus supply) is $Az - w$. Writing

(8.17) $Az - w + d - e = 0,\ d,e \geq 0,\ d^T e = 0$

d will denote the vector of possible excess supplies of primary goods and *e* the vector of possible excess demands. (The nonlinear condition $d^T e = 0$ sees to it that *d* and *e* cannot be positive at the same time; we shall in a moment see how this condition will automatically be taken care of in the programming formulation to follow.)

The purpose of activity analysis is to trace the frontier of efficient vectors of final deliveries *Bz*. As explained and illustrated by a numerical example in section 4.1, each such efficient vector can be obtained as the optimal solution to a mathematical programming problem, using a vector of fixed prices of all final goods, say the vector $p = [p_i]$. In the present instance we are then led to the problem

(8.18) $$max \; p^T Bz - \sum_{r \in R} \int Q_r(w_r)dw_r + \sum_{r \in R} (\underline{q}_r d_r - \overline{q}_r e_r)$$

subject to

$$Ax - w + d - e = 0$$

$$z \geq \overline{z}$$

$$z,w,d,e \geq 0$$

The objective function is the difference between the value of all final deliveries, and the total cost of supplying all primary goods actually used up as inputs. The cost of excess supplies of primary goods are not included. The cost of excess demands for primary goods is included.

The first set of constraints are the market relations (8.17). The second set of constraints are capacitating conditions, with $\overline{z} = [\overline{z}_m]$ being a given vector of capacity bounds.

As signaled, note that the optimals d_r^* and e_r^* cannot both be positive at the same time, so that the condition $d_r^* e_r^* = 0$ is indeed satisfied. (If they were both positive, it would be possible to increase the value of the maximand by subtracting some small positive constant from both.)

Rather than dealing with program (8.18), we immediately proceed to a somewhat more involved case also featuring the possibility of disequilibrium in the markets for productive capacity—that is, in the markets for existing real capital.

There are many ways in which existing real capital can be brought inside the purview of the present modeling effort, and one way certainly would be to treat various categories of real capital as primary goods $r \in R$. Another is to associate the upper bounds on operating capacity

(8.19) $z \leq \bar{z}$

with the amounts of installed real capital. Assuming that there is a one-to-one correspondence between operating capacity and the amount of installed real capital, the vector of capacity bounds $\bar{z}$ will then also measure the vector of existing real capital in the partial economy being studied. Further—and this was the theme of section 5.4—real investment leads to increased capacity.

Refer again to figure 8.4; the lower panel illustrates the supply of capacity to produce using activity m. The supply curve is kinked, consisting of one horizontal segment and one vertical segment. If the demand for capacity is sufficiently strong, equilibrium will be established at a point along the vertical segment. Existing capacity will be fully used $z_m^* = \bar{z}_m$, and the implicit unit cost charge of capacity can be read off the diagram along the vertical axis. It is the optimal value s_m^* of the Lagrangean multiplier of the capacitating condition.

If the demand for capacity is weaker, however, the utilization of capacity may fall below its full potential. In model (8.18), as in all similar models involving capacity limits, the Lagrangean multiplier of the capacitating condition will then drop to zero.

From an economic point of view, this result is quite unsatisfactory. Why should capacity suddenly become a free good, just because it is not employed up to its existing limit? In the real world, wages do not fall to zero in the presence of unemployment. Nor does the price of a dry dock in a shipyard or a convector oven in a steel mill fall to zero just because the utilization of such real capital is below capacity.

If the (actual or implied) market price of excess capacity were zero, managers would feel no qualms about getting rid of it, dumping it on the market for free. There would be no reason why they should not take a book loss right away. But the fact of the matter is that managers feel a psychological resistance against realizing unrealized book losses and that they would rather hang on to excess capacity, hoping that better times will come along in the future. The implied market price of excess real capital does not fall to zero. It is sticky downward. Let us assume, then, that it is bounded from below:

(8.20) $s_m \geq \underline{s}_m, \; m \in M$

The lower bound $\underline{s}_m$ is the horizontal segment of the supply curve in figure 8.4. If the demand for capacity is weak and the demand curve for capacity intersects the supply curve along this horizontal segment, the cost charge of capacity s_m has fallen to its floor $\underline{s}_m$. At this price, there is an excess capacity that is not employed. The market for existing real capital is in disequilibrium.

Write

(8.21) $z + z_d = \bar{z}, z_d \geq 0$

where $z_d = [z_{dm}]$ is the vector of possible excess capacities.

We now want to extend program (8.18) so that it accounts for the presence of rigid prices of capacities as well as rigid prices or primary goods. The general strategy of approach is the same as before: the economic potential function is suitably adjusted so that the desired price constraints (in this case constraints (8.20)) are generated on the dual side, from the Kuhn–Tucker conditions. The required program is

(8.22) $max \; p^T Bz - \sum_{r \in R} \int Q_r(w_r) dw_r + \sum_{r \in R} (\underline{q}_r d_r - \bar{q}_r e_r)$

$+ \sum_{m \in M} \underline{s}_m z_{dm}$

subject to

$Ax - w + d - e = 0$

$z + z_d = \bar{z}$

$z, w, d, e, z_d \geq 0$

Denote the Lagrange multipliers of the two sets of constraints by $q = [q_r]$ and $s = [s_m]$, respectively. They are all unrestricted in sign. We shall identify the optimal q^* with the market prices of all primary goods, and the optimal s^* with the unit cost charges of productive capacity. The Kuhn–Tucker conditions are listed below.

(i)   The market for each primary good may fail to clear. If the price ceiling for a good is binding, there will occur an excess demand. If the price floor is binding, there will occur an excess supply. But if the price of the good falls between the ceiling and the floor, there is equilibrium in the market.

For

(8.23) $Ax^* - w^* + d^* - e^* = 0$

and there is also the set of conditions

(8.24a) $q_r^* \geq \underline{q}_r, d_r^*(q_r^* - \underline{q}_r) = 0, r \in R$

(8.24b) $-q_r^* \geq -\overline{q}_r, e_r^*(-q_r^* + \overline{q}_r) = 0, r \in R$

As desired, we here recoup the price bounds (8.16) together with their corresponding conditions of complementary slackness.

If the price ceiling for a primary good r is binding, presumably the price floor is slack (cf. n. 3 attached to the similar relations (8.6)) and d_r^* must be zero. There is then a non-negative excess demand for this good equal to e_r^*. Conversely, if the price floor is binding, presumably the ceiling is slack and $e_r^* = 0$. There is a non-negative excess supply equal to d_r^*. If neither the ceiling nor the floor is binding, both d_r^* and e_r^* vanish, and the market clears.

    (ii)   The suppliers of all primary goods are adjusted in the following sense. The supply price of a primary good cannot fall short of the market price. If supply is positive, the supply price actually equals the market price. But if the supply price exceeds the market price, the primary good is not offered on the market.

The conditions now stated are contained in

(8.25) $q_r^* \leq Q_r(w_r^*), w_r^*(q_r^* - Q_r(w_r^*)) = 0, r \in R$

    (iii) The imputed profit of operating any activity is nonpositive. For the purpose of the calculation of the imputed profit, the possible charges for hitting the capacity limits of activities have to be included among the costs. If the activity is operated, the profit vanishes. But if the profit is negative, the activity is not operated.

This is the standard no-profit condition of activity analysis. Mathematically,

$$(8.26) \qquad A^T q^* + s^* \geq B^T p, \; z^{*T}(A^T q^* + s^* - B^T p) = 0$$

Finally,

(iv) The level of operation of any activity cannot exceed its capacity limit. There is a unit capacity cost charge that can never fall short of some stated threshold level. If an activity is operated at less than its capacity limit, the capacity charge equals this minimum threshold level. But the capacity charge may also be greater than this; in that case the activity is operated at its capacity limit.

These conditions are

$$(8.27) \qquad z^* + z_d^* = \overline{z}$$

and

$$(8.28) \qquad s^* \geq \underline{s}, \; z_d^{*T}(s^* - \underline{s}) = 0$$

which recoups (8.21) together with complementary slackness.

To sum up, we have indeed been able to recoup both the desired bounding conditions on the prices of all primary goods, and the bounds on the imputed capacity charges, from the dual side of program (8.22). As explained, this property provides the rationale for forming that direct program in quantity variables in the first place.

Exercise 8.2

In the 1980s most U. S. observers seemed to accept quite readily the phenomenon of unemployment in the "smokestack" industries of coal and steel. Many of these production facilities had been built a long time ago and represented technologies that were no longer competitive. Also, U. S. wages had been propped up by expensive labor contracts. So, it seemed to be in the nature of things that these industries should gradually succumb to the competition from young, aggressive developing nations possessing advanced technology.

The U. S. public was in for a shock, however, when in the early 1980s the pride of the nation, its computer industry, ran into bad times, laying off computer engineers, systems analysts, and other specialized labor. The programming models developed in the present chapter can be used to explain why this could happen, and why no category of labor can ever be shielded from the potential threat of unemployment.

The numerical example below mimics these events. An activity analysis model of the data industry is developed, featuring a limited supply of four categories of skilled labor: computer engineers $(r = 1)$, system analysts $(r = 2)$, computer programmers $(r = 3)$, and sales personnel $(r = 4)$. The industry manufactures and delivers two main categories out output: (1) personal computers, disk drives, printers, and other hardware $(i = 1)$, and (2) computer software $(i = 2)$. The market prices of these outputs are set in fierce international competition, and must be taken as fixed and given by the domestic industry. The computer industry had been booming during the 1970s in the face of strong prices. But eventually an international overcapacity developed, and the bottom fell out of the market for computer chips. In the face of flagging prices, the domestic computer industry contracted. There were layoffs.

This particular example illustrates another interesting feature of the modern high-tech economy: the rising importance of the service industry. The computing boom brought with it a proliferation of computer consulting firms of all kinds. These consultants compete head-on with the large computer manufacturers, buying hardware from many different manufacturers and packaging hardware and software to suit the customer. In the terminology of activity analysis, such services constitute an intermediate good. In the example below, there is a group of software consulting firms. The intermediate good is software consulting services $(j = 1)$.

There are four different activities:

- the buyer himself negotiating with the various hardware manufacturers and designing the hardware configuration that he needs $(m = 1)$
- the buyer himself negotiating with various software manufacturers and designing himself the software solution that he needs $(m = 2)$
- the buyer signing a contract with a software consulting firm $(m = 3)$
- the software consulting firm selecting and developing the software that the customer requires $(m = 4)$

The description of the activities listed above can be made more precise with reference to the input requirements and the outputs of each activity. The unit input requirements are listed in the matrices below. A^P is the matrix of unit input requirements of primary goods; A^I is the matrix of unit input requirements of intermediate goods.

$$A^P = [a_{rm}^P] = \begin{bmatrix} 20 & 0 & 0 & 0 \\ 0 & 4 & 0 & 4 \\ 0 & 24 & 0 & 26 \\ 2.4 & 12 & 0 & 6 \end{bmatrix}$$

$$A^I = [a_{jm}^I] = \begin{bmatrix} 0 & 0 & 1 & 0 \end{bmatrix}$$

The figures show that two kinds of specialized labor are needed to sell and install hardware: computer engineers and sales personnel (first column). Three kinds of specialized labor are needed to design software: systems analysts, programmers, and sales personnel (second column). When the consulting firm packages the services, more programming hours are needed but the requirement of sales personnel is halved (fourth column).

The unit outputs are shown next. B^F is matrix of outputs of final goods; B^I is the matrix of intermediate goods.

$$B^F = [b_{im}^F] = \begin{bmatrix} 1 & 0 & 0 & 0 \\ 0 & 1 & 1 & 0 \end{bmatrix}$$

$$B^I = [b_{jm}^I] = \begin{bmatrix} 0 & 0 & 0 & 1 \end{bmatrix}$$

Let the supply price functions of specialized labor be

Computer engineers	$0.0006w_1^2$
Systems analysts	$0.0008w_2^2$
Programmers	$0.00015w_3^2$
Sales personnel	$0.0004w_4^2$

where w_r, $r = 1,2,3,4$, is the amount of labor of category r supplied, and the reservation wages below which these persons will not accept employment:

Computer engineers   37.5

Systems analysts	70
Programmers	25
Sales personnel	25

measured in thousands of dollars per year.

The prices—or rather, unit valuations—of final goods are

hardware	*900*
software	*1800*

The numerical example now being developed highlights the possible scarcity of specialized labor. All other inputs, including all hardware equipment and real and financial capital, are assumed to be procured at fixed and known market prices. The unit valuations listed above are calculated net of the unit costs of such inputs. They therefore reflect only the costs of specialized labor sunk into each product.

Program (8.18) now reads

$$max \; 900z_1 + 1800(z_2 + z_3) - 0.0002w_1^3 - 0.000267w_2^3 - 0.0005w_3^3$$

$$- 0.000133w_4^3 + 37.5d_1 + 70d_2 + 25d_3 + 25d_4$$

subject to

$$z_3 - z_4 \qquad\qquad = 0$$

$$20z_1 \qquad\qquad -w_1 + d_1 = 0$$

$$4z_2 + 4z_4 \qquad\qquad -w_2 + d_2 = 0$$

$$24z_2 + 26z_4 \qquad\qquad -w_3 + d_3 = 0$$

$$2.4z_1 + 12z_2 + 6z_4 \qquad\qquad -w_4 + d_4 = 0$$

$$z, w, d \geq 0$$

The optimal solution is

$$z_1^* = 13.23, \; z_2^* = 0, \; z_3^* = 22.80, \; z_4^* = 22.80$$

$$w_1^* = 264.58, \; w_2^* = 295.80, \; w_3^* = 592.69, \; w_4^* = 250.00$$

$$d_1^* = 0, \; d_2^* = 204.62, \; d_3^* = 0, \; d_4^* = 81.48$$

Activity $m = 2$ will not be operated. The consulting firms are doing a better job in packaging the software services than the customer himself could do developing the required software designs and programs in-house.

There is some unemployment for two categories of labor: systems analysts and sales personnel. So, in this example, unemployment is not a low-wage phenomenon. Quite the contrary, it hits people with top pay. Why? Because the supply of systems analysts is comparatively abundant and they have a grossly inflated reservation wage.

The optimal values of the last four Lagrange multipliers (say q_1, q_2, q_3, and q_4, respectively) are $q_1^* = 42.00$, $q_2^* = 70.00$, $q_3^* = 52.69$, $q_4^* = 25.00$.

Note that the annual wages here obtained are in all cases not less than the reservation wages, as stipulated. The optimal wage coincides with the reservation wage for two categories of labor: systems analysts and sales personnel. That is as it should be: there is less than full employment for these two categories of labor, and the excess supply forces the wage down into equality with the reservation wage.

NOTES

1.   Hayek [8].
2.   If only lower bounds have been specified, the upper bounds may be taken to be some sufficiently large positive number. If only upper bounds have been specified, the lower bounds may be taken to be zero.

3.   It is tacitly assumed that $\underline{p}_h < \overline{p}_h$. If, on the contrary, the two bounds are equal, the mentioned conclusion does not follow. The dual of the equality is unconstrained in sign, so that both an excess supply and an excess demand is possible.
4.   See e.g., Lindahl [9].
5.   See Sion [16].

BIBLIOGRAPHIC NOTES

For a recent study of price disequilibrium in the market for a single good, see Greenberg and Murphy [7]. They set out to provide "a unified framework for computing equilibria in mathematical programming models involving government policies that affect market prices" (p. 935). Starting out from Samuelson's extremal principle which—as we have seen in earlier chapters—is capable of dealing with the standard case of equilibrium, they propose an algorithm of successive adjustments of quantities and prices. The algorithmic mechanism is inspired by the cobweb (or hog cycle) pattern of dynamic adjustments in a single market. Greenberg and Murphy apply this tool for the numerical solution of market models involving price rigidities and the presence of taxes. Each step of the algorithm involves the solution of a concave program. However, as recognized by the authors, the success of this procedure is limited by some nontrivial assumptions that have to be made to see to it that the cobweb-like dynamic sequence actually converges.

Fortunately, there is no need to insist on the convergence of Greenberg and Murphy's algorithm at all. Instead, as shown in the main text, all cases of disequilibrium in a single market may be solved directly from a simple nonlinear mathematical program. For the numerical computation of the solution, a standard nonlinear software code may be employed. No assumptions are required beyond standard properties of the individual demand and supply curves (that the demand price function be positive, nonincreasing, and differentiable, and the supply price function positive, nondecreasing, and differentiable).

The quantity formulation of spatial disequilibrium belongs to Thore [19]. The nonintegrable case was dealt with by Nagurney and Zhao [14].

The quantity formulation of price disequilibrium in an activity analysis model—dealt with in section 8.3 in the main text—was pioneered by Morgenstern and Thompson (see [11] and [12] and their subsequent book [13], chap. 4). Dealing with an open, expanding von Neumann model, these two authors present a simple linear program which solves for the optimal vector of activity levels when the price of each good is not to exceed the import price and not to fall short of the export price. Their objective function simply is the value of exports (valued at the export prices) minus the value of imports (valued at the import prices).

For empirical applications of the disequilibrium format, see Faxén and Thore [6] (education and retraining of labor with reservation wages), Thore and Isser [20] (energy markets with given and fixed import prices), and Thore, Kozmetsky, and Burtis [21] (a Leontief input-output model with rigid wage rates).

See also the recent survey by Thompson and Thore [18], which discusses these earlier developments and also deals with the case of nonintegrable demand and supply functions so that a mathematical programming formulation of disequilibrium does not exist. (Disequilibrium must then rather be solved by the use of complementarity methods.)

The disequilibrium approach to economics has recently experienced a renaissance under the guidance of economists like Drèze [5], Barro and Grossman [1], and Malinvaud [10]. In a way, this modern school can be seen as the blossoming of early efforts along similar lines by J. R. Hicks and economists of the Stockholm school, writing in the 1930s. It is important to point out with E. Lindahl ([9], pp. 60ff.) that the choice of equilibrium or disequilibrium as a vehicle for the economic modeling of a dynamic economic process is one of economic method only and reflects nothing about the nature of the real-life economic phenomena to be modeled. Adopting the disequilibrium method of analysis, an economic dynamic process is seen as a sequence of market situations in disequilibrium. Adopting the equilibrium method of analysis (temporary equilibrium), the very same process is portrayed instead as a sequence of equilibria. It was only with the formulation of the much admired Drèze's theorem that these early propositions were given a precise context. Consider a disequilibrium economy with price rigidities (each price being bounded by a floor and a ceiling). Then it is possible to construct a system of rationing (direct demand and/or output constraints) so that all markets in the former disequilibrium model are actually cleared. For the formulation and proof of Drèze's theorem as applied to spatial disequilibrium, see Thore [19].

Whereas the interest of the present volume is partial economics and sector economics, the so-called fixed-price models of Drèze [5], Benassy [2], Barro and Grossman [1], Malivaud [10], and others deal with disequilibrium in an entire interdependent system of markets or in a macroeconomic model. Assuming that wage rates and prices are rigid in the short run, these authors worked out the details of some dynamic process of tâtonnement in quantities (a fixed point of this tâtonnement being a "temporary equilibrium"). Here, we are only concerned with the initial possible occurrence of ex ante market gaps (excess supplies or excess demands). How these gaps are eventually resolved ex post, with the economic agents modifying their market behavior in the light of perceived quantity constraints (rationing), has not been dealt with.

REFERENCES

[8.1]   Barro, R. J., and H. I. Grossman. "A General Disequilibrium Model of Income and Employment," *American Economic Review* 61 (1971): 82–92.

[8.2]   Benassy, J. P. "Neokeynesian Disequilibrium in a Monetary Economy," *Review of Economic Studies* 42 (1975): 502–23.

[8.3]   Charnes, A. "Constrained Games and Linear Programming," *Proceedings of the U. S. National Academy of Sciences* 39 (July 1953): 639–41.

[8.4]   Charnes, A., P. R. Gribik, and K. O. Kortanek: "Polyextremal Principles and Separably-Infinite Programs," *Zeitschrift fur Operations Research* 4 (1980): 211–34.

[8.5]   Drèze, J. "Existence of an Exchange Equilibrium under Price Rigidities," *International Economic Review* 16 (1975): 301–20.

[8.6]   Faxén, K. O., and S. Thore. "Retraining in an Interdependent System of Labor Markets: A Network Analysis," *European Journal of Operational Research* 44 (1990): 349–56.

[8.7]   Greenberg, H. J. and F. H. Murphy: "Computing Market Equilibria with Price   Regulations Using Mathematical Programming," *Operations Research* 33/5 (1985): 935–54.

[8.8] Hayek, F. A. "Price Expectations, Monetary Disturbances and Malinvestments." In *Readings in Business Cycle Theory,* ed. American Economic Association. London: Allen and Unwin, 1950.

[8.9] Lindahl, E. *Studies in the Theory of Money and Capital.* London: Allen and Unwin, 1939.

[8.10] Malinvaud, E. *The Theory of Unemployment Reconsidered.* Oxford: Basil Blackwell, 1977.

[8.11] Morgenstern, O., and G. L. Thompson. "Un Modèle de Croissance en Économic Ouverte," *Économics et Societés* 5 (1971): 1703-28.

[8.12] Morgenstern, O., and G. L. Thompson. "A Note on an Open Expanding Economy Model," *Naval Research Logistics Quarterly* 19 (1972): 557–59.

[8.13] Morgenstern, O., and G. L. Thompson. *Mathematical Theory of Expanding and Contracting Economies.* Lexington, Mass.: D.C. Heath, 1976.

[8.14] Nagurney, A. and L. Zhao. "Disequilibrium and Variational Inequalities," research report 89-11 (1988), Cambridge, Mass: Department of Civil Engineering, Massachusetts Institute of Technology.

[8.15] Schultze, C.L. "Microeconomic Efficiency and Nominal Wage Stickiness," *The American Economic Review* 75/1 (1985): 1–15.

[8.16] Sion, M. "On General Minimax Theorems," *Pacific Journal of Mathematics* 8 (1958): 171–76.

[8.17] Thompson, G. L., and S. Thore. "Economic Disequilibrium by Mathematical Programming," *Journal of Optimization Theory and Applications,* in press Oct. 1991.

[8.18] Thore, S. "Spatial Disequilibrium," *Journal of Regional Science* 26/4 (1986): 661–75.

[8.19] Thore, S. and S. Isser. "A Goaling Format for National Energy Security," *Mathematical Modeling* 9/1, (1987): 51–62.

[8.20] Thore, S., G. Kozmetsky and M. Burtis. "Effects of Defense Spending on the Texas Economy: An Example of Concave Programming," *Journal of Policy Modeling* 6/4 (1984): 573–86.

9

Chance-Constrained Activity Analysis and Chance-Constrained Production and Distribution Systems

Uncertainty is an important aspect of reality. There is uncertainty attached to each single link in the logistics chain: uncertainty about the availability of supplies, about the technological relationships involved in production, and about the demand for output.

It is a trivial observation to note that even established and well-known technologies are subject to random disturbances. For example, the harvest of agricultural produce depends upon the weather, plant diseases, and the like.[1] Indeed, the entire science of statistical quality control attests to the fact that there is statistical variation in the quality (and presumably also the quantity) of output. However, the concept of technological uncertainty has taken on additional significance in a modern world where producers have to develop new technologies, new products, and new channels of marketing just to survive. Innovations no longer necessarily arise spontaneously as the result of the lone inventor and the lone capitalist who happen to strike a lucky venture. Innovations are planned—in great numbers. Many of them fail but a few survive. It is an entirely new numbers game that the modern producer has to play: the uncertainty of the technological relations that are going to hold tomorrow is much greater; the stakes are much higher.

Uncertainty is needed in order to explain an important part of the supply process that has so far been left unaccounted for: the accumulation of inventory at all stages of the supply chain to be kept as a contingency against uncertainty—what one may call holdings of precautionary inventories, excess capacity, and planned slack in the productive processes. Paraphrasing well-known terms used by Keynes to explain the demand for money, one may say that the treatment of inventory and the warehouse model provided in chapter 5 refer to the speculation motive for holding inventories. We now reach the precautionary motive (and possibly even a transactions motive) for holding inventories and excess capacity.

Conventional economic theory is not well equipped to handle uncertainty in production and distribution. Instead, it has been left to operations research and management science to mount a systematic study of the role of uncertainty in these areas. Particularly germane to our present investigation are a number of operations research studies of product development and technological and market uncertainty. Drawing upon these developments, we propose here to sketch the main features of activity analysis and activity networks in a setting of uncertainty.

Many different analytical techniques have been developed in operations research and management science to deal with uncertainty: simulation, mean variance analysis, stochastic programming, and so on. Here, we shall restrict the treatment to one particular technique—chance-constrained programming, developed by Charnes, Cooper, and Symonds in 1958 (in reference [5], see also [3] and [4]).

A so-called chance constraint may be violated without violating feasibility, provided the violations do not occur too frequently. For instance, one may desire to impose an upper limit on the storage capacity at some warehouse. The purpose of a chance constraint is to express those constraints that the manager normally must reckon with in some standard mode of operations; one may require the inventory on hand to be less than or equal to the maximal storage capacity in 95 percent of all cases. Such a formulation excludes the remaining five percent of all cases, when the manager may have to look for an ad hoc arrangement to handle the accumulation of exceptional volumes of merchandise, like renting additional storage facilities, holding an inventory sale to free existing warehouse capacity, or shipping inventory to dealers.

Chance-constrained programming does not specify the various recourse strategies that the manager may resort to when the chance constraint is violated. All possible states of the world are not specified explicitly. Rather, the chance constraint just excludes the exceptional cases from consideration. From the point of view of the modeling effort, this limitation may often appear as an advantage, in that the modeler avoids extreme situations where the standard pattern of behavior may break down anyhow.

Uncertain input and output coefficients typically arise when the activities involve new technologies.

When input coefficients are uncertain there is no guarantee that the total inputs required to operate a given activity can be accommodated by a fixed supply. Consider for instance the inputs required to run a nuclear power plant. Because of technical uncertainties, and because of uncertainties about the norms that the regulatory authorities are going to enforce, the volume of cooling water required may be uncertain. An adjacent lake designed to receive the cooling water of the plant may therefore not be large enough to prevent the temperature of the water in the lake from rising to unacceptable levels. Hence, the requirement that the available supply should cover the demand as an expected value may need to be supplemented by one or more chance constraints to ensure that the risks of moving to unacceptable temperature are kept at a sufficiently small level; there is, of course, a risk that such constraints may be violated but we may specify in advance that violation must not occur in more than five percent of all cases.

When output coefficients are uncertain one cannot be sure that any deterministic delivery of final goods will satisfy final demand. In a study of health care delivery systems, for instance, one particular activity may represent heart operations by means of some specific newly developed by-pass technique. The inputs and their respective costs (surgeons, operating rooms, hospital care facilities) may be known but the output (the success rate as a percentage of all patients treated) may be uncertain. A chance constraint requiring the number of successful operations to exceed some lower threshold is included in the program in the form of a policy constraint or as a result of some known properties of this kind of surgery.

The analytical treatment of a chance constraint may be undertaken in various ways. A convenient and often used way involves converting the original chance constraint into a so-called certainty equivalent. Even if the constraint itself is linear, the certainty equivalent typically is nonlinear. The overall optimization problem becomes an instance of optimization with nonlinear constraints. The original linear activity analysis format becomes transformed into one with nonlinear constraints.

How do decision makers act in the face of uncertainty? A common hypothesis in economics is that less uncertainty is preferred to more uncertainty, all other factors being equal. As applied in the conventional theory of stock portfolios, this maxim leads to the conclusion that portfolio managers will select a balanced portfolio providing some optimal tradeoff between return and risk. Firms will seek to establish a balanced portfolio of uncertain production activities to secure some optimal tradeoff between return and risk.

In the hospital and health care delivery example mentioned a moment ago, no hospital will do just heart by-pass operations. Instead, there will exist an optimal mix of activities in each operating room, blending well-established surgical procedures with some experimental ones. In a similar fashion, there will exist in any line of manufacturing or trade some optimal mix of well-established production techniques and the development of new ones.

As discussed in chapter 4, Koopmans' activity analysis format is too general for the purpose of many applications. To obtain further specification, it is often helpful to spell out the details of the generalized network of production and distribution. In section 9.2 below we provide a chance-constrained formulation of such a network, imbedded inside a conventional activity analysis format. Rather than allowing every single good to require every other good as an input, one is then left with a series of concatenated activities along the links of a network. When the attenuation (or amplification) factors along each link are uncertain, one can no longer insist a priori that the Kirchhoff condition at each node be satisfied in all cases. Instead, each Kirchhoff condition will be conceived of as a chance constraint, stating that the total outflow from a node can most of the time not exceed the total inflow into the same node.

The network formulation enables the analyst to investigate the effects of innovation and technological change in the entire production and distribution chain, and the possible hierarchical cascading of innovations along this chain.

SYMBOLS USED IN CHAPTER 9

$i \in I$	final goods
$j, k \in J$	intermediate goods
$r \in R$	primary goods (resources)
$m \in M$	activities
P as superscript	primary goods (resources)
I as superscript	intermediate goods
F as superscript	final goods
$A = [a_{rm}], A^P = [a^P_{rm}], A^I = [a^I_{jm}]$	matrix of input coefficients
$B = [b_{im}], B^F = [b^F_{im}], B^I = [b^I_{jm}]$	matrix of output coefficients
z_m	level of operation of activity m
x_i	quantity demanded of final good i
w_r	quantity supplied of resource r
$P_i(x_i)$	demand price function for final good i
$Q_r(w_r)$	supply price function for resource r
μ_i, ν_r	"spacer" variables, at the optimal point to be identified with optimal inventories
p_i, q_r	Lagrange multipliers of market balances for final goods and resources, respectively
ω_i, ρ_r	Lagrange multipliers

For modified notation employed in section 9.3, see separate list at the beginning of the section.

9.1. TECHNOLOGICAL UNCERTAINTY

The basic premise of activity analysis is that the producer has available to him a number of technologically well-defined activities, and that his decision variables are the levels at which each one of these activities is going to be operated. Once these decisions have been made—assuming known input and output coefficients—it is a matter of simple arithmetic to compute the inputs required and the outputs obtained.

If the input and output coefficients are uncertain, the result of this exercise will be uncertain too: the total inputs required and the total outputs obtained become stochastic variables. For instance, in the case of farming, the decision variables are decisions about what kind of crops to grow on various pieces of land, on methods of irrigation and cultivation, on the use of agricultural machinery, and the like. Presumably the input coefficients can be treated as deterministic. But, due to weather and plant diseases, the output coefficients are stochastic.

A revolution is sweeping the modern industrial world. There is a scramble to develop new production methods, new products, new distribution and marketing techniques. Many of these production techniques are imprecisely known and the relationship between inputs and outputs cannot be specified in deterministic mathematical terms. Both the input coefficients and the output coefficients may be stochastic.

When Schumpeter coined the term "innovation,"[2] he was thinking of large discrete jumps in manufacturing techniques (such as the introduction of high-power transmission lines or commercial aviation) and the introduction of entirely new products (such as movie theaters). While such innovations still occur (the electronic chip, heart transplants), a new type of innovation has become characteristic in the second half of the twentieth century: a very large number of small changes in technology and design are launched in the marketplace; many of these fail in the modern competitive environment but a few succeed and are quickly imitated by other producers who in their turn find successful improvements or succumb (examples include the development and marketing of new breakfast cereals, razor blades, and portable personal computes). The very fact that these changes are numerous opens up new possibilities of mathematical modeling: such innovations can be characterized as probabilistic with accompanying smooth behavior rather than a discrete deterministic jump.

This ongoing improvement of technology and product requires producers to maintain considerable *R&D* facilities. Typically, the benefits of *R&D* accrue to the producer as a time stream of small adjustments possibly interspersed with a few somewhat larger discrete jumps. From a bookkeeping point of view, the implementation of small adjustments of production will appear as current costs rather than capital investments. These are costs of changing designs, modifying the engineering or chemical specifications of the product, and marketing the new characteristics. Looking at the problem of planning production ex ante, these are uncertainties in the production relationships, that is, in the production functions.

Continuing the argument now in terms of activity analysis, a stream of small modifications of technology can be represented as stochastic variability in the unit input coefficients and/or output coefficients of any given activity. These stochastic changes may involve smaller input requirements for some inputs, and larger ones for others (and, in particular, positive requirements of some inputs that previously were not used at all); and they may result in less of some outputs and more of others (including, in particular, some outputs or economic characteristics that were not previously produced at all).

With these introductory comments we turn now to a formal presentation of activity analysis with probabilistic input and output coefficients. Using the same notation as in chapter 4, let a_{rm} denote the quantity of input r required to operate activity m at unit level $(r \in R; m \in M)$ and b_{im} the quantity of output i obtained when operating activity m on unit level $(i \in I; m \in M)$. Let both a_{rm} and b_{im} be probabilistic variables, defined by some suitable joint probability distribution. The actual realization of empirical coefficients will be thought of as random drawings from this distribution.

The vector of levels of activities will simply be denoted $z = [z_m]$, $m \in M$. These are decision variables to be determined a priori. The vectors of input requirements and outputs are then Az and Bz, respectively; they are both probabilistic because the coefficients a_{mr} and b_{mi} are no longer constant but random variables.

The symbol $x = [x_i]$, $i \in I$ is used to denote the vector of demand for final goods; the symbol $w = [w_r]$, $r \in R$ is the vector of supplies of primary goods.

The seemingly innocent requirement that the total output must suffice to cover the quantity demanded will now need some interpretation. We can no longer always insist that the condition

$$(9.1) \qquad Bz \geq x$$

be fulfilled at all times; as long as the joint probability distribution of all b_{im} gives positive weight to numerically small non-negative unit outputs there is the risk of violation of the stipulated inequality to be considered. However, we may insist that such violations do not occur too often, say not more often than in five percent of all cases, so we can write

(9.2) $Prob \left(\sum_{m \in M} b_{im} z_m \geq x_i \right) \geq 0.95,\ i \in I$

Each condition (9.2) is a so-called chance constraint. A violation of any chance constraint (9.2) may be referred to as a supply failure—a failure of the quantity of a final good produced to meet the demand for it.

Similarly, the requirement that the total use of inputs not exceed the availability of inputs needs interpretation. We can no longer always insist that the condition

(9.3) $Az \leq w$

be fulfilled at all times when the matrix A has elements that are random variables. If the joint probability distribution of all z_{rm} includes at least some possible very large positive unit input requirements there is always a risk of violation of the inequality. However, we may insist that such violations do not occur too often, say

(9.4) $Prob \left(\sum_{m \in M} a_{rm} z_m \leq w_r \right) \geq 0.95,\ r \in R$

Each condition (9.4) is a chance constraint. A violation of this constraint may also be referred to as a supply failure—a failure of the forthcoming supply of a primary good to cover the demand for it.

The demand price function for each final good i is written $P_i(x_i)$; the supply price function for each primary good r is written $Q_r(w_r)$. The former is assumed to be positive, differentiable, and nonincreasing; the latter nonnegative, differentiable, and nondecreasing. As we have developed at some length in earlier chapters (see sec. 3.4 and 4.1), the crucial assumption here is that the demand price functions and the supply price functions are all integrable. Although much more general mathematical forms of these functions are permissible, these simple functional expressions have been chosen just for convenience.

The chance-constrained activity analysis model we now examine is

(9.5) $max \sum_{i \in I} \int P_i(x_i) dx_i - \sum_{r \in R} \int Q_r(w_r) dw_r$

subject to $Prob(\sum_{m \in M} x_i - b_{im}z_m \leq 0) \geq 0.95, i \in I$

$Prob(\sum_{m \in M} a_{rm}z_m - w_r \leq 0) \geq 0.95, r \in R$

$x,z,w \geq 0$

Program (9.5) instructs us to maximize a certain mathematical potential function (which we have used repeatedly in the past) subject to two sets of chance constraints. The first of these sets states that the supply of each final good must be covered in at least 95 percent of all cases. The second set states that the supply of each primary good must suffice to cover the demand for it in at least 95 percent of all cases.

Note that no restrictions are placed on the joint distribution of the a_{rm} and the b_{im} other than that it should be known. In order to simplify the presentation below, however, it will be assumed that the joint distribution is normal.

The chance constraints (9.2) and (9.4) can be converted into deterministic equivalents in various ways by reference to different classes of decision rules that may be used. Here we shall simply insist that a deterministic choice regarding the level of operation of each activity has to be made a priori, before the outcome of the random coefficients has been observed (a so-called zero-order decision rule[3]).

Each chance constraint (9.2) may then be replaced by its so-called certainty equivalent in the following manner. First, note that the stochastic variable $\sum_m b_{im}z_m$ has the mathematical expectation and the standard deviation

(9.6a) $E(\sum_{m \in M} b_{im}z_m) = \sum_{m \in M} Eb_{im}z_m$

(9.6b) $s.d.(\sum_{m \in M} b_{im}z_m) = \{ \sum_{m \in M} \sum_{n \in M} z_m Cov(b_{im}, b_{in}) z_n \}^{1/2}$

respectively. Form the standardized variable

$$(9.7) \qquad \zeta_i = \frac{\sum_{m \in M} (b_{im} - Eb_{im})z_m}{s.d.(\sum_{m \in M} b_{im}z_m)}$$

When all b_{im} are normally distributed, this variable is also normal and has its mathematical expectation equal to zero and its standard deviation equal to unity. This is, or course, one of the best-known probability distributions in theoretical statistics. The distribution function is commonly denoted F.

The chance constraints (9.2) can now be written

$$(9.8) \qquad Prob \left\{ \zeta_i \geq \frac{x_i - \sum_{m \in M} Eb_{im}z_m}{s.d.(\sum_{m \in M} b_{im}z_m)} \right\} \geq 0.95, i \in I$$

or, equivalently, by the definition of F,

$$(9.9) \qquad 1 - F \left\{ \frac{x_i - \sum_{m \in M} Eb_{im}z_m}{s.d.(\sum_{m \in M} b_{im}z_m)} \right\} \geq 0.95, i \in I$$

Collecting terms, one finds that $F \leq 0.05$. Noting that F is non-negative and monotonically increasing over its entire range, one may then invert to obtain

$$(9.10) \qquad \frac{x_i - \sum_{m \in M} Eb_{im}z_m}{s.d.(\sum_{m \in M} b_{im}z_m)} \leq F^{-1}(0.05) = -1.645$$

The value $F^{-1}(0.05)$ is defined as the algebraically smallest outcome of a random variable with the cumulative probability distribution F that has the property that at least 5 percent of all cases fall below it. It is negative, and since F is symmetric around the origin, $F^{-1}(0.05) = F^{-1}(0.95)$. Consulting a table on the normal distribution, one finds that $F^{-1}(0.95)=1.645$ and $F^{-1}(0.05) = -1.645$.

Next, since the standard deviation appearing in (9.10) is positive, we can multiply through by the dominator and rearrange terms to obtain

$$(9.11) \qquad \sum_{m \in M} Eb_{im}z_m - 1.645 \left\{ \sum_{m \in M} \sum_{n \in M} z_m Cov(b_{im},b_{in})z_n \right\}^{1/2} \geq x_i$$

This is the deterministic equivalent to (9.2) in the sense that a choice of all z_m that satisfies this expression will satisfy (9.2) at the indicated probability levels. In economic terms it states that the expected output of each final good minus a risk term must be large enough to cover demand. The risk term or safety margin serves as a contingency against the variability of the unit outputs.

One may go one step further and interpret the safety margin appearing in (9.11) as a buffer inventory that the producers want to hold as a contingency against unexpected low unit output coefficients.

The general idea that inventory serves as a contingency against random variability in demand is of course well known in economics. So, while the particular application of chance-constrained programming in the present context may be new to the economics literature, the nature of the results certainly is in accordance with well-known principles of economic behavior under uncertainty.

Note finally that the programming format not only provides a rationale for the existence of such precautionary holdings, but actually provides a mathematical formula for the numerical calculation of their magnitude.

Next turning to each chance constraint (9.4), it may be also be converted into a certainty equivalent. Proceeding as a moment ago, one this time gets

$$(9.12) \qquad \sum_{m \in M} Ea_{rm}z_m + 1.645 \left\{ \sum_{m \in M} \sum_{n \in M} z_m Cov(a_{rm},a_{rn})z_n \right\}^{1/2} \leq w_r$$

This relation states that a supply failure must not occur too often. Hence, some safety margin must be added to the expected use of each input. This margin serves as a contingency against the variability of the input requirements. It may be interpreted as a buffer inventory. In the case of real capital used as an input, the same term is in the nature of excess capacity, held as a contingency against unexpected additional capacity needs.

Reflecting on the nature of the two certainty equivalents (9.11) and (9.12), we may make the following general observation. Uncertain input coefficients require putting aside stocks of raw materials and other inputs and maintaining excess capacity; uncertain output coefficients require buildup of stocks of finished goods.

(We are currently disregarding the presence of intermediate goods. As will be seen in sec. 9.3, uncertain coefficients of inputs or outputs of intermediate goods lead to the need to hold stocks of intermediate goods as well.)

Formally, we are now in a position to replace the two sets of chance constraints in program (9.5) by their certainty equivalents (9.11) and (9.12). Before doing so, however—in order to facilitate subsequent interpretations and also with the purpose of obtaining a convex constraint set—we make additional transformations in the following fashion. Defining new non-negative spacer variables μ_i,[4] each constraint (9.11) is split into the two constraints

$$(9.13) \qquad \sum_{m \in M} E b_{im} z_m - \mu_i \geq x_i$$

$$\mu_i \geq 1.645^2 \; s.d.(\sum_{m \in M} b_{im} x_m)$$

or, replacing the last inequality by its square (which is certainly permitted since both sides are non-negative)

$$(9.14) \qquad \sum_{m \in M} E b_{im} z_m - \mu_i \geq x_i$$

$$\mu_i^2 \geq 1.645^2 \; var(\sum_{m \in M} b_{im} z_m)$$

where var is the variance operator. As will be seen in a moment, the mathematical program to be written will see to it that, at the point of optimum, the spacer variable will be brought into equality with the corresponding contingency buffer of inventory held so that the last inequality of the pair becomes binding.

Dealing with the certainty equivalents (9.12) in an analogous manner, defining non-negative spacer variables v_r, each constraint can be replaced by the pair

(9.15) $\sum_{m \in M} Ea_{rm}z_m + v_r \leq w_r$

$$v_r^2 \geq 1.645^2 \, var(\sum_{m \in M} a_{rm}z_m)$$

The certainty equivalent to the entire program (9.5) now reads

(9.16) $max \sum_{i \in I} \int P_i(x_i)dx_i - \sum_{r \in R} \int Q_r(w_r)dw_r$

subject to

$x_i - \sum_{m \in M} Eb_{im}z_m + \mu_i \leq 0, \, i \in I$

$1.645^2 \, var(\sum_{m \in M} b_{im}z_m) - \mu_i^2 \leq 0, \, i \in I$

$\sum_{m \in M} Ea_{rm}z_m + v_r - w_r \leq 0, \, r \in R$

$1.645^2 \, var(\sum_{m \in M} a_{rm}z_m) - v_r^2 \leq 0, \, r \in R$

$x, z, w, v, \mu \geq 0$

The maximand is concave. The constraints are linear, and quadratic forms of the unknowns. We make the elementary observation that quadratic forms are convex functions. Hence the entire constraint set is convex.

For the question regarding the existence of an optimal solution to program (9.16), we refer to the Kuhn–Tucker theorem for extremization over a nonlinear constraint set.[5] To eliminate the possibility of trouble from the so-called constraint qualifications, assume that there exists an interior point in the constraint set to (9.16) for which all constraints are slack (i.e., they all hold with < signs). (The observant reader will here recognize the well-known Slater conditions which indeed see to it that the constraint qualifications are fulfilled.[6])

Program (9.16) will then have an optimal solution $x^*, z^*, w^*, \mu^*, v^*$ if and only if there exists non-negative multipliers $p^* = [p_i^*]$, $\omega^* = [\omega_i^*]$, $q^* =$

$[q_r*]$, $\rho* = [\rho_r*]$ (corresponding to the four sets of constraints, respectively) satisfying the following Kuhn–Tucker conditions:

(i) There is equilibrium in the market for each final good in the following sense: The expected output of each good should suffice to cover demand plus some contingency buildup of stocks of the finished good. If the price of the good is positive, total output must actually equal total demand now mentioned. If output exceeds total demand, the price must have dropped to zero.

The conditions now stated are contained in the Kuhn–Tucker conditions

(9.17a) $x_i* - \sum_{m \in M} Eb_{im}z_m* + \mu_i* \leq 0, i \in I$

(9.17b) $p_i*(x_i* - \sum_{m \in M} Eb_{im}z_m* + \mu_i*) = 0, i \in I$

where the optimal p_i* is identified with the market price for final good i, $i \in I$.

Also, there will be equilibrium in the market for each resource in the following sense: The expected use of each resource as inputs plus the quantity set aside as a buffer inventory cannot exceed the available supply. If the resource price is positive, total demand now mentioned must actually equal total supply. But if total demand falls short of supply, the price must have dropped to zero.

Mathematically,

(9.18a) $\sum_{m \in M} Ea_{rm}z_m* + v_r* \leq w_r, r \in R$

(9.18b) $q_r* (\sum_{m \in M} Ea_{rm}z_m* + v_r* - w_r) = 0, r \in R$

(ii)   The quantity of each final good set aside as a buffer inventory is given by the formula:

$$(9.19) \qquad \mu_i^* = 1.645 \; s.d.(\sum_{m \in M} Eb_{im}z_m^*)$$

and the quantity of each resource set aside as a buffer is

$$(9.20) \qquad v_r^* = 1.645 \; s.d.(\sum_{m \in M} Ea_{rm}z_m^*)$$

(Since the spacer variables μ_i and v_r do not appear in the maximand of program (9.16), and since any decrease of a spacer variable is advantageous in that it will permit the expansion of final demand or additional use of resources, one will clearly want to drive each spacer variable down to its lower bound.)

(iii)   The consumers and the resource owners are adjusted to equilibrium in the following sense. The market place of any final good cannot fall short of the demand price. If a positive quantity of the final good is consumed, the market price equals the demand price; if the market price exceeds the demand price, nothing will be consumed. Further, the market price of a resource cannot exceed the supply price. If a positive quantity of the resource is supplied, the market price equals the supply price; in the case that the market price actually falls short of the supply price, nothing of the resource will be supplied.

The conditions now stated are all contained in the standard relations

$$(9.21) \qquad p_i^* \geq P_i(x_i^*), \; x_i^*(p_i^* - P_i(x_i^*)) = 0, \; i \in I$$

and

$$(9.22) \qquad q_r^* \leq Q_r(w_r^*), \; w_r^*(q_r^* - Q_r(w_r^*)) = 0, \; r \in R$$

(iv)   The value of the expected output obtained when operating an activity at unit level cannot exceed the expected input costs plus a risk premium reflecting the stochastic variability of both the input coefficients and the output coefficients. If the activity is to be operated on a positive level, the value of the output must equal the cost elements now mentioned. In this sense, the producers must make an expected profit per unit level of operation that exactly matches the risk premium. If the expected profit falls short of the risk premium, the activity will not be operated:

(9.23a) $- \sum_{i \in I} p_i \cdot Eb_{im} + 1.645^2 \sum_{i \in I} w_i^* \sum_{n \in M} 2\, Cov(b_{im}, b_{in}) z_n^* +$

$+ \sum_{r \in R} q_r^* \, Ea_{rm} + 1.645^2 \sum_{r \in R} \rho_r^* \sum_{n \in M} 2\, Cov(a_{rm}, a_{rn}) z_n^*$

$\geq 0,\ m \in M$

(9.23b) $- \sum_{i \in I} p_i^* \, Eb_{im} z_m^* + 1.645^2 \sum_{i \in I} \omega_i^* \sum_{n \in M} 2\, z_m^*$

$Cov(b_{im}, b_{in})\, z_n^* + \sum_{r \in R} q_r^* \, Ea_{rm} z_m^*$

$+ 1.645^2 \sum_{r \in R} \rho_r^* \sum_{n \in M} 2\, z_m \, Cov(a_{rm} a_{rn})\, z_n^* = 0,$

$m \in M$

Rearranging equation (9.23b) and summing over all activities m, note also that the total expected profit in the entire activity model comes out as

(9.24) $1.645^2 \sum_{m \in M} \sum_{i \in I} 2 \omega_i^* \, var(Eb_{im} z_m^*) +$

$$+ 1.645^2 \sum_{m \in M} \sum_{r \in R} 2\rho_r^* \, var(Ea_{rm}z_m^*)$$

(v)   Finally, one finds the Kuhn–Tucker conditions

(9.25) $p_i^* - 2\mu_i^* \, \omega_i^* \geq 0, \; \mu_i^*(p_i^* - 2\mu_i^* \, \omega_i^*) = 0, \; i \in I$

and

(9.26) $q_r^* - 2v_r^* \rho_r^* \geq 0, \; v_r^* \, (q_r^* - 2v_r^* \rho_r^*) = 0, \; r \in R$

which we shall use for the proof of theorem 9.1.

To sum up, we have now discussed two features of the chance-constrained activity analysis model: The holding of inventories of inputs and the presence of profits. Inventories are held as a contingency against uncertainty. A surplus of expected sales revenues above costs is necessary to finance the holdings of such inventories. There exists a precise relationship between the total value of all inventories held and the total expected profit, as stated by the following:

> **Theorem 9.1.** At a point of optimum of program (9.16), the total value of all inventories put aside as a contingency against uncertain developments exactly equals the total profit made in the economy. Or, to put the matter slightly differently, the profits occurring exactly suffice to finance the desired buildup of inventories.

Proof. We have already calculated total profit in the economy as being given by the expression (9.24). Making use of the formulas (9.19) and (9.20), this can be further simplified to read

(9.27) $$\sum_{m \in M} \sum_{i \in I} 2\omega_i^*(\mu_i^*)^2 + \sum_{m \in M} \sum_{r \in R} 2\rho_r^*(v_r^*)^2$$

Finally, making use of the conditions (9.25–26), the same expression simply reduces to

(9.28) $$\sum_{i \in I} p_i^* \mu_i^* + \sum_{r \in R} q_r^* v_r^*$$

which is the value of all inventories of final goods and resources.

Theorem 9.2. At an optimum for program (9.16), the total value of all final demand equals the total market value of all resources supplied.

Proof: This theorem is obtained as a corollary to the preceding one. We have already established that the difference between the total value of all expected output and the total market value of all expected inputs used equals the market value of all inventories of both final goods and resources set aside. Rearranging terms, the excess of the expected value of output above the value of the buffer stocks of final goods equals the market value of all expected inputs plus the value of the buffers of resources:

(9.29) $$\sum_{i \in I} \sum_{m \in M} p_i^* E b_{im} z_m^* - \sum_{i \in I} p_i^* \mu_i^* =$$

$$\sum_{r \in R} \sum_{m \in M} q_r^* E a_{rm} z_m^* + \sum_{r \in R} q_r^* v_r^*$$

Remembering (9.17b) on sees that the left-hand side of (9.29) simply equals the total value of all final demand. Similarly, remembering (9.18b), the right-hand side clearly equals the total market value of all resources:

(9.30) $$\sum_{i \in I} p_i^* x_i^* = \sum_{r \in R} q_r^* w_r^*$$

Q.E.D.

Exercise 9.1

The personal computer industry produces three kinds of hardware:

	Expected Average Price($)
Desktop personal computers	*1500*
Portable personal computers	*2000*
Printers	*1200*

The market is very large, both nationally and internationally, and the demand curves are approximately horizontal at the indicated price levels. Output is limited by the availability of scarce resources, primarily computer engineers and electronic chips. There is rapid product development and average costs are falling, creating considerable uncertainty about technical coefficients (input requirements per unit of output), as indicated in the following table.

	Engineer Hours	Chips	Capital Hours
Desktop units	*(4, 0.8)*	*10*	*(300, 20)*
Portable units	*(6, 1.4)*	*8*	*(250, 15)*
Printers	*(4, 0.3)*	*3*	*(150, 5)*

The input requirements of engineer hours and capital hours are believed to be normally distributed and stochastically independent. Each double entry *(a, b)* in the table should be interpreted as follows: *a* refers to the mathematical expectation and *b* to the variance.

The use of the normal distribution is, of course, an approximation. The true distribution is truncated from below; in any case there will exist some minimum threshold requirement of inputs.

Total available inputs are 800,000 engineer hours, 1,250,000 chips, and 40,000,000 capital hours. Find the optimal manufacturing program in the industry.

Solution: Defining the unit level of operation of each activity as the manufacture of one hardware unit, the expected value of the gross revenue from output produced can be written

$$1500 \, z_1 + 2000 \, z_2 + 1200 \, z_3$$

The objective is to maximize this expression subject to the constraints

$$
\begin{aligned}
4z_1 + 6z_2 + 4z_3 + 1.645 \, (0.8z_1^2 + 1.4z_2^2 + 0.3z_3^2)^{1/2} &\leq && 800{,}000 \\
10z_1 + 8z_2 + 3z_3 &\leq && 1{,}250{,}000 \\
300z_1 + 250z_2 + 150z_3 + 1.645 \, (20z_1^2 + 15z_2^2 + 5z_3^2)^{1/2} &\leq && 40{,}000{,}000
\end{aligned}
$$

The final terms on the left-hand side denote the safety margin of each resource that has to be set aside as a contingency against possible unfavorable stochastic variation in the unit input requirements.

Finally, all unknowns have to be non-negative.

At the optimum 74,920 desktop personal computers, 52,300 portable computers, and 27,470 printers are produced. All available resources are used in production, as follows:

	Expected Input Requirements	Set Aside as Buffer Stock	Sum
Engineer Hours	*723,370*	*76,630*	*800,000*
Chips	*1,250,000*	*---*	*1,250,000*
Capital Hours	*39,631,510*	*368,490*	*40,000,000*

The first column exhibits the mathematical expectation of the input requirements. The second column shows the planned quantities above this average that will be set aside as a buffer. Thus even if the average is exceeded, the production plan can be realized most of the time (i.e., 95 percent of the time) on the hypothesized probability distribution.

The Lagrange multipliers indicate the equilibrium prices of the three resources. Engineer hours fetch the highest price ($262.38). The price of chips is $11.41, and the price of a capital hour is $0.65. The expected manufacturing costs can then be calculated as follows:

$$\text{expected cost of one desktop unit} = 262.38 \times 4 + 11.41 \times 10 + 0.65 \times 300 = 1356.98$$

$$\text{expected cost of one portable unit} = 262.38 \times 6 + 11.41 \times 8 + 0.65 \times 250 = 1836.68$$

$$\text{expected cost of one printer} = 262.38 \times 4 + 11.41 \times 3 + 0.65 \times 150 = 1180.42$$

The expected unit profits thus come out as $143.02, $173.32, and $19.58, respectively.

The interested reader may check the relationships established in theorems 9.1–2 numerically.

9.2. ACTIVITY PORTFOLIOS

The problem of managing the modern firm including the development of new technologies, new products, and new marketing channels can be described as a portfolio problem. Just as an investor in the stock market may try to select an optimal vector of stocks, the manager of a firm may aim at determining an optimal vector of production activities to be operated. Given the background of the firm, its current line of production, the available technologies, and the image of the firm in the eyes of customers, there are some production activities that can presumably be operated with very little uncertainty; there may also be a number of product development efforts underway; and finally there is the possibility (indeed typically) of a need to initiate a stream of entirely new product designs. The modern firm no longer just produces. It must also generate new technologies. A framework for optimal selection among such new technologies may then be required to effect a rational approach to this problem. It is helpful to imagine the management of such a firm choosing a portfolio of activities, with some reasonable tradeoff between return and risk being provided to guide these choices.

The uncertainty at issue here is a complex weave of both technological and market factors. A manufacturer of shaving blades may be engaged in the development of a new type of adjustable steel-blade razor; at the current stage of development there are still a number of outstanding technical problems like the grade of plastics to be employed, the design of the plastics molds, and so on. There is also the question of the marketing of the new design and the magnitude of the possible demand.

Just as in the case of the stock portfolio problem it is not sufficient for management simply to go for the minimal possible risk. The solution to the stock portfolio problem is not to put all funds in gilt-edged government bonds, nor is the solution to the activity portfolio problem to choose well-established and well-mastered activities alone. In the modern competitive environment risks must be taken in order to survive. The manager of the modern firm must embark upon a series of product development projects although one knows in advance that some proportion of them will yield little return or may even fail entirely. The problem at hand is one of selection among alternative risky development projects.

In order to develop the argument further, it is now helpful to say a few words about the concept of efficiency in the presence of risk. The concept of efficiency is used in economics in many ways. In Koopmans' deterministic formulation of activity analysis, the efficient point or points are input-output combinations such that no output can be increased without decreasing other outputs or increasing inputs. In the mathematical programming formulation of activity analysis—which we have reviewed in chapter 4—the efficient points are determined as the optimal solution to a linear program involving explicit recognition of resource constraints in which all coefficients are knows constants.

Building upon pioneering contributions by J. Tobin and H. M. Markowitz (see references [21] and [13], respectively), the concept of efficiency as used in modern portfolio theory refers to an optimal tradeoff between return and risk. When prices of assets are stochastic, the market value of an entire portfolio of assets is also stochastic variable.

The efficiency frontier under risk continues to be the locus of efficient points. However, this is now stated in terms of mean variance relations. For any given variance that the investor is willing to accept, the portfolio to be efficient must provide the maximum attainable mathematical expectation of return (e.g., profit). Conversely, for any given mathematical expectation that the investor feels he requires, the chosen portfolio if efficient will provide the minimal variance that can be achieved.

Although this is the standard formulation in economics, it has drawbacks in that the variance (being a symmetric measure) does not adequately distinguish between "better than expected" and "worse than expected" returns. Markowitz therefore introduces concepts like the semivariance but these do not seem to provide what is needed.

Note that the chance-constrained activity analysis format discussed in the preceding section also establishes a tradeoff between mathematical expectation and risk. Program (9.5) trades off the optimal value of the program against the risk of supply violation. In other words, the risk is measured by the tail of the probability distribution rather than by the variance. The risk is a one-sided one that refers to extreme outcomes in one direction only. In particular, it is oriented toward avoidance of undesirable outcomes. So, what we have accomplished in the present context using chance-constrained programming might be worth following up in financial portfolio theory as well.

Extending the concept of efficiency, we now propose to refer to an optimal solution of program (9.5) as an efficient point. Whereas Koopmans assumed that a feasible collection of production plans must be accommodated by the availability of primary resources and labor, the extended definition permits supply failures to occur now and then, but it also allows us to plan in a way that makes it possible to control the risk of such occurrences.

In the formulations (9.2) and (9.4) we have assumed that supply failures must not occur in more than 5 percent of all cases. If the tolerance against supply violations is lowered, say to one percent of all cases only, the certainty equivalent (9.13) is changed parametrically, and there will be a new efficient point. In other words, the concept of efficiency now depends parametrically upon our willingness to accept specific rates of supply violations.[7] Such parametric changes define an entire efficiency frontier of optimal tradeoffs between the program value and the planner's tolerance of supply violations.

9.3. CHANCE-CONSTRAINED ACTIVITY NETWORKS

In order focus on the nature of the production chain which transforms primary goods into final goods, that is, on the successive transformation of a good from one intermediate stage into another, we now turn to the network format outlined in section 4.2. The nodes of the network represent the various stages of the production and distribution of a product. Each link or arc represents a distinct technology. Several links leading into the same node represent alternative available technologies.

It will be sufficient here to deal with the simple case when all activities of the model can be represented as directed links in a network (4.26). Modifying our current notation slightly, let now

$i,j,k \in I$	=	stages of production, whether primary, intermediate, or final
G	=	graph of network
x_i	=	final demand of good located at stage i
w_i	=	primary supply of good located at stage i
$P_i(x_i)$	=	demand price function at stage i
$Q_i(w_i)$	=	supply price function at stage
c_{jk}	=	unit cost along link (j,k)
t_{jk}	=	quantity leaving node j en route for node k
δ_{jk}	=	amplification/attenuation factor along link (j,k)
M	=	incidence matrix
p_i,q_i,u_i	=	Lagrange multipliers of market balance at node i

In a generalized network some transformation occurs to the commodity as it travels along the links of the network. This transformation may take the form of refining, processing, or subassembly of semifinished goods, packaging, marketing, and the like. Mathematically, we capture such change by a factor of attenuation or amplification δ_{jk} of the flow of the commodity along each link (j, k) belonging to the network. When there is technological uncertainty present, these amplification or attenuation factors δ_{jk} are uncertain.

As before we define the incidence matrix M of the generalized network in the following manner. The matrix has one row for each node in the network and one column for each link. The entries in column (j,k) are -1 in row j and δ_{jk} in row k, and zeroes in all other positions.

In the deterministic case we can write the Kirchhoff conditions as Mt = vector of effluxes and influxes where $t = [t_{jk}]$ is the vector of quantities transported along each link (j,k) of the network. The vector of effluxes and influxes appearing on the right-hand side of the equation is entered as follows. Influxes are entered with a minus sign and effluxes with a plus sign. If at a given node there is neither an influx nor an efflux the figure zero is entered.

But when the factors δ_{jk} are stochastic, the Kirchhoff conditions require attention. They will still hold ex post, of course, stating that all flow actually entering a node must equal all flow leaving the node. But how can we give a meaning to the Kirchhoff conditions ex ante before the stochastic outcome of the uncertain attenuation or amplification factors has been recorded? How is it possible to plan for fixed and deterministic flows leaving each node when the magnitude of the flows entering the node is uncertain?

Answering this question, we shall now elect to interpret the Kirchhoff conditions as chance constraints, stating that the inflow into each node must suffice most of the time to cover the flow leaving the same node:

$$(9.31) \qquad \text{Prob} \{- \sum_{i:\, (i,j) \in G} \delta_{ij} t_{ij} + \sum_{k:\, (j,k) \in G} t_{jk} \leq x_j - w_j\} \geq 0.95$$

for each node j in the graph G of the network

(The notation $i:\, (i,j) \in G$ means all nodes having a link leading directly to j, and the notation $k:\, (j,k) \in G$ means all nodes which receive flow directly from j.)

Extending program (4.26) to the stochastic case, one then has

$$(9.32) \qquad max \sum_{j \in I} \int P_j(x_j) dx_j - \sum_{j \in I} \int Q_j(w_j) dw_j - \sum_{(j,k) \in G} c_{jk} t_{jk}$$

subject to

$$\text{Prob} \{- \sum_{i:\, (i,j) \in G} \delta_{ij}\, t_{ij} + \sum_{k:\, (j,k) \in G} t_{jk} \leq x_j - w_j\} \geq 0.95$$

$$x_j, w_j \geq 0, j \in I$$

$$t_{jk} \geq 0, (j,k) \in G$$

The mathematics becomes quite elaborate, and we shall leave the matter here. The reader will readily see, however, how it is possible to proceed as before, converting each chance constraint in (9.32) into a certainty equivalent, defining Lagrange multipliers, and writing the Kuhn–Tucker conditions. (For an illustration and interpretations, see exercise 9.2).

It will be remembered that in the deterministic network there are equilibrium conditions stating that if a positive flow is transmitted along a link of the network, the appreciation of value along the link must equal the unit cost along the link. The appreciation of value along a link (j,k) was defined as the arrival value at node k of one unit of the commodity departing from node j minus the departure value of the same unit (see the last two paragraphs of sec. 4.2). In the stochastic case one will rather find that the appreciation along link *(j,k)* will generate some positive profit above the unit cost c_{jk}. Furthermore, these profits will be used to accumulate buffer inventories of intermediate goods. For the economy as a whole there is a counterpart result to theorem 9.1 stating that total profits in the economy equal the value of all inventory and excess capacity held.

Exercise 9.2

There has been rapid technological development in almost all phases of the production and distribution of seafood during the last several decades, spurred by breakthroughs in marine biology, breeding technology, packaging, and air freight. An instructive example of this development is provided by the crayfish industry. The State of Louisiana accounts for 85 percent of the world's harvest of crayfish (called crawfish in Louisiana). The state's Atchafalaya Basin is a vast wetland where the crayfish finds an ideal natural habitat. In addition, industrial breeding in ponds has become important and during the last decade the pond acreage in Louisiana has tripled.

The production process, however, is quite risky. A certain parasitic fungus can rapidly kill the entire population of crayfish in a breeding pond. Distribution is also precarious, since the crayfish is a perishable commodity.   Through packaging and air transportation, it is possible to reach distant export markets. U.S. crayfish exports to Sweden alone in 1987 amounted to close to two thousand metric tons.

For a schematic illustration of the production and distribution, we shall use a simple network containing five nodes and four links. The nodes signify various stages in the production and distribution, as follows:

> *Node 1:*   *Crayfish in its natural habitat*
>
> *Node 2:*   *Crayfish in breeding ponds*
>
> *Node 3:*   *Harvested crayfish*
>
> *Node 4:*   *Crayfish for sale in U. S. supermarkets*
>
> *Node 5:*   *Exports*

There are links from nodes 1 and 2 leading to node 3, and links from node 3 leading to nodes 4 and 5. Each link represents a separate technology, as follows:

> *Link (1,3):* *Harvesting of crayfish located in its natural habitat*
>
> *Link (2,3):* *Harvesting of crayfish located in breeding ponds*
>
> *Link (3,4):* *Transporting and distributing crayfish to U.S. supermarkets*
>
> *Link (3,5):* *Exporting*

Consider now the following numerical example. Consider (in line with conventional activity analysis) the supply of crayfish in its natural habitat w_1 as an endowment of nature, say w_1 = twenty thousand metric tons. But the supply in breeding ponds w_2 is an unknown, to be determined. Such supply can be increased by supplying new pond acreage. Let the supply price function for crayfish in breeding ponds be

$1 + 0.2w_2$ dollars per kilogram (there are one thousand kilograms in a metric ton)

The unit cost of production and transportation along the four links are $c_{13} = 4, c_{23} = 6, c_{34} = 2, c_{35} = 10$, respectively.

Attenuation of flow along the links of the network occurs as crayfish die or are destroyed. The attenuation factors δ_{jk} are uncertain, as explained, as follows:

$$E\delta_{13} = 0.9, E\delta_{23} = 0.7,$$

$$var(\delta_{13}) = 0.01, Cov(\delta_{13}, \delta_{23}) = 0.01, var(\delta_{23}) = 0.04$$

$$E\delta_{34} = 0.9, E\delta_{35} = 0.7$$

$$var(\delta_{34}) = 0.01, var(\delta_{35}) = 0.04$$

Domestic U. S. demand is given by the demand price function $30 - 0.5x_4$ dollars per kilogram, where x_4 is the quantity sold in thousand metric tons. The export price is \$24 per kilogram. The demand curve in the export market is horizontal ("infinite demand").

Determine the level of operation of each activity, the quantity sold domestically, and the volume of exports. Determine the price to be charged in U. S. supermarkets.

Solution. Program (9.29) simply reads

$$max\ 30x_4 - 0.25(x_4)^2 + 24x_5 - w_2 - 0.1(w_2)^2 - 4t_{13} - 6t_{23}$$

$$-2t_{34} - 10t_{35}$$

subject to

$$t_{13} \leq 20$$

$$t_{23} - w_2 \leq 0$$

$$Prob\ (t_{34} + t_{35} - \delta_{13}t_{13} - \delta_{23}t_{23} \leq 0) \geq 0.95$$

$$Prob\ (x_4 - \delta_{34}t_{34} \leq 0) \geq 0.95$$

$$Prob\ (x_5 - \delta_{35}t_{35} \leq 0) \geq 0.95$$

$$x_4, x_5, t_{13}, t_{23}, t_{34}, t_{35}, w_2 \geq 0$$

The first two terms of the maximand represent the social payoff of domestic demand. The third term is the social payoff of export demand; it simply equals the value of export demand. The negative terms are the cost of breeding crayfish in ponds (obtained by integrating marginal costs), and all costs of transportation and distribution.

There is one market constraint for each node of the network. In the case of nodes 1 and 2, it simply states that the harvest cannot exceed the supply. As to nodes 3, 4, and 5, the constraint is of a more complicated nature, since the availabilities at these nodes are stochastic. The market constraint is written as a chance constraint stating that the quantity available must suffice to cover the local demand at the node at least 95 percent of the time. A supply violation must not occur more than 5 percent of the time.

Converting the three chance constraints into certainty equivalents, and also introducing a spacer variable μ_3 at the third node of the network, one gets

$$t_{34} + t_{35} - 0.9t_{13} - 0.7t_{23} + \mu_3 \leq 0$$

$$1.645^2\ (0.01t_{13}^2 + 0.02\ t_{13}\ t_{23} + 0.04\ t_{23}^2) - \mu_3^2 \leq 0$$

$$x_4 - 0.9\ t_{34} + 1.645 \times 0.1\ t_{34} \leq 0$$

$$x_5 - 0.7\ t_{35} + 1.645 \times 0.2\ t_{35} \leq 0$$

For simplicity, it has been assumed that the stochastic attenuation factors are all normally distributed.

The entire program may now be written

$$max\ 30x_4 - 0.25\ (x_4)^2 + 24x_5 - w_2 - 0.1(w_2)^2 - 4t_{13} - 6t_{23} - 2t_{34} - 10t_{35}$$

subject to

$$t_{13} \leq 20$$

$$t_{23} - w_2 \leq 0$$

$$t_{34} + t_{35} - 0.9t_{13} - 0.7t_{23} + \mu_3 \leq 0$$

$$1.645^2\ (0.01\ t_{13}^2 + 0.02t_{13}t_{23} + 0.04\ t_{23}^2) - \mu_3^2 \leq 0$$

$$x_4 - 0.9\ t_{34} + 1.645 \times 0.1\ t_{34} \leq 0$$

$$x_5 - 0.7\ t_{35} + 1.645 \times 0.2\ t_{35} \leq 0$$

$$x_4, x_5, t_{13}, t_{23}, t_{34}, t_{35}, w_2, \mu_3 \geq 0$$

Solving, one finds the optimal solution

$$x_4^* = 11.84, x_5^* = 0,$$

$$t_{13}^* = 20.00, t_{23}^* = 2.75, t_{34}^* = 16.11, t_{35}^* = 0$$

$$w_2^* = 2.75, \mu_3^* = 3.82$$

So, it turns out that the optimal solution calls for holdings of buffer inventory at nodes 3,4,5 amounting to, respectively, 3.82, 1.645 x 0.1 x 16.11 = 2.65, and 0.

The optimal direct solution may then be summarized as follows (all quantities measured in thousands of metric tons):

Node 1:	*Inflow 20, outflow 20*
Link (1,3):	*Flow entering link 20, flow leaving link 18*
Node 2:	*Inflow 2.75, outflow 2.75*
Link (2,3):	*Flow entering link 2.75, flow leaving link 1.93*
Node 3:	*Inflows 18 and 1.93. Inventory held at node 3.82.*
	Outflow 16.11
Link (3,4):	*Flow entering link 16.11, flow leaving link 14.50*
Node 4:	*Inflow 14.50. Inventory held at node 2.65. Outflow 11.84*
Link (3,5):	*No flow*
Node 5:	*No flow*

Furthermore, for the Lagrange multipliers (say $q_1, q_2, u_3, \omega_3, p_4, p_5$, respectively) one finds

$$p_4^* = 24.08, p_5^* = 24.00$$
$$q_1^* = 7.61, q_2^* = 1.55, u_3^* = 15.71, \omega_3^* = 15.04$$

The imputed prices at the various nodes of the network, and the expected imputed appreciation along links are exhibited below (all prices measured in dollars per kilogram):

Node 1:	*Imputed price 7.61*
Node 2:	*Imputed price 1.55*
Node 3:	*Imputed price 15.71*
Link (1,3)	*Imputed appreciation $0.9 \times 15.71 - 7.61 = 6.53$; unit cost = 4;*
	imputed unit profit = 2.53
Link (2,3):	*Imputed appreciation $0.7 \times 15.71 - 1.55 = 9.45$; unit cost = 6;*
	imputed unit profit = 3.45

Node 4:   *Imputed price 24.08*

Node 5:   *Price 24*

Link (3,4):   *Imputed appreciation $0.9 \times 24.08 - 15.71 = 5.96$;*

unit cost = 2; imputed unit profit = 3.96

Link (3,5):   *Imputed appreciation $0.7 \times 24 - 15.71 = 1.09$; unit cost = 10.*

Imputed appreciation does not even cover unit cost; flow along this link is not warranted.

Also note that

Value of all inventories held in the system $= 15.71 \times 3.82 + 24.08 \times 2.65 =$
$$= 123.82$$

and

Total profit in the system $= 2.53 \times 20 + 3.45 \times 2.75 + 3.96 \times 16.11$ $= 123.89$. The small discrepancy is due to rounding errors.

As the optimal solution shows, airlifting crayfish for exports is still too costly and too risky. But suppose now that there occur innovations in packaging and airfreight and distribution that (i) lower the expected spoilage rate $1 - E\delta_{35}$ from 0.3 to 0.1 and lower the attendant risk $var\delta_{35}$ from 0.04 to 0.01, and (ii) lower the unit shipping cost c_{35} from 10 to 6. The reader is asked to solve the problem again. This time exports are warranted.

A Theory of Innovation and Technological Change

Within the context of activity networks, innovation and technological change may be thought of as a displacement of the optimal flow through the network, rerouting production and/or distribution away from one or several established activities and starting up the operation of a single new link or a succession of new links that has not been utilized before.

The conventional Schumpeterian way of looking at such change would no doubt be to declare that new links in the network emerge spontaneously. The present setting of analysis under uncertainty, however, invites another interpretation: that these "new" links actually have been in existence all the time, but that the uncertainty attached to the amplification or attenuation factors was earlier prohibitive; further, that some technical or managerial improvement has now reduced this uncertainty so that optimization will lead to some positive flow along the link.

To make these ideas specific, we may place ourselves in the position of a manager who wants to evaluate the possible operation of a particular activity represented by a link in the network. The Kuhn–Tucker conditions have taught us to carry out such an evaluation by calculating the imputed appreciation of the commodity being processed along the link, and comparing it to the incurred processing cost. Operation of the activity will be warranted if the imputed appreciation is sufficient to both cover the cost and provide a unit profit large enough to cover the risk incurred. There will therefore exist, for each link leaving a given node, some cut-off level of uncertainty. If the uncertainty is greater than the threshold level, the activity will not be operated. If the uncertainty stays within the threshold level, however, the activity will be operated.

A change of the joint probability distribution of all risk factors, taking the form of a reduction in the covariances of the required inputs and/or the resulting outputs may then, if the reduction is of sufficient numerical magnitude, lead to the initiation of the operation of an activity that has not been operated earlier.

Formally, innovation and technological change may also come about even under unchanging risk conditions if, for some reason presently to be discussed, the manager increases his subjective tolerance of risk, that is, becomes willing to accept a greater frequency of supply violations. In the mathematical programs in this chapter, we have assumed throughout that the supply constraints were to be satisfied in at least 95 percent of all cases. This figure was chosen as a numerical example only. If for some reason the manager becomes willing to accept more frequent violations, say in 10 percent of all cases so that the supply constraints need only be satisfied 90 percent of the time, reoptimization of the same program may now lead to the positive use of one or several uncertain processes that were formerly considered too risky.

What determines the willingness of managers to accept a given risk? Leaving the realm of the specific mathematical programs developed here, one may identify several institutional factors that affect these decisions. Tax policy, the availability of venture capital and borrowed funds, and the general state of confidence in the economy all play a part.

Note finally that the theory sketched here also provides a framework for the understanding of a cascading series of innovation and technological change throughout an industry or economic sector. The network representation allows us to investigate not just the introduction of a new single link in the network but shifts that may involve the dismantling of an entire path of successive links (creative destruction) and the appearance of an entirely new chain of links featuring a series of new production processes.

NOTES

1. See, e.g., Borch [1].
2. The standard reference is Schumpeter [15].
3. The treatment follows Charnes and Cooper [3] and [4].
4. See Charnes and Cooper [4].
5. See Kuhn and Tucker [2.5]. The account of the Kuhn–Tucker theorem provided in section 2.3 was limited to the case of a linear constraint

set; in the general case of a convex constraint set a so-called constraint qualification condition is also required.

6.   See Slater [16].

7.   See Land, Lovell, and Thore [11] for a discussion of the relative willingness of management to accept supply violations in a capitalist economy and in a setting of state socialism.

BIBLIOGRAPHIC NOTES

The material in this chapter draws upon developments in both economics and operations research.

The original formulation of activity analysis (see Koopmans [9] and [10]) was of a deterministic nature. The interest in stochastic disturbances in input and output coefficients arose somewhat later in connection with the study of intertemporal formulations involving dynamic Leontief models, turnpike theory, and multisector growth models. For a representative formulation of stochastic activity analysis in this literature, see Majumdar and Radner [12], sec. 2.

Developments in OR literature have unfolded from another end. Here the emphasis is on practical problems of management and resource allocation in the face of uncertainty. Many of these studies were not expressly formulated as activity analysis, but can be so translated. The OR literature was quick to recognize the necessity to build up inventory stock as a contingency against uncertainties, both at the level of primary resources and of finished products.

The original development of chance-constrained programming by Charnes, Cooper, and Symonds [5] involved a case of providing heating oil to customers with variable customer demand and storage constraints. Applications of chance-constrained programming have later been reported in the literature relating to problems of staffing hospitals, operating railroads, determining reservoir capacities in irrigation projects, determining optimal cropping patterns in agriculture, planning investment in electricity generating plants, and the like. All these various applications can—at least in principle—be reformulated in an activity analysis format with uncertain parameters.

The optimal price structure in a linear programming formulation of activity analysis is obtained from the corresponding dual program. Each market price is the dual of a corresponding market constraint. In an analogous fashion, it became clear in the chance-constrained programming literature that optimal prices can be determined as the Lagrange multipliers of the certainty equivalents of the market constraints. See in particular Charnes, Kirby, Littlechild, and Raike [6] and Charnes, Kirby, and Raike [7].

The first attempt to straddle the heritage from Koopmans and the more recent developments in chance-constrained programming is Thore [17].

In a remarkable paper by Charnes and Stedry [8], a chance-constrained programming model was developed to represent the planning of organized research in different research areas. The treatment in the main text of the planning of product innovation in an uncertain context follows similar lines. The work by Charnes and Stedry goes much further, however, in that it also allows for unexpected research breakthroughs and real-time modification of the original research plans due to such unexpected events.

The developments in section 9.1 are brought from Thore [18]. See also Land, Lovell, and Thore [11] and Thore [19].

The idea of an activity portfolio, presented in section 10.2, is well known in the literature of management planning under uncertainty. For the use of chance-constrained programming in portfolio analysis, see Naslund and Whinston [14] and Burnham [2].

Section 9.3 draws on Thore [20].

REFERENCES

[9.1]   Borch, K. *The Economics of Uncertainty*. Princeton, N. J.: Princeton University press, 1968.

[9.2]   Burnham, J. M. "Conditional Chance-constrained Programming Techniques in Portfolio Selection," Ph. D. diss., The University of Texas at Austin, 1970.

[9.3]   Charnes, A., and W. W. Cooper. "Chance Constrained Programming," *Management Science* 15 (1959): 73–79.

[9.4]   Charnes, A., and W. W. Cooper. "Chance Constraints and Normal Deviates," *Journal of the American Statistical Association* 57 (1962): 134–48.

[9.5]   Charnes, A., W. W. Cooper, and G. H. Symonds. "Cost Horizons and Certainty Equivalents: An Approach to Stochastic Programming of Heating Oil," *Management Science* 4 (1958): 235–63.

[9.6]   Charnes, A., M. J. L. Kirby, S. C. Littlechild, and W. M. Raike. "Chance-constrained Methods for Transport Pricing and Scheduling under Competition," *Transport Science* 2 (1968): 57–76.

[9.7]   Charnes, A., M. J. L. Kirby, and M. W. Raike. "Chance-constrained Generalized Networks," *Operations Research* 14 (1966): 1113–20.

[9.8]   Charnes, A., and A. Stedry. "A Chance-constrained Model for Real-Time Control in Research and Development Management," *Management Science* 12/8 (Apr. 1966) B353–B362.

[9.9]   Koopmans, T. C., ed. *Activity Analysis of Production and Allocation.* Cowles Commission Monograph, no. 13. New York: Wiley, 1951.

[9.10]   Koopmans, T. C. *Three Essays on the State of Economic Science.* New York: McGraw-Hill, 1957.

[9.11]   Land, K. C., C. A. K. Lovell, and S. Thore. "Chance-constrained Efficiency Analysis," Paper presented at the National Science Foundation Conference on Parametric and Nonparametric Approaches to Frontier analysis, Chapel Hill, N. C., Sept. 1988.

[9.12]   Majumdar, M., and R. Radner. "Stationary Optimal Policies with Discounting in a Stochastic Activity Analysis Model," *Econometrica* 51/6 (Nov. 1983): 1821–38.

[9.13]   Markowitz, H. M. "Portfolio Selection," *Journal of Finance* (Mar. 1952): 77–91.

[9.14]   Naslund, B., and A. Whinston. "A Model of Multi-Period Investment under Uncertainty," *Management Science* 8 (1961): 184–200.

[9.15]   Schumpeter, J. A. *Business Cycles.* London and New York: McGraw-Hill, 1st ed. 1939.

[9.16]   Slater, M. "Lagrange Multipliers Revisited: A Contribution to Nonlinear Programming," *Crowles Commission Discussion Paper, Math. 403,* Nov. 1950.

[9.17]   Thore, S. "A Dynamic Leontief Model with Chance-constraints." In *Risk and Uncertainty,* eds. K. Borch and J. Mossin. New York: Macmillan, 1968.

[9.18]   Thore, S. "Chance-Constrained Activity Analysis," *European Journal of Operational Research* 30/3 (1987): 267–69.

[9.19]   Thore, S. "Generalized Network Spatial Equilibrium: The Deterministic and the Chance-Constrained Case," *Papers of the Regional Science Association* 59 (1986): 93–102.

[9.20]   Thore, S. "Koopmans' Activity Analysis as a Network of Uncertain Technology Portfolios," *Proceedings of the First International Conference of Technology Management,* University of Miami, Feb. 1988, Interscience Enterprises Ltd., Geneva, 1988.

[9.21]   Tobin, J. "Liquidity Preference as Behavior toward Risk," *Review of Economic Studies* 25 (Feb. 1958): 65–86.

10

The Production and Distribution System as an Infinite Game

Uncertainty in the marketplace is not just uncertainty about the parameters of production. It is above all uncertainty about competitors and market reactions for which, as observed at the close of chapter 2, the theory of games provides an approach.

At this point, the reader is asked to review the basic concepts of a two-person zero-sum game (see sec. 2.5). The gaming format that we presently need is that of a two-person game. One player controls the use of all primary resources, production, and the distribution of outputs. To him, all prices are uncertain. The other player is a fictitious market player who sets all prices. To him, all quantity decisions are uncertain.

The games that will be dealt with here are called infinite games in that each player can choose from infinitely many strategies. The player controlling all quantity variables can choose any combination of production inputs and production outputs that satisfies the given technological relationships. The price player can choose any combination of non-negative prices.

When the theory of games as developed by von Neumann and Morgenstern was first published, there was a belief among economists that it would dramatically change the approach to economic science (J. Marschak [9]; L. Hurwicz [8]). But such a dramatic reevaluation never came about, partly because the theory of games itself became a field for specialists. This was unfortunate. Game theoretical results that have been known to specialists for a long time still await their proper appreciation by the economics profession at large. The material to be covered in this chapter offers one example. We shall review some theory of infinite two-person games that was developed more than twenty-five years ago and yet is still not well known in economics. Such theory, however, has implications for use by economists who wish to understand the formation of markets and market prices.

In the case when each player controls just one single decision variable, each player may select from a continuum of choices over some given closed interval. The field of possible choices by both players may then be represented as a square, with each player controlling the choices along one side of it. If each player has many available decision variables, the field of possible choices may be represented as a hypersquare (the intersection of the intervals of possible choices of each player).

The payoff function is assumed to be continuous and concave-convex. The deterministic problem then has a saddle-point. A mixed strategy for a player takes the form of a probability density function over his interval of possible choices.

The basic theoretical result is quite attractive: It states simply that this mixed strategy game has a solution in pure strategies. The solution point is given by the saddle-point to the deterministic problem.

This establishes a logical link between infinite games and deterministic models. The optimal solution to many deterministic programming models may alternatively be arrived at as the solution to an implied infinite two-person game. In particular, most of the deterministic models of production and distribution that have occupied us in the earlier chapters in this volume, may alternatively be represented as the optimal outcome of such a game.

To illustrate this proposition, the conventional transportation model may alternatively be represented as an infinite two-person game. One player controls all quantity variables, the other controls all price variables.

The games are zero-sum in the sense that the payoff of one player has to come from the pocket of the other player. But the value of these market games will in general not be zero. There is nothing inherently fair in the market duel between resource owners and producers and consumers on the one hand, and the fictitious market player on the other. As we shall see, the payoff function consists of the sum of all consumers' surplus, all suppliers' surplus (to be defined), and all profit.

Who is the fictitious price player? Is he just a hypothetical analytical device, perhaps reminiscent of the famous Maxwell's demon in thermodynamics, or is he a flesh-and-blood person? The final section of the chapter offers some comments and discusses the role of brokers in markets.

SYMBOLS USED IN CHAPTER 10

$0 \leq x \leq M$	choice variable of player $\mathcal{P}_1$ (dummy variable: t)
$0 \leq y \leq N$	choice variable of player $\mathcal{P}_2$ (dummy variable: u)
ϕ, ψ	mixed strategies of players $\mathcal{P}_1$ and $\mathcal{P}_2$, respectively
$\mathcal{F}(x,y)$	payoff function of the game

v, v_1, v_2	value of game, value to player $\mathcal{P}_1$, value to player $\mathcal{P}_2$
$h \in H, k \in K$	origins and destinations, respectively
x_k	demand at destination k
w_h	supply at origin h
t_{hk}	quantity transported from origin h to destination k
p_k, q_h	prices at destinations and origins, respectively
c_{hk}	unit transportation costs
$i \in I$	final goods
$r \in R$	resources
$m \in M$	activities
$A = [a_{rm}]$	matrix of input coefficients
$B = [b_{im}]$	matrix of output coefficients
z_m	level of operation of activity m
x_i	quantity demanded of final good i
w_r	quantity supplied of resource r
p_i, q_r	prices of final goods and of resources,respectively
$P_k(x_k), P_i(x_i)$	demand price function
$Q_h(w_h), Q_r(w_r)$	supply price function
$(\bar{\ })$	upper bounds on quantities and prices; throughout the chapter, these upper bounds are assumed to be redundant so that they can be added or deleted as desired

10.1. INFINITE TWO-PERSON GAMES PLAYED ON A SQUARE

Section 2.5 outlined the basic setting of a two-person game. There are two players, say $\mathcal{P}_1$ and $\mathcal{P}_2$; each player controls a choice variable or decision variable. There are a number of alternative possible choices for each player. Each such choice represents a pure strategy. We also formalize the concept of a mixed strategy for each player as a probability distribution over the various pure strategy choices.

The games that we shall study in the present chapter are more complicated than those discussed in chapter 2 in that the decision variable of each player will typically allow for infinitely many alternative possible values and are not restricted to just a finite number of different choices. More specifically, we shall assume that each player has available to him a continuum of pure strategies, represented as points in an interval. Assume that player $\mathcal{P}_1$ controls the decision variable x over the interval $0 \le x \le M$ and player $\mathcal{P}_2$ controls the decision variable y over the interval $0 \le y \le N$. Each player controls a single variable and the joint decisions of both players may then be represented as a point in x,y-space located in the square

$$(10.1) \qquad 0 \le x \le M$$

$$0 \leq y \leq N$$

The payoff function $\mathcal{F}(x,y)$ defined over the square (10.1) is assumed to be real-valued, continuous, concave in x for each y, and convex in y for each x. If $\mathcal{F}(x,y) > 0$ then the payment is from player $\mathcal{P}_2$ to player $\mathcal{P}_1$, while if $\mathcal{F}(x,y) < 0$ the payoff is from $\mathcal{P}_1$ to $\mathcal{P}_2$. The gain of one player equals the loss of the other so the game is zero-sum.

Any deterministic choice of the variable x by player $\mathcal{P}_1$ will be referred to as pure strategy for him. Any deterministic choice of y is a pure strategy for player $\mathcal{P}_2$.

The deterministic saddle-point problem

(10.2) $\underset{x}{max} \ \underset{y}{min} \ \mathcal{F}(x,y)$

subject to $0 \leq x \leq M$

$$0 \leq y \leq N$$

has a saddle point. (The key observation here is that both constraint sets are convex, bounded, and closed. See sec. 2.1.) The saddle point need not be unique.

We proceed to define the concept of a mixed strategy for each player. Instead of confining the choices of player $\mathcal{P}_1$ to pure strategies like "always choose $x = x_0$," we shall allow $\mathcal{P}_1$ to choose a probability density function $\phi(x)$ of the continuous random variable x, defined over the interval $0 \leq x \leq M$. The probability density function is defined so that:

(i)   The density function is non-negative over the interval of allowable strategy choices defined for the random variable in question:

(10.3) $\phi(x) \geq 0 \ \ for \ 0 \leq x \leq M.$

(ii)   The probability density function is interpreted such that the mass quantity allotted to any interval represents the probability that the random variable takes a value belonging to the interval:

(10.4) $$\int_{x_1}^{x_2} \phi(t)\, dt = Prob(x_1 \leq x \leq x_2)$$

where x_1 and x_2 are any two points satisfying $0 \leq x_1 \leq x_2 \leq M$, and where t is a dummy variable used as the variable of integration.

(iii)   In particular, over the entire interval $0 \leq x \leq M$ one gets

(10.5) $$\int_0^M \phi(t)\, dt = 1$$

that is, the value of the random variable must be chosen with probability one from the interval $0 \leq t \leq M$.

Once the probability density function has been defined, the corresponding cumulative distribution function

(10.6) $$\int_0^x \phi(t)\, dt$$

is also determined for any $0 \leq x \leq M$.

Note that the pure strategy $x = x_0$ may always formally be regarded as a special case of a mixed strategy with the cumulative distribution

(10.7) $$\int_0^{x_0 - \varepsilon} \phi(t)\, dt = 0$$

for all $\varepsilon \geq 0$, but

(10.8) $$\int_0^{x_0 + \varepsilon} \phi(t)\, dt = 1$$

for all $\varepsilon \geq 0$. In other words, the choice "always choose $x = x_0$" continues to be admissible, as before, and this pure strategy choice also continues to be available in those cases where it is "best" for $\mathcal{P}_1$. More generally, the problem for $\mathcal{P}_1$ is to choose the best density function $\phi(x)$ satisfying (10.3–4).

Similarly, the mixed strategy for player $\mathcal{P}_2$ will be defined by the probability density function $\psi(y)$ of the continuous random variable y, defined over the interval $0 \leq y \leq N$. It is required that this density function is non-negative over the interval of variability

$$(10.9) \qquad \psi(y) \geq 0 \qquad \text{for } 0 \leq y \leq N$$

but zero elsewhere, and that

$$(10.10) \qquad \int_{y_1}^{y_2} \psi(u)du = Prob(y_1 \leq y \leq y_2)$$

where y_1 and y_2 are two arbitrary points satisfying $0 \leq y_1 \leq y_2 \leq N$, and where u is as the variable of integration.

The corresponding cumulative distribution function for player $\mathcal{P}_2$ is

$$(10.11) \qquad \int_0^y \psi(u)\, du$$

We are now ready to calculate the expected payoff of the game under different scenarios. If player $\mathcal{P}_1$ uses the pure strategy x_0 while player $\mathcal{P}_2$ uses the mixed strategy φ, the expected payoff is

$$(10.12) \qquad \int_0^N \psi(u)\, \mathcal{F}(x_0,u)\, du,$$

where the value of $\mathcal{F}(x_0,u)$ is the payoff associated with the choice x_0,u. If $\mathcal{P}_2$ uses the pure strategy y_0 and $\mathcal{P}_1$ uses the mixed strategy ϕ, the expected payoff is

$$(10.13) \qquad \int_0^M \psi(t) \, \mathcal{F}(t,y_0) \, dt$$

Finally, if $\mathcal{P}_1$ uses ϕ and $\mathcal{P}_2$ uses ψ one gets the expected payoff

$$(10.14) \qquad \int_0^M \int_0^N \phi(t)\psi(u) \, \mathcal{F}(t,u)dtdu$$

We now formulate the problem of optimal strategy choices for each player in the following terms. Player $\mathcal{P}_1$ may fear that $\mathcal{P}_2$ will discover his choice of strategy. If this should happen, then $\mathcal{P}_2$ will certainly choose some pure strategy y_0 that will minimize the expected payoff (to $\mathcal{P}_1$) of the game, that is, that would give

$$(10.15) \qquad \min_{y_0} \int_0^M \phi(t) \, \mathcal{F}(t,y_0)dt$$

This, then, is $\mathcal{P}_1$'s expected gain-floor. Hence, $\mathcal{P}_1$ should use a mixed strategy ϕ to maximize this expression, yielding him

$$(10.16) \qquad v_1 = \max_{\phi} \, \min_{y_0} \int_0^M \phi(t) \, \mathcal{F}(t,y_0)dt$$

In other words, he seeks the maximum strategy that would produce the expected payoff (10.16). The expected payoff (10.16) is the value of the game to player $\mathcal{P}_1$.

From the point of view of player $\mathcal{P}_2$, the situation is exactly the opposite. His fear is that $\mathcal{P}_1$ will discover his strategy. If that were to happen, $\mathcal{P}_1$ would choose some pure strategy x_0 that would maximize his expected payoff of the game, that is, that would attain

$$(10.17) \qquad \max_{x_0} \int_0^N \psi(u) \, \mathcal{F}(x_0,u) \, du$$

This is P_2's loss-ceiling. P_2 tries to reduce it to a minimum, yielding

(10.18) $v_2 = \displaystyle\min_{\psi} \max_{x_0} \int_0^N \psi(u) \, \mathcal{F}(x_0, u) du$

This choice of ψ with the given x_0 is the minimax strategy of player P_2 and the expression (10.17) is the value of the game to this player. Evidently,

(10.19) $v_1 \leq v_2$

We shall simply say that the game has a value if solutions to the saddle-point problems (10.16) and (10.18) always exist and are finite, and if the optimal value v_1 of the maximin problem equals the optimal value v_2 of the minimax problem.

In the applications that we are going to encounter later in this chapter, the games are inherently skewed in the sense that player P_1 may expect to win some positive or negative amount (the expected payoff) from player P_2 during each round of the game. But, the games are still zero-sum in the sense that any gain of player P_1 is a loss to player P_2.

Theorem 10.1.   Under the assumptions listed, the mixed strategy game has a value, say $v = v_1 = v_2$.

The key assumptions are that the game is played on the square given by (10.1) and that the payoff function is continuous. The assumption that the payoff function is concave-convex is not needed now.

The proof of the theorem proceeds by approximating the given infinite game by a finite one with a large number of discrete choices for each player. This finite game has a value. As the number of choices is increased for each payer, the approximation can be made arbitrarily close.

To give analytical form to what has now been said, let us replace the intervals $0 \leq x \leq M$ and $0 \leq y \leq N$ for the two players by the discrete alternatives (the grid)

(10.20) $x_m = m/\omega, \; m = 0, M, 2M, \ldots, \omega M$

$$y_n = n/\omega, \; n = 0, \, N, \, 2N, \ldots, \omega N$$

that is, the unit interval of each player is divided into ω equal parts.

One then has the following finite game (as seen from the point of view of player $\mathcal{P}_1$):

$$(10.21) \quad \min_{q} \; \max_{p} \; \sum_{m=1}^{m=M} \sum_{n=1}^{n=N} p_m \, \mathcal{H}\!\left(\frac{m}{\omega}, \frac{n}{\omega}\right) q_n$$

subject to

$$\sum_{m=1}^{m=M} p_m = 1$$

$$\sum_{n=1}^{n=N} q_n = 1$$

$$p_m \geq 0, \; m = 1, 2, \ldots, M$$

$$q_n \geq 0, \; n = 1, 2, \ldots, N$$

where p_m, $m = 1, 2, \ldots, M$ is the mixed strategy to be determined for player $\mathcal{P}_1$, and q_n, $n = 1, 2, \ldots, N$ is the mixed strategy to be determined for player $\mathcal{P}_2$.

Rather than permitting a continuum of choices for each player over an entire square in the x-y plane, we are now narrowing down the options of the players by requiring the game to be played on only a finite number of discrete grid points in the x-y plane. Let the optimal solution to this approximate game be the mixed strategies

$$(10.22) \quad p_m{}^*, \; m = 0, \, M, \, 2M, \ldots, \omega M$$

$$q_n{}^*, \; n = 0, \, N, \, 2N, \ldots, \omega N$$

for the two players P_1 and P_2, respectively, and let the value of this approximate finite game be v_ω.

The purpose of the mathematical development to follow is to demonstrate that the value v_ω is close to the value v_1 of the original infinite game to player 1. Also, v_ω is close to the value v_2 of that same infinite game to player P_2. If the approximating grid in the x-y plane is made sufficiently fine, v_ω can in fact be brought arbitrarily close to both v_1 and v_2. Hence, by limiting arguments as we shall show, $v_1 = v_2$.

Let player P_1 play the mixed strategy $p_m{}^*$, all m, and consider two alternatives: (1) player P_2 plays the pure strategy y_0 which may not be a grid point; and (2) player P_2 plays the pure strategy n/ω which is a "close" grid point in the sense that

$$(10.23) \qquad \left| \sum_{m=1}^{m=M} p_m{}^* \, \mathcal{F}(m/\omega, y_0) - \sum_{n=1}^{n=N} p_m{}^* \, \mathcal{F}(m/\omega, n/\omega) \right| < \varepsilon$$

where the vertical strokes indicate an absolute value and ε is some given small positive number. (Because $\mathcal{F}$ is continuous, it is always possible to find such a grid point by choosing the grid fine enough, that is, by making ω sufficiently large and positive.)

Examining the just given alternative (2) a bit further, the suggested play for player P_2 will in general be a nonoptimal play for him (his optimal play is $q_n{}^*$, $n = 0, N, 2N, \ldots, \omega N$). Hence the value of the objective function of the finite game outlined in case (2) will in general be greater than the minimax value:

$$(10.24) \qquad \sum_{m=1}^{m=M} p_m{}^* \, \mathcal{F}(m/\omega, n/\omega) \geq v_\omega$$

Combination of (10.23) and (10.24) yields (multiplying through the first equation by -1, adding, and making use of the elementary rule $|a + b| \leq |a| + |b|$ for absolute values)

$$(10.25) \qquad \sum_{m=1}^{m=M} p_m{}^* \, \mathcal{F}(m/\omega, y_0) > v_\omega - \varepsilon$$

This result holds for any pure strategy y_0 for player $\mathcal{P}_2$.

To continue the argument, let us now return to the original infinite game played on the square $0 \leq x \leq N, 0 \leq y \leq M$. In particular, then, the inequality (10.25) holds for that optimal y_0 which solves (10.16) and which player $\mathcal{P}_1$ must fear that his opponent might use as a pure strategy against him and for which

$$(10.26) \qquad v_1 \geq \sum_{m=1}^{m=M} p_m{}^* \; \mathcal{F}(m/\omega, y_0)$$

Comparing (10.25) and (10.26) we obtain

$$(10.27) \qquad v_1 > v_\omega - \varepsilon$$

In a similar way, it can be shown that

$$(10.28) \qquad v_2 < v_\omega + \varepsilon$$

and hence

$$(10.29) \qquad v_1 > v_\omega - \varepsilon > v_2 - 2\varepsilon$$

But by (10.19) $v_1 \leq v_2$ *and* $\varepsilon > 0$ is arbitrary. Hence, $v_1 = v_2$. We also see that

$$(10.30) \qquad v_1 = v_2 = \lim_{w \longrightarrow +\infty} v_\omega$$

We are now ready to develop theorem 10.2, which is the main result. This theorem deals with the mixed strategy game (10.14) which obtains when both players are allowed to choose probability distributions as optimal mixed strategies. As the theorem states, an optimal strategy to each player is actually a pure strategy. The optimal strategy to player $\mathcal{P}_1$ is the pure strategy x^*, and the optimal strategy to player $\mathcal{P}_2$ is the pure strategy y^*, where (x^*, y^*) is the saddle-point to the deterministic problem (10.1).

Theorem 10.2.   Under the assumptions listed, the pure strategies (x^*, y^*) solve the mixed game.

The key assumptions are that the game is played on the square (10.1) and that the payoff function is continuous and concave-convex.

By virtue of this theorem, if each player plays the deterministic strategy (x^*, y^*), player $\mathcal{P}_1$ will do at least as well as if he were to use any mixed strategy. There is no reason for any of the players to use a mixed strategy. They can confine themselves to deterministic choices and the deterministic saddle-point problem (10.2) actually solves the mixed strategy game too.

The assertion of the theorem may seem quite surprising in that one of the singular achievements of the theory of finite games is precisely the realization that a finite game can in general not be solved by deterministic play, but that the solution requires a recourse to mixed strategies for each of the two players. Essentially the mixed strategy achieves an interpolation between the discrete alternatives available to each player. In an infinite game, no such interpolation is necessary because the entire continuum of moves over a given interval is available to each player.

Proof: First, note that theorem 10.1 applies, so that the mixed strategy game has a value, say $v = v_1 = v_2$. As before, v_1 is defined as the value of the game to player $\mathcal{P}_1$ when he uses the mixed strategy ϕ; v_1 is given by the expression (10.16). Also, v_2 is the value of the game to player $\mathcal{P}_2$ when he uses the mixed strategy ψ; v_2 is given by (10.18).

Now we define the expected move of each player as

$$(10.31) \qquad \bar{x} = \int_0^M t\phi(t)dt$$

$$\bar{y} = \int_0^N u\psi(u)du$$

This makes it possible to show that each player will do at least as well when he replaces his mixed strategy by the expected move (10.31). The expected move is an instance of a pure strategy. Hence, each player will do at least as well with this pure strategy, and it must follow that the optimal solution to the game is a pure strategy for each player.

In order to initiate the proof, we first need a simple property of a concave function. The property is this: if a continuous function $f(x)$ is concave, there must exist some α such that the function $f(x) - \alpha x$ attains its maximum value at any $x^\#$ chosen in advance.[1]

Returning now to the main line of argument, given any y, there exists some α such that the function

$$(10.32) \qquad f_y(x) = \mathcal{F}(x,y) - \alpha x$$

attains its maximum at $\bar{x}$. Let player $\mathcal{P}_1$ use the mixed strategy ϕ while player $\mathcal{P}_2$ uses some pure strategy y. The expected payoff of the game is then

$$(10.33) \qquad \int_0^M \phi(t)\, \mathcal{F}(t,y)dt = \int_0^M \phi(t)f_y(t)dt + \alpha \int_0^M \phi(t)tdt$$

$$= \int_0^M \phi(t)f_y(t)dt + \alpha\,\bar{x}$$

The function $f_y(x)$ has its maximum at $\bar{x}$, hence the first integral is at most equal to $f_y(\bar{x})$. Thus

$$(10.34) \qquad \int_0^M \phi(t)\, \mathcal{F}(t,y_0)dt \leq f_y(\bar{x}) + \alpha\,\bar{x} = \mathcal{F}(\bar{x},y)$$

In simple words, the pure strategy $\bar{x}$ to player $\mathcal{P}_1$ is at least as good as the mixed strategy ϕ against any y.

Now, let player $\mathcal{P}_2$ choose the particular $y = y_0$ determined in (10.16). This is the pure strategy y_0 that player $\mathcal{P}_1$ must fear that player $\mathcal{P}_2$ may choose. Relation (10.34) then reads

(10.35) $$\int_0^M \phi(t)\, \mathcal{F}(t,y_0)\,dt \leq \mathcal{F}(\bar{x},y_0)$$

Thus even if player $\mathcal{P}_2$ discovers the strategy of player $\mathcal{P}_1$, the pure strategy $\bar{x}$ is at least as good for player $\mathcal{P}_1$ as any mixed strategy.

In the same fashion it is demonstrated that the pure strategy $\bar{y}$ is at least as good for player $\mathcal{P}_2$ as any mixed strategy. Thus, $\bar{x}$ and $\bar{y}$ are optimal pure strategies.

Remark: The account in the present section, and the two theorems, readily extends to the case when each player controls an entire vector of variables.

10.2. THE CONVENTIONAL TRANSPORTATION MODEL AS AN INFINITE GAME

To see how the theory of infinite games can be brought to bear on deterministic economic models such as those in chapters 3–8, consider the case of the conventional transportation model (sec. 3.2). A good is to be shipped from $h \in H$, a set of origins, to $k \in K$, a set of destinations. The supplies w_h at all origins and the quantities x_k demanded at all destinations are known. One wants to determine the optimal transportation patterns, say t_{hk}, $h \in H$, $k \in K$, that would minimize total transportation costs $\Sigma \Sigma c_{hk} t_{hk}$.

We propose now to demonstrate that this problem can be represented alternatively as the optimal solution to the following two-person infinite game. Player $\mathcal{P}_1$ controls all quantity variables t_{hk} to be determined over the interval

(10.36) $0 \leq t_{hk} \leq T_{hk}$, $h \in H$, $k \in K$

The upper bounds T_{hk} may not be part of the given problem. Since the sum total of all demand at all destinations is finite, however, the quantity transported along any particular route (h,k) must also be finite. It must therefore in fact be possible to find along each route (h,k) some large positive number $\bar{r}_{hk}$ so that the bounding condition (10.36) remains satisfied at the optimum point that we are looking for. Further, we may actually assume that this bounding condition remains slack at the point of optimum, so that the upper bound is redundant and may be inserted or deleted as desired.

Player $\mathcal{P}_2$, a fictitious player (the market) controls all price variables to be determined: the prices q_h at all origins $h \in H$ and the prices p_k at all destinations $k \in K$, over the intervals

$$(10.37) \qquad 0 \leq p_k \leq \bar{P}_k, \, k \in K$$

$$0 \leq q_h \leq \bar{q}_h, \, h \in H$$

Again, the upper bounds may not belong to the given problem, but for the purpose of economic interpretation it is not harmful to limit the analysis to cases where the solution prices are finite. There will then certainly exist some large positive number $\bar{P}_k$, $k \in K$ and $\bar{q}_h$, $h \in H$ satisfying (10.37) and we may assume that these upper bounds remain slack at the point of optimum.

The game is played on the hypersquare that is formed by (10.36) and (10.37) jointly.

The payoff of the game is defined as the value of all supply at the origins, the value of all shipping profit, and the negative of the value of all demand. So, it equals the surplus of the cost value of all goods supplied at the destinations above their sales value.

There is no obvious a priori reason why the payoff of the game should be formed in this manner. There is a general principle involved here, however, which will eventually become clear as we gain experience from this and other examples. For the moment we only show that this payoff function will actually solve the problem at hand.

The mathematical expression of the payoff is

$$(10.38) \qquad \mathcal{F}(t;p,q) = \sum_{h \in H} q_h w_h + \sum_{h \in H} \sum_{k \in K} (p_k - q_h - c_{hk}) t_{hk} -$$

$$- \sum_{k \in K} p_k x_k$$

The first term stands for the value of all supply at the origins. The second term is all shipping profit, being formed by adding total profit along each link (h,k), over all origins h and all destinations k. The last term is the negative of the value of all demand.

The payoff function is continuous; also, it is concave in the choice variables of player $\mathcal{P}_1$ (actually, it is linear in these variables) and it is convex in the choice variables of player $\mathcal{P}_2$ (it is linear here too).

The theorem to follow compares the infinite game now specified with the conventional transportation problem [2]

$$(10.39) \qquad min \sum_{h \in H} \sum_{k \in K} c_{hk} t_{hk}$$

$$\text{subject to} \qquad \sum_{k \in K} t_{hk} \leq w_h$$

$$\sum_{h \in H} t_{hk} \geq x_k$$

$$t_{hk} \geq 0, \, h \in H, \, k \in K$$

Theorem 10.3. Consider the following infinite two-person game. Player $\mathcal{P}_1$ controls the quantity variables t over the interval (10.36). Player $\mathcal{P}_2$ controls the price variables p and q over the interval (10.37). The payoff function is given by (10.38). The solution to this infinite game is given by the following pure strategies for the two players, respectively. Player $\mathcal{P}_1$: the optimal pure strategy is t^* which solves the conventional transportation problem (10.39). Player $\mathcal{P}_2$: the optimal pure strategy is p^*, q^* which are the optimal values of the dual variables (price variables) of the same transportation problem.

Proof. The proof is immediate. Application of theorem 10.2 shows that the mixed strategy game has an optimal solution in pure strategies. These are the pure strategies that solve the deterministic saddle-point problem

$$(10.40) \qquad max_{t} \; min_{p,q} \; \mathcal{F}(t; p,q)$$

subject to $0 \leq t \leq \bar{t}$

$0 \leq p \leq \bar{p}$ and $0 \leq q \leq \bar{q}$

Next, note that $\mathcal{F}(t;p,q)$ can be written, with some elementary rearrangement of terms:

$$(10.41) \qquad - \sum_{h \in H} \sum_{k \in K} c_{hk} t_{hk} + \sum_{k \in K} p_k \left(-x_k + \sum_{h \in H} t_{hk}\right)$$

$$+ \sum_{h \in H} q_h \left(w_h - \sum_{k \in K} t_{hk}\right)$$

Also, since by construction the upper bounds $\bar{t}, \bar{p}, \bar{q}$ are redundant (that is why we introduced them in the first place), problem (10.40) may alternatively be written

$$(10.42) \qquad \max_{t} \ \min_{p,q} \ - \sum_{h \in H} \sum_{k \in K} c_{hk} t_{hk}$$

$$+ \sum_{k \in K} p_k (-x_k + \sum_{h \in H} t_{hk}) + \sum_{h \in H} q_h (w_h - \sum_{k \in K} t_{hk})$$

subject to $t \geq 0$

$p,q \geq 0$

Now, the Kuhn–Tucker theorem states that t^* solves (10.39) if and only if there exist non-negative p^*,q^* so that (t^*,p^*,q^*) is a saddle-point to (10.42). But this saddle-point—as has been explained—actually solves the given infinite game. So, the solution to this game solves the given transportation problem and its dual.

Again appealing to the Kuhn–Tucker conditions, one further conclusion follows. The value of this infinite game simply reduces to

(10.43) $v = - \sum\limits_{h \in H} \sum\limits_{k \in K} c_{hk} t_{hk}^*$

since the two last terms in the expression (10.40) both vanish at the point of optimum. Thus, as seen in (10.43), the value of the game equals the negative of total transportation costs. Interpreting this as the payment from $\mathcal{P}_2$ to $\mathcal{P}_1$, it is seen that in this game player $\mathcal{P}_1$ will lose total transportation costs to player $\mathcal{P}_2$.

The Generalized Transportation Problem

In order to obtain a better understanding of the way the payoff function of the infinite game is formed, it is instructive to extend our analysis to the case when the supply at each origin and the demand at each destination is price-dependent rather than fixed and given. This corresponds to the generalized transportation problem described in section 3.2. Using the same assumptions as given in chapter 3, let the demand price function at each destination be

(10.44) $p_k = P_k(x_k), \ k \in K$

and the supply price function at each origin be

(10.45) $q_h = Q_h(w_h), \ h \in H$

As in chapter 3, it is also assumed that the demand price functions are all positive, differentiable, and nonincreasing. The supply price functions are differentiable and nondecreasing.

Consider the following infinite two-person game. Player $\mathcal{P}_1$ controls all consumer demand x_k, all shipments from origins to destinations t_{hk}, and all supplies w_h, over the intervals

(10.46) $0 \leq x_k \leq \bar{x}_k, \ k \in K$

$0 < t_{hk} \leq \bar{t}_{hk}, \ h \in H, \ k \in K$

$$0 \leq w_h \leq \overline{w}_h, \ h \in H$$

Player $\mathcal{P}_2$ controls the price variables p_k (at all destinations) and q_h (at all origins) over the intervals (10.37), as before. In brief, player $\mathcal{P}_1$ controls all quantity variables and player $\mathcal{P}_2$ controls all price variables. Also, in order to conform with our analysis of an infinite two-person game, it has been assumed that these unknown variables are all bounded from above, so that the game is played on a square (hypersquare). In other words, it is assumed that the optimal solution that we are looking for is finite. To an economist, such an assumption comes easily and naturally. There will then exist some large positive numbers $\overline{x}_k$, $\overline{t}_{hk}$, and $\overline{w}_h$ that may be used as upper bounds in the intervals (10.46).

The payoff of the game is defined as the sum of all consumers' surplus at destinations, all shipping profit, and all suppliers' surplus at origins.

A few explanations are in order. The terms "consumers' surplus" and "producers' surplus" were briefly mentioned in section 3.2, in relation to the discussion of the economic potential function (3.7). These terms have a long and complicated history in economic thought. In the general treatment in this book, we have tended to avoid the issue of the interpretation of concepts like "social payoff," "quasi-welfare," and "consumers' surplus." It has in general been sufficient for our purposes to consider entities like these as economic potential functions or drivers of the partial economy under investigation.

We did point out in section 3.2, however, that if the good is a produced good, it may sometimes be possible to identify the supply price of the good with its marginal cost. The integrated supply price function then equals total costs. Form "suppliers' surplus" at origin h:

$$(10.47) \qquad q_h w_h - \int_{w_{h0}}^{w_h} Q_h(\eta_h) d\eta_h = q_h w_h - \int Q_h(w_h) dw_h$$

(The first term is the income of the suppliers from the sale of quantity w_h. The second term is an integral. The lower limit of integration is an arbitrary point w_{h0}. The upper limit of integration is w_h. The dummy variable η_h is used as a variable of integration. The complete notation is given to the left; the abbreviated notation as an indefinite integral to the right.) Suppliers' surplus then equals the net profit of these suppliers, defined as the difference between their gross revenue and their costs.

It was also pointed out that a similar interpretation on the demand side may sometimes be possible. If the good is a producer good (i.e., employed as an input by other producers downstream the logistics chain), one may be able to identify the demand price of the good of these latter producers with the value of its marginal product. The integrated demand price function then equals total revenue. Form the mathematical expression of consumers' surplus at destination k:

$$(10.48) \qquad \int_{x_{k0}}^{x_k} P_k(\xi_k)d\xi_k - p_k x_k = \int P_k(x_k)dx_k - p_k x_k$$

(The indefinite integral used on the right-hand side has been spelled out in some detail to the left. The lower limit of integration is an arbitrary point x_{k0}. The upper limit of integration is x_k. The dummy variable ξ_k is used as a variable of integration. The second term of the expression simply is the negative of total consumer expenditure.) "Consumers' surplus" then simply equals the net profit of these "consumers" (they are actually producers, demanding the good as an input for production) at the destination in question.

Using the interpretation now explained, the payoff of the game would simply equal the sum of all profit in the system: the profit of the manufacturers making the good at the various origins, the profit of the shippers, and the profit of all producers located at the destinations, demanding the good as an input for further processing.

Collecting the three terms, the payoff of the game is

$$(10.49) \qquad \mathcal{F}(x,t,w;p,q) = \sum_{k \in K} \{\int P_k(x_k)dx_k - p_k x_k\}$$

$$+ \sum_{h \in H} \sum_{k \in K} (p_k - q_h - c_{hk})t_{hk} + \sum_{h \in H} \{q_h w_h - \int Q_h(w_h)dw_h\}$$

This payoff function is continuous. It is concave in the choice variables of player $\mathcal{P}_1$ and it is convex in the choice variables of player $\mathcal{P}_2$.

The theorem to follow compares the infinite game now described with the generalized transportation problem:[3]

$$(10.50) \quad max \; \sum_{k \in K} \int P_k(x_k) dx_k - \sum_{h \in H} \int Q_h(w_h) dw_h - \sum_{k \in K} \sum_{h \in H} c_{hk} t_{hk}$$

$$\text{subject to} \quad x_k - \sum_{h \in H} t_{hk} \leq 0, \; k \in K$$

$$-w_h + \sum_{k \in K} t_{hk} \leq 0, \; h \in H$$

$$x_k, t_{hk}, w_h \geq 0, \; h \in H, \; k \in K$$

Theorem 10.4. Consider the following infinite two-person game. Player $\mathcal{P}_1$ controls the quantity variables x, t, w over the interval (10.46). Player $\mathcal{P}_2$ controls the price variables p and q over the interval (10.37). The payoff function is given by (10.49). The solution to this infinite game is given by the following pure strategies for the two players, respectively. Player $\mathcal{P}_1$: the optimal pure strategy is x^*, t^*, w^* which solves the generalized transportation problem (10.50). Player $\mathcal{P}_2$: the optimal pure strategy is p^*, q^* which are the optimal values of the Lagrange multipliers (price variables) of the same generalized transportation problem.

Proof: The proof is as before, noting that the payoff function (10.49) by elementary rearrangement can be written

$$(10.51) \quad \sum_{k \in K} \int P_k(x_k) dx_k - \sum_{h \in H} \int Q_h(w_h) dw_h - \sum_{h \in H} \sum_{k \in K} c_{hk} t_{hk}$$

$$+ \sum_{k \in K} p_k \left(-x_k + \sum_{h \in H} t_{hk} \right) + \sum_{h \in H} q_h \left(w_h - \sum_{k \in K} t_{hk} \right)$$

Noting that this is the very expression that would appear as objective function in the Kuhn–Tucker saddle-point problem that corresponds to (10.5), the proof is continued as before.

The value of the game equals the optimal value of consumers' surplus and suppliers' surplus. (By the Kuhn–Tucker conditions, profits vanish.) This is the sum of money that player $\mathcal{P}_1$ wins from player $\mathcal{P}_2$.

10.3.   ACTIVITY ANALYSIS AS AN INFINITE GAME

It is natural now to ask if the interpretation of the transportation model as an infinite game is just a mathematical coincidence, or have we here encountered a mathematical principle of some more general bearing? In order obtain an answer to this question, we now turn to activity analysis as another standard deterministic model of production and distribution that has figured prominently in this book. Further, in order to concentrate on fundamentals, let us first take a look at Koopmans' original version of activity analysis involving a given and known vector of endowments of all resources, a set of linear production activities, and given and known prices of all consumer goods.

Section 4.1 provided an outline of a Samuelson-type mathematical programming formulation of a partial activity analysis model. Since our present purpose is only to establish the fundamental equivalence between the deterministic model and the infinite game formulation, we shall here make further simplifying assumptions.

Let $M = \{m\}$ be the set of individual production activities available, $R = \{r\}$ be the set of primary goods and services (resources), and $I = \{i\}$ be the set of final goods and services. No explicit account will be made of the presence of intermediate goods in the present development, since the necessary extensions to handle commodities which are both inputs and outputs should be obvious to the reader and need not delay us here.

Define the matrices

$$A = [a_{rm}] \quad (r \in R, m \in M)$$

$$B = [b_{im}] \quad (i \in I, m \in M)$$

The input coefficient a_{rm} measures the quantity of resource r which is used when activity m is operated at unit level; the output coefficient b_{im} measures the quantity of output i which is obtained when activity m is operated at unit level.

Denote the vector of activity levels to be determined $z = [z_m]$ $(m \in M)$. Each element z_m is required to be non-negative. The vector of inputs of primary goods and services is Az. The vector of outputs of final goods and services is Bz. Let the vector $w = [w_r]$ represent quantities of labor and other primary goods supplied. These are given and known endowments.

Imagine now the following game situation. There are two players, $\mathcal{P}_1$ and $\mathcal{P}_2$. Player $\mathcal{P}_1$ controls all production decisions, that is, he controls

$$(10.52) \qquad 0 \leq z_m \leq \overline{z}_m, \, m \in M$$

We have earlier discussed at length the significance of capacity limits and how they may be increased through the formation of new productive capital. But the upper bounds $\bar{z}_m$ featured in (10.52) must be accorded another meaning. They are given the meaning of large positive numbers— so large, in fact, that we know in advance that these upper bounds will certainly be slack at the point of optimum. By construction, then, they are redundant. It must surely be possible to find such large positive numbers, if each activity is indeed limited by existing capacity.

Player $\mathcal{P}_2$ controls all unknown prices. Not all prices are unknown, however. Following the spiral method of Charnes and Cooper for the representation of the activity analysis economy as the optimal solution to a linear programming problem with given prices of all final goods and services (see chap. 4 for further elaboration of this matter), it is assumed that the vector $p = [p_i]$ has already been established. Given these prices, it is our task to determine the efficient combination of outputs that the producers will then elect to supply. But the prices of labor and other primary resources, say the vector $q = [q_r]$ is unknown and is to be determined. It is controlled by player $\mathcal{P}_2$, over the interval

(10.53) $0 \leq q_r \leq \bar{q}_r, r \in R$

where it is assumed that these prices will turn out to be finite so that there will exist some large positive numbers $\bar{q}_r$ satisfying (10.53).

The game is played on the hypersquare formed by (10.52) and (10.53).

The payoff function of the game is defined as the sum of all profit and the market value of all resource endowments. Mathematically,

(10.54) $\mathcal{F}(z,q) = (p^T B - q^T A)z + q^T w$

This payoff function is continuous and concave-convex (actually, it is bilinear).

In preparation of the theorem to follow, we write the deterministic activity analysis problem:[4]

(10.55)   *max $p^T B z$*

subject to $Az \leq w, z \geq 0$

Theorem 10.5. Consider the following infinite two-person game. Player $\mathcal{P}_1$ controls the quantity variables z over the interval (10.52). Player $\mathcal{P}_2$ controls the price variables q over the interval (10.53). The payoff function is given by (10.54). The solution to this infinite game is given by the following pure strategies for the two players, respectively. Player $\mathcal{P}_1$: the optimal pure strategy is z^*, which solves the deterministic activity analysis problem (10.55). Player $\mathcal{P}_2$: the optimal pure strategy is q^*, which is the vector of optimal values of the dual variables of the same problem.

The proof is immediate. We know from theorem 10.2 that the mixed strategy game has an optimal solution in pure strategies that solves the deterministic saddle-point problem

$$(10.56) \qquad \max_{z} \ \min_{q} \ \ \mathcal{F}(z,q)$$

$$\text{subject to} \quad 0 \leq z \leq \overline{z}$$

$$0 \leq q \leq \overline{q}$$

Note that with some elementary rearrangement of terms $F(z,q)$ can be written

$$(10.57) \qquad p^T B z + q^T (w - Az)$$

Also, since the upper bounds $\overline{z}$ and $\overline{q}$ are redundant by construction, problem (10.56) may alternatively and equivalently be written

$$(10.58) \qquad \max_{z} \ \min_{q} \ p^T B z + q^T (w - Az)$$

$$\text{subject to } z, q \geq 0$$

The Kuhn–Tucker theorem states that z^* solves (10.55) if and only if there exists a non-negative q^* such that (z^*, q^*) is a saddle-point to (10.58).

This is the saddle-point that solves the infinite game and the solution to this game solves the activity analysis model (10.55) and its dual.

Finally, it may be noted that the value of the game equals $p^T B z^*$. Player $\mathcal{P}_1$ will win the value of final demand from player $\mathcal{P}_2$.

It may be helpful to the reader at this point to spell out in nontechnical terms what has now been accomplished. The infinite game outlined in theorem 10.5 pits the producers and resource owners against a fictitious price player. The payoff represents the direct concerns of the parties of the first player: the sum of all profit and the market value of all resource endowments. Jointly, the producers and the resource owners would strive to maximize this total payoff. The choice variable controlled by the first player is the vector of all activities, z. The second player has a different aim. He controls the vector of all resource prices q, and would like to minimize the payoff to the parties represented by the first player. In other words, he is an adversary, trying to bring both profits and the market value of the resources as low as possible. Indeed, by choosing his optimal strategy, he is able to wipe out all profits in the system. In his attempts to counter the moves of the first player, it happens that he will opt for prices that will clear all resource markets. In short, this mixed strategy adversary confrontation results in exactly the same optimal solution as the conventional deterministic activity analysis model.

In order to reveal the principles involved in forming the payoff function, we also deal briefly with the more general case involving price-dependent consumer demand and resource supply. That is, rather than assuming all demand curves to be horizontal with the demand prices fixed at $p = [p_i]$, we permit the demand price to be given by

$$(10.59) \qquad p_i = P_i(x_i), \, i \in I$$

and rather than assuming resource supply curves to be vertical at the fixed levels $w = [w_r]$, we shall use supply price functions of the form

$$(10.60) \qquad q_r = Q_r(w_r), \, r \in R$$

As usual, these demand price functions and supply price functions are partial relationships assuming given incomes and given prices of all consumer goods and resources outside the current modeling effort. Also, the demand and supply of each good is supposed to depend only upon its own price. More general formulations are possible, the only assumption of substance being that the demand price functions and the supply price functions all be integrable. (See sec. 4.1 for a detailed discussion of these issues.)

The demand price functions are taken to be positive, differentiable, and nonincreasing. The supply price functions are differentiable and nondecreasing.

We then formulate the following infinite two-person game. Player $\mathcal{P}_1$ controls all consumer demand x_i, all production activities z_m, and all resource supply w_r, over the intervals

$$(10.61) \qquad 0 \leq x_i \leq \bar{x}_i \ , \ i \in I$$

$$0 \leq z_m \leq \bar{z}_m \ , \ m \in M$$

$$0 \leq w_r \leq \bar{w}_r \ , \ r \in R$$

It is assumed that the optimal solution that we are looking for is finite so that all these upper bounds exist and that they turn out to be redundant. Player $\mathcal{P}_2$ controls all consumer prices p_i and all resource prices q_r over the intervals

$$(10.62) \qquad 0 \leq p_i \leq \bar{p}_i \ , \ i \in I$$

$$0 \leq q_r \leq \bar{q}_r, \ r \in R$$

A similar assumption is made about these upper bounds.

The payoff of the game is defined as the sum of all consumers' surplus, all profit, and all resource-owners' surplus.

At this point, we again remind the reader that the supply price function of a produced input may sometimes be interpreted as the marginal cost of this input.[5] The integrated supply price function is then the total cost of producing the input, and resource-owners' surplus from supplying resource r

$$(10.63) \qquad q_r w_r - \int Q_r(w_r) dw_r$$

equals the net profit collected by the producer of the input. (The resource is now a produced good, and the resource owner is actually a producer.)

In some applications it may be possible to interpret the demand price of a good that is demanded by a producer as an input for further processing as the value of the marginal product of that producer. The integrated demand price function then is the total revenue garnered by this producer, and consumers' surplus arising from the demand of commodity i

$$(10.64) \qquad \int P_i(x_i)dx_i - p_ix_i$$

equals the net profit of the same producer.

The payoff of the game may then be thought of as the sum of all profit arising at the resource stage of the vertical network, all manufacturing profit being generated from operating the various production activities of the network, and all profit cumulating at the final demand stage.

Collecting terms, total payoff is obtained as

$$(10.65) \qquad \mathcal{F}(x,z,w;p,q) = \sum_{i \in I} \{\int P_i(x_i)dx_i - p_ix_i\} + (p^TB - q^TA)z$$

$$+ \sum_{r \in R} \{q_rw_r - \int Q_r(w_r)dw_r\}$$

This payoff function is continuous and concave-convex.

In order to state theorem 10.6 we also need the activity analysis type partial model with price-dependent final demand and resource supply:

$$(10.66) \qquad max \quad \sum_{i \in I} \int P_i(x_i)dx_i - \sum_{r \in R} \int Q_r(w_r)dw_r$$

subject to $\qquad x - Bz \leq 0$

$$Az - w \leq 0$$

$$x,z,w \geq 0$$

Theorem 10.6. Consider the following infinite two-person game. Player $\mathcal{P}_1$ controls all quantity variables x,z,w over the intervals (10.61). Player $\mathcal{P}_2$ controls the price variables p and q

over the interval (10.62). The payoff function is given by
(10.65). The solution to this infinite game is given by the
following pure strategies for the two players, respectively.
Player $\mathcal{P}_1$: the optimal pure strategy is x^*,z^*,w^*, which solves
the activity analysis type partial model (10.66). Player $\mathcal{P}_2$: the
optimal pure strategy is p^*,q^*, which are the optimal values of
the Lagrange multipliers of the same program (10.66).

The general approach of the proof should by now be familiar to the
reader. It should therefore be sufficient to point out that by elementary
rearrangement the payoff function (10.65) may be rewritten

$$(10.67) \qquad \sum_{i \in I} \int P_i(x_i)dx_i - \sum_{r \in R} \int Q_r(w_r)dw_r$$

$$+ p^T(-x + Bz) + q^T(- Az + w)$$

Note that total profits vanish at the point of optimum. Hence, the
value of the infinite game equals the sum of all consumers' surplus and all
resource owners' surplus.

A General Principle for Forming the Payoff of the Infinite Game

All models of production and distribution covered in chapters 3
through 8 can be written as infinite games. The payoff function is always
formulated as the sum of consumers' surplus, resource owners' surplus (or
suppliers' surplus, as the case may be), and all profit. In some models the
mathematical expression for consumers' surplus or for resource owners'
surplus collapses into a simpler expression—if a demand price or a supply
price is fixed and known (horizontal demand or supply curve, respectively),
the surplus vanishes; if a demand is fixed and given (vertical demand
curve), consumers' surplus equals the negative of the consumer expenditure;
finally, if a supply is fixed and given (vertical supply curve), resource
owners' surplus equals the market value of the resource. And profits
include profits from production, transportation, and any other activity which
is represented in the model.

Further simplification of these expressions may be possible when the
current modeling effort has not been traced back to the use of original
nonproduced resources but rather starts out with given supply price
functions of one or several produced goods that are treated along the lines of

resources. As discussed, resource owners' surplus may in this case sometimes be identified with the net profit arising in the production of this produced resource. Similarly, the modeling effort may not extend all the way to the delivery of finished consumer goods but rather end with the production of one or several producer goods and a given demand price function for each such producer good. It may then be possible to identify consumers' surplus with the net profit associated with the production of this final good (which really is an intermediate good).

If capacity limits on quantities transported or on activities are present, shipping profit or manufacturing profit has to be calculated net of the imputed costs of the possible violation of such bounds. At the point of optimum, all shipping profit and all manufacturing profit are wiped out. Hence, the value of the game equals just the sum of all consumers' surplus and all resource owners' surplus.

10.4. WHO IS THE PRICE PLAYER?

As long as economists have reflected on the nature of market formation, they have felt a need to imagine the presence of some hypothetical agent who brings the market formation to fruition. To Adam Smith it was "the invisible hand," to Edgeworth it was "the actioneer."

In modern equilibrium theory consumers are supposed to be price takers who determine their optimal consumption plans. Producers are price takers who determine their optimal production plans. But if all economic agents in the system are price takers, then who sets prices? In comparative statics theory and in dynamic economic theory, the movements of price are studied in terms of "tâtonnement"—a process of "groping" for the equilibrium solution. But who is groping?

The idea of describing the formation of markets in game theoretic terms is as old as the theory of games itself. In *The Theory of Games and Economic Behavior,* von Neumann and Morgenstern envision an entirely new theoretical machinery for the analysis of economic markets based on the concepts of game theory. And in their seminal paper on the existence of equilibrium for a competitive economy, Arrow and Debreu [1] propose to characterize general equilibrium as an abstract economy, which includes concepts related to those of the theory of games. The abstract economy includes a "fictitious participant who chooses prices and who may be termed the market participant" (p. 274).

Note that, whereas consumers, firms, and resource owners take all prices as given and formulate optimal plans for the quantity variables under their control, the price player acts in an opposite fashion. The price player takes all quantity decisions as given and sets prices. It so happenes that there are economic agents in the real world who perform their economic roles in this same manner. These agents are the dealers or brokers that one finds in many commodity markets and in almost all financial markets. A broker typically quotes both an ask price and a bid price, that is, he is willing to deal both ways in the market. The broker may hold a small inventory of the commodity of his own. If his inventory cumulates he will tend to mark down the price; if the inventory is being depleted he will tend to adjust the price upwards.[6]

The game theoretic formulations that we have provided may be interpreted in terms of a hypothetical situation in which all commodities at all stages of resource supply, production, and distribution are handled by brokers. Whenever a resource owner, distributor, or firm wants to sell a product, the transaction must be handled through a broker. Whenever a distributor, firm, or consumer wants to buy a product, this, too, must be done through a broker.

Player $\mathcal{P}_1$ would then represent all resource owners, distributors, shippers, producers, and consumers. Player $\mathcal{P}_2$ would be all brokers. All possible profit would be wrested from the brokers.

This may sound extravagant. In our search for the identity of the price player, we have been lured along a tricky path of theoretical constructions. Perhaps the entire enterprise of trying to identify the price player is misdirected from the beginning. Remembering Samuelson's admonitions not to try to put any economic content into the concept of social net payoff, we should perhaps consider the infinite games in this chapter as just a mathematical artifact that happens to deliver the desired market solutions.

One way to breathe more realism into these gaming models would be to allow explicitly for different ask and bid prices, so that the economic operations of the brokers could be represented more truthfully (for some attempts in this direction, see Bradfield and Zabel [4]).

In any case the game theoretic approach provides a unifying principle, a kind of grand design for all the material developed in the present volume, and more. It is of considerable interest that such a unifying principle exists. The mathematical prototypes that we have covered together form an illustration of the concept of integrated modeling. Using another term, we could speak of a production and distribution paradigm.

NOTES

1.   A definition of concavity was given in sec. 2.1. As an exercise, the reader may want to show that the stated property follows from the definition given. Note in particular that the function $f(x)$, although continuous, need not be differentiable, so that the solution slope cannot always be taken to be equal to the gradient of f at point $x^{\#}$.

2.   This reproduces program (23.13).
3.   See program (3.12).
4.   For this and more general activity analysis formats, see chap. 4.
5.   See sec. 4.1.
6.   For some recent attempts to describe the role of brokers in competitive markets, see the bibliographic notes.

BIBLIOGRAPHIC NOTES

The account of infinite two-person games played on a square in section 10.1 follows quite faithfully Owen [10], chap. 4. Owen's treatment is based on earlier work by Borel [3], Bohnenblust, Karlin, and Shapley [2], Duffin [7], and others. The idea to present market equilibrium as a solution in pure strategies to an infinite two-person game featuring a fictitious price player was used in Charnes, Kortanek, and Thore [5].

In economic theory there is general agreement that game theory must play an important role in an analysis of market formation. Unfortunately, however, there is no consensus on exactly how this should be done. The dilemma is well illustrated by the path-breaking works by Arrow and Debreu [1] and the ensuing monograph by Debreu [6]. As has already been pointed out in the main text, Arrow and Debreu proposed to characterize general equilibrium as an abstract economy which includes concepts related to those of the theory of games. However, Debreu later abandoned this approach. In an interesting paper [11], Shubik later forcefully argued that there were no game aspects left in [6], and that this version could just as well be interpreted as a centralized economy with set and fixed prices. The gaming element of market formation had somehow vanished along the way.

For the role of brokers of dealers in market formation, see Bradfield and Zabel [4]. They call brokers "security specialists." The profit of the specialists occurs as a markup between bid and ask prices.

REFERENCES

[10.1]   Arrow, K. J., and G. Debreu. "Existence of Equilibrium for a Competitive Economy," *Econometrica* 22/3 (1954): 265–90.

[10.2]   Bohnenblust, H. F., S. Karlin, and L. S. Shapley. "Games with Continuous Convex Payoff." In *Contributions to the Theory of Games I*, eds. H. W. Kuhn and A. W. Tucker. Annals of Mathematics Studies, no. 24. Princeton, N. J.: Princeton University Press, 1950.

[10.3]   Borel, É. "Sur les jeux ou interviennent le hasard et l'habilité des joueurs," *Éléments de la Theorie des Probabilitiés*. 3d, ed. Paris: Librairie Scientifique, 1924.

[10.4]   Bradfield, J., and E. Zabel.   "Price Adjustment in a Competitive Market and the Securities Exchange Specialist." In *General Equilibrium, Growth and Trade,* eds. Green and Scheinkman. New York: Academic, 1979.

[10.5]   Charnes, A., K. O. Kortanek, and S. Thore.   "An Infinite Constrained Game Duality Characterizing Economic Equilibrium," *Research Report CCS 386,* Center for Cybernetics Studies, The University of Texas at Austin, Mar. 1981.

[10.6]   Debreu, G. *Theory of Value.* New York: Wiley, 1959.

[10.7]   Duffin, R. J. "Infinite Programs," In *Linear Inequalities and Related Systems,* eds. H. W. Kuhn and A. W. Tucker.   Annals of Mathematics Studies, no. 38. Princeton, N. J.: Princeton University Press, 1956.

[10.8]   Hurwicz, L. "Game Theory and Decisions," *Scientific American* 192 (Feb. 1955): 75–83.

[10.9]   Marschak, J. "Neumann's and Morgenstern's New Approach to Static Economics," *Journal of Political Economy* 54 (1946): 97–115.

[10.10] Owen, G. *Game Theory.* New York: Academic, 1982.

[10.11] Shubik, M. "Competitive and Controlled Price Economies: The Arrow–Debreu Model Revisited." In *Equilibrium and Disequilibrium in Economic Theory*, ed. G. Schwödiauer, Dordrecht, Holland: D. Reidel, 1977.

Index

About the Author

STEN THORE is a Senior Research Scientist and the Gregory A. Kozmetsky Centennial Fellow at the IC² Institute at the University of Texas at Austin. His articles have appeared in numerous journals, including the *Journal of Regional Science, Mathematical Modeling, European Journal of Operations Research*, and the *Journal of Forecasting*.